Pharmaceutical Industry 4.0: Future, Challenges & Application

RIVER PUBLISHERS SERIES IN BIOTECHNOLOGY AND MEDICAL RESEARCH

Aiming primarily at providing detailed snapshots of critical issues in biotechnology and medicine that are reaching a tipping point in financial investment or industrial deployment, the scope of the series encompasses various specialty areas including pharmaceutical sciences and healthcare, industrial biotechnology, and biomaterials. Areas of primary interest comprise immunology, virology, microbiology, molecular biology, stem cells, hematopoiesis, oncology, regenerative medicine, biologics, polymer science, formulation and drug delivery, renewable chemicals, manufacturing, and biorefineries.

Each volume presents comprehensive review and opinion articles covering all fundamental aspect of the focus topic. The editors/authors of each volume are experts in their respective fields and publications are peer-reviewed.

For a list of other books in this series, visit www.riverpublishers.com

Pharmaceutical Industry 4.0: Future, Challenges & Application

Editors

Rishabha Malviya

School of Medical and Allied Sciences
Galgotias University, Greater Noida, India

Sonali Sundram

School of Medical and Allied Sciences
Galgotias University, Greater Noida, India

Shivkanya Fuloria

AIMST University, Malaysia

Dhanalekshmi Unnikrishnan Meenakshi

National University of Science and Technology
Muscat, Sultanate of Oman

River Publishers

Routledge
Taylor & Francis Group
NEW YORK AND LONDON

Published 2023 by River Publishers
River Publishers
Alsbjergvej 10, 9260 Gistrup, Denmark
www.riverpublishers.com

Distributed exclusively by Routledge
605 Third Avenue, New York, NY 10017, USA
4 Park Square, Milton Park, Abingdon, Oxon OX14 4RN

Pharmaceutical Industry 4.0: Future, Challenges & Application / by Rishabha Malviya, Sonali Sundram, Shivkanya Fuloria, Dhanalekshmi Unnikrishnan Meenakshi.

Routledge is an imprint of the Taylor & Francis Group, an informa business

ISBN 978-87-7022-843-5 (hardback)
ISBN 978-87-7022-998-2 (paperback)
ISBN 978-10-0096-518-6 (online)
ISBN 978-10-0344-249-3 (master ebook)

Contents

Preface

Today's pharmaceutical manufacturing technologies continue to evolve as the internet of things, artificial intelligence, big data, deep learning, cloud computing, robotics, and advanced computing begin to challenge the traditional approaches, practices, and business models for the manufacture of pharmaceuticals. The application of these technologies has the potential to dramatically improve the efficiency, agility, flexibility, and quality of the industrial production of medicines.

This book explains how advanced technologies and emerging trends such as blockchain, robotics, bioinformatics, big data, artificial intelligence, deep learning, cloud computing, will impact the manufacturing and distribution of pharmaceuticals in order to build a better future of healthcare.

This book will help many pharmaceutical companies, IT companies and researchers to explore how evolution of industry 4.0 can be effectively utilized to revolutionize the pharmaceutical sector and healthcare. This book gives wide variety in topics which represent the opportunity and application of industry 4.0 in pharmaceutical field. This book contains 12 chapters subdivided into various section that is written by profound researchers and academicians from many parts of the world. The book is profusely referenced and copiously illustrated. This should be noted that all chapters were deliberately reviewed and all were suitably revised once or two times. So, the content presented in this book is of greatest value and meets the highest standard of publication.

This book should present useful source for researchers and industrialists working in clinical research, pharmaceutical manufacturing, scientist working in R&D.

We sincerely believe that the book will prove to be useful contribution to pharmaceutical science.

Finally comes the best part to thank you everyone who helped to make this book possible. First and foremost, we express our heartfelt gratitude to the authors for their contribution, dedication, participation, and willingness to share their significant research experience in the form of written testimonials, which would not have been possible without them. lastly, we are feeling fortunate to express our gratitude to River Publishers for his unwavering support.

Editors:

Rishabha Malviya
School of Medical and Allied Sciences,
Galgotias University, Greater Noida, India.

Sonali Sundram
School of Medical and Allied Sciences,
Galgotias University, Greater Noida, India.

Shivkanya Fuloria
AIMST University, Malaysia.

Dhanalekshmi Unnikrishnan Meenakshi
National University of Science and Technology,
Muscat, Sultanate of Oman.

Acknowledgement

Having an idea and turning it into a book is as hard as it sounds. The experience is both internally challenging and rewarding. At the very outset, we fail to find adequate words, with limited vocabulary to our command, to express our emotion to almighty, whose eternal blessing, divine presence, and masterly guidelines helps us to fulfill all our goals.

When emotions are profound, words sometimes are not sufficient to express our thanks and gratitude. We especially want to thank the individuals that helped make this happen. Without the experiences and support from my peers and team, this book would not exist.

No words can describe the immense contribution of our parents, friends, without whose support this work would have not been possible.

Last but not least, we would like to thank, our publisher for their support, innovative suggestions and guidance in bringing out this edition.

List of Figures

List of Tables

List of Contributors

Ahamad, Javed, *Department of Pharmacognosy, Faculty of Pharmacy, Tishk International University, Iraq*

Anand, Anubhav, *Department of Pharmaceutics, Hygia Institute of Pharmaceutical Education and Research, India*

Babu, Rekha Naresh, *Nirmala College of Pharmacy, India*

Bairagee, Deepika, *Oriental College of Pharmacy and Research, Oriental University, India*

Budha, Roja Rani, *Department of Pharmacology, Institute of Pharmaceutical Technology, Sri Padmavati Mahila Visvavidyalayam, India*

Dahiya, Rajiv, *School of Pharmacy, Faculty of Medical Sciences, The University of the West Indies, Trinidad & Tobago*

Dahiya, Sunita, *Department of Pharmaceutical Sciences, School of Pharmacy, University of Puerto Rico, USA*

Dua, Kamal, *Faculty of Health, Australian Research Centre in Complementary and Integrative Medicine, University of Technology Sydney, Australia*

Dwivedi, Sumeet, *Faculty of Pharmacy, Oriental University, India*

Fatima, Hajeera, *Joginpally B.R. Pharmacy College, India*

Fuloria, Neeraj Kumar, *Faculty of Pharmacy, AIMST University, Malaysia*

Gupta, AVSSS, *Joginpally B.R. Pharmacy College, India*

Jain, Neelam, *Faculty of Pharmacy, Oriental University, India*

Jain, Neetesh Kumar, *Oriental College of Pharmacy and Research, Oriental University, India*

Jayasree, P., *Joginpally B.R. Pharmacy College, India*

Malviya, Rishabha, *Department of Pharmacy, School of Medical and Allied Sciences, Galgotias University, India*

Mishra, Prem Shankar, *School of Medical and Allied Sciences, Galgotias University, India*

Mishra, Rakhi, *Noida Institute of Engineering and Technology (Pharmacy Institute), India*

Mishra, Sudhanshu, *Department of Pharmaceutical Science & Technology, Madan Mohan Malaviya University of Technology, India*

Naim, Mohammad Javed, *Department of pharmaceutical Chemistry, Faculty of Pharmacy, Tishk International University, Iraq*

Ojha, Smriti, *Department of Pharmaceutical Science and Technology, Madan Mohan Malviya University of Technology, India*

Padarthi, Pavan Kumar Arya, *Department of Computer Science in Artificial Intelligence and Robotics, University of Hertfordshire, United Kingdom*

Pandey, Akanksha, *Department of Pharmacy, School of Medical and Allied Science, Galgotias University, India*

Pingali, Sirisha, *IPT, Lonza Biologics, United Kingdom*

Rao, GSN Koteswara, *Department of Pharmacy, School of Medical and Allied Sciences, Galgotias University, India*

Rawat, Shilpa, *Department of Pharmacy, School of Medical and Allied Science, Galgotias University, India*

Saini, Manoj, *Department of General Medicine, All India Institute of Medical Science, India*

Saraogi, Gaurav, *Department of Pharmacy, Sri Aurobindo Institute of Pharmacy, India*

Sekar, Mahendran, *Department of Pharmaceutical Chemistry, Faculty of Pharmacy and Health Sciences, Royal College of Medicine Perak, Universiti Kuala Lumpur, Malaysia*

Sharma, Akanksha, *Monad College of Pharmacy, Monad University, India*

Sharma, Urvashi, *Faculty of Pharmacy, Medi-Caps University, India*

Singh, Aditi, *Ashoka Institute of Pharmacy, Ashoka Engineering Chauraha, India*

Singh, Nishita, *Madhu Vachaspati Institute of Pharmacy, India*

Singh, Nitu, *Faculty of Pharmacy, Oriental University, India*

Singh, Shilpa, *Department of Pharmacy, School of Medical and Allied Science, Galgotias University, India*

Subramaniyan, Vetriselvan, *Faculty of Medicine, Bioscience and Nursing, MAHSA University, Malaysia*

Sundram, Sonali, *Department of Pharmacy, School of Medical and Allied Science, Galgotias University, India*

Telikicherla, Karteek, *Whitbread, United Kingdom*

Verma, Ashish, *School of Pharmacy, Monad University, India*

Verma, Poojashree, *Faculty of Pharmacy, Oriental University, India*

Verma, Swati, *Department of Pharmacy, School of Medical & Allied Science, Galgotias University, India*

Yadav, Shalini, *Dr. MC Saxena College of Pharmacy, India*

List of Abbreviations

FIR	Fourth industrial revolution
ACN	Australian center for nanomedicine
ADMET	Absorption, distribution, metabolism, excretion, and toxicity
AE	Autoencoder
AI	Artificial intelligence
AN	Artificial neuron
AOUP	Azienda ospedaliero-universitaria pisana
AQI	Air quality index
AR	Augmented reality
ASPECTS	Alberta stroke program early CT score
AUC	Area under the curve
BASN	Body area sensor network
BBB	Blood–brain barrier
BBN	Bayesian belief network
BCT	Blockchain technology
BE	Bio equivalence
BMI	Body mass index
BP	Boiling point
BPNN	Back propagation neural network
CAD	Computer-aided diagnosis
CAD	Computer-assisted detection
CAD	Computer aided design
CAGR	Compound annual growth rate
CAR	Chimeric antigen receptor
CBI	Clinical bioinformatics
CCD	Charge-coupled device
CCU	Critical care unit
CD	Constellation of differentiation
CDMO	Contract development and manufacturing organization
CFCN	FCN in a cascade

CGM	Continuous glucose monitoring
CI	Confidence interval
CNC	Computer numerical control
CNN	Convolutional neural network
CNS	Central nervous system
CPS	Cyber–physical system
CPT	Current procedural terminology
CPT	Common proficiency test
CPV	Continuous process verification
CRNs	Residual convolutional networks
CSC	Chatbot-based symptom checker
CTEPH	Chronic thromboembolic pulmonary hypertension
CV	Cardiovascular
CV	Computer vision
CVD	Cardiovascular disease
CXR	Chest radiography
DApps	Decentralized applications
DCNN	Deep convolutional neural network
DCNs	Deep convolutional networks
DDCS	Decentralized data centers
DDS	Drug delivery system
DFT	Density functional theory
DILI	Drug-induced liver injury
DL	Deep learning
DLT	Distributed ledger technology
DNNs	Deep neural networks
DoS	Denial of service
DT	Decision tree
DTI	Drug–target interaction
ECG	Electrocardiogram
EHR	Electronic health records
EMR	Electronic medical records
EPA	Environmental protection agency
ERPS	Enterprise resource planning system
ES	Expert systems
FAIR	Findable, accessible, interoperable, and reusable
FDA	Food and drug administration
FMA	Foundational model of anatomy

GAMP	Good automated manufacturing processes
GANs	Generative adversarial networks
GDA	Gene-disease associations
GDPR	General data protection regulation
GLIMS	General laboratory information management system
GMP	Good manufacturing practice
GNN	Graph neural networks
GP	General practitioner
GPUs	Graphical processing units
GRU RNN	Gated recurrent units RNN
GxP	Good practices
H & E	Hematoxylin and Eosin
HALS	Hindered amine light stabilizers
HC	Hierarchical clustering
HCPCS	Healthcare common procedure coding system
HDFS	Hadoop distributed file system
HF	Heart failure
HGP	Human genome project
HIA	Human intestinal absorption
HIPAA	Health insurance portability and accountability act
HIPI	Hadoop image processing interface
HIV	Human immuno virus
HOG	Histogram of oriented gradients
HTX	Hematoxylin
HVAC	Heating, ventilation, and air-conditioning
I2B2	Informatics for integrating biology & the bedside
ICD	International classification of diseases
ICD-9	International classification of diseases, ninth revision, clinical modification
ICU	Intensive care unit
IHC	Immunohistochemistry
IIoT	Industrial internet of things
ILSC	Intelligent laser speckle classification
ILSVRC	ImageNet large scale visual recognition challenge
IoS	Internet of services

IoT	Internet of things
ISO/TC 307	International organization for standardization/technical committee 307
ISPE	International society for pharmaceutical engineering
IT	Information technology
ITC	Information and communication technology
ITH	Intratumor heterogeneity
KNN	K-nearest neighbor
LBP	Local binary pattern
LgR	Logistic regression
LOINC	Logical observation identifiers names and codes
LPU	Local processing unit
LR	Linear regression
LR	Logistic regression
LSTM	Long short-term memory
LVO	Large vessel occlusion
MAE	Mean absolute error
MAM	Multi-attribute monitoring
MGECNN	Molecular graph encoding convolutional neural networks
MHRA	Medical products regulatory agency
MI	Mutual information
MIS	Medical image segmentations
MIT	Massachusetts institute of technology
ML	Machine learning
MLP	Multilayer perceptron
MM	Molecular mechanics
MNA	Multilevel neighborhoods of atoms
MNT	Molecular nanotechnology
MoH&FW	Ministry of Health and Family Welfare
MP	Melting point
MPM	Medical practice management
MRI	Magnetic resonance imaging
MS	Mass spectrometry
MW	Molecular weight
NB	Naive Bayes
NDC	National Drug Code
NETTAB	Network tools and applications in biology

NFC	Near field communication
NHCAA	National Health Care Anti-Fraud Association
NLP	Natural language processing
NMEs	New molecular entities
NMSC	Nonmelanoma and melanoma skin cancer screening techniques
NS	Network structures
NSCLC	Non-small cell lung cancer
NSCLC	Non-small cell lung carcinoma
OEE	Overall equipment effectiveness
ORB	Oriented FAST and rotated BRIEF
OT	Operational technology
PAI	Pre-approval inspections
PAT	Process analytics technology
PC	Personal computer
PCA	Principal component analysis
PCPs	Primary care providers
PDA	Personal digital assistance
P-gp	P-glycoprotein
PHI	Protected health information
PHR	Personal health record
PI	Pharmaceutical industry
PLS	Partial least squares
PMS	Patient management system
PMS	Patient monitoring system
PMS	Practice management system
PNN	Probabilistic neural networks
PPB	Plasma protein binding
PR	Paper record
pRAS	Psoriasis risk assessment systems
PTLR	Plain thoracolumbar radiography
PWDs	Person with diabetes
QA	Quality assurance
QC	Quality control
QR	Quick response
QSAR	Quantitative structure-activity relationship
R&D	Research and development
RASAR	Read across structure-activity relationship
RBM	Restricted Boltzmann machine

RECIST	Response evaluation criteria in solid tumors
RF	Random forest
RFID	Radio frequency identification
RFL	Random forest learning
RNN	Recurrent neural networks
ROI	Region of Interest
RPA	Robotic process automation
RPET	Recycled polyethylene terephthalate
RPM	Remote patient monitoring
SC	Smart contract
SGDClassifier	Stochastic gradient descent classifier
SIG	Special Interest Group
SMILES	Simplified molecular-input line-entry system
SNGP	Spectral-normalized neural Gaussian processes
SNOMED-CT	Systemized nomenclature of medicine – clinical terms
SSS	Safe, secure, and scalable
STE	Speckle-tracking echocardiography
SVM	Support-vector machine
SWOT	Strength, weakness, opportunity, and threat
TB	Tuberculosis
TBI	Translational bioinformatics
TDM	Typical drug makers
TM	Template matching
TPI	Terahertz pulsed imaging
TTD	Therapeutic target database
UCSF	University of california at san francisco
UM	Universal marker
UMA	Un-mixing algorithm
UQ	Uncertainty quantification
VAEs	Variational autoencoders
VDA	Variant disease associations
VDF	Van de Graaff factor
VF	Vertebral fracture
VR	Virtual reality
WDs	Wristwatches
WHO	World health organization
ZRSS	Zenith robotic surgical method

1

Digitalization in the Pharmaceutical Industry: Prioritization Throughout the Digital Transformation

Sudhanshu Mishra[1*], Shalini Yadav[2], Nishita Singh[3], Rajiv Dahiya[4], Swati Verma[5], and Shivendra Mani Tripathi[1]

[1]Department of Pharmaceutical Science & Technology, Madan Mohan Malaviya University of Technology, India
[2]Dr. MC Saxena College of Pharmacy, India
[3]Madhu Vachaspati Institute of Pharmacy, India
[4]School of Pharmacy, Faculty of Medical Sciences, The University of the West Indies, Trinidad & Tobago
[5]Department of Pharmacy, School of Medical & Allied Science, Galgotias University, India
*Corresponding author: Department of Pharmaceutical Science & Technology, Madan Mohan Malaviya University of Technology, Gorakhpur, Email: msudhanshu22@gmail.com, Contact: +91-8377836989.

Abstract

The development of a manufacturing industry's production process is impossible without including digitalization. Automated and computerized processes are part of digitalization, which results in cost savings as well as increased accuracy and efficiency. Due to a lack of training and a wide range of research and manufacturing procedures, the pharmaceutical industry (PI) has been a staunch opponent of digitalization. Traditional and new pharmaceuticals are becoming more popular, so there's little doubt that PI will need to be digitized. Because of this, contract development manufacturing organizations have specific problems when it comes to implementing new technologies. GMP should be closely linked to PI digitalization and CDMO in particular, and success in PI digitalization demands a constant focus on GMP.

Another key part of CDMO digitalization is ensuring that the company's stakeholders are kept up to date on the company's progress. This article will talk about the benefits and drawbacks of digitizing CDMOs, focusing on practical ways to keep going digital.

Keywords: Digitalization and process improvements, pharmaceutical industry, GMP, contract development manufacturing organization.

1.1 Introduction

By 2020, pharmaceutical business is expected to produce $122.845 billion in global revenues, making it the top-most fastest-expanding financial sector. Since 2017, the pharmaceutical industry has expanded at an annual rate of 5.9%. By 2017, the pharmaceutical business earned $1.143 billion in sales and is predicted to generate $1.462 billion by 2021. The utilization of information from systems integration and linked devices to better recognize and assess consumer wants and improve supply chain performance is referred to as "digitalization." In the future, pharmaceutical Industry business 4.1 will offer intelligent automation technologies and may help enhance production, for instance, tailored medication, additive manufacturing, and localized 3D printing of therapy. Digitalization technology is now more crucial than ever in enabling companies of all sizes to enhance their performance by raising manufacturing efficiency, enhancing competitive capabilities, improving budgeting, scheduling accuracy, and ensuring financial sustainability [1]. Old product-oriented business models are under strain because of variables such as patent expirations, greater customer demand, more competition, and increased pricing pressures. It is no secret that digital transformation is currently reshaping industries as digital services other than products become increasingly ubiquitous. According to digitalization and "connected health," the "triple goal" of enhancing treatment, improving quality of care, expanding access to care, and lowering per capita costs may all be accomplished through "connected health" [2, 3]. This industry is known for its high profitability and low risk, as well as its extensive and expensive R&D periods and intense marketing. Computer modeling can assist in cutting costs in the pharmaceutical industry, where production interruptions and digitalization are typical [4, 5]. Through the Internet of Things, machine-to-machine connectivity and machine learning artificial intelligence [6] provide frictionless operations, automated remedial actions, and predictive maintenance. Small mistakes in the pharmaceutical manufacturing environment can have life-changing consequences for patients as well as substantial financial, legal, and reputational consequences for the corporation [7].

In the PI, digitalization can benefit both small and large firms [8]. Manufacturers may be able to maintain quality while also complying with upcoming serialization standards if the serial numbers of the supply chain are used by the manufacturers to digitalize medications that are bogus-proof. Digitalization can be the topmost way to meet the demand of pharmaceutical businesses rising from global markets [9, 10]. Using automated sensor technologies, social networking sites, and health applications, it is also feasible to track medication compliance and predict demand across areas [11]. Cloud-based information exchanges may be used to stay in compliance with laws, discover manufacturing proficiencies to save money, and engage with suppliers and distributors more promptly.

Digitalization technologies must be employed to deploy PI. Digitalization is critical if medical items are to fulfill the ever-increasing demand of a changing world and people. PI has been active in digitalization for a longer length of time and with less success than other industries. As a result, the purpose of this research is to look into the notions of successful digitalization and how they might be used for PI. This article focuses on contract development and manufacturing organizations (CDMOs). Because GMP is such an important component of industrial digitalization, general aspects of GMP in PI are also investigated and discussed. It is mostly a review article on Good Manufacturing Practices and processes that are crucial to the digitalization of the pharmaceutical sector. Because this is an introductory post, we won't go to great length regarding various technologies.

1.2 Good Manufacturing Practice (GMP) within Pharmaceuticals

Regulations all around the globe use GMP, or "Good Manufacturing Practices," to keep tabs on the approval and licensing of new products [12]. Additional safeguards can be taken to guarantee the safety and efficacy of pharmaceuticals and medical equipment, as well as food and plasma, under these laws. A quality-oriented approach to production is necessitated by GMP rules, allowing organizations to avoid or eradicate errors and inaccuracies. Thus, the buyer is shielded against receiving substandard or even hazardous products [13]. Other quality-based operations controls, such as accurate screening and high-quality raw materials, recognition, and deviation investigation, are included in GMP systems. GMP regulations include everything from records management to employee certifications to sanitation, apparatus certification, cleanliness, and process validation [14].

1.2.1 Enforcement of GMP

Even if a pharmaceutical manufacturer is situated in another nation, GMP must be followed for their goods to be sold in the European Union. In the United Kingdom, GMP inspections are overseen by the Medical Products Regulatory Agency (MHRA), whereas in Canada, GMP inspections are overseen by the Health Product and Food Branch Inspectorate. Day-to-day assessments are carried out by each appointed officer to verify that medications are manufactured correctly and safely according to GMP guidelines. The FDA has recently begun inspecting Chinese pharmaceutical manufacturing plants to check that GMP rules are being followed [15, 16]. Several countries around the world conduct GMP inspections regularly to ensure that medications are manufactured in a contaminant- and error-free environment. Before allowing new pharmaceuticals to be commercialized, several nations conduct GMP compliance checks as part of pre-approval inspections (PAI). Because this is an introduction post, we will focus on illustrious technology [17, 18].

It is believed by the PI that a primary goal of GMP is risk reduction in pharmaceutical manufacturing, as this cannot be accomplished by analysis of the final product. Mistakes in packaging or labeling can result in patients receiving the wrong medication as well as unanticipated and unwelcome product contamination and too much or too little of a component [19]. There are many different types of pharmaceutical manufacturing processes that are covered by GMP [20, 21]. This includes everything from raw materials and infrastructure to training and cleanliness.

Based on the kind of GMP violation and pharmaceuticals implicated, penalties might vary. There's little likelihood that a pharmaceutical that has been prepared in violation of GMP would be hazardous or ineffective. As a result, healthcare providers will be better equipped to consider the advantages and disadvantages of various treatment options for their patients because of the FDA and maybe other regulatory bodies issuing guidance that is more contextually relevant.

1.2.2 The pharmaceutical industry's five GMP principles

Product safety and high quality are two of the primary concerns for the PI, and the five GMP principles (5Ps) address each of these concerns. The GMP 5Ps is a useful framework for thinking about the most important aspects of compliance. People, Processes, Procedures, Premises, Equipment, and Products comprise the GMP's five Ps. To comply with GMP, the industry generally agrees that these five criteria must be prioritized [23, 24]. These

Figure 1.1 Schematic representation of 5Ps of GMP.

five principles are essential to any discussion about best practices. When it comes to pharmaceutical product production, GMP is designed to help keep risks to a minimum, especially those that can't be prevented once the final pills have been consumed. The pharmaceutical sector and businesses that produce consumables are heavily influenced by GMP and the 5Ps. A schematic representation of the GMP 5Ps is shown in Figure 1.1, with more information provided below.

1.2.2.1 People

Every person involved in the pharmaceutical production process must be made aware of their responsibilities and obligations. The approach requires employees to be trained and their performance to be assessed. To maintain their effectiveness in ensuring that their staff is adequately trained and competent, manufacturers must evaluate their training methodologies regularly. A manufacturing company is nothing without the people who run it. That is why it is so important. Employees must be trained in how to achieve the desired results. To increase productivity and efficiency, roles and duties are distributed among workers. Depending on their talents, competencies, and experience, each employee is given a unique assignment. When we say "written documentation and monitoring," we mean timely reporting of deviations from protocols and any other important aspects that need to be tracked. Because of this, all employees should be able to see and understand the processes that are in place. Regular reviews of employees must be conducted to make certain that they are in the wake of established procedures and meeting the company's requirements. To ensure product safety and decrease the risk of contamination, these quick inspections need to be implemented. Early detection of any inconsistencies is good for businesses, even if the requirements and methods aren't the same.

1.2.2.2 Procedures

An instruction manual is a set of guidelines for ensuring that a technique or a part of a process is carried out consistently. To keep things running properly, every employee in an industrial organization must adhere to the regulations and processes in place [25]. Regular data collection at important phases of production will make it simpler to establish the cause of any quality issue if a group looks to have a problem that must be canceled [26]. To ensure that a company's activities meet the required standards, both processes and procedures must be developed and documented. It is imperative that all procedures are well stated and adhered to. Disturbances from the predetermined routine must be properly investigated.

1.2.2.3 Process

A process is a series of linked operations that convert inputs to outputs. It is a collection of well-organized tasks that must be followed precisely to get maximum production and rewards. Different techniques and activities may be used to speed up the manufacturing process, allowing for the creation of a bigger quantity of goods in a shorter amount of time. However, extensive investigations and inspections of the credibility and potential of newly chosen tactics in this respect should be conducted early on to ensure that quality is not compromised.

1.2.2.4 Premises and equipment

In contrast to "equipment," which refers to machines and healthcare appliances that are accustomed to monitoring, curing, or preventing an individual's health or ailments, "premises" refers to any structure, building as well as any equipment or apparatus physically attached or incorporated into the building frame. Every effort should be made by manufacturing companies to construct their facilities and equipment so that they can be cleaned effectively and cross-contaminated. The location, design, construction, maintenance, and modification of the facility should be tailored to the specific needs of the business [27].

Documentation of cleaning procedures for every facility and piece of equipment must be kept. Protocols for preventing cross-contamination and documented calibration instructions must be in place [28]. To make sure that a facility's equipment is performing as intended and producing consistent results, these requirements must be taken into account during the construction process. In addition to routine equipment and machinery inspections, sanitation checks are required [29]. Equipment must be cleaned, dried, and washed regularly to ensure that it does not damage anything.

1.2.2.5 Products

There are several ways to increase the quality and consistency of items that customers will use. Ensure that all commodities enter and depart the facility in excellent shape; it is also an end-to-end responsibility [30]. When it comes to raw materials and components, manufacturers, for example, need to set standards. Repetitive processes are essential for all stages of R&D: processing, monitoring, manufacturing, testing, sampling, packing, and record keeping. In the context of a manufacturing company, this conveys the magnitude of the issue they are trying to solve. As a result, research was conducted, and resources such as manpower, money, and other materials were allocated [31]. An organization's inability to provide products that meet the needs of its customers is an extremely significant threat to its long-term viability and integrity [32]. As a result, there is a significant demand for assets, intermediates, components, and final goods. For production, packaging, sampling, testing, archiving stability data, and monitoring status, look for the most efficient, hygienic techniques [33].

It is possible to limit the probability of cross-contamination and mistakes in the manufacturing of medicines and other consumables if the 5 Ps are handled appropriately. Making sure that the necessary ingredients are in the right proportions for the intended effect is dependent on a consistent pharmaceutical production strategy and technology. Quality cannot be "tested into" drugs retrospectively, as we are constantly told. Instead, the only way to achieve precision and dependability in large-scale medication manufacturing is to adhere to set criteria by appropriately educated and accountable people [34, 35]. That is why it is important to keep the GMP 5 Ps in mind while implementing digitalization procedures.

1.3 Traditional Drug Production vs. Contract Development and Manufacturing Organizations

Drug development and manufacturing services are provided by CDMOs, which are corporations that have a contract with pharmaceutical firms. Outsourcing drug development and production is a common practice among

CDMOs and pharmaceutical companies. All customer's demands are taken into consideration. For pre-clinical, Phase I, and late-stage clinical trials, materials for formal stability and scale-up, commercial manufacturing, batch registrations, serialization, and shipment are all part of CDMO services.

Developing and executing GMP and digitalization processes must take CDMOs' variations from conventional drug manufacturers into account. Subsequent sections cover some of these subjects in greater depth. It provides a comprehensive array of services. CDMOs have a far broader range of experience and competence than typical drug makers (TDM). Large CDMOs also spend heavily on equipment. According to TDM, internal drug design and manufacturing present challenges for pharmaceutical businesses, whether they are looking to expand capacity, introduce a new medication, or change the frequency at which they manufacture [36].

On the other hand, businesses that outsource to a CDMO get access to a vast array of equipment and facilities without having to pay ownership expenses. Also recognized for helping pharmaceutical companies scale up, CDMOs are well-positioned to assist with this process as well. Pharmaceutical firms may be put in jeopardy if production volumes are altered or a new medicine type is introduced. Working with a CDMO reduces the risk and length of time involved in making these kinds of decisions. Companies of all sizes have the opportunity to flourish thanks to outsourcing pharmaceutical development and manufacturing. They can operate lean and efficient operations since they know that medication development and manufacturing will not cost a lot of money for pharmaceutical businesses of all sizes [37].

1.4 Digitalization of CDMO

Digital transformation plans, high levels of digital diffusion, and staff upskilling should all result in the projected productivity improvement. It has never been a better time for businesses of all sizes to embrace digitalization, since our economic well-being depends on it, of course. Cybersecurity, artificial intelligence, and other activities will be necessary for your organization to undertake as part of the digitalization and digital transformation process. You'll need a current skill set to keep up with these new technologies and put them to good use as soon as they arrive. You may significantly improve your game by learning new skills and going to training sessions. All businesses, not just a select few, must embrace digitalization and technology to increase productivity.

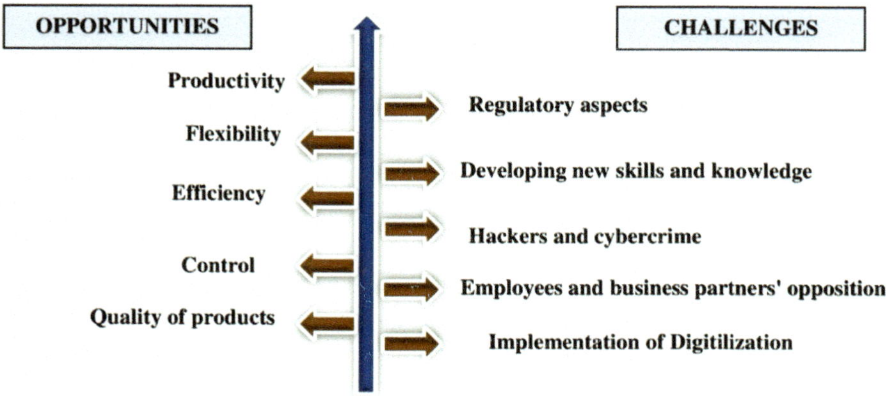

Figure 1.2 Opportunities and challenges of digitalization.

The digital revolution will hurt businesses that do not adopt new technologies. As a result of the consequences, these firms may be left behind. There must be a real digitalization of all businesses and organizations to have a substantial influence. So, big corporations need to face their technical demons and design a strategy to overcome their adoption obstacles. Small and medium-sized businesses need to start integrating technology to remain competitive. Digital transformation of business models and the whole industry and value chain will need a productivity strategy for companies. There is an overarching digital transformation strategy behind every major reform, training program, and digitalization effort.

Organizations face both possibilities and problems when it comes to dealing with change. As the most difficult issue, and maybe the most common error, managers regard change as a short-term phenomenon. Change is a continuous process, not a one-time event, in any business. A company's long-term success depends on its ability to deal with and negotiate with these issues on an ongoing basis [37, 38]. The digitalization process necessitates regular updates to services, procedures, and ways of operation. Also, there are both advantages and disadvantages to it. It is vital to anticipate and prepare for obstacles to deal with them successfully. Figure 1.2 shows pros and cons of digitalization.

1.5 Opportunities

Organizations face both possibilities and problems when it comes to dealing with change. As the most difficult issue, and maybe the most common error, managers regard change as a short-term phenomenon. Change is a continuous process, not a one-time event, in any business. A company's long-term success depends on its ability to deal with and negotiate with these issues on an ongoing basis. The digitalization process necessitates regular updates to services, procedures, and ways of operation. Also, there are both advantages and disadvantages to it. It is vital to anticipate and prepare for obstacles to deal with them successfully. As a result, digitalization's pros and downsides are examined. The fear that robots will replace workers is a common occurrence in the industrial sector, but the focus should instead be on how individuals and machines can work together to generate the best results possible. You can get the most out of your smart factory's production processes and labeling if your employees are more tech-friendly. Human–computer symbiosis is the basis of human–machine interaction. A project should be started to see if machines and software can boost system productivity in ways that are more intelligent and physical than either human or machine productivity alone.

Pharmaceutical companies must adhere to exacting standards and laws and safeguard their data with great care. These companies might benefit from finding a strategy that is both reliable and efficient. Industrial processes may be monitored, regulated, and optimized with the aid of a digitalization plan, resulting in increased productivity and efficiency. The use of GMP digitalization may improve several business components, as will be shown in the following paragraphs.

1.5.1 To put it another way, productivity

In recent years, pharmaceutical manufacturing has expanded its global reach. The demand for both national and imported goods will be at its peak with the mere expansion in the sector of healthcare, economics, and insurance. Demand for pharmaceuticals is rising along with the variety of pharmaceutical needs as emerging nations battle noncommunicable illnesses that are more prevalent in wealthy countries. AIDS, malaria, and tuberculosis are just a few of the infectious diseases that continue to wreak havoc in many underdeveloped nations. In addition, as individuals live longer, the worldwide population of adults aged 65 and older is expected to expand. It is also important that the product can be produced in large enough quantities and quickly enough to meet these requirements throughout time. This is especially true in the PI, where the medicine is often lifesaving and requires constant access. These challenges in the industrial sector necessitate a new set of tactics to deal with them. Through the use of digitalization, new and more effective ways to fulfill increased production demand may be found through the use of digitalization, which improves manufacturing processes and speeds them up while maintaining product quality.

1.5.2 The product's quality

Pharmaceutical companies must collect operational data to ensure the quality of their products. On the other hand, many firms are still using paper-based systems, which increases the likelihood of human error in data collection and management. As a result, it is more difficult to absorb this information in written form. By reducing human errors and enhancing data collection efficiency, digitalization technology can help decrease data entry errors. For example, pharmaceutical companies may use digitalization methods such as machine learning to acquire, standardize, and analyze data from many sources. When a batch is finished, basic quality assurance reports are immediately available [37, 38]. To sum up, digitalization has the potential to increase quality control's efficiency and reliability. Early batch results are now available during the completion of the manufacturing process by the application of digitalization [39].

1.5.3 Control

The quality control standards at the PI are among the most demanding in the industry. From product development through packaging and labeling to equipment cleaning, every step in the process must be strictly controlled. The pharmaceutical industry frequently employs the batch process, in which products are manufactured in batches rather than continually. One disadvantage is that even a minor mistake might ruin an entire batch. Negative consequences can include serious bodily injury, penalties, and litigation, as well as a considerable loss of reputation if a defective batch is not discovered by the manufacturer in time.

Effective batch control is needed to avoid these and other potentially harmful outcomes. Digitalization makes it possible to better manage the process and boost output in this case [40]. Digitalization can also assist you in streamlining your production's packaging phase. It's easier to find methods to improve your packaging process when it's managed, monitored, and visualized in the same manner that batch manufacturing can be. You may also monitor and oversee your business from any location by accessing data remotely. The pharmaceutical industry's profitability relies heavily on the digitalization of control tasks. Profitability is immediately increased by reducing the consumption of raw materials, human resources, and time, as well as reducing the risk of low-quality final products because of digitally automated control systems [40].

1.5.4 Cost-effectiveness

Efficiency may be described as the time, money, and resources needed by a business to produce a specific amount of output. As a result, productivity and efficiency are inseparably linked. As a result of digitalization, you'll be able to get a complete picture of your operating efficiency. The data and reports you collect can be used to pinpoint areas in which your procedures and infrastructure need to be enhanced. Your organization can also use it to automate some processes. If you use digitalization, you can do the same amount of work with less time, effort, and resources. With real-time alerts, for example, operators can reply quickly with automated warnings [41, 42]. The pharmaceutical industry relies heavily on validation due to the stringent rules and regulations that must be followed. In this industry, digitalization also contributes to efficiency [43]. You don't have to review or update your processes before you can change or enhance them, which saves you time and money [43].

1.6 Challenges

Supply chain and operational improvements for pharmaceutical firms face several challenges. Because of the quick rate of technological change, they must work with a wide range of external partners throughout the supply chain to find solutions [44]. To overcome long-standing working patterns and the resistance of organizations and employees used to decades-old procedures, businesses will have to be exceedingly transparent. Additionally, there's a lot of hype and possible dangers to be aware of [45]. There are various crucial success factors on this journey. As a starting point, enterprises should familiarize themselves thoroughly with the ecosystem and the rapidly evolving technology inside it. Companies in the pharmaceutical industry must also have the appropriate resources, such as a diverse team of specialists and investment funds, to be successful. The supply chain must be completely connected, and players must work with their partners to do so.

For the most part, companies must recognize that this is a process that requires choosing a few activities, adopting an experimental mentality, and learning by doing. The pharmaceutical industry will also face several important challenges. Cybersecurity is one of the most pressing issues in digital operations [46, 47].

1.7 Execution of the Digital Transformation

The pharmaceutical industry will be affected by technological advancements. Because of the digitalization of industrial production, the manufacturing process may be more self-organized, and useful data can be collected [48]. This is made possible by current information and communication technology. Preparing for the future requires pharmaceutical and biotech firms to take into consideration technological advancements such as digitalization [36]. A good illustration of this is the need for CDMOs to stay on top of these changes. When they get involved early in the process, they have the opportunity to become a valuable partner for their consumers. The following criteria and aspects must be addressed to achieve a successful implementation as outlined in the next paragraphs.

1.7.1 Focus on value

Digitalization is a term that encompasses a broad range of data in CDMOs. Data analytics software in R&D, for example, is not linked to the value chain. It is necessary to categorize digitalization to have a clear view of the problem. When it comes to digitalization at a visual inspection workstation, it is like switching from a paper book to a tablet. Employees would instead utilize a tablet to submit the findings of their inspections into the Enterprise Resource Planning System (ERPS). A more complex solution, such as integrating formerly paper-based duties into the new application, is also possible [49]. Using analog to digital data transmission in a laboratory, for example, may be linked. Measurement equipment data would be automatically sent to the software, where it would be stored and processed for future use. Digitalization has led to several new trends and technologies, including machine learning, artificial intelligence, blockchain, and big data. Despite their immense potential, these technologies should only be used when necessary [50]. Projects should be chosen based on whether or not they will improve efficiency and effectiveness and thus add value to the company and its all-important partners, such as customers and suppliers, rather than on how often and how many times they happen. The pharmaceutical industry will be affected by technological advancements. Because of the digitalization of industrial production, the manufacturing process may be more self-organized, and useful data can be collected [48]. This is made possible by current information and communication technology. Preparing for the future requires pharmaceutical and biotech firms to take into account technological advancements such as digitalization [36]. A good illustration of this is the need for CDMOs to stay on top of these changes. When they get involved early in the process, they have the opportunity to become a valuable partner for their consumers. The following criteria and aspects must be addressed to achieve a successful implementation as outlined in the next paragraphs.

1.7.2 Holding the adaptability

While standardization can assist a CDMO in minimizing the complexity of its entire operation, flexibility is required to meet the demands of varied clients. It is possible to adjust paper-based procedures to handle numerous filling techniques depending on the customer's requirements. As an alternative, a digital system may limit flexibility by standardizing procedures so that they can be managed by the system [49]. In their manufacturing requirements, clients of a CDMO, for example, may use a variety of terminologies. If they are not standardized, different wordings lead to a plethora of process variances that must be documented digitally. Uniformity and flexibility can be achieved by using pre-programmed text modules with all the essential components. CDMOs can stay adaptable even if they are digitalized, but it is important to keep this in mind while designing systems [51].

1.7.3 Prioritize the quality

In the world of high-priced injectables, the first and most important need is quality. As a result, patients are getting the same medications that CDMOs produce for their pharmaceutical and biotechnology clients. Because pharma digitalization boosts productivity while simultaneously enhancing safety and convenience, one way to get there is to focus on the global supply chain up to implementation and contemplate several single pharmaceutical manufacturing stages overall. However, digitalization will not be completed linearly and must instead be tackled as a comprehensive program. As a result of several subprojects, the phases of the process inside an organization become increasingly intertwined. Pharmaceutical companies, in particular, are particularly hard hit by this. To ensure compliance with regulations, even minor changes in procedures must be taken into consideration. The quality and efficiency of these operations can always be better, even if they are done well.

1.7.4 Standardization of process

In the world of high-priced injectables, the first and most important need is quality. As a result, patients are getting the same medications that CDMOs produce for their pharmaceutical and biotechnological clients. Because pharma digitalization boosts productivity while simultaneously enhancing safety and convenience, one way to get there is to focus on the global supply chain up to implementation and contemplate several single pharmaceutical manufacturing stages overall. However, digitalization will not be completed linearly and must instead be tackled as a comprehensive program. As a result of several subprojects, the phases of the process inside an organization become increasingly intertwined. Pharmaceutical companies, in particular, are particularly hard hit by this. To ensure compliance with regulations, even minor changes in procedures must be taken into consideration. Even if they are done well, the quality and efficiency of these operations can always be improved. Digitalization in the pharmaceutical industry has the potential to improve both the security and the efficiency of documentation processes. By definition, CDMOs are separate from their biopharmaceutical customers, and these distinctions may become more apparent as digitalization takes hold. The utilization of laboratory testing equipment is one example. Laboratory testing equipment is determined by customers, not CDMOs [52].

In the wake of the wide range of testing approaches, net connectivity and execution of processes over the digital platform have become more challenging. As a consequence of the wide variety of goods and services that CDMOs provide, they often have to employ a wide variety of process variations, including a wide range of documentation techniques. Attempting to implement all of these paper-based documentation methods into the digital system at once would result in a major loss of system reliability and efficiency. As a result, harmonizing and standardizing procedures is essential before using software to digitalize activities. In most cases, digitalization is not completed in a single effort. Instead, it's considered a multi-project, all-encompassing initiative. Interdependence and operational linkages are common among these smaller initiatives. So, it is important to identify the presence of any synergies or project dependencies. Even more difficult than one may think is defining who controls the corporate practices. Therefore, it is important to figure out what cross-divisional responsibilities there are and who is in charge of them to digitize operations [53].

1.7.5 An illustration of digitalization

There is a slew of extra-legal and administrative hurdles to jump over first. Following the production process, every filled item procured by the client is subjected to a final graphical examination. The aseptically prefilled cartridges, vials, and syringes are subjected to an independent quality examination after compounding and filling and before packaging. For illustration's sake, consider the Vetter Pharma Corporation. The inspection reports containing all the findings were reported before the introduction of the System Application and Products system. There are around 60,000 manufacturing standards that SAP produces each year for use by the Visual Inspection team. It was then the shift coordinator's responsibility to manually enter the results into the SAP software systems and batch analysis. When it comes to adopting and implementing digitalization, employees can be classified as either digital or non-digital natives. This includes management, employees who will be touched by this new policy, and their union representatives, as well as those who support or oppose it. Any time soon is better than never when it comes to setting up a dedicated transformation team [54].

1.8 Conclusions

In today's technological, industrial, and economic climate, the digitalization of manufacturing processes is universally accepted as essential. Because of this, pharmaceutical sector digitalization is being held back by the resistance of PI, which has led to delayed progress. Lower prices, improved quality, and reduced capacity restrictions are some of the advantages of digitalization in PI. For the most part, pharmaceutical businesses have been loath to utilize arithmetical manufacturing methods because they think their systems, data, and employees are not ready for it now. However, many firms have realized that waiting is no longer an option and have begun to experiment with digitalization. Using a digital platform has various advantages, including the ability to track multiple manufacturing components, collect data, and discuss experiment findings in real-time. When it comes to digitalization, pharmaceutical companies and CDMOs have a lot in common. Commodities and operations of a CDMO can be improved through digitalization if done effectively. Digitalization in the pharmaceutical sector can enhance product and process quality when implemented correctly. This involves dealing with complexity while being adaptable for our customers, providing a smooth-out modification for all employees, and improving the whole value chain for

CDMOs. To improve pharmaceutical development, contemporary CDMOs may establish stronger personal relationships with the many professions they serve by centralizing all of their services.

Acknowledgments

I'd like to express my gratitude to my co-authors for their contributions of expertise and effort, as well as their participation in compiling the work.

Conflicts of Interest

There are no conflicts of interest declared by the authors.

Funding

No funding required

References

[1] Faraj, S., Renno, W., & Bhardwaj, A. (2021). Unto the breach: What the COVID-19 pandemic exposes about digitalization. *Information and Organization*, *31*(1), 100337. DOI: 10.1016/j.infoandorg.2021.100337

[2] Iglehart, J. K. (2014). Connected health: emerging disruptive technologies. *health affairs*, *33*(2), 190-190. DOI: 10.1377/hlthaff.2014.0042

[3] Fecha, P. M. S. (2017). *The Return of the Investment of the Digital Channels in Pharmaceutical Industry* (Doctoral dissertation, Universidade de Coimbra).

[4] Schaufelberger, D. E., Koleck, M. P., Beutler, J. A., Vatakis, A. M., Alvarado, A. B., Andrews, P., ... & Forenza, S. (1991). The large-scale isolation of bryostatin 1 from Bugula neritina following current good manufacturing practices. *Journal of natural products*, *54*(5), 1265-1270. DOI: 10.1021/np50077a004

[5] Anthony Jnr, B., & Abbas Petersen, S. (2021). Examining the digitalisation of virtual enterprises amidst the COVID-19 pandemic: a systematic and meta-analysis. *Enterprise Information Systems*, *15*(5), 617-650. DOI: https://doi.org/10.1080/17517575.2020.1829075

[6] Ngamvichaikit, A. (2021). Leveraging design thinking for pharmaceutical digital marketing. *Asian J. Business Res*, *2021*, 11. DOI: 10.14707/ajbr.210102

[7] Sehlstedt, U., Bohlin, N., de Maré, F., & Beetz, R. (2016). Embracing digital health in the pharmaceutical industry. *International Journal of Healthcare Management*, *9*(3), 145-148. DOI: https://doi.org/10.1080/20479700.2016.1197513

[8] Lakshmi, B., & Patel, S. (2020). Digital Marketing in Pharmaceutical Industry–An Overview and Assessment.

[9] Lakshmi, B., & Patel, S. (2020). Digital Marketing in Pharmaceutical Industry–An Overview and Assessment.

[10] Rosenbaum, M. S., Ramírez, G. C., Edwards, K., Kim, J., Campbell, J. M., & Bickle, M. C. (2017). The digitization of health care retailing. *Journal of Research in Interactive Marketing*. DOI: 10.1108/JRIM-07-2017-0058

[11] van Velthoven, M. H., Cordon, C., & Challagalla, G. (2019). Digitization of healthcare organizations: the digital health landscape and information theory. *International journal of medical informatics*, *124*, 49-57. DOI: 10.1016/j.ijmedinf.2019.01.007

[12] Cramer, M. M. (2006). *Food plant sanitation: design, maintenance, and good manufacturing practices*. CRC Press. DOI: https://doi.org/10.1201/9781420005943

[13] Patel, K. T., & Chotai, N. P. (2011). Documentation and records: harmonized GMP requirements. *Journal of young pharmacists*, *3*(2), 138-150. DOI: 10.4103/0975-1483.80303

[14] Patel, K. T., & Chotai, N. P. (2008). Pharmaceutical GMP: past, present, and future–a review. *Die Pharmazie-An International Journal of Pharmaceutical Sciences*, *63*(4), 251-255. DOI: 10.1691/ph.2008.7319

[15] World Health Organization. (2007). *WHO guidelines on good manufacturing practices (GMP) for herbal medicines*. World Health Organization.

[16] Harris, J., & Hill, R. (2010, April). Building a trusted image for embedded systems. In *Proceedings of the Sixth Annual Workshop on Cyber Security and Information Intelligence Research* (pp. 1-4).

[17] Rangarajan, A. (2015). The FDA and Worldwide Current Good Manufacturing Practices and Quality System Requirements: Guidebook for Finished Pharmaceuticals. *Quality Progress*, *48*(4), 60. https://asq.org/quality-press/display-item?item=H1458

[18] Haleem, R. M., Salem, M. Y., Fatahallah, F. A., & Abdelfattah, L. E. (2015). Quality in the pharmaceutical industry–A literature review. *Saudi pharmaceutical journal*, *23*(5), 463-469. DOI: 10.1016/j.jsps.2013.11.004

[19] Abhinaya, N., Thunga, G., Muddukrishna, B. S., Pai, R., Shenoy, U. R., Khan, S., & Pai, K. G. (2019). Research on effective management of manufacturing defects to avoid product recalls: a challenge to pharmaceutical industry. *Research Journal of Pharmacy and Technology, 12*(12), 6124-6132. DOI: 10.5958/0974-360X.2019.01064.3

[20] Abou-El-Enein, M., Römhild, A., Kaiser, D., Beier, C., Bauer, G., Volk, H. D., & Reinke, P. (2013). Good Manufacturing Practices (GMP) manufacturing of advanced therapy medicinal products: a novel tailored model for optimizing performance and estimating costs. *Cytotherapy, 15*(3), 362-383. DOI: 10.1016/j.jcyt.2012.09.006

[21] Taylor, P. (2008). Pharmaceutical excipients: where now for GMP. *RAJ Pharma, 19*(12), 815-818. DOI: 10.1007/s40005-017-0354-4

[22] Kumar, N., & Jha, A. (2019). Application of principles of supply chain management to the pharmaceutical good transportation practices. *International Journal of Pharmaceutical and Healthcare Marketing*. DOI: 10.1108/IJPHM-09-2017-0048

[23] George, B. V. C. D. (2012). Improvement of manufacturing operations at a pharmaceutical company. A lean manufacturing approaches. *J. Manuf. Technol. Manag, 23*(1), 56-75. DOI: https://doi.org/10.5772/59027

[24] Lee, F. S., Wang, X., & Fu, P. P. (2010). Quality assurance and safety protection of traditional Chinese herbs as dietary supplements. *Funct. Foods East, 431*. DOI: 10.1080/10590500902885676

[25] Joseph, D. N. (Ed.). (2000). *Good Manufacturing Practices for Pharmaceuticals: A Plan for Total Quality Control from Manufacturer to Consumer*. CRC Press.

[26] Zacharia, Z. G., & Mentzer, J. T. (2004). Logistics salience in a changing environment. *Journal of Business Logistics, 25*(1), 187-210. DOI: 10.1108/IJLM-10-2012-0113

[27] Phelps, C. E., & Madhavan, G. (2017). Using multicriteria approaches to assess the value of health care. *Value in Health, 20*(2), 251-255. DOI: 10.1016/j.jval.2016.11.011

[28] Krekora, M. (2008). *Contract manufacturing of medicines*. Kluwer Law International BV.

[29] Aghayan, H. R., Arjmand, B., & Burger, S. R. (2016). GMP facilities for clinical cell therapy product manufacturing: a brief review of requirements and design considerations. *Perinatal Tissue-Derived Stem Cells*, 215-227. DOI: 10.5812/ans.68497

[30] Reinhardt, I. C., Oliveira, J. C., & Ring, D. T. (2021). Industry 4.0 and the future of the pharmaceutical industry. *Pharm. Eng.*

[31] Jaiganesh, V., & Sudhahar, J. C. (2013). Sketching out the hidden lean management principles in the pharmaceutical manufacturing. *International Journal of Scientific and Research Publications*, *3*(2), 1-12.
[32] NAYEREH, N., JORDI, B., & VESAL, T. (2012). Good Manufacturing Practice: A New Approach for the 21st Century. *Управління, економіка та забезпечення якості в фармації*, (3), 37-44.
[33] Karmacharya, J. B. (2014). Good manufacturing practices (GMP) for medicinal products. *Promising Pharmaceuticals*, 101-148. DOI: 10.5772/49096
[34] Peng, Z., Wu, D., & Zheng, Q. (2013). A level-value estimation method and stochastic implementation for global optimization. *Journal of Optimization Theory and Applications*, *156*(2), 493-523.
[35] Vugigi, S. K., Thoithi, G. N., Ogaji, J. I., & Onuonga, S. O. (2019). Good manufacturing practices in the Kenyan pharmaceutical industry and impact of facility upgrading on domestic and international sales. *East and Central African Journal of Pharmaceutical Sciences*, *22*(3), 77-84.
[36] Awad, A., Trenfield, S. J., Gaisford, S., & Basit, A. W. (2018). 3D printed medicines: A new branch of digital healthcare. *International journal of pharmaceutics*, *548*(1), 586-596. DOI: 10.1016/j.ijpharm.2018.07.024
[37] Capel, A. J., Rimington, R. P., Lewis, M. P., & Christie, S. D. (2018). 3D printing for chemical, pharmaceutical and biological applications. *Nature Reviews Chemistry*, *2*(12), 422-436. DOI: https://doi.org/10.1038/s41570-018-0058-y
[38] Patidar, A., Vinchurkar, K., & Balekar, N. (2018). Digitalisation in Pharmacy. *International Journal of Research in Pharmacy and Pharmaceutical Sciences*, *3*(5), 37-43.
[39] Shah, N. (2004). Pharmaceutical supply chains: key issues and strategies for optimisation. *Computers & chemical engineering*, *28*(6-7), 929-941. DOI: 10.1016/j.compchemeng.2003.09.022
[40] Lexchin, J., Bero, L. A., Djulbegovic, B., & Clark, O. (2003). Pharmaceutical industry sponsorship and research outcome and quality: systematic review. *bmj*, *326*(7400), 1167-1170. DOI: 10.1136/bmj.326.7400.1167
[41] Alloghani, M., Al-Jumeily, D., Hussain, A., Aljaaf, A. J., Mustafina, J., & Petrov, E. (2018, September). Healthcare services innovations based on the state-of-the-art technology trend industry 4.0. In *2018 11th*

International Conference on Developments in eSystems Engineering (DeSE) (pp. 64-70). IEEE. DOI: 10.1109/DeSE.2018.00016

[42] Steinwandter, V., Borchert, D., & Herwig, C. (2019). Data science tools and applications on the way to Pharma 4.0. *Drug discovery today*, *24*(9), 1795-1805. DOI: 10.1016/j.drudis.2019.06.005

[43] Arden, N. S., Fisher, A. C., Tyner, K., Lawrence, X. Y., Lee, S. L., & Kopcha, M. (2021). Industry 4.0 for pharmaceutical manufacturing: Preparing for the smart factories of the future. *International Journal of Pharmaceutics*, *602*, 120554. DOI: 10.1016/j.ijpharm.2021.120554

[44] Sarkis, M., Bernardi, A., Shah, N., & Papathanasiou, M. M. (2021). Emerging challenges and opportunities in pharmaceutical manufacturing and distribution. *Processes*, *9*(3), 457. DOI: https://doi.org/10.3390/pr9030457

[45] Chowdary, B. V., & George, D. (2012). Improvement of manufacturing operations at a pharmaceutical company: a lean manufacturing approach. *Journal of Manufacturing Technology Management*. DOI: https://doi.org/10.5772/59027

[46] Pandya, E. J., & Shah, K. V. (2013). CONTRACT MANUFACTURING IN PHARMA INDUSTRY. *Pharma Science Monitor*, *4*(3).

[47] Sokolov, M. (2020). Decision making and risk management in biopharmaceutical engineering—opportunities in the age of covid-19 and digitalization. *Industrial & Engineering Chemistry Research*, *59*(40), 17587-17592. DOI: 10.1021/acs.iecr.0c02994

[48] Rantanen, J., & Khinast, J. (2015). The future of pharmaceutical manufacturing sciences. *Journal of pharmaceutical sciences*, *104*(11), 3612-3638. DOI: 10.1002/jps.24594

[49] Ganesh, S. (2020). *Continuous Pharmaceutical Manufacturing: Systems Integration for Process Operations Management* (Doctoral dissertation, Purdue University Graduate School).

[50] Mendenhall, D. W., & Kontny, M. J. (2010). CDMO Industry Update.

[51] Hurter, P., Thomas, H., Nadig, D., Emiabata-Smith, D., & Paone, A. (2013). Implementing continuous manufacturing to streamline and accelerate drug development. *AAPS newsmagazine*, *16*, 15-19.

[52] Coyle, D., & Nguyen, D. (2020). No plant, no problem? Factoryless manufacturing, economic measurement and national manufacturing policies. *Review of International Political Economy*, 1-21. DOI: https://doi.org/10.1080/09692290.2020.1778502

[53] May, M. (2021). Adaptability of CDMOs Sorely Tested by COVID-19: surviving and thriving though COVID-19-imposed rigors, contract

development and manufacturing organizations are confident of meeting future challenges. *Genetic Engineering & Biotechnology News*, *41*(6), 60-62. https://www.genengnews.com/insights/adaptability-of-cdmos-sorely-tested-by-covid-19/

[54] Chircu, A. M., Sultanow, E., & Sözer, L. D. (2017). A reference architecture for digitalization in the pharmaceutical industry. *INFORMATIK 2017*. DOI: 10.18420/in2017_205

Biographies of Authors

Sudhanshu Mishra

Sudhanshu Mishra received his M. Pharm (Pharmaceutics) from Rajiv Gandhi Proudyogiki Vishwavidyalaya and is presently employed as a teaching faculty member at the Madan Mohan Malaviya University of Technology in Gorakhpur. During his M. Pharm studies, he concentrated on developing a herbal topical formulation for the treatment of arthritis. At present, he is working on a variety of literature projects, including authoring review articles for various innovative approaches and technologies for treating chronic disorders. He has taken part in international seminars, conferences, workshops, and oral presentations, among other things. This book chapter is one of the most influential contributions to his interest in technology and future study.

Shalini Yadav

Shalini Yadav received her bachelor's degree from Dr. M.C. Saxena College of Pharmacy, Lucknow. She gained interest in writing papers during her graduation and have also presented oral and poster presentations and attended a variety of online and offline conferences, webinars, and other events. She have always prioritized learning new technology and developing innovative approaches to combating chronic conditions. One of the significant influences to her interest in technology has been this book chapter.

Nishita Singh

Nishita Singh is positioned today as an Assistant professor at Madhu Vachaspati Institute of Pharmacy, Prayagraj. She has been active in the field of pharmacy since 2013. She has completed her pharmacy graduation from Chandra Shekhar Singh College of Pharmacy, which is affiliated to A.K.T.U. Lucknow, was approved by A.I.C.T.E, and completed in the year 2016. During her B. Pharm graduation, she was the topper in her college. She has done hospital training for my project work on the topic “Diabetes Mellitus” and also patient counseling for six months in D.R.S. Hospital, Prayagraj, during her college period. This book chapter is one of the most interesting topics on which she has worked.

2

Applications of Industry 4.0 in the Pharmaceutical Sector

Urvashi Sharma[1*], Nitu Singh[2], Poojashree Verma[3], Sumeet Dwivedi[4], Neelam Jain[5], and Javed Ahamad[6]

[1]Faculty of Pharmacy, Medi-Caps University, India
[2]RGS College of Pharmacy, Lucknow, U.P., India
[3]Pacific College of Pharmacy, Pacific University, Udaipur, Rajasthan, India
[4]Acropolis Institute of Pharmaceutical Education and Research, Indore, India
[5]Faculty of Pharmacy, Oriental University, India
[6]Department of Pharmacognosy, Faculty of Pharmacy, Tishk International University, Iraq
*Corresponding Authors: Faculty of Pharmacy, Medi-Caps University, Indore, Indore-453331, Madhya Pradesh, India,
Email: urvashi.ekta12@gmail.com.

Abstract

Industry 4.0 indicates the fourth industrial revolution which is continuously bringing up drastic changes in the manufacturing industry around the globe. This is the recent technological trend occurring for digitalization and automation of the entire manufacturing sector. In the present era, an amalgamation of novel information technologies like the Internet of Things (IoT), artificial intelligence (AI), and cloud computing together with modern manufacturing processes have played a crucial role in economically transforming the entire production process. This mutual interaction helps in analyzing the data to predict any failure and further reconfigure, thereby supporting while adapting the changes. Implementation of Industry 4.0 in the pharmaceutical sector has been referred to as Pharma 4.0. This evolution has allowed sustainable, autonomous, integrated, and self-organizing manufacturing systems to operate independent of human involvement with much-enhanced efficacy. Pharma

4.0 offers numerous advantages such as enhanced transparency, quality, efficiency, and safety with increased speed for industrial drug production. Some of the applications of Industry 4.0 to the pharma sector are electronic log books, digital line clearance, online microbial-testing systems, etc., and these are being furnished by several startups namely OptiworX, GoSilico, and QbDVision, working with stringent compliance with pharmaceutical regulations. This chapter summarizes Pharma 4.0 and various applications of Industry 4.0 in the pharmaceutical sector.

Keywords: Industry 4.0, Internet of Things, artificial intelligence, cloud computing, Pharma 4.0, OptiworX, GoSilico, QbDVision.

2.1 Introduction

The development of science and technology has taken place in many fields and is having an impact on all the major spheres of human life. Smart grids, which use digital and advanced technology to generate, transmit, and distribute power, as well as advancements in other fields like healthcare, transportation, and education, among others, are simplifying day-to-day life and increasing productivity. With time, the adoption of technologies across a number of sectors has also helped the numerous interconnected sectors to operate in synchronicity with one another [1].

The manufacturing industry must adopt new technologies, digitalization, and process intelligence in the era of ambiguity, disruption, and complexity in order to improve customer service models, modularize supply chain networks, and foster network collaboration. The production and manufacturing sectors are currently moving away from mass production and toward customized manufacturing. The development of industrial technologies has raised the level of dedication to quality and productivity across all goods and services [2].

Revolution simply refers to the significant socioeconomic changes that initiated the modifications in many industries in order to increase industrial output. The industrial revolution encompasses the advancements that followed and had a significant impact on the economy and society of the time. Mechanization, which is used to produce things, agriculture, and transportation, makes all of this feasible. The industrial revolution notifies the start of capitalism, an advanced economic system, and a financial system that currently rules the entire world and supports changing the social structure and the rise of the proletariat, a new social group [3].

The industrial revolution first started in England between 1750 and 1760. It is among the most significant turning points in human civilization ever occurred. During this time, machinery such as steam engines, spinning machines, tin plating, rolling processes to produce iron, etc., replaced the technologies that used human and animal labor. The goal of reviving the industrial revolution throughout time is economic expansion, which includes growing production of goods and services, among other things, to satisfy consumer demand. The communication and transportation networks using roads, canals, and trains have all improved as a result of the timely amendment of industrial methods. To help businesses and trading firms operate efficiently, banking and other financial systems have also been updated. In addition, this has decreased infant and child mortality rates, which has had a significant impact on population growth [4]. After that, industrial revolutions persisted for a while, and every nation adopted them to improve its manufacturing capabilities.

2.1.1 Industrial revolutions in different eras

Several industrial revolutions evolve as follows:

1. **First industrial revolution**
   The introduction of machinery, water power, and the use of energy for production in manufacturing marked the beginning of the first industrial revolution in the latter half of the 18th century (1760–1840). This led to improvements in manual manufacturing, and industries also used steam engines to make things easier. In addition, it greatly aided agriculture and brought about great development in the textile industry [5].
2. **Second industrial revolution**
   The second evolution took place in the 19th century between 1870 and 1914 as a result of the creation of electricity with the development of railway and telegraph industries as well. This revolution introduced innovation to chemistry and associated sectors while aiming to introduce bulk production [6].
3. **Third industrial revolution**
   Between 1950 and 1970, there was a third revolution that focused on integrating digital technologies into the manufacturing industry. This aided in the conversion of an analog system to a mechanical one. Modern advancements in information technology (IT), computers, and communication were unveiled during this era. It implemented dynamic and tailored manufacturing solutions, utilizing a variety of manufacturing technologies that were running separately using the computer systems, to generate another level of automation in the production system [7].

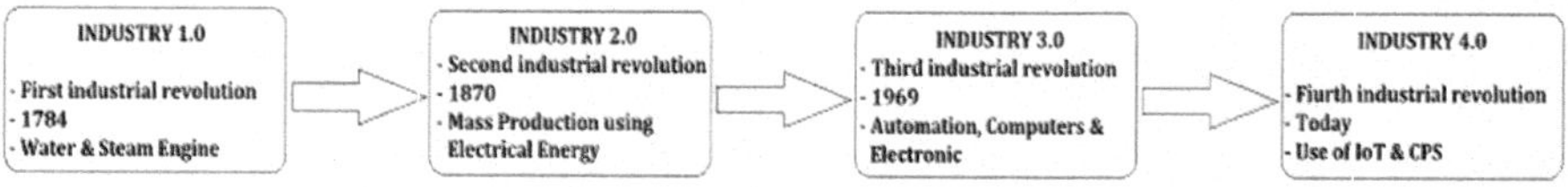

Figure 2.1 Evolution of Industries 4.0.

4. **Fourth industrial revolution**
   In order to satisfy the cutting-edge demands of the industrial sector, the fourth revolution began in the year 2020. The Internet of Things, 3D printing, artificial intelligence, cloud computing, and robots are just a few of the novel concepts and technological advancements that are crucial to this revolution. Industry 4.0 is built on a new manufacturing pattern that integrates intelligent manufacturing equipment to use new production techniques more effectively and efficiently. Overall, it creates a smart factory that can be quickly and effectively modified as needed. This will completely alter a number of industrial and commercial models [8].

Figure 2.1 [6] depicts various industrial revolutions that have taken place. These revolutions have had a noticeable impact on society because they laid the groundwork for the current manufacturing system and, to a large extent, for social and economic organization. By combining the human–machine interface, these revolutions have improved production or value-added activities while reducing waste production [3].

2.1.2 Industry 4.0

Due to ongoing technological advancements and changes in production techniques, the global industrial environment has undergone significant changes in recent years [9]. The industrial revolution of the 21st century is known as Industry 4.0, and it focuses on creating a concept for an intelligent manufacturing environment inside the production sector [10].

With a focus on connection, automation, machine learning, and real-time data, operational technology (OT) and information technology (IT) are effectively combined in the industrial sector. For companies that prioritize production and supply chain management, Industry 4.0 can occasionally include IIoT or smart manufacturing, which blends physical manufacturing and operational processes with digital technologies, machine learning, and big data [11].

Germany first launched the idea of “Industry 4.0” in 2011, heralding the start of a new phase in the industrial revolution. European scholars and manufacturing firms went to tremendous lengths to accept the concept when it was initially introduced. They were captivated by the idea since, with Industry 4.0, production will become more efficient and less expensive. All of this can be obtained by combining the production control and devices that function simultaneously and intelligently through interoperability and by facilitating easy information interchange [12].

By merging the physical and virtual components, Industry 4.0 enables the production sector to switch to digital sensing devices and produce goods much more effectively while still employing the same manufacturing equipment. All industries throughout the world might change to advance much more quickly and with greater impact by merging digital data and physical items with connected data analysis within a system [13].

At a CAGR of 20.6% from 2021 to 2026, the market for Industry 4.0 is anticipated to grow from USD 64.9 billion in 2021 to USD 165.5 billion by 2026. The main causes of this increase include increased deployment of the Internet of Things (IoT) and artificial intelligence (AI) in the production sector, increased demand for industrial robots in the medical device and pharmaceutical manufacturing industries, increased government funding for 3D printing and additive manufacturing, and quicker adoption of blockchain technology in the production sector. Most notably, the market for Industry 4.0 has a chance to expand as a result of the growing and expected demand for wearable medical devices [14].

Therefore, it can be claimed that the fourth industrial revolution and the notion of Industry 4.0 are the results of ongoing technological advancement. It also makes use of the technology developments from earlier digitalization and automation revolutions to provide improved manufacturing and other services [15].

2.1.3 Benefits of Industry 4.0

Industry 4.0 simply implies the transformation of traditional industrial and production platforms into automated, networked systems that are capable of continual automation and improvement. The development of technologies like the Internet of Things (IoT), Industrial Internet of Things (IIoT), and various connected devices on cyber-physical networks made this kind of transition conceivable [16]. The manufacturing industries and the businesses implementing it in their systems have benefited greatly from this automation. The following are some of Industry 4.0's many advantages that have been discussed:

1. **Increased productivity**
   Industry 4.0 technologies enable larger, more rapid manufacturing while consuming fewer resources. This simply means the technologies will enable the efficient and profitable utilization of allotted inputs to produce more material at a much faster rate. The manufacturers will be able to continuously improve with the least amount of waste thanks to the increased automation capabilities. Improved machine monitoring and automated decision-making will help the facility to become an Industry 4.0 smart factory, by improving the overall equipment effectiveness (OEE) [16].
2. **Enhanced efficiency**
   Industry 4.0 will enable several production lines to operate effectively in less time. Production efficiency will rise as a result of the ability to produce more goods more quickly and with less downtime for the machines. The production facility will be continuously observed to reduce errors and produce higher-quality goods. Other instances of improved efficiency include quicker batch changeovers and automated tracking, tracing, and reporting procedures. As a result, both company decision-making and the introduction of new products are improving [17].
3. **Greater knowledge sharing and fluid collaboration**
   Industry 4.0 technologies enable the interconnection between various departments like production lines, business processes, and even the managerial levels, devices, and people to communicate irrespective of time zone, place/geographical conditions, platform, or other factors. Most importantly, it can be done automatically such as from machine to machine and system-to-system, excluding the interference by any human. In short, data acquired from the sensor can immediately improve numerous manufacturing lines situated anywhere around the globe [18]. Conventional production practices were only allowed in the plant or a single unit. Because of minimal collaboration inside the company, there was less scope for exchanging the information or knowledge acquired by the individual facility with others. Industry 4.0 technologies make it possible for departments like manufacturing lines, corporate processes, and even administrative levels, devices, and people to communicate with one another regardless of the time zone, location, or other circumstances. This allows the dissemination of information that has been acquired by a sensor in a single plant within the whole organization. The most crucial aspect is that it can be done automatically, without any interference

from humans, such as from machine to machine and system to system. In brief, information obtained from the sensor can instantly enhance a variety of production processes located anywhere in the world [18].

4. **Flexibility and enhanced agility**
   Today's needs are expanding and shifting at a far faster rate, making it challenging for businesses to keep up. Demands for the newest designs, features, and technology are tough to satisfy every few months using the same conventional method. Flexibility and agility are increased thanks to Industry 4.0. For example, this technology makes it simpler to boost or lower production in an intelligent plant. This makes it simpler to introduce new items onto the production line and opens up the possibility of one-off build cycles, high-mix manufacturing, etc. [19].
5. **Facilitate compliance**
   It is not always necessary to use only manual processes to comply with regulations in sectors like pharmaceuticals and those that deal with medical equipment or devices. And by including traceability, quality checks, serialization, data logging, and other features, Industry 4.0 technology also enables automatic compliance [19].
6. **Better customer experience**
   The technology provides several chances for customer service enhancement, which raises customer happiness. For instance, one can promptly fix the issues with automated tracking and tracing tools. In addition, there won't be as many issues with product accessibility, which will improve the product's quality and give clients more options [20].
7. **Reduced expenses and high-profit margin**
   A significant investment is required to become a smart factory that uses Industry 4.0 technologies. However, this one-time expenditure will reduce the overall costs of manufacturing that are incurred at each location. Lower operational costs, effective resource use, increased output with top-notch product quality, little waste, and less downtime are the major factors driving cost reduction. Industry 4.0 technologies also make it possible to produce items of a higher caliber using more creative methods, which will increase the profit margin in a few years. With the use of these technologies, buyers can obtain customized goods using the same method that is used for the mass manufacture of comparable goods [20, 21].
8. **Enhanced business oversight**
   Real-time reporting, a collection of enormous amounts of data, improved data processing, and its display in consumable formats are all made

possible by Industry 4.0 technology. This information also acts as a source of knowledge for manufacturing and business operations, resulting in better decisions. In addition, this data aids in pinpointing areas for improvement, enables better resource allocation, and provides predictive analytics, such as patient demand projections during the product development process, aiding organizations in long-term planning [22, 23].

9. **Potential for innovations**
Industry 4.0 is entirely based on innovations; it provides deeper insight into the manufacturing process, supply chains, distribution chains, business performance, and even the products that are being made. This develops ample opportunities for innovation by either modifying a business process or creating a new product, optimizing a supply chain, etc. [23].
10. **Higher return and income**
Increased income for industrial facilities is another benefit of Industry 4.0. For instance, a new transition can be implemented with lower staff costs, needed to supply rising demand, or while vying for a new assignment by using a completely automated manufacturing line and applying the Industry 4.0 idea. There may also be a satisfactory return on investment from these transforming technologies [23].
As Industry 4.0 have multiple benefits, it is now crucial for the manufacturing sectors to equip facilities and personnel with the most upgraded technologies in order to compete in the market. This need of an hour is pushing all the manufacturing units like food, drugs, etc., to switch to Industry 4.0 techniques to reap lifetime benefits.

2.1.4 Technological pillars of Industry 4.0

Industry 4.0 is the manufacturing technology of the future. The technological system is being used in the era of digitalization to transform factories and goods into digital ones. Future technologies that can be used for mass production in smart factories include robotics, 3D printing, the Internet of Things, cloud computing, and others [24]. Industry 4.0's technological foundations are described in detail.

1. **Big data analytics**
In Industry 4.0, big data analytics is favorable for predictable production and is essential for the advancement of industrial technology through the quicker expansion of Internet infrastructure. Big data is a

compiled bundle of extensive, complex data that is massive in volume and evolves progressively over time. Large amounts of information may now be produced and retrieved quickly, which is not possible with conventional methods because it would take humans and their teams a long time to process it. Therefore, big data has recently turned up to be a point of discussion in Industry 4.0. Other applications might become more significant if the massive data management capabilities of current approaches improve. Big data involved the use of digital technology analytics. In industries, big data is gathered from a variety of sources, including factory floor IoT sensors, sales data, electrical systems, and other supply chain-relevant variables including climate, weather, and political environment. The level of effectiveness will increase as the number of data increases. For instance, according to statistics, social media sites' databases daily use more than 500 terabytes of new data generated by message forwarding, photo and video uploads, commenting on postings, etc. [25, 26].

Big data can be utilized by companies to reveal trends or consumer patterns and to identify consumer behavior. One of the famous companies that use big data is Google. Apart from its access to Chrome browser and Gmail products, it also gets data from search engines. This data is used by the company to develop algorithms related to sentence framing, correcting the spellings, etc., which help them to understand the fundamental search tasks and what the user wants to search exactly [27].

2. **Internet of Things**

The term "Internet of Things" simply refers to the link between a rapidly expanding network of physically connected things, such as integrated sensors, with the internet. These sensors can gather and distribute real-time data. As a new expression of cooperation between current IoT technology and the production industry, Industry 4.0 was created. Industry 4.0 is a result of integrating IoT and the Internet of Services (IoS) in the manufacturing process. Usually, IoT provides upgraded connectivity among physical objects, systems, and services, enabling proper communication and data sharing between various components. By automating and managing certain elements like lighting, heating, and remote monitoring in a variety of sectors, IoT can be acquired. Smart factory equipment, biometric cybersecurity scanners, wireless inventory monitors, and wearable devices for health monitoring are some examples of this technology [28, 29].

3. **Cyber-physical system**
   A computer system called a "cyber-physical system" (CPS), also referred to as an "intelligent system" or "cyber manufacturing," enables a mechanism to be controlled or monitored by computer-based algorithms. It denotes a production environment governed by Industry 4.0 that offers real-time data gathering, analysis, and transparency between each component of a manufacturing operation. Industry 4.0 can be seen as a study of cyber-physical systems in which Industry 4.0 is created by the growth and development speed of communication. Every CPS manufacturing system has sensors installed in every physical component that allows physical items to be connected to virtual models. In order to ensure that the CPS exhibits stability and has a correlation when used with AI, that is, artificial intelligence, it is important to note that the cyber-physical system is widely accepted by the general public and appears to interact with humans. The IoT, which can be used to create the Internet of Services, is built on the CPS (IoS). Therefore, in the future, it will be easier for companies to establish global networks linking CPS storage systems, machinery, and manufacturing facilities [30].
4. **Autonomous robots**
   The idea of autonomous robots is developing as Industry 4.0 advances. Robots that can manage their jobs intelligently with minimum intervention from humans are said to be autonomous. Except for maintenance, they can complete repetitive, delicate, or difficult jobs quickly and without any downtime. These autonomous robots can range in size and functionality from mobile pick-and-place robots to scanning drones. They are employed in production lines in the manufacturing sector to hold and move larger objects, preventing human injuries [31].
5. **Industrial IoT**
   The links between data, machinery, and people in the manufacturing industry are referred to as the "Industrial Internet of Things." To gather and keep track of an organization's real-time data, it uses computer tools like sensors with everything from lighting to HVAC (heating, ventilation, and air-conditioning) systems to factory floor machines. Sensors and RFID tags are used by physical items including machinery, devices, robots, and equipment to provide real-time information about the environment, position, and performance. This aids industries in running supply chains, making design changes, keeping track of inventories, and creating product listings, among other things [31, 32].

6. **Artificial intelligence**
   Artificial intelligence is a concept in which an algorithm is used by computers to carry out activities and draw conclusions that would otherwise need human intellect, such as voice recognition, visual perception, or decision-making, without any help from a person or inbuilt program. These automated systems gather information from data and make precise predictions. Since artificial intelligence is so good at foreseeing market shifts for manufacturers, it is commonly employed in the production sector to forecast demand and do predictive maintenance. The use of technology is also frequently seen in things like face recognition and navigational maps [32].
7. **Simulation or digital twins**
   A digital twin, also known as simulation modeling, is the technology of developing a simulation of a real-world object or concept within a digital space. It is a method of developing or assuming the outcome of the modeled process or system employing a virtual system or process. By using real-time data to depict the real world in a simulation model, including people, products, and machines, it includes a three-dimensional portrayal of physical objects, structures, and operating systems throughout an entire facility. Operators can thus improve the machine configuration in a virtual simulation before applying it in the real world. These speed up machine setup and improve product quality. The current innovations in the simulation modeling paradigm allow the modeling of production and other systems through the idea of the virtual factory. Moreover, through simulations, it is also possible to realize advanced artificial intelligence (cognitive) in the control of processes, including autonomous adaptations to operating systems [32, 33].
8. **Cloud computing**
   Cloud offers numerous advantages to the user such as storage of vast amounts of data, easy and timely access irrespective of geographical location, elimination of the needs of physical infrastructure, etc. Through the use of networks, cloud computing makes offsite hardware or software available when needed. The basic cloud computing models are Software as a Service, Infrastructure as a Service, and Platform as a Service. Amazon (Amazon Web Services), Microsoft (Azure), Apple (iCloud), Google (Google Drive), etc., are the top cloud service providers [34].

9. **Augmented reality**
   The use of augmented reality, commonly referred to as mixed reality, allows one to virtually place a digital object in the physical world. The idea behind Industry 4.0 is to overlay virtual visuals on real-world objects. This is known as superimposing digital content. In an augmented reality system, employees use mobile devices or smart glasses to view real-time IoT data, digital parts, training materials, repair or assembly instructions, etc., while looking at physical items, like a product or a piece of equipment. Although augmented reality is still developing, it has a significant impact on technician training, technician safety, quality control, and maintenance services. Google ARCore, a mobile app that supports augmented reality, is among the better ones that can be found online. To create virtual characters that completely mimic the real world, motion tracking, environmental awareness, and light estimation are primarily used [31, 35].
10. **Additive manufacturing or 3D printing**
   Intelligent manufacturing systems and enhanced data technologies are being driven by Industry 4.0. As a result, 3D printing and additive manufacturing are crucial tools for implementing Industry 4.0. Economic competitiveness is significantly influenced by the use of innovative production techniques to incorporate information technologies. The advent of information technology has motivated the transformation to Industry 4.0. The trend of using additive manufacturing to find new products on the market is growing right now. Several key attributes of a product can be acquired easily using metallic components and smart materials. The use of Industry 4.0 strongly depends on additive manufacturing technologies. The medical sector is also greatly impacted by 3D printing, where projects ranging from constructing a replica of the human heart to creating tailored prosthetic legs have shown amazing results [36, 37].

2.2 Pharma 4.0

As a result of stringent rules put in place by numerous stakeholders, Industry 4.0 techniques are now being used in the pharmaceutical industry to ensure the security, safety, and general well-being of society. The majority of pharmaceutical businesses have been using batch manufacturing procedures rather than continuous manufacturing for many years. Lack of an on-site quality control facility and flexible manufacturing are the two biggest problems in ensuring a steady supply of medicines, which frequently results in product shortages in emergencies. As pharmaceuticals are considered vital products, their approachability and affordability directly impact the patient's quality of life; it is important to note that pharmaceutical makers have a responsibility to make drugs more accessible to every patient [38, 39].

Traditional batch production imposes many hazardous effects on the environment, such as chemical pollution, pollutants emission into the air, sewage and residual waste, etc., in addition to availability issues in comparison to effective and tensile continuous production, which requires a lesser consumption of raw materials and less hazardous solvents. The pharmaceutical industry is the second-largest emitter of greenhouse gases; as a result of its increased emissions, the potential impact on the climate, and strict regulations, the industry is now more focused than ever on reducing its energy use and emissions throughout the life of its drug substances. Because of the limitations of conventional manufacturing practices, the pharmaceutical industry is presently adopting the Industry 4.0 idea for updating the production processes, making the processing sustainable with zero defects to the environment. This has given life to Pharma 4.0 [39].

Industry 4.0 enables localized 3D printing of medications, tailored medicine, additive manufacturing, and augmented manufacturing in the pharmaceutical sector, and provides a glimpse of the manufacturing process in which humans are not directly involved. Only via collaboration between industry, academia, and research institutions, it will be feasible to advance Industry 4.0 deployment and progressive research in all facets of the pharmaceutical industry [40].

This industrial approach covers every element of the industrial operating model, including managerial responsibilities and interactions with governing agencies. The innovative technologies of Industry 4.0 technologies that are emerging nowadays encourage the development of sustainable values and subsequently aid toward the agile, intelligent, and tailored pharmaceutical unit, giving pharma businesses a competitive advantage. In order to adapt future pharmaceutical operational and managerial processes throughout the life cycle, the pharmaceutical supply chain must be made more sustainable [41].

Manufacturing has radically changed in the pharmaceutical sector, moving from bulk production to customization. The driving trends for Industry 4.0 emphasize the industry's utilization of technology including supply chain integration, control techniques, and data integrity by design. Industry 4.0 redefines the roles of labor in the industrial sector, enabling the use of computers and physical systems to work together productively and to develop smart factories [41].

Pharma 4.0 is a framework for implementing digital technologies in the context of pharmaceutical manufacturing in order to boost productivity, foster connectivity between various departments, and does so by streamlining regulatory compliance and compiling production data in a way that will enable problem-solving as it arises. In order to apply the principles of Industry 4.0 to the manufacturing of pharmaceuticals, the International Society for Pharmaceutical Engineering created the Special Interest Group (SIG) known as International Society for Pharmaceutical Engineering (ISPE) Pharma 4.0 in 2017. Pharma 4.0 offers a variety of effective automated processes that can be batch, continuous, or a hybrid of the two, all of which are controlled by a single integrated production strategy. Pharma 4.0's primary objective is to make pharmaceutical product manufacturing along the entire value chain safer and significantly more efficient [42].

This operating model may be adopted using the concepts of Industry 4.0 technical breakthroughs, from research to product development and up to commercial manufacture by adding pharma-specific modifications at the operational and regulatory levels. Direct communication between various organizational levels is made possible, guaranteeing total transparency throughout the management of the product life cycle. Furthermore, a paperless, data-driven approach to identify and resolve various production challenges is made possible by the high connectivity of various information systems, devices, and machines [43]. With the help of Pharma 4.0, production processes may be continuously and in real time monitored, making it possible to anticipate and correct any deviation from established standards. By offering insights and removing related downtime or product loss, this technique aids in predictive analysis and various other analytics, thereby increasing the growth and wealth of business, which is currently unavailable because of dispersed, unorganized, and incomplete data [44].

2.2.1 Elements of Pharma 4.0

The new paradigm Pharma 4.0 is a universal operational model for managing the pharmaceutical industry and handling the future supply chain, as per the basis of digital maturity and data integrity by design. These serve as the key enablers of Pharma 4.0 within any industrial organization.

1. **Digital maturity**
   The digital maturity of an organization explains the ability to work inside the industrial parameters or especially within Pharma 4.0^{TM}. Pharma 4.0^{TM} SIG has framed a precise model for the pharmaceutical

industry enabling the companies to assess their current situation, the range of feasible comprehensive control measures, and the best course for developing future capabilities. Digital maturity is the fundamental enabler in moving an agile data-driven organization. Although their methods of execution will vary, all industrial phases share the same four operational model components. For shifting to Pharma 4.0^{TM}, an industry requires transparency, data visibility, predictability, and adaptability. Novel technologies like collaborative robotics, paperless execution systems, augmented reality, virtual reality (VR), etc., can leverage resources, but nothing worthwhile can be produced unless all four components of the Pharma 4.0 operating model are equally developed [45]. This has four fundamental components, as seen in Figure 2.2 [47]:

A. **Resources:** By physical and tangible assets, we mean things like labor, facilities, machinery, raw materials, and finished goods.
B. **Information systems:** The socio-technical systems that provide information based on economic standards gathered from either the populace or information and communication technology. The information may be prepared, processed, gathered, and transferred [46].
C. **Organization and processes:** This refers to the company's internal structure, which comprises its operational and structural procedures as well as its place in the value network. This establishes

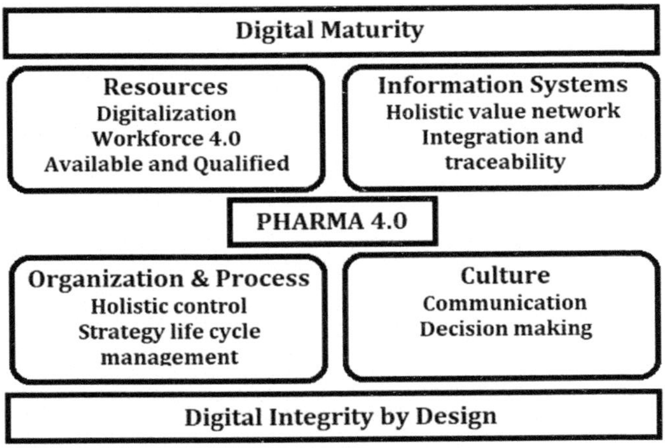

Figure 2.2 Elements of Pharma 4.0.

Table 2.1 Comparison of digital maturity models in different industrial evolutions.

Industrial Evolutions	Resources	Information systems	Organization & processes	Culture
1.0	Mechanical	Unit operation	Craft shop	Adaptive behavior, internal focus,
2.0	Electrical	Production process	Taylorism*	Stabilizing behavior, internal focus
3.0	Digitalization	Computerization	Connectivity	Stabilizing behavior, external focus
4.0	Visibility	Transparency	Predictive	Adaptive behavior, external focus

the standards necessary for internal and external cooperation in the business.

D. **Culture:** Culture highlights the facets of collaboration and incorporates the company's value system. Organization and culture should cooperate since they are interdependent [48]. Table 2.1 [48] compares digital maturity models across several industry evolutions.

2. **Data integrity by design**
The second component that ensures legal compliance and the accuracy of the shared data is data integrity. Data integrity can act as a motivating element while creating new procedures or altering current ones. Even in the days of physical labor, this was crucial, and regulatory organizations value it as well. Data collection occurs in the pharmaceutical industry from all angles, but maintaining its integrity is never simple. In addition to facilitating successful inspections, data integrity also provides the highest possible product quality, adequate and correct content, data life cycle, etc. To prevent any error, misunderstanding, or mix-up, each excipient, for example, must have a distinct name and reference number within the company's network. Data integrity requires a clearly defined methodology and risk management principles that are based on prior knowledge and research [44, 48].

2.3 Applications of Industry 4.0 to Pharmaceutical Sectors

Industry 4.0, a digitization strategy being implemented by every industry to boost productivity, has several applications in the pharmaceutical industry.

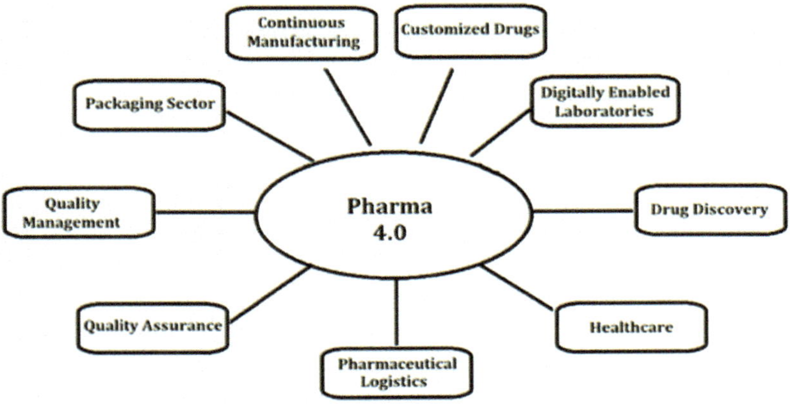

Figure 2.3 Applications of Industry 4.0 in the pharmaceutical sector.

Figure 2.3 lists some of the most important applications, which are covered in this section.

2.3.1 Continuous manufacturing

Continuous manufacturing is a manufacturing process where raw materials are provided continuously into a production unit and prepared final goods are continuously withdrawn, amid the operational duration of manufacturing processes. This technology automates many activities which streamline the process while placing the least amount of effort on human operators [49].

The pharmaceutical industry has begun the employment of Industry 4.0 technology only a few years ago. Batch production had been used for more than 50 years before this. However, the conventional batch approach takes a long time because every stage of manufacturing is often stopped for quality testing and sampling. The material is frequently stored in containers during this holding period or transferred to other internal or external facilities, even in other nations for completion of the production process. Each pause lengthens delivery timeframes and raises the risk of contamination, flaws, and mistakes [50].

In the pharmaceutical industry, continuous production, or feeding materials through a fully integrated component assembly line, reduces holding periods between the various stages of product creation in the pharmaceutical sector by transferring the substances without pause inside the same facility. Continuous production, as depicted in Figure 2.4 [50], decreases the likelihood of human errors and contamination while also freeing up time to react

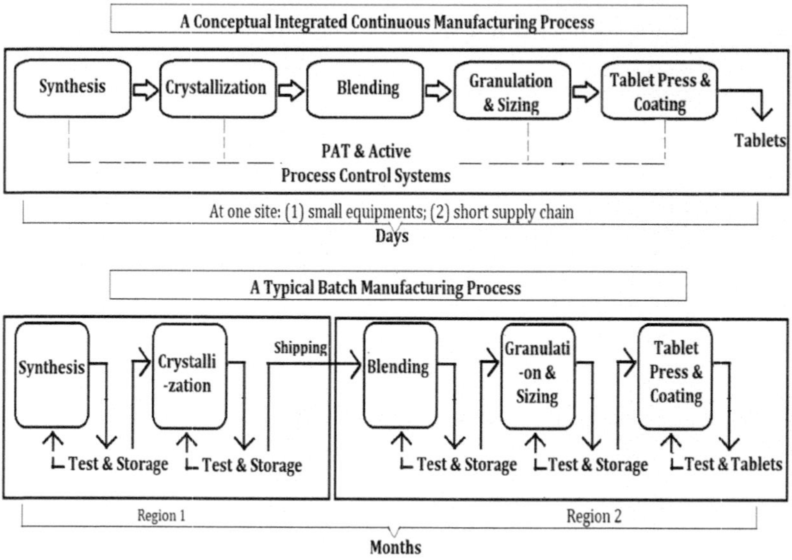

Figure 2.4 Representation of a comparison between continuous manufacturing and batch manufacturing.

more swiftly to market fluctuations. In addition, it can run for longer periods, reducing the probability of a drug shortage [51].

Continuous manufacturing has a number of benefits, including increased productivity and efficiency made possible by improved automation of unit operations like synthesis, crystallization, blending, etc.; improved product quality and safety due to continuous automated process monitoring; decreased waste production lowering negative impact on the environment; and smaller equipment sizes necessitating less space. Even though the initial financial requirement may be higher than with batch manufacturing, running costs are reduced, which boosts the overall economic efficiency of the company [52].

The development of several technologies has increased the viability of implementing continuous production. Process analytics technology (PAT), a general name for technologies used to monitor reaction behaviors in real time during manufacturing processes, including reaction progress, temperature, and pressure, is essential for resolving issues with real-time monitoring. Soft sensors, a type of virtual measurement technique, have gained attention in PATs. These soft sensors make it possible to determine data that would otherwise be problematic to evaluate in real time while employing a simulation

Table 2.2 Major pharmaceutical companies employing Pharma 4.0 concept.

Name of the Company	Project Details
Johnson & Johnson's	By operating on a continuous production technique, Janssen drug unit gained the approval from Food and Drug Administration (FDA) in 2016 for the production of HIV drug Prezista via continuous manufacturing.
Novartis	In 2007, Novartis initiated collaborative research along with the Massachusetts Institute of Technology (MIT) and developed CONTINUOUS Pharmaceuticals to motivate the introduction and development of a continuous manufacturing process.
Novartis	Novartis started the service of technology transfer among its continuous manufacturing facilities, i.e., from CONTINUOUS Pharmaceuticals to "Technikum," the purpose of which is to build new ideas and equipment.
Eli Lilly	Ireland-based plant of Eli Lilly took an initiative and used a continuous process to prepare drugs for clinical trials of phases I and II.
Vertex	Manufacturer of Orkambi, a drug for cystic fibrosis, Vertex employed the continuous manufacturing systems from July 2015.
Pfizer	Officially started a continuous tablet manufacturing plant in May 2017 in Freiburg; however, bulk production was halted a month later because of regulatory considerations.
Glatt's	In November 2016, continuous solid-dosage processing systems were started and are running at Glatt's Innovation Center in Germany.
GSK	GSK in 2014, initiated a continuous pilot plant.

technique. Since it is becoming more and more accepted as a viable alternative to actual measurements using real sensors, several manufacturers are urging the development of soft sensor technologies. Future plans call for the creation of soft sensors, which are essential foundational technology for the implementation of continuous manufacturing and can monitor reactions with complicated processes [53].

Some of the renowned pharmaceutical companies implementing continuous manufacturing initiatives are discussed in Table 2.2 [51].

2.3.2 Customized drugs and biopharmaceuticals

Today is the era of personalized medicine, "where medicines need to be manufactured with unique characteristics and supplied more quickly to the individuals who require them." Pharmaceutical businesses do not require production in large batches because producing them in lesser quantities will satisfy the needs of a smaller population that only wants a particular drug in a specific dose. Certainly, batch production is unable to resolve such needs but flexible, interconnected, intelligent, and precise continuous production can be a solution. Along with the motivation of regulatory bodies to shift to customized drugs, the market exerts significant pressure on the pharmaceutical business by requiring it to use Industry 4.0 technologies [51, 54].

Currently, the biopharmaceutical industry is moving from the one-size-fits-all drug paradigm to personalized bioproducts. This is happening because of the therapies targeting particular (stratified) patient groups or (personalized) individuals, as is the case with patient-specific autologous cells and genes. This necessitates a comparable shift in manufacturing toward customized, small-scale, and agile production that can be manufactured to order profitably. For instance, the cells are obtained from the patients at the hospital for the chimeric antigen receptor (CAR) T-cell therapy, which has been approved for the treatment of leukemia and lymphoma. These cells are delivered to a manufacturing facility for engineering before being pumped into the patient to specifically target their cancer [55].

Autologous cell therapies are another example. If the initial cell content needed for a particular patient's treatment is higher than expected and the product has a lower cell concentration than anticipated in the donor source material, Industry 4.0 can immediately decide and inform about extending the time needed for culturing (within validated limits) to produce the final required number of cells. To consistently achieve the desired product quality attributes, control of feedback, such as the use of assays for cellular characterization and online assessment to govern the cell culture operation, will be required. This will not only enhance yields and minimize waste, but it will also make a significant difference between successfully treating a patient with a life-threatening illness and failing to do so, particularly in the case of patient-specific cell and gene treatments. Since patients' health is already immunocompromised, it might not be able to repeat the manufacture using bulk manufacturing, especially if starting material from a new patient is required [56].

In addition, as patient-centered therapies are becoming more popular, a significant amount of high-quality data, batch production records, reviews, and release testing will be generated. If Industry 4.0 technologies are being used, this data may be easily kept and compiled. For instance, real-time continuous release techniques will be necessary to automate QC/QA tasks in order to handle a greater volume of patients annually and prevent creating a bottleneck. The delivery of healthcare is affected from both the patient and provider perspectives by advances in genomics and personalized treatment [56, 57].

2.3.3 Digitally enabled laboratories

The majority of processes used to regulate the quality of R&D and manufactured goods result in higher-quality, massive volumes of data that need to be analyzed and computed. This data must be gathered in order for pharmaceutical companies to better comprehend the concepts underlying each step of a drug's research and production. And this is the only way to control and improve the quality [58].

Digitally equipped labs carry out paperless procedures that use less than 80% paper throughout the entire process. Despite the former manual data transcription and second-person verification required between equipment and GLIMS, i.e., General Laboratory Information Management System, laboratories are now converting to automated data transcription. The laboratories use powerful real-time data analytics and continuous verification operations to monitor market trends, avert any deviations from specifications, and simplify the planning. These turn standard operating procedures into an in-depth visual manual that explains the steps needed for each process using digital tools like smart glasses. A digital twin of the laboratory is also generated to forecast the impacts before any physical modification. The current state of these modern technologies makes an impact on each instance in just three months. By achieving the horizon of the digitally enabled laboratory, an average quality control laboratory can cut costs by up to 25 to 45%. It is possible to save between 15 and 35% in a typical microbiology lab [59].

For instance, scientists frequently use a variety of analytical techniques when monitoring a reaction during production. These include chromatography using ion chromatography for liquid, gas, or other media. Mass spectrometry (MS) is increasingly used to monitor reactions, making it easier to combine multiple phases of analysis into a single test, reducing the possibility of human mistakes and increasing the accuracy and confidence in results. In order to obtain better analytical results in fewer steps, it is anticipated that more pharmaceutical manufacturers would use high-resolution mass spectrometry-based techniques like multi-attribute monitoring (MAM) in the approaching years. Currently, several MS-based monitoring systems are being replaced with modern sensors as well, simplifying test procedures, enhancing data security, and increasing operational effectiveness. However, the majority of the required sensors still need to be created [60].

Better use of data can be made possible by the combination of analysis and informatics in Pharma 4.0, which can increase efficacy and efficiency across the board for the pharmaceutical industry, including medication research and manufacturing. Scientists occasionally need more sophisticated analytical approaches like artificial intelligence, particularly in research and development labs. Large datasets are necessary for the majority of artificial intelligence (AI) and machine learning (ML) tools. In addition, the considerable amount of data produced by pharmaceutical production processes are typically not large or well-formatted enough to meet the requirements of many AI or ML algorithms. Consequently, a few modules are being created to enable dealing with the datasets that are present in the pharmaceutical business in order to address this issue [60, 61].

Collaboration between professionals in the analytical and instrumentation fields could help pharmaceutical companies create more efficient production testing techniques that adhere to regulatory authorities' laid-down criteria. For instance, some companies are implementing such advanced techniques in assessing drug release, hoping to combine near-infrared technology for determining the time needed to dissolve a tablet with modeling to create in-line dissolution testing rather than performing the offline test using dissolution apparatus [60].

2.3.4 Drug discovery

Pharmaceutical companies are most reliable in innovation and research for drug development. It is highly typical for new revolutionary digital capabilities to be used in drug research in order to decrease the likelihood of failure, save time, and boost productivity. Machine learning and artificial intelligence are powering the early stages of drug research, and the market for drug discovery apps is also employing these technologies. Machine learning algorithms are also being used by scientists to shorten the development process and create a stable and long-lasting medicine. In pharmaceutical laboratories, machine learning algorithms are now accessible because of the ongoing growth of cloud computing. This offers a glimpse of laboratories in the future that will operate on digital connectivity and focus on introducing new lead compounds to healthcare markets. Artificial intelligence-powered dashboards assist sectors in monitoring recent updates from health authorities and compliance with them [62, 63].

A new drug's market entry takes 12 to 14 years and practically enormous financial resources. The cost of drug discovery can be reduced by up to 70% by automating the process. For instance, a London-based company that used artificial intelligence to look into two possible drug targets for Alzheimer's inspired other pharmaceutical companies to use these techniques in its research and development division. Exscientia, a company that designs drugs, employs an artificial intelligence platform to design and pick the lead molecule assisting in the discovery of new drugs. These technologies efficiently create and examine minuscule quantities of materials that can aid in modern designs and model refinement. Cloud computing, the Internet of Things, machine learning, etc., are suited for offering a quicker, more affordable, and more effective solution while searching for novel compounds [64].

Over the past two decades, the rapid development of data processing segments has resulted in the creation of sophisticated algorithms that make it easier to conduct research on new drugs by collecting data from clinical trials, devices, and patients and categorizing it for cloud categorical storage. These have been analyzed and used at every stage of the drug discovery process and by the time they are delivered, the costs involved in the drug discovery process will be drastically reduced. Drug companies are now embracing patient-driven biology and data collection instead of the traditional trial-and-error method of drug discovery in order to make more accurate predictions. In order to look for any hidden patterns, artificial intelligence is used to process this vast amount of data. Multiple pieces of information are connected to remember the behavior pattern of the investigational molecule during the drug discovery process using databases. It aids in anticipating the nature of the substance based on its impact on the patient and previously stored data for the substance being tested. Only one substance out of 1000 that was first believed to be a safe medicine receives FDA approval [64, 65].

The traditional drug discovery method costs much and is also time taking. Future drug research will be governed by the confluence of new technologies, with sophisticated intelligent hardware systems controlling the entire process of drug discovery and clinical trials. Through the Internet, the IoT collaborates with people, systems, data, and objects. Information technology (IT), operations technology, and data are all integrated as part of the digital transformation process in order to improve productivity and provide improved understanding. Though scientists are struggling to use digitization to its fullest extent, cultural inertia still holds it back. Pharmaceutical firms are embracing digital transformation to innovate new personalized therapies and medicines. IoT-based methods that have been put into practice enable for more affordable production of both new and conventional pharmaceuticals as well as the funding of more creative drug production concepts. IoT-based drug discovery systems enable smoother study replication while limiting human intervention, hence lowering the possibility of human error in the process and tests [66, 67].

2.3.5 Healthcare

Industry 4.0 and the revolution in healthcare are occurring at the same time. In this situation, a cyber-physical system equipped with radio frequency identification (RFID), Internet of Things (IoT), medical robots, smart sensors, wearable and other types of healthcare devices, etc., is used to deliver healthcare services. This system is also combined with Industry 4.0 technologies like big data analytics, artificial intelligence, cloud computing, and decision support techniques to more intelligently acquire interconnected healthcare. This system helps link together all the equipment and gadgets, together with the patient's location and his community, in addition to the healthcare organizations and institutions like hospitals, clinics, etc. [68].

IoT drastically influences the healthcare sector; in other words, the modern healthcare industry is a component of Healthcare 4.0, which is a subset of Industry 4.0 and used in several areas. The term "digital databases" in healthcare refers to the IoT, which is the fastest-adopting technology and explains remote monitoring services, especially for patients. In addition, historically it was a little difficult for patients to meet with their doctor and schedule an appointment. Even in life-threatening situations where the patient needs rapid medical attention for chest discomfort, bleeding, and shortness of breath, the patient may experience difficulties. In such times, accessible, convenient, affordable, and customized medical facilities can be delivered by deploying IoT in digital healthcare [69].

Wearable IoT devices include smartwatches made by Apple Watch and smart glasses like Hololens and Google Glass. Smartwatches can easily track and display a person's heart rate, pulse rate, daily step count, and even more. These gadgets are built with wireless sensors that provide information to a central server, which then shows results to individuals. The term "fabric and flexible devices" now refers to inexpensive, disposable IoT-based patches that are typically worn for a few days. A few examples of such flexible disposable patches are BP monitor, iRhythm, Biostamp, electro pads, UV sense, etc. The

Australian Center for Nanomedicine (ACN) and the University of New South Wales in Sydney recently developed a wearable sensor to alert the user to UV light exposure [70].

The term "ambient IoT" refers to Internet of Things (IoT) gadgets like door, motion, video, pressure, sound, and object sensors that are not wearable. By adopting remote monitoring, these IoT environmental gadgets help doctors immediately connect with their patients. IoT adoption in the healthcare industry had a significant impact both from an industrial and commercial perspective. Various networks of interconnected devices are used in IoT industries to exchange data; data analysis for the system includes data collecting and result generation. AI-based data processing algorithms can also be used to observe ECG, as a result of which IoT devices make it simple to detect health problems [69].

Many processes are time-consuming and hence documented in the electronic health record; even the manual activities such as purchase order entry and digitized electronic post-visit summary are being computerized in much less time with better efficiency [71]. In addition, by exploiting the current computer networks, telemedicine and teleassistance are becoming feasible and electronic visits are being replaced by in-person encounters. The recent scenario of the COVID-19 pandemic has intensified the demand for telemedicine and virtual visits. All of these brought a number of innovative changes in the healthcare sector [68].

2.3.6 Pharmaceutical logistics

Pharmaceutical manufacturers themselves control outbound transportation; thereafter, the drug transit is carried out by distributors and wholesalers. The fundamental social duty of the pharmaceutical supply chain is to increase the accessibility of medications in order to reduce the risk of a drug shortage at any time [72]. The distribution process can benefit from "smart logistics," becoming considerably more coordinated and visible over time. Cloud computing, the Internet of Things, and cyber-physical systems give superior networking and traceability for both the physical and data flows [73].

Despite the typical retrospective management, pharmaceutical supply chain logistics managers can share information, organize tasks, and take real-time actions utilizing ledgers or cloud-based computers, which aids in the establishment of virtual enterprise resource planning systems. Real-time data exchange with other businesses makes it possible to assemble consumption statistics, which not only increases the flexibility but also makes it possible to better meet customer demand for drugs by making them more readily available and accessible. In addition, merchants can have far more flexible and automated supply and management of inventories, even in cases of insufficient manpower or the absence of decision-makers, by employing more precise real-time data that is backed up by a cyber-physical system. It is possible to record how sensitive indicators respond, such as humidity, temperature, cleanliness, air pressure, etc., and anomalous data is recorded automatically. While intelligent logistics allows for smaller buffer levels, a higher level of collaboration can be attained [74].

As stated by European Union in 2018, prescription drugs must have an exclusive serial number, such as China has its own inherent code for each drug under the "Drug Electronic Supervision Code." By doing this, data on product distribution is gathered and stored in cloud-operated computer systems, allowing each patient to quickly access the whole pharmaceutical supply chain by scanning the package's barcode, QR code, or another unique identifying number. The widespread usage of radio frequency identification (RFID) in pharmaceutical logistics is due to its lower risk of error and higher cost-effectiveness. Despite being more expensive than conventionally printed labels, IT systems utilizing RFID technologies are nonetheless used throughout the pharmaceutical supply chain, from producers to merchants. Small and medium-sized businesses are therefore very reluctant to adopt RFID readers, IT databases, and sensors [75].

The real-time information collected using RFID tracking may support the producers working in conjunction with recent distributors to ensure the real needs in the proper amount, delivery time, and product location, given that proper intercommunication can result in better utilization of the available spaces in the warehouse and also reduce the possibility of transaction error by shortening the prediction time for demand. In addition, RFID can provide information on the expiration date, which is thought to be the primary reason for drug returns and can thus intimate about the return of expired or soon-to-expire medications. As a result, each PSC member must cooperate in order to administer RFID using the procedures and generic database. Although detection is possible with RFID tags for serialization, it should be highlighted that prolonged exposure to radio frequency signals might reduce the effectiveness of biopharmaceutical goods. Another significant issue with such novel technologies as cloud computing, RFID, etc., is that in order to prevent any variation, they must adhere to internationally recognized standards [75, 76].

2.3.7 Quality assurance

Pharmaceutical 4.0 ideas from Industry 4.0 also apply to quality assurance (QA), and their application offers significant room for improvement in the industry's production and manufacturing processes. Data that is already available can be collected right away with enhanced analytics and information technologies. Training in quality assurance includes instruction in data handling as well. The data automation and its digitization increase information accessibility with fewer restrictions on searching and using the collected data. When opposed to testing that is solely conducted in laboratories, which is less accurate, real-time online testing may increase efficiency and feedback collection. The utilization of simulation and process digitization focuses mainly on improving the productivity of the supply chain, in addition to good practices (GxP) and guidelines by FDA, etc. This suggests an idea for better growth of the quality assurance sector to work with greater accuracy [77].

GxP documentation can shift from manual documentation to electronic documents if the process keeps moving in the same direction. Every stakeholder in the pharmaceutical value chain can access information in digital form. Instead of keeping data isolated within the corporate walls, information technology allows it to be dispersed and shared across diverse industry personnel. When working in the future with new businesses or industries, this data may be useful as reference backup material or in the event of increased workload. This is an ingenious way for the industry to continue with pharmaceutical production capable of satisfying a greater number of market demands with numerous benefits. Data can be used to extend this internal communication among various company personnel and create a strong link. The opportunity to combine resources and findings from every process imaginable through this collaboration may make it a far more significant component of the effort in pharmaceutical quality assurance and a greater source of knowledge [77].

2.3.8 Quality management

Quality 4.0 is based on the concept of Industry 4.0, which alludes to the future of quality management through the adoption of emerging technology in many sectors of the economy This type of quality-based shift can be driven by the industrial sector adopting more digital working practices, which will increase process robustness and efficiency [78]. Paper-based processes and procedures are still prevalent in many businesses. Even now, the Quality Assurance (QA) and Quality Control (QC) divisions still use paper-based or manual techniques for a number of data management tasks. To ensure product quality standards and data integrity while using such traditional ways to keep important quality records, additional manual checks are required. These methods require a lot of time, are prone to human mistakes, and over time, improper storage options might result in data loss [79].

Manual quality inspections are much more expensive and tedious in high-volume environments. For example, to determine particle size in bulk solids, sampling inspection will be carried out, which includes assessing the quality of the whole production batch by examining a minute fraction of the product at one time. Traditionally, the distribution of particle size is evaluated on-site using a sieve analysis or another procedure. By continually measuring the particle size online to enable automated inspection, particle size analyzers like Eyecon2 offer an evolutionary step forward. Continuous Process Verification (CPV) is a technique that demonstrates the process's validity by allowing continuous verification of the performance of a manufacturing process. Real-time particle size data can be dynamically obtained using PAT, such as Eyecon2, and is included in process knowledge. CPV is essential for real-time release testing because it lowers overheads and results in more productive workloads [79, 80].

Therefore, it can be claimed that Quality 4.0 opens the door to the Smart Factory, where employing digital techniques can enhance the productivity and flexibility from the workshop to the larger company. Digital technologies can enhance quality as they provide modern tools to companies to monitor operations and collect data in real time, conduct analyses, and foresee quality issues. These technologies give the assurance to tackle quality in a proactive rather than a reactive manner. With Eyecon2, automated digital tools, and a governance control system, companies can simply create better, quicker products at a cheaper cost. Online quality measures that optimize quality control, digitize quality control labs, and lessen the need for paper-based systems are provided by recent process analytical technologies (PATs) that can be included in the process. Data can be gathered and processed in real time, shared with the wider team for evaluation, or securely kept for convenient retrieval in the future when used in conjunction with a fully automated control system. In this approach, an effort to implement Industry 4.0 as a whole results in the removal of stages that do not add value and the augmentation of quality requirements [80].

Pharma 4.0 technologies can transform the entire value chain by allowing producers to trust findings gathered from real-time data. Digitization also supports the formulator in assuring better product quality by decreasing human errors. For instance, businesses related to publishing and archiving are now becoming fully paperless and rely totally on electronic ways of archiving. Hence, the technologies of Pharma 4.0 assure the maintenance of data integrity throughout their life cycle [62].

2.3.9 Packaging sector

In order to successfully meet customer needs, the pharmaceutical manufacturing business must continue to develop toward Industry 4.0, as well as its supporting supply chains, particularly the packaging industry, without which no products can be supplied. Today's packaging equipment must be fully modular, automatic, intelligent, and able to increase a manufacturing company's packaging efficiency while producing personalized goods quickly and effectively [81].

In today's time, thinking about packaging and packaging machines has entirely changed and constantly adopting innovations, while moving away from designing only the package appearance toward designing the packaging machines. Before cutting any metal, creating a "digital twin" facilitates thorough simulation and virtual image construction. As a result, whole new operational platforms have been developed that, by default, require significantly reduced energy usage, less material use, flexibility to handle a variety of pack sizes, increased production rates, and extremely quick changeover times. This digital twin remains in the Internet of Things and continuously monitors the physical twin to ensure that everything is operating as intended. The issue of downtime is resolved by rapidly identifying and implementing the preventive solution in the event of any issue [82].

In order to implement 4.0, manufacturers must examine the fundamental platform around which the packing machine is built, re-examine their workflow, and reconsider the materials they have been relying on for a long time. The new packaging equipment enables manufacturers to adaptably assess the materials they are using for packing, enabling them to evaluate hybrid packaging made of recycled polyethylene terephthalate (RPET) and corrugated cardboard. A robust package that is suitable for shipping and simpler to handle and open can be created by combining the high strength of corrugated cardboard with the presentation features of the RPET. Utilizing RPET even improves product exposure since most consumers are more interested in the product's content than its packaging.

The cold-stuffing method: The cold wrapping technology can improve the efficiency of the delivery system by inserting a third component as a thin film in combination with RPET trays. Plain corrugated sleeves and thin film offer more flexibility to modify pack size following store demand and customized product requirements, without incurring high source and printing costs [83].

Product personalization and safety can advance to new heights by allowing smart digital communication among patients and product packaging, with improving the communication with machines in manufacturing. These goods enhance patient communication by utilizing Near Field Communication (NFC) chip technology, which is incorporated inside the box. As long as the "read" terminal is within the range, the NFC chip transmits information [84].

2.4 Service Providers of Industry 4.0 to Pharmaceutical Sectors

The Pharma 4.0 market is being served by a large number of creative businesses that are utilizing these emerging technologies to provide the best solution for the transformation of the pharmaceutical sector from industrialization to digitalization. Table 2.3 [85] discusses a few of them.

2.5 Conclusion

Industry 4.0 is the globally accepted paradigm that is bringing revolutions in the field of the manufacturing sector. This concept is playing a crucial role in transforming the manufacturing industry toward digitalization by utilizing the technologies like robotics, augmented reality, the Internet of Things (IoT), simulation, cloud computing, etc. This explains the future industrial scenario where the entire life cycle of the product will be more controlled and organized. Though the concept is in a very early stage as it got introduced in 2011 only, every business is adopting it due to its immense benefits. The pharmaceutical industry, one of the quickly expanding sectors, is also implementing this concept to guarantee the timely delivery of medication items in a more synchronized manner.

Pharma 4.0 ensures the continuous and real-time monitoring of prepared products on the manufacturing line itself, ensuring that any deviation from the norm will be corrected right away without wasting any time or material. Increased productivity, improved efficiency, information sharing, timely access from anywhere, the potential for innovations, and reduced human intervention are just a few of the advantages that Pharma 4.0 offers. Offering personalized drug items aids the manufacturing sector in meeting the rising demand for medicines.

Table 2.3 Service providers of Industry 4.0.

Name of the Company	Description of Services
Goodly Innovations	Used augmented reality technology to develop OptiworX, a product that offers services to the manufacturing industry. Offering assistance with the production, filling, and packaging of pharmaceutical items enables operators and technical personnel to work effectively.
QbDVision	Utilizing machine learning and artificial intelligence (AI) algorithms enables analysis and evaluation of the vast set of data. This has been created to impart knowledge and solutions for drug development. The technology allows the product to launch at a much faster rate. The software evaluates the involved risk and also enables the process visualization [86].
Electrosan Technologies	Pharmaceutical firms can benefit from Electrosan Technologies, which adheres to GAMP 5 (Good Automated Manufacturing Processes) and 21 CFR compliance criteria. Producers can evaluate downtime, cost of investment, and production efficiency using IoT-based sensors and predictive features [87].
GoSilico	This product helps biopharma firms by offering creative ideas for drug discovery, development, and packaging. It does this by utilizing big data and artificial intelligence. The "in silico" experiment, which is far less expensive and quicker, is made possible by creating digital twins of bioprocesses [88].
Smart Factory	Smart Factory developed the automated cloud-based FLEXIM solution to help the pharmaceutical packaging industry. The operation of numerous stations allows for the automation and ongoing supervision of each process [89].

Pharma 4.0 is being used to its fullest capacity in a number of target industries, including packaging, digitally equipped labs, continuous manufacturing, customized product formulation, and pharmaceutical logistics. Industry 4.0 has simplified the laborious lab work, lowered investment costs, and provided results with much higher accuracy about the safety and efficacy of lead compounds. In addition, the idea is being applied in the healthcare industry to support telemedicine and real-time patient care. This is being used by numerous well-known pharmaceutical companies, including Pfizer, Johnson & Johnson, Novartis, Eli Lilly, GSK, and others, in a variety of ways to update their manufacturing, drug discovery, pilot plant study, and other processes for the continuous delivery of safe and effective medications on time to mass.

Acknowledgment

The authors are thankful to Dean Pharmacy Dr. Sanjay Jain and the Management of Medi-Caps University, Indore for their gracious assistance and cooperation needed for the completion of this work.

Conflict of Interest

The authors declare that there is no conflict of interest.

Funding

No funding is received.

References

[1] Paul, S., Rabbani, M. S., Kundu, R. K. and Zaman, S. M. R. –2014) "A review of smart technology (Smart Grid) and its features," *in the proceedings of the International Conference on Non-Conventional Energy (ICONCE 2014)* Kalyani, India, 200–203.
[2] Adhikari, I., and Singhal, N. (2020) Industry 4.0 preparedness in Indian pharmaceutical companies - A review and agenda for future research. *MDIM Business Review*. 1-1, 39-45.
[3] Eurotransis: The Industrial Revolution. Was it so important?. Available at: https://eurotransis.com/en/the-industrial-revolution-was-it-so-important/ [accessed Jan 5, 2022].
[4] Mohajan, H. K. (2019) The First Industrial Revolution: Creation of a New Global Human Era. *Journal of Social Sciences and Humanities*. 5-4, 377-387.
[5] Groumpo, P. P. (2021) A Critical Historical and Scientific Overview of all Industrial Revolutions. IFAC-PapersOnLine, 54-13, 464–471. DOI: https://doi.org/10.1016/j.ifacol.2021.10.492.
[6] Kagermann, H., Helbig, J., Hellinger, A., Wahlster, W.(2013) Recommendations for Implementing the Strategic Initiative Industry 4.0: Securing the Future of German Manufacturing Industry. *Final Report of the Industry 4.0 Working Group Forschungsunion*.
[7] Mohd, J., Haleem A. (2019) Industry 4.0 applications in medical field: A brief review. *Curr. Med. Res. Pract.* 9,102-109. DOI: https://doi.org/10.1016/j.cmrp.2019.04.001.

[8] Sharma, A., and Singh, B. J. (2020) Evolution of Industrial Revolutions: A Review. *International Journal of Innovative Technology and Exploring Engineering*, 9. 66-73.

[9] Recommendations for Implementing the Strategic Initiative Industries 4.0: Final Report of the Industries 4.0 Working Group. Available at: https://www.din.de/blob/76902/e8cac883f42bf28536e7e8165993f1fd/recommendations-for-implementing-industry-4-0-data.pdf [accessed Jan 5, 2022].

[10] Crnjac, M., Veža, I. (2017) From concept to the introduction of Industry 4.0. *Int. J. Ind. Eng. Manag.* 8-1, 21-30.

[11] Epicor:What is Industry 4.0—the Industrial Internet of Things (IIoT)?. Available at: https://www.epicor.com/en-in/resources/articles/what-is-industry-4-0/ [accessed Jan 5, 2022].

[12] Qin, J., Liu, Y., Grosvenor, R. A. (2016) Categorical Framework of Manufacturing for Industry 4.0 and beyond. *Procedia CIRP*. 52, 173–178. DOI: https://doi.org/10.1016/j.procir.2016.08.005.

[13] Mrugalska, B., Wyrwicka, M. K. (2017) Towards Lean Production in Industry 4.0. *Procedia Eng.* 182, 466–473. DOI: https://doi.org/10.1016/j.proeng.2017.03.135.

[14] Market & Market: Industry 4.0 Market. Available at: https://www.marketsandmarkets.com/Market-Reports/industry-4-market-102536746.html [accessed Jan 5, 2022].

[15] Adebayo, A. O., Chaubey, M. S., Numbu, L. P. (2019) Industry 4.0: The fourth industrial revolution and how it relates to the application of Internet of Things (IoT). *J. multidiscip. eng. sci. technol.* 5-2, 2477-2482.

[16] LabhGroup: 6 Key Benefits of Industry 4.0 for Businesses. Available at: https://labhgroup.com/insights/6-benefits-of-industry-4-0/_[accessed Jan 5, 2022].

[17] The Main Benefits and Challenges of Industry 4.0 Adoption in Manufacturing. Available at: https://www.infopulse.com/blog/the-main-benefits-and-challenges-of-industry-4-0-adoption-in-manufacturing [accessed Jan 5, 2022].

[18] Industry 4.0 And Smart Factory: How These Can Benefit Businesses. Available at: https://www.tm-robot.com/en/blog/industry-4-smart-factor-business-benefits/ _[accessed Jan , 6 2022].

[19] Prescient Technologies: Benefits of Industry 4.0. Available at: https://www.pre-scient.com/knowledge-center/industry-4-0/benefits-of-industry-4-0.html _[accessed Jan 6, 2022].

[20] Woboton: 5 Key Benefits of Industry 4.0 for Factories. Available at: https://woboton.com/5-key-benefits-of-industry-40-for-factories/ [accessed Jan 6, 2022].

[21] Industrial Internet of things (IIoT) and Industry 4.0: Are you ready for it?. Available at: https://radixweb.com/blog/what-is-industry-4-0 _[accessed Jan 5, 2022].

[22] How can Industry 4.0 benefit my business?. Available at: https://www.bdc.ca/en/articles-tools/technology/invest-technology/how-can-industry-benefit-my-business [accessed Jan 5, 2022].

[23] SLCONTROLS: Benefits of Industry 4.0. Available at: https://slcontrols.com/en/benefits-of-industry-4-0/ _[accessed Jan 6, 2022].

[24] Gajdzik, B., Grabowska, S., Saniuk, S. (2021) A Theoretical Framework for Industry 4.0 and its Implementation with Selected Practical Schedules. *Energies*. 14-4, 940. DOI: https://doi.org/10.3390/en14040940.

[25] Guru99: What is Big Data? Introduction, Types, Characteristics, Examples. Available at: https://www.guru99.com/what-is-big-data.html [accessed Jan 6, 2022].

[26] Witkowski, K. (2017) Internet of Things, Big Data, Industry 4.0 – Innovative Solutions in Logistics and Supply Chains Management. *Procedia Eng*. 182, 763 – 769. DOI: https://doi.org/10.1016/j.proeng.2017.03.197.

[27] Builtin:17 Big Data Examples and Applications. Available at: https://builtin.com/big-data/big-data-examples-applications [accessed Jan 6, 2022].

[28] Zhong, R. Y., Xu, X., Klotz, E., Newman, S. T.N (2017) Intelligent Manufacturing in the Context of Industry 4.0: A Review. *Engineering*. 3-5, 616–630. DOI: https://doi.org/10.1016/J.ENG.2017.05.015.

[29] Builtin: 27 Top Internet of Things Examples You Should Know. Available at: https://builtin.com/internet-things/iot-examples [accessed Jan 6, 2022].

[30] Tay, S. I., Lee, T. C., Hamid, N. A. A, Ahmad, A. N. A. (2018) An Overview of Industry 4.0: Definition, Components, and Government Initiatives. *J. Adv. Res. Dyn. Control Syst.* 10-14, 1379-1387.

[31] SAP: What is Industry 4.0?. Available at: https://insights.sap.com/what-is-industry-4-0/ [accessed Jan 6, 2022].

[32] Machinemterics: Emerging Industry 4.0 Technologies with Real-World Examples. Available at: https://www.machinemetrics.com/blog/industry-4-0-technologies [accessed Jan 6, 2022].

[33] Vaidya, S., Ambad, P., and Bhosle, S. (2018) Industry 4.0 – A Glimpse. *Procedia Manuf.* 20, 233-238. DOI: https://doi.org/10.1016/j.promfg.2018.02.034.

[34] Netcov: What is Cloud Computing?. Available at: https://www.netcov.com/what-is-cloud-computing/_[accessed Jan 6, 2022].

[35] StudiousGuy: 11 Examples of Augmented Reality in Everyday Life. Available at: https://studiousguy.com/examples-augmented-reality/ [accessed Jan 6, 2022].

[36] Dilberoglu, U. M., Gharehpapagh, B., Yaman, U., Dolen, M. (2017) The Role of Additive Manufacturing in the Era of Industry 4.0. *Procedia Manuf.* 11, 545-554. DOI: https://doi.org/10.1016/j.promfg.2017.07.148.

[37] NeoMetrix Technologies: 7 Examples of 3D Printing in the World Today. Available at: https://3dscanningservices.net/blog/7-examples-of-3d-printing-in-the-world-today/ [accessed Jan 7, 2022].

[38] Woodcock, J. (2004) The Concept of Pharmaceutical Quality. Am. Pharm. Rev. 7-6,10-15.

[39] Stegemann, S. (2016) The future of pharmaceutical manufacturing in the context of the scientific, social, technological and economic evolution. *Eur. J. Pharm. Sci.* 90, 8-13. DOI: 10.1016/j.ejps.2015.11.003.

[40] Weichhart, G., Molina, A., Chen, D., Whitman, L., and Vernadat, F. (2015) Challenges and Current Developments for sensing, Smart and Sustainable Enterprise Systems, Computers in Industry. Comput Ind. 79, 34-46, DOI: 10.1016/j.compind.2015.07.002.

[41] Reinhardt, I. C., Oliveira, J. C., and Ring, D. T. (2021) Industry 4. 0 and the Future of the Pharmaceutical Industry. *Pharm. Eng.* 41-2.

[42] Herwig, C., Woelbeling, C., Zimmer, C. (2017) A Holistic Approach to Production Control. *Pharm. Eng.*

[43] Markarian, J. (2018) Pharma 4.0. *Pharm. Technol.* 42-4. 1-24.

[44] Interfacing: What is Pharma 4.0?. Available at: https://www.interfacing.com/pharma-4-0 [accessed Jan 6, 2022].

[45] Vimachem IIOT Pharma 4. 0 AI Platform: A practical guide to pharma 4. 0 realization, Available at: https://www.vimachem.com/resources/pharma-4-0/ [accessed Jan 7, 2022].

[46] From Industrie4. 0 to Pharma 4. 0 Operating model and The Holistic ICH Control Strategy. Available at https://gosgmp.ru/download/Materialy/ivgmp/2019-09-23/04-en/Volbeling_angl.pdf [accessed Jan 6, 2022].

[47] Manzano, T., and Langer, G. (2018) Getting Ready for Pharma 4.0^{TM}. *Pharm. Eng.* 72-79.

[48] ISPE Connecting Pharmaceutical Knowledge, Pharma 4.0^{TM}: Hype or Reality?. Available at: https://ispe.org/pharmaceutical-engineering/july-august-2018/pharma-40tm-hype-or-reality [accessed Jan 7, 2022].

[49] Inada, Y. (2019) Continuous Manufacturing Development in Pharmaceutical and Fine Chemicals Industries. Mitsui & Co. Global Strategic Studies Institute Monthly Report.

[50] U.S. Food and Drug Administration, Modernizing the Way Drugs Are Made: A Transition to Continuous Manufacturing. Available at: https://www.fda.gov/drugs/news-events-human-drugs/modernizing-way-drugs-are-made-transition-continuous-manufacturing [accessed Jan 7, 2022].

[51] Tefen Management Consulting: The Impact of Industry 4. 0 on the Pharma Industry. Available at: https://www.tefen.com/insights/industries/Patient_Care/the_impact_of_industry_40_on_the_pharma_industry [accessed Jan 6, 2022].

[52] Domokos, A., Nagy, B., Szilágyi, B., Marosi, G. and Nagy, Z. K. (2021) Integrated Continuous Pharmaceutical Technologies—A Review. *Org. Process Res. Dev*. 25-4, 721–739. DOI: https://doi.org/10.1021/acs.oprd.0c00504.

[53] Hock, S. C., Siang, T. K. and Wah, C. L. (2021) Continuous manufacturing versus batch manufacturing: benefits, opportunities and challenges for manufacturers and regulators. *GaBI Journal.*10-1, 44-56. DOI: 10.5639/gabij.2021.1001.004

[54] John Klaess, 8 Trends in Pharmaceutical Manufacturing to Watch in 2022, Available at: https://tulip.co/blog/pharmaceutical-manufacturing-trends-to-watch/[accessed Jan 8, 2022].

[55] Veeva: How Digital Quality Management is Transforming Pharma Manufacturing, Available at: https://www.veeva.com/wp-content/uploads/2020/05/Transforming-Pharma-Manufacturing [accessed Jan 6, 2022].

[56] Branke, J., Farid, S. S., and Shah. N. (2016) Industry 4.0: A vision for personalized medicine supply chains?. *Cell gene ther. Insights*. 263-270.DOI: 10.18609/cgti.2016.027.

[57] Narayanan, H. et al. (2020) Bioprocessing in the Digital Age: The Role of Process Models. *Biotechnol J.* 15-1, e1900172. DOI: 10.1002/biot.201900172.

[58] Hariry, R. E., Barenji, R. V., and Paradkar A. (2022) From Industry 4. 0 to Pharma 4.0: Handbook of Smart Materials, Technologies, and Devices. *Drug Discov. Today*. 27-1, 315- 325.DOI: 10.1007/978-3-030-58675-1_4-1.

[59] Digitization, automation, and online testing: The future of pharma quality control. *McKinsey & Company*. Available at: https://www.mckinsey.com/industries/life-sciences/our-insights/digitization-automation-and-online-testing-the-future-of-pharma-quality-control _[accessed Jan 8, 2022].

[60] Grumbach, E. Emerging Technologies Required for Pharma 4.0. Available at: https://www.technologynetworks.com/drug-discovery/articles/emerging-technologies-required-for-pharma-40-346220 [accessed Jan 6, 2022].

[61] Hole, G., Hole, A. S., and McFalone-Shaw, I. (2021). Digitalization in pharmaceutical industry: What to focus on under the digital implementation process?. *Int J Pharm X*. 3-100095. DOI: https://doi.org/10.1016/j.ijpx.2021.100095

[62] Krishnamurthy, S. Pharma 4.0: Redefining Product Development and Regulatory Operations. *Pharmexec.com*. Available at: https://www.pharmexec.com/view/pharma-4-0-redefining-product-development-and-regulatory-operations [accessed Jan 7, 2022].

[63] Alagarsamy, S., Kandasamy, R., Subbiah., L., and Selvamani, P. (2019) Applications of Internet of Things in Pharmaceutical Industry. *SSRN Electronic Journal*. 1-14. DOI: 10.2139/ssrn.3441059.

[64] Gralla, P. Speeding drug discovery with AI and big data. Available at: https://www.hpe.com/us/en/insights/articles/speeding-drug-discovery-with-ai-and-big-data-1802.html _[accessed Jan 7, 2022].

[65] Tripathi, M. K., et al. (2021) Evolving scenario of big data and Artificial Intelligence (AI) in drug discovery. Mol Divers. 25, 1439–1460. DOI: https://doi.org/10.1007/s11030-021-10256-w.

[66] Abel, J. Digital Transformation of Pharma and Biotech. Arc Report Abstract. Available at: https://www.arcweb.com/blog/digital-transformation?pharma-biotech_ [accessed 7, 2022].

[67] Pharma IQ: Automation, IoT and the future of smarter research environments. Available at: https://www.pharma-iq.com/preclinical-discovery-and-development/news/automation-iot-and-the-future-of-smarterresearch-environment [accessed Jan 7, 2022].

[68] Jingshan. L., Carayon, P. (2021) Health Care 4.0: A vision for smart and connected health care, *IISE Trans Healthc Syst Eng*. 11-3, 171-180. DOI: 10.1080/24725579.2021.1884627.

[69] Paul, S. et al. (2021) Industry 4.0 Applications for Medical/Healthcare Services. *J. Sens. Actuator Netw*. 10-3, 43. DOI: https://doi.org/10.3390/jsan10030043.

[70] Jayaraman, P. P. et al. (2019) Healthcare 4.0: A review of frontiers in digital health. *WIREs Data Min Knowl Discov.* 10-2, e1350. DOI: https://doi.org/10.1002/widm.1350.

[71] Wetterneck, T. B. et al. (2011). Factors contributing to an increase in duplicate medication order errors after CPOE implementation. *J Am Med Inform Assoc.* 18-6, 774-82. DOI: 10.1136/amiajnl-2011-000255.

[72] Nematollahi, M. et al. (2016) Economic and social collaborative decision-making on visit interval and service level in a two-echelon pharmaceutical supply chain. *J. Clean. Prod.* 142-4, 3956-3969. DOI:10.1016/j.jclepro.2016.10.062.

[73] Trappey, A. J. C., Trappey, C. V., Fan, C. Y., Hsu, A. P. T., Li, X. K., Lee, I. J. Y. (2017). IoT patent roadmap for smart logistic service provision in the context of Industry 4.0. *J. Chin. Inst. Eng*. 40-7, 1–10. DOI:10.1080/02533839.2017.1362325.

[74] Hofmann, E., Rüsch, M. (2017) Industry 4. 0 and the current status as well as future prospects on logistics. *Comput Ind.* 89, 23-34. DOI: https://doi.org/10.1016/j.compind.2017.04.002.

[75] Ding, B. (2018) Pharma Industry 4.0: Literature review and research opportunities in sustainable pharmaceutical supply chains. *Process Saf Environ Prot.* 119,115-130. DOI: https://doi.org/10.1016/j.psep.2018.06.031.

[76] Mohamed B. D., Hassini, E. and Bahroun, Z. (2019) Internet of things and supply chain management: A literature review. *Int. J. Prod. Res.* 57:15-16, 4719-4742. DOI: 10.1080/00207543.2017.1402140.

[77] Toronto Institute of Pharmaceutical Technology: 3 Ways Pharma 4. 0 Could Change Pharmaceutical Quality Assurance and Quality Control. Available at: https://www.tipt.com/blog/3-ways-pharma-4-0-could-change-pharmaceutical-quality-assurance-and-quality-control/ [accessed Jan 8, 2022].

[78] Srikrishna S. 5. 0 Ways Quality 4. 0 Will Improve Manufacturing. Available at: https://www.pda.org/pda-letter-portal/home/full-article/5.0-ways-quality-4.0-will-improve-manufacturing_[accessed Jan 8, 2022].

[79] Pharmaceutical online: Achieving Integrated Quality Through A Continued Process Verification Program. Available at: https://www.pharmaceuticalonline.com/doc/achieving-integrated-quality-through-a-continued-process-verification-program-0001 [accessed Jan 8, 2022].

[80] Innopharma technology: What Is Quality 4.0?. Available at: https://www.innopharmatechnology.com/news/revolutionise-quality-through-quality-4 [accessed Jan 8, 2022].

[81] Five things to consider for building an Industry 4.0-compatible supply chain. Available at: https://www.pharmaceutical-technology.com/sponsored/building-industry-40-compatible-supply-chain/ [accessed Jan 8, 2022].

[82] Arden, N. S. et al. (2021) Industry 4. 0 for pharmaceutical manufacturing: Preparing for the smart factories of the future, *Int. J. Pharm.* 602, 120554. DOI: https://doi.org/10.1016/j.ijpharm.2021.120554.

[83] Gardner, E. The next industrial revolution: Packaging and 'Industry 4.0', Packaging Gateway. Available at: https://www.packaging-gateway.com/features/next-industrial-revolution packaging-industry-4-0/_[accessed Jan 8, 2022].

[84] Hammer, C. (2018) Digitisation & Industry 4. 0 in Pharma Production. *ONdrugDelivery Magazine*. 83, 81-83.

[85] Startups Insights: 5 Top Emerging Pharma 4. 0 Impacting The Industry, Available at: https://www.startus-insights.com/innovators-guide/5-top-emerging-pharma-4-0-startups-impacting-the-industry/ [accessed Jan 8, 2022].

[86] QbDVision, Available at: https://www.qbdvision.com/# [accessed Jan 9, 2022].

[87] Electrosan Technologies. Available at: https://electrosan.co.in/ [accessed Jan 9, 2022].

[88] Gosilico, Available at: https://www.linkedin.com/company/gosilico/ [accessed Jan 9, 2022].

[89] Smart factory, Available at: https://www.smartfactory.it/flexim-en.html [accessed Jan 9, 2022].

3

Blockchain in the Pharmaceutical Industry: Opportunities and Challenges

Deepika Bairagee[1,2*], Poojashree Verma[1,2], Gaurav Saraogi[3], Neelam Jain[1], Neetesh Kumar Jain[1], and Mohammad Javed Naim[4]

[1]Oriental College of Pharmacy and Research, Oriental University, India
[2]Pacific College of Pharmacy, Pacific University, India
[3]Department of Pharmacy, Sri Aurobindo Institute of Pharmacy, India
[4]Department of pharmaceutical Chemistry, Faculty of Pharmacy, Tishk International University, Iraq
*Corresponding Author: Oriental College of Pharmacy and Research, Oriental University, Sanwer Road, Jakhiya, Indore-453555, Madhya Pradesh, India, Email: bairagee.deepika@gmail.com, Mobile No.: +91-9158841091.

Abstract

Blockchain is a dispersed digital ledger skill that has the prospective to change healthcare by improving data management, provenance, and security. Outstandingly, blockchain is a data construction with far-reaching applications beyond Bitcoin, the cryptocurrency that popularized the technology by relying on it. Various players in the health industry are exploring blockchain to improve business operations, cut charges, recover patient consequences, increase obedience, and permit improved usage of healthcare-related data. The necessity to confirm that blockchain plan features incorporate genuine healthcare demands from the varied viewpoints of clients, patients, workers, plus managers is dangerous in analyzing whether blockchain can live up to the publicity of knowledge described as "revolutionary" and "disruptive." In addition to meeting the genuine demands of health sector investors, blockchain solutions can be sensitive to the particular obstacles that healthcare has in comparison to other industries. In this regard, it is critical to make sure that a health blockchain is "fit-for-the-purpose." This idea is the cornerstone for this essay, in which we present the viewpoints of a varied collection of experts at the front of blockchain invention, growth, and disposition.

Keywords: Blockchain, pharmaceutical industry, healthcare, patient, fit-for-purpose, data management, technology.

3.1 Introduction to Blockchain

Daily, a vast amount of data is created, retrieved, and shared in the healthcare industry. Due to the delicate nature of data and restricting limits such as safety and secrecy, storing and distributing this massive amount of data is both necessary and troublesome [1, 2].

In the medical profession and clinical settings, data exchange that is safe, secure, and scalable (SSS) is crucial for analysis and joint clinical decision-making. The data-sharing plan is critical for healthcare practitioners to be able to convey their clients' clinical data to the appropriate authorities quickly. These providers and family physicians must be able to send their patients' clinical data safely and swiftly, ensuring that both patients and healthcare practitioners have the most up-to-date health information.

Telemedicine and electronic health, on either hand, are two prominent fields in which clinical data is sent to a specialist for review (at a remote location). The patient's data is provided using "store-and-forward technology" or digital actual clinical surveillance in these multiple online clinical settings [2, 3] (e.g., telemonitoring, telemetry, and the like). Clinical practitioners employ these online clinical settings and clinical data to diagnose and treat patients remotely. Because of the specific instance character of patient information, safety, responsiveness, and confidentiality of clinical data are some of the key difficulties that may arise in any clinical setting. Diagnostic accuracy and treatment efficacy are improved because secure data transfer facilitates clinical conversation by receiving recommendations or verification from a community of healthcare practitioners.

Furthermore, this industry is plagued by serious interoperability issues daily. The clinical data transfer that is safe, secure, and effective between healthcare organizations or research institutes, for example, could face significant operational issues. All parties participating in such healthcare data transfers must cooperate in a comprehensive, trustworthy, and healthy manner. The sensitivity of healthcare data, data sharing agreements, protocols, advanced patient matching algorithms, ethical standards, and regulatory

Table 3.1 Blockchain technology's main components.

Key Elements	**Functionality Description**
Decentralized	Anyone connecting to the network has open access to a database system.
Transparent	On numerous platforms, the data may be retrieved, checked, saved, and modernized.
Immutable	Potential users may see the data that has been captured and kept on the blockchain, and it can be quickly updated. Blockchains' transparent nature may likely avoid data from being tampered with or taken.
Autonomy	Once saved, the archives are reserved indefinitely and can't be accessed deprived of concurrent regulators of greater than 51% of the node.
Open Source	It is self-contained and independent, which means that individual nodes may safely admit, hand over, stock, and upgrade data, making it reliable and permitting outside interference.
Anonymity	Because data is sent from node to node, the individual's identity stays anonymous, making the system more safe and dependable.

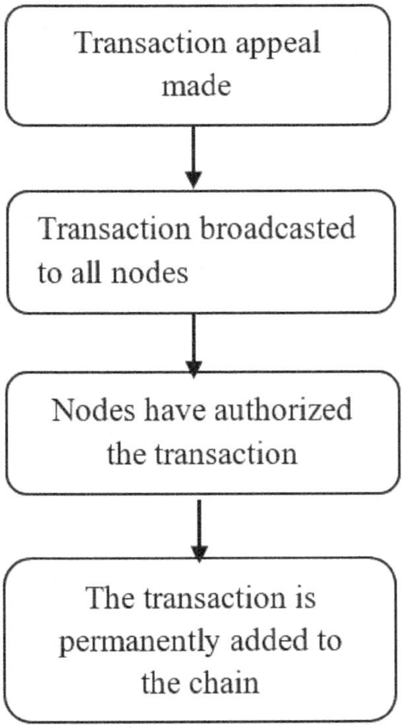

Figure 3.1 A general workflow of the blockchain method.

norms are all potential roadblocks. Before any clinical data exchange can take place, these are some of the key factors that must be mutually agreed upon [5].

Researchers have attempted to use the internet of things, artificial intelligence, machine learning, and computer vision to assist clinicians in diagnosing and treating many chronic illnesses (Table 3.1) [6, 1].

Each new transaction must be confirmed by someone who is a member of the system. Each deal in a blockchain block becomes increasingly immutable as it is verified by all of the network's nodes. The process of blockchain is depicted in Figure 3.1.

By combining all real-time clinical data on a patient's health and presenting it as an up-to-date reliable and safe setup, blockchain [1, 7, 8] may be a technology that helps in the future with individualized, dependable, and secure healthcare.

3.1.1 Definition of blockchain

Although the underlying blockchain technology was envisioned and released in Nakamoto's white paper in 2008, a widely recognized definition was not included in the publication and was not established until today [10]. Jeffries compiles impressions from numerous disciplines and uses cases, including governments, banking, law, and so on, in her paper "'Blockchain' is meaningless," and concludes that "creating a precise definition will help clear up some (of these) misunderstandings" [11].

The ambiguity of the terminology used to describe the technology, according to Walch [12], can be due to several factors, including "word taint," the phenomenon of some terms acquiring undesirable meanings; technology variation, the continuous development of all underlying technology that blockchain is based on; and "cross-field communication," the fact that terms are used across multiple fields and industries with varying degrees of technological expertise [13]. The International Standards Organization is presently working on ISO/TC 307, a standard that attempts to define and standardize several elements of a blockchain and distributed ledger technology, including terminology, security, privacy, and smart contract interactions [14]. The following is a definition of blockchain proposed by Seebacher and Schuritz [15], which will also be used in this paper:

"A blockchain is a community platform that allows users to share and agree on a distributed database. It's made up of a chain of blocks that hold timestamped contacts that are protected by public-key encryption and confirmed by the system public."

Information may be kept on the blockchain and dispersed throughout the network's nodes, resulting in a decentralized network. Before entering the blockchain network, all participating nodes agree on a set of rules and follow them [16]. The nature, purpose, and functioning of the network are governed by the rules' specifications. One of the most important characteristics of a blockchain network is robustness, which implies that all data produced is permanent and can only be changed at a very high cost. There are several different types of blockchain networks. They are classified as decentralized (public, not permission), hybrid (consortium, permissioned), or centralized (private/governed by a single entity, permissioned) based on the consensus and governance methods used [13, 17].

3.2 Cryptography

Cryptography, unlike other techniques of information concealment, aims to make transmitted signals unreadable to outsiders. The following are the primary information security goals it pursues:

- Confidentiality: ensuring that content is only accessible to those who are permitted.
- Data integrity: preventing data tampering by unauthorized individuals.
- Authentication: covers entity authentication as well as information and data identification; there is a reliable process in place to ensure that entities are who they say they are and that data has not been tampered with by unauthorized parties.
- Non-repudiation: prevents prior acts or transactions from being denied.

These qualities are also important for blockchain and combined they make up one of its most valuable components. When sending information through insecure channels, secrecy is achieved by the use of an encryption system.

Unkeyed encryption, symmetric-key encryption, and asymmetric-key encryption are three of the most common encryption methods (also recognized as public-key encryption).

3.2.1 Unkeyed encryption

The employment of cryptographic hash functions to ensure data integrity and message authentication is ubiquitous. They are also one of the building elements of blockchain due to their properties. They accept a message as an input and output a hash value or just a hash. "The core principle behind cryptographic hash meanings is that a hash-value performance is a compact representation of an input string that can be utilized as if it were uniquely identified with it." The following steps would be followed in a typical application of an unkeyed hash function:

- A message's hash value is calculated and then safely saved.
- A new hash of the original message is calculated at a later time.
- A comparison is made between the first hash and the freshly produced hash. If they're the same, it's safe to presume the original message's integrity hasn't been compromised.

Two key aspects of a hash function are:

- Compression: the function accepts an arbitrary length input and outputs a bit length that is fixed.
- The simplicity of computation: regardless of the original input, the hash is simple to compute [13, 18].

3.2.2 Symmetric-key encryption

The fact that the same key is used to encrypt and decode data sent between parties through an unsecured channel distinguishes symmetric-key encryption. Block cyphers and stream cyphers are the two types of functions that are often employed in practice. When utilizing key-based encryption, it is often thought that the only information that must be kept secret is the key itself. In the case of symmetric-key encryption, this implies that both parties must ensure that their keys (also known as secret-key cyphers) are kept secret since they are identical, and disclosing one would undermine the communication's secrecy and authenticity. The so-called key distribution problem is the most difficult problem for symmetric-key encryption. To ensure the integrity of the key exchange operation, the secret key is frequently encrypted in a separate key, signaling that the receiver already has that key. Despite this difficulty, the main advantages of using symmetric-key cryptography are the ability to create cyphers with high data throughput; the use of relatively short, yet inexpensive, keys that provide a high level of protection; algorithms that are relatively inexpensive to process in comparison to others; and the ability to use cyphers to create stronger cyphers through simple transformations [13, 19].

3.2.3 Asymmetric-key encryption

The presence of a pair of keys, specifically a private key and a public key, each granted to an enterprise that desires to electronically authenticate its authenticity or encryption keys, is the basis of governmental cryptography, also known as asymmetric-key cryptography. The technique implies that the public key will be made public while the secret key will be kept private. Only the private key associated with the public key may decode messages encrypted with it. The following are the most significant benefits of using public-key cryptography:

- The transmission of encrypted data across insecure channels with the receiver's capacity to decode the data once it arrives.
- Non-repudiation: the sender cannot dispute that the data was sent or that the data was changed at any stage during the transmission [13, 20, 21].

3.2.4 Signatures

Digital signatures can be used for authentication, data reliability, and non-repudiation, in addition to the aforementioned encryption techniques. "A message's digital signature is a number based on a secret known only to the signer, as well as the content of the message being signed." This permits the message's origin to be digitally linked. One of the most important applications of such signatures is to verify the identities of public key owners and, as a result, to prevent the sender of a message from subsequently denying the transaction. A private key functions as a digital signature, validating the provenance of communication sent over the internet. The communication's receiver may then decode the message using the public key, therefore validating the sender's identity. If a sender disputes authorship of communication, a match between his or her private key and the public key used to decode the message suffices as proof [13, 15].

3.3 Characteristics of Blockchain

Blockchain technology, according to Seebacher and Schuritz's literature assessment, offers an ecosystem that is decentralized and trust-inspiring. Further elements form these qualities as a result of the system's design and the technology it was built on, as shown in Figure 3.2. Transparency, data integrity, and immutability underpin trust, although isolation, dependability, and adaptability bolster the benefits of decentralization.

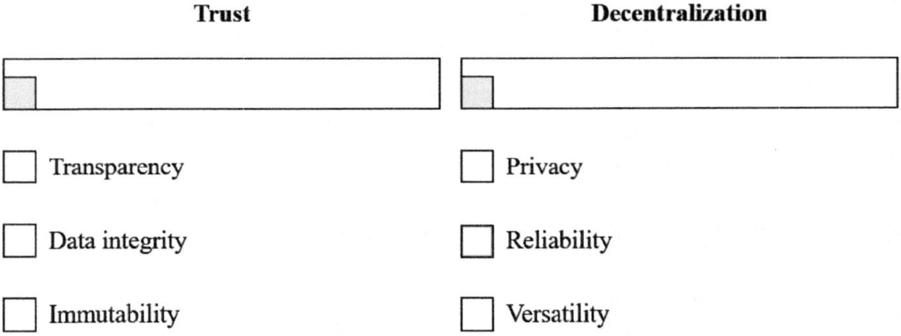

Figure 3.2 Blockchain characteristics.

This section will go through each aspect in further depth.

3.3.1 Trust

The peer-to-peer aspect of the network on which blockchain is constructed is believed to provide transparency by allowing shared and public interactions among the members. All transactions are publicly available and broadcast to the whole network, allowing all actors on the system to obtain fast and comprehensive information. Transparency and trust are the fundamental elements of a blockchain since a central authority that might single-handedly influence transactions, authorize, dismiss, or amend them is replaced with a trust model based on network-wide consensus [13, 15, 16].

The dependence on public-key encryption and hashing provides high-security levels, data integrity and govern direct connection with data stored on the system.

The third significant feature of a blockchain that contributes to trust establishment is its so-called immutability. A transaction cannot be amended once it has been authorized by network participants, additional to a block, and the block has been put on the blockchain. Because of consensus approaches like evidence of work and stake, which allow contributors to demonstrate their trustworthiness [13], this shift occurs.

3.3.2 Decentralization

Transparency, data integrity, and immutability are all important factors for the establishment of a decentralized network; hence, trust and decentralization are linked in the context of blockchain. Decentralization, on the other hand, is required to ensure participant engagement, since it includes elements such as privacy, dependability, and adaptability. To explain, privacy is integrated into a blockchain-based system through the usage of public and private keys, which verify individuals without revealing their true identities. While transactions may be traced back to a single key, the network remains pseudonymous, allowing for anonymity. Blockchain's dependability is another feature that is characterized as "emergent" because of certain hazards that although unlikely and computationally tough, yet exist. The claim of dependability is founded on two factors: first, the dispersed nature of the information and transactions throughout the network, and second, the automated structure of the system. However, Conte de Leon et al. suggest that if the blockchain has been tampered with, for example, by an adversary taking over 51% or more of the processing power in the network, such an assault can be left undiscovered, therefore jeopardizing the dependability of future transactions [13, 22].

3.4 Blockchain Structure

3.4.1 Blockchain

The blockchain as a concept refers to the data structure as a whole rather than any single application, which is made up of blocks. It preserves a record of all transactions that have happened, packed in linked timestamped blocks, called a sequential transaction database (Figure 3.3). The initial block in any blockchain is known as a genesis block, and it is determined by the blockchain's developers. Any modifications made to the blockchain after the acceptance of a specific block may be tracked back due to the interlinking of all blocks based on hashes, as all blocks share the same genesis chunk. The confusion of the preceding chunk is included in each new block. As a result, if anything is changed, the hashes will no longer match, indicating an error [23, 24].

3.4.2 Block

Each block in the chain, as shown in Figure 3.3, has two objects: a block header with information and a bundle of transactions. The header of the block aids in verifying the legitimacy of the transactions included inside it. It usually comprises the following information: the current block's version, the preceding chunk's header confusion, the Merkle root confusion (hash of all dealings in the block), a period stamp, and a nonce (a random value miners modify to solve the computational puzzle). Every transaction that is fresh to

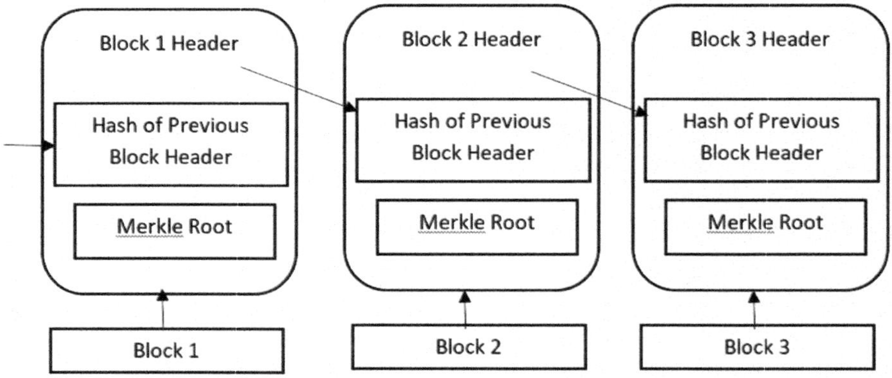

Figure 3.3 Simplified blockchain structure

the network is typically included in the most recent block. Blocks were put into the blockchain network to improve its operations and efficiency, allowing nodes to process bundles of numerous transactions constituting a block at the same time instead of confirming individual transactions on the network. Block size is one factor that affects network operations since it indirectly determines the number of transactions in a block, which affects the system's overall throughput. For example, bigger blocks result in slower propagation, which leads to more "stale" blocks and a less secure network. Because of disputes, stale blocks are excluded from the longest chain. They can cause chain splits, slowing down the blockchain's overall growth and endangering its performance and security by giving possible attacks like double-spending an advantage [13, 25, 26].

3.4.3 Transaction

A transaction is the smallest building block of a blockchain. There is a sender address, a receiver address, and a value. Each transaction is subject to a set of rules. One of them specifies that input must equal output for each transaction on the blockchain, where input and output can represent any physical or immaterial value. Additional rules are frequently implemented using a scripting language, such as Forth in Bitcoin, and are dependent on the individual blockchain application. These rules also serve as the foundation for keen agreements, which will be discussed in further complexity in the subsequent unit [13, 23].

On the blockchain, every transaction changes the status of the whole chain. Because of the ledger's shared, decentralized, and distributed character, all nodes on the blockchain, each of which has a copy of the chain, must process transactions to acquire an updated copy. As previously stated, transactions are grouped into blocks and dispersed over the network.

Following that, each node checks them for accuracy and validity using pre-defined criteria. At least one input and one output are included in each transaction. To ensure that no partially unspent transactions occur, the entire charge of all contributions must equal the entire worth of all outputs. As a result, every value that is not transferred to another entity is referred to as an output (unspent transaction). The sole difference between permissible input and output, when input is greater, is to account for contract fees remunerated to the miner who creates the block [27].

3.5 Applications

Blockchain technology (BCT), which is best recognized for its applications in banking and cryptocurrency, is now finding interest in a variety of other fields, including medicine. By stabilizing and safeguarding the dataset with which users may engage through various types of transactions (as depicted in the model, shown in Figure 3.4), blockchain technology has shown promise in the fields of medical, genome sequencing, telehealth, telemonitoring, electronic health, cognitive science, and customized healthcare applications (as illustrated in the framework, shown in Figure 3.4) [28].

3.5.1 Blockchain in electronic health records (EHR)

In the past ten years, medical practitioners, hospitals, and healthcare equipment have all pushed for the digitization of medical health information, since it provides for simpler access and exchange, as well as a basis for better and faster decision-making. Electronic medical records [29] are the most prevalent submission of blockchain knowledge in the health sector.

Patients' data is dispersed among multiple institutions as their lives take them away from one provider's data and away from straightforward access to past data. Many scholars have proposed adopting blockchain technology to manage EHRs in response to a pressing demand for a novel approach to handling EHRs that encourages consumers to interact with their existing and past healthcare data. To manage authentication, confidentiality, integrity, and data interchange, a prototype known as "MedRec" makes use of unique

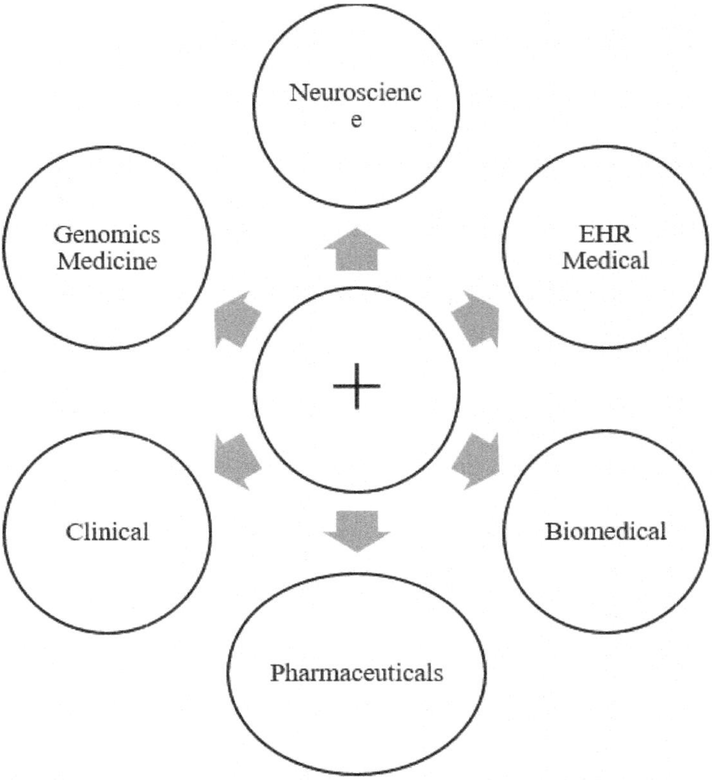

Figure 3.4 Blockchains in healthcare applications

blockchain capabilities. It's based on a decentralized archives administration structure that has rights to give patients a complete, unchangeable medical past as well as quick access to their information from a range of doctors and treatment centers. "MedRec" does not require any medicinal records or a modification period. It creates a blockchain record and notifies the patient, who is ultimately answerable for the evidence's movement. The mark ensures that a perfect copy of the record was obtained. It also shifts control from the organization to the patient, weighing and enabling the patient to take responsibility. Management links are developed to act as patient representatives for those patients who would rather not engage with their information. Individual patient entrances now have a lot of bulky plans, which take more time and have different user interfaces in each foundation [30, 31]. Major limitations on medical data transmission can occur as a result of EHR adoption, like damage of switch over data, data origin, audits, and protected data tracing. With these limits in mind, Xia et al. [25] built MeDShare, a harmless and secure blockchain system for digital assets. Untrustworthy parties are sharing medical data. Medical records and information can be shared through MeDShare. Manage e-health chronicles between cloud vendors, clinics, and pharmaceutical research organizations with stronger information origin, tailored inspection regulators, and minimum data security and privacy concerns. EHRs often include extremely sensitive and crucial patient data that is routinely exchanged among doctors, radiologists, healthcare providers, pharmacists, and researchers to offer active judgment and action. The patient's treatment could be jeopardized as a result of the storage, transfer, and circulation of this extremely sensitive patient info across numerous organizations, posing substantial dangers to the patient's health and the capacity to maintain track of their medical history. Because chronic disease patients have had a long history of pre/post, so their risk of consequences may be higher (e.g., cancer and HIV). As a result, keeping track of a patient's medical history is essential for effective treatment. To circumvent these limitations, a blockchain-based system for gathering, saving, and transferring electronic medical information for cancer patients has been proposed. To get entry to, manage, and retain protected customer records, they used planned and implemented blockchain solutions. These protocols may have been used to incorporate blockchain solutions into clinical practice to gain access to and manage the safety and confidentiality of patient data and histories.

Estonia's blockchain-based medical record endeavor is another historical milestone. In 2016, by presenting the importance of holding billions of health records confidential while keeping them available to the public healthcare professionals and private insurers, Estonia established itself as a global leader in blockchain technology. Possibly the purpose for the rapid adoption of blockchain knowledge in a prescription through the ecosphere is a solid guarantee to patients that employing this kind of expertise would make their medical records unchangeable and unchanged. Any access or modification effort may be instantly tagged and identified across the blockchain. This is important not just for patient integrity, but also for recognizing any prohibited activities, such as wholesale deception or record adulteration. Furthermore, exchanging and reviewing approved pharmaceutical service records would be much easier. When a patient visits, the bulk of that patient's suppliers are likely to notice it right away. Medication issues, allergy symptoms, and pharmaceutical remedies can be adapted very quickly across all blockchain records utilizing accurate patient-caring algorithms, eliminating the need for time-consuming pharmaceutical compromise forms. As a result, blockchain technology will improve treatment accessibility, medical record management, clinical data validity, confidentiality, and treatment plan [1].

3.5.2 Blockchain in clinical research

Information privacy, the integrity of data, sharing of information, maintaining records, patient information, and other issues might arise during clinical studies. As the next version of the web, blockchain can overcome these issues. Healthcare practitioners are working to overcome these issues by utilizing blockchain knowledge. Blockchain knowledge, AI, and ML are expected to revolutionize the healthcare industry. In the education presented by Timothy et al., p2p Ethereum, a blockchain platform that allows for keen agreement capabilities, is used in combination with clinic-based data administration schemes. The primary purpose of the education was to find a solution to the patient enrollment challenge. The education discovered that Ethereum smart contracts allowed for quicker payments than bitcoin, pointing to the fact that Ethereum smart contracts might be utilized to increase the openness of clinical trial data management systems. As a result, one of the current blockchains used in clinical research is patient enrollment [32]. Another study provided a system for procurement of knowledgeable consent from patients and recording and storing data in a safe, publicly demonstrable, and unfalsifiable way. Blockchain technology was used to develop the approach.

3.5.3 Blockchains in medical fraud detection

Management of medicinal medication supply chains is one of the most important applications of blockchains in the medical business. Stockpile management is a key issue in many businesses, but it is especially important in healthcare owing to its growing difficulty. This is because any disturbance in the supply chain has a detrimental influence on a patient's health. Distribution channels are unstable and vulnerable to fraud due to the numerous moving elements and persons involved. Blockchains, by providing increased data transparency and improved product traceability, deliver a harmless and protected stage to address this difficulty and, in certain circumstances, eradicate scams. Manipulation of a blockchain record is difficult because it can only be confirmed and altered using a smart contract [33, 34].

3.5.4 Neuroscience blockchains

The quantity of media and study devoted to blockchain technologies is fast expanding, and neuroscience is undoubtedly engaged. Modern brain technologies are attempting to invent a fresh model in which apparatus and data are handled by mental instructions rather than mechanical interaction with the environment. Based on data from a person's activity in the brain, these neural devices can identify a person's current mental state, as well as analyze mind movement patterns and decode them into instructions for operating exterior equipment. Neurological data provided online with several sensitive sensors, computer processors, and Wi-Fi devices address the problem of analyzing and understanding brain signals. They would read the mind's function, which would then be interpreted and communicated to the control system. Everything happens in a single gadget that the user wears on his or her head. To capture such brain impulses on the neural interface, analyze data collection methods and big data will use blockchain theory. One of the companies that have expressed its plan to utilize blockchain technology is Neurogress. The company, located in Geneva, specializes in neural-control technologies that allow users to control artificial limbs, drones, household sensors, and AR/VR (augmented reality/virtual reality) equipment using just their minds [35].

To increase the precision of its brain reading, Neurogress' control technique depends on learning algorithms, which demands maintaining 90% of neurological information to educate the system's AI. In those other respects, "huge information of user cerebral function" is required, with "exabytes (1 exabyte = 1 billion gigabytes) of memory" mentioned in the Human Brain Project's whitepaper as an instance of storage capability. As a result, it's no surprise that Neurogress plans to adopt blockchain, which, according to the company, "simply handles the issues related to data storage confidentiality and protection." When user information is recorded on a blockchain system, it becomes significantly more secure and private. Similarly, blockchain enables the Neurogress system to be "open and transparent to future Neurogress platform services consumers." The technology will "guarantee the integrity and privacy of private information" [36] since aberrant behavior will be detected promptly.

As a result, blockchains are a type of info technology with many key potential applications, including brain augmentation, brain simulation, and brain thinking. A complete human brain must be digitized, which necessitates the use of a medium to stock it, and here is where blockchain knowledge comes into play once more. Mindfiles might be stored in a peer-to-peer network file system with historical versioning and used as data construction blocks in personal thought chains, according to one idea. This sort of blockchain thought is characterized as an insight computational system with a set of characteristics that allow for artificial intelligence, human augmentation, or a combination of both. A connected network of computers may link arms on at frequent basis to certify the provenance and integrity of a ledger using blockchain. This type of trust mechanism may allow networks of neurons to store and retrieve information with precision and trust of what is subjective vs. objective of a specific event if we were to create a brain from the ground up. The safe building of a quantitative information commons for people as a public blockchain can be enabled by a combination of many authentication and a personal idea chain. A data commons reduces human data silos while permitting each individual to retain control over their privacy and sharing of their experience, possibly for financial gain, without the requirement for a third party or centralization of authority. We may be able to reconstruct their activities in the future to be more objective about the events of that instant by consuming an augmented version of this technology when more than two people observe a similar time from particular viewpoint. In an ideal world, this would allow for the fabrication of virtual replicas of earlier memories, as well as the ability to subjectively experience life through the eyes of someone else. We'll move data from the senses onto this future blockchain after we have a more elastic grasp of individual mappings to emotions and sensory experiences as contributing to a specific memory (i.e., sight, smell, and so forth.). The technologies required to make this a reality are currently being developed. In the not-too-distant future, wearable technology, brain and nerve implants, biofeedback imaging, and any other sensors that allow a multi-factor fingerprint specific to a given human's record of temporal experience will be available. Research might be done to improve decision making, learning, remembering, and rehabilitative treatments expending this knowledge as a preliminary point [37, 38].

3.5.5 Blockchains in pharmaceutical industry and research

The drug companies are the quickest expanding in the world, and it plays a major role in healthcare distribution. The medicinal industry not only assists in the development of novel and promising therapies but also ensures the safety and efficacy of medical devices and pharmaceuticals available to the general public. In addition, the pharmaceutical industry assists in the study and production of safe drugs, allowing patients to recover more quickly.

Table 3.2 Blockchain technology's applications in healthcare.

Uses	Summary
Electronic Health Records	The authenticity of an electronic EHR on a dispersed network of an authorized blockchain is ensured without human intervention from the point of information products to the fact of information recovery.
Clinical Research	Blockchain, based on the clinical investigation, provides a decentralized and secure platform for any data exchange that might also occur. This tool enables researchers to securely communicate data with one another.
Medical Fraud Detection	Since blockchain is irreversible, it aids in fraud prevention by prohibiting transaction duplication or change, resulting in a transparent and safe transaction.
Neuroscience	Blockchain as technology will help a slew of novel apps, such as brain advancement, brain re-enactment, and brain starting to think. A media for storing an entire human brain is necessary for digitalizing the whole human mind, and here is where blockchain innovation comes into the equation.
Pharmaceutical Industry and Research	The source of the drug, its mechanisms, and possession are routinely acknowledged at the separate phase of the pharmaceutical supply chain, utilizing blockchain's capabilities of complete tracking to eliminate sheet metal forming.

In most situations, pharma businesses experience difficulties tracking their goods on time, which can pose serious hazards by allowing counterfeiters to damage manufacturing or infiltrate the system with fake medications. Whenever it comes to giving effective and safe medications to patients, here is an urgent need to track, analyze, and safeguard the whole procedure of developing and delivering pharmaceutical therapies using electronic technologies all over the world, particularly in poor countries. A computerized drug control system may be a long-term solution to preventing counterfeit pharmaceuticals in this location (DDCS). Three prominent pharmaceutical firms, Sanofi, Pfizer, and Amgen, have established a combined pilot initiative to discover and assess novel medications using a blockchain-based DDCS [39, 40]. Table 3.2 summarizes the benefits of adopting blockchain to further biology and medicine.

3.6 Challenges

Blockchain is a digital technology with a lot of potentials that is gaining popularity in a range of sectors. This innovation, on the other hand, carries

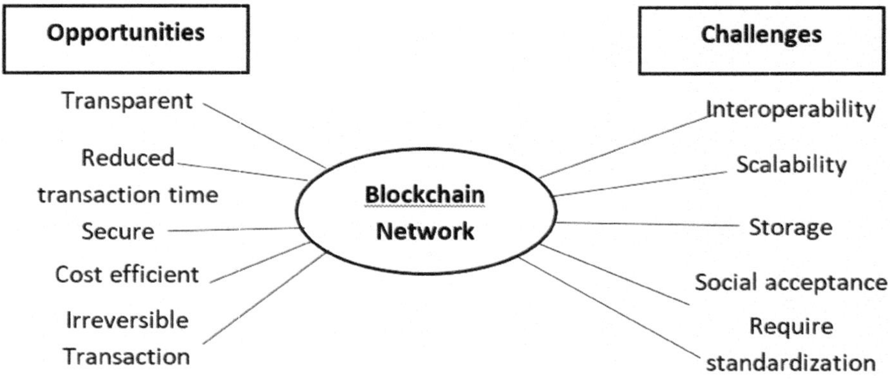

Figure 3.5 Blockchains in healthcare: opportunities and challenges

with it its individual usual of difficulties that must be lectured (as shown in Figure 3.5). We'll look at a few of the most significant challenges in this part [41, 42].

3.6.1 Safety and confidentiality of data

The first and most critical issues are data confidentiality. Using blockchain-based apps removes the need for an intermediary to execute a transaction. Since blockchain technology enables the whole society, instead of a single trusted source, to authenticate the archives in a blockchain construction, the data converts are exposed to confidentiality and safety problems. Because all nodes will be talented to see the info broadcast by a single node, private information will be jeopardized. In the lack of an approved third party, the patient must appoint one or more leaders to have direct connections to his or her info and/or remedial past in the instance of backup. This individual can now provide a large number of other access to the same patient's documents, possibly resulting in a big data leak. The safety and confidentiality of individuals are jeopardized. Due to the general elevated methods used in the data, there are stumbling obstacles in transporting data from one block to another, giving recipients entry due to the lack of or inadequate data. Such as 51% of attacks may be employed by the blockchain networks. This approach is carried out by a team of mineworkers that control extra than half of the blocks on a blockchain network. If the mineworkers do not acquire permission, they gain system power and have the capacity to inhibit any new transactions from taking place. So according to CoinDesk, this hack has recently attacked five currencies. A medical file may potentially contain sensitive data that should not be stored on the blockchain [42, 43].

3.6.2 Storage capacity management

Storage capacity management is another challenge that emerges in this area. Because it was meant to capture and process transaction data with a limited scope, blockchain does not require a lot of storage. Storage difficulties became obvious as it grew into the field of healthcare. The healthcare business must process a large volume of data daily. All data in the blockchain paradigm, including patient records, health histories, and test results, as well as MRI scans, X-rays, and other medical imagery, will be obtainable to all nodes in the chain, needing a vast amount of interplanetary storage. Furthermore, since blockchain requests are transactional, the systems that support this innovation are projected to grow. The speed with which records can be searched and accessed slows as databases grow in size, which is uncomfortable, and hence unsuitable for time-sensitive transactions. As a result, the use of a blockchain solution is essential. It must be scalable and dependable [44].

3.6.3 Interoperability issues

Interoperability, which requires the creation of blockchains from multiple communicating providers and services to communicate with one additional in a seamless and suitable manner, is another issue with blockchain. This problem makes it difficult to communicate data effectively.

3.6.4 Standardization challenges

Because blockchain knowledge is static in its early stages, it will face standardization challenges as it approaches widespread implementation in medicine and healthcare. International standardization organizations would have to produce many well-validated and approved standards. These guidelines could help determine the amount, kind, and structure of data transferred in blockchain applications. These guidelines will serve as both an evaluation and a safety measure for the shared data.

3.6.5 Social challenges

Because blockchain skill is static in its initial stages, it is confronted with societal difficulties such as cultural shifts in addition to the technological challenges stated above. Accepting and implementing skill that is fundamentally dissimilar from traditional work methods is not ever simple. Though the medical profession is rapidly becoming more digital, it still has a long way to go before completely embracing new technologies, particularly blockchain, which has yet to be scientifically validated. It will take time and effort to persuade doctors to abandon paper in favor of technology. The technology and strategies provided are generally untrustworthy due to their little implementation rate in the health industry. We can't yet declare it a feasible and worldwide answer to all healthcare concerns because of all of these challenges and risks. We used a SWOT analysis technique to better understand, appraise, and recognize the powers, flaws, chances, and threats that blockchain knowledge faces in the healthcare market (as illustrated in Figure 3.6).

To address these concerns, this Forum paper proposed a "fit-for-purpose" health blockchain layout framework to address critical questions about basic blockchain new designs, sharing of information and top managers, and supervisory options, as well as identifying innovative ideas which can be used to improve blockchain intent and attempting to describe the ultimate goal of the blockchain-based system. If all these risks are appropriately handled, blockchain technology will be more likely to be "fit-for-purpose"

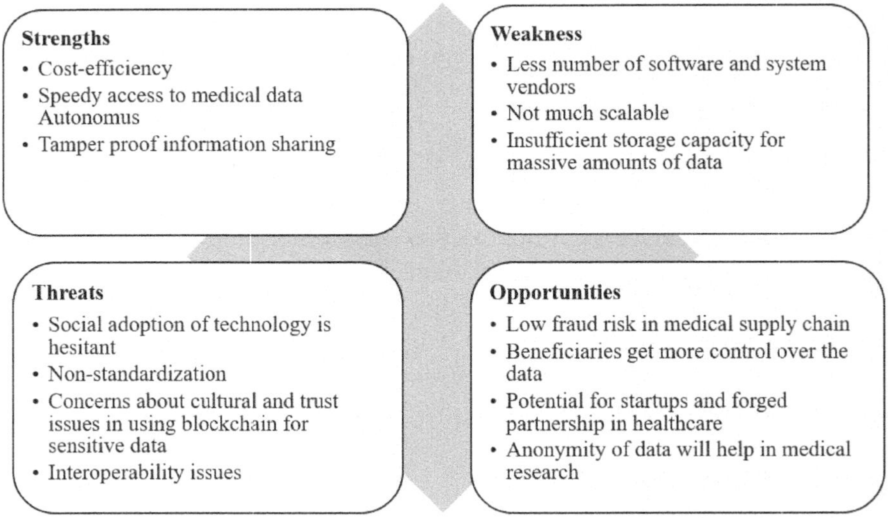
Strengths
• Cost-efficiency
• Speedy access to medical data Autonomus
• Tamper proof information sharing
Weakness
• Less number of software and system vendors
• Not much scalable
• Insufficient storage capacity for massive amounts of data
Threats
• Social adoption of technology is hesitant
• Non-standardization
• Concerns about cultural and trust issues in using blockchain for sensitive data
• Interoperability issues
Opportunities
• Low fraud risk in medical supply chain
• Beneficiaries get more control over the data
• Potential for startups and forged partnership in healthcare
• Anonymity of data will help in medical research

Figure 3.6 Blockchains in healthcare: a SWOT analysis

for whatever health concern is uncovered. The foundation issues are built on the following six concepts:

1. **Types of blockchains:** Choose between a public blockchain (available to everyone and without permissions), an isolated blockchain (with incomplete contribution and authorization assemblies), or a fusion blockchain (blockchain schemes with mutually private and public designs).
2. **Information exchange and accessing:** The exchange and availability of mental well-being data in healthcare are governed by a range of security, legal, and regulatory requirements (for example, HIPAA and GDPR). It must be specified how data will be transmitted with and among members; whether data will be exchanged; whether data will be kept on-chain, off-chain, or even on a side-chain; and what approvals groups would be used.
3. **Blockchain governance decisions:** A blockchain system's governance is an important part of its architecture. The blockchain's nodes, users, peers, and/or validators must be determined, as well as if the blockchain will be made up of individual associates, a consortium of players, community organizations, or supervisors, and whether clients/consumers/the general community will be included. Lastly, it will be required to determine in what way these individuals will make choices on how the blockchain should be run (counting options for consensus processes, permissions, and data governance).
4. **Additional technology to improve blockchain functionality:** As stated previously, the blockchain structure can enable the use of supplemental knowledge of the subject, such as the creation of an application-level that interconnects with the blockchain, its use of gentle arrangements to standardize processes if certain agreed-upon conditions are met, through the use of a cryptocurrency/tokens to motivate campaign contribution that preferably delivers able to share earnings to all attendees.
5. **Definitive healthcare objective of blockchain:** Defining the blockchain's ultimate objective to improve healthcare is a key difficulty that must be addressed, despite its seeming clarity. Aside from the intrinsic advantages of a distributed, permanent, transparent, and higher-trust system, the unique benefits that a blockchain network for healthcare procedures may give over other current technologies should be evaluated. Each blockchain will be created for a different purpose(s). These could merely

be designed to reduce healthcare transaction fees by enhancing and automating procedures (for example, through the use of smart contracts), eliminating intermediaries, or lowering administrative expenses. Others could focus on devising revenue-generating tactics.

6. **The importance of a blockchain:** In healthcare-related problems, if another sort of technology would be more appropriate than blockchain, then go for it; if it is not, then you finally require blockchain.

Though the list of "fit-for-purpose" blockchain outline deliberations above isn't complete, it may be used as a starting point for considering how blockchains might be created to achieve common goals like bettering healthcare and, ultimately, patient outcomes. It provides a compendium of important usage cases in health sector, constructed on continuing investigation, printed studies, and actual experiences, to help the reader to better understand what a "health" blockchain would appear identical to in the nearby forthcoming. The purpose of this paper is to look at many points of view on key planning aspects, challenges, possibilities, and best practices again for the personal health blockchain ecosystem. The report puts together an interdisciplinary group of experts from academia, industry, healthcare startups, and high-quality goods and services affiliations to explain cases in healthcare records, clinical trial managerial staff, medical credentialing and licensure, genomics and precision medicine, pharmaceutical supply chain, and biomedical research to accomplish this. The significance of adopting technological and industry standards is then discussed in order to guarantee that blockchain in healthcare evolves and fulfills its promise as a transformative force in 21st-century healthcare [47].

3.7 Future Perspectives

In many ways, blockchain technology might benefit the medical business. Comparable to how the internet transformed health services and ushered in telemedicine, blockchain technology has the possibility to take medical advances to the next level by lowering the prices of checking, conformation, and having a dominant server for data, as well as the administration that manages medical data. Due to the obvious global ledger's availability, when a patient enrolls in a study, the whole assortment of information will be accessible at the same moment, drastically lowering processing time.

Furthermore, because doctors may access true, original, and slightly elevated source-documented information in real time, they need not have anxiety about enduring delivering an accurate medicinal past, lowering the possibility of medical history errors. So because data is public, patients didn't have anxiety about receiving an additional view from the additional doctor. Patients should be able to interact with others from all over the globe who are struggling with identical medical issues, which will not only improve their health but will also make them feel welcomed, encouraged, and inspired to combat the illness. Patients will have whole control over their data and will be willing to part it with anyone they choose. The next phase, according to Richie Etwaru, who coined the slogan "Freedom-As-A-Service [1]" during a book launch in 2016, can be labeled "Freedom-As-A-Service [2]."

3.8 Implications and Conclusions

Although healthcare lags behind other industries in terms of innovation, the integrity of possible data might be a cause to adopt blockchain in the near future. There may be a few essential issues to consider when it comes to storing electronic health information on the blockchain. The usage of keen agreements that have been highlighted urges us to adopt and use them in the healthcare business for every little and large transaction. Keen agreements would build an indestructible sequence of chunks that would account for personalized care while remaining compliant with healthcare criteria. Converged healthcare systems would leverage a blockchain smart contract to prevent duplication in the parent centralized system. Researchers may benefit from blockchain since it can give verified and timestamped versions of scientific studies. Researchers would be able to preserve a long-term history of their discoveries using a documented blockchain record, similar to how smart contracts let patients save pathway of their data. Blockchain is a must-have technology in the large pharmaceutical segment.

Every medicinal association report distribution may be encrypted and saved on a blockchain using blocking technology. This strategy will increase the speed of data preparation; assure the accuracy of collection distribution; and limit the risk of archive damage, damage, or fabrication. These crucial issues are under the power of innovation: It is not possible to edit or remove the created block. Because of the blockchain, data will not be tampered with. Any offer of counterfeit or inferior medications will be rejected. This is done by tightly controlling all areas of the pharmaceutical supply chain, including manufacturing, transportation, and distribution.

Health professionals, healthcare providers, R&D experts, healthcare individuals, and medical scientists will advantage from the practical submission of blockchain technology in the healthcare domain because it will allow them to more effectively disseminate large amounts of data, share scientific knowledge, and interconnect references while maintaining better safety and confidentiality guard. If blockchain technology is effectively deployed in clinical settings, it will surely open up new avenues for biomedical research. In precision medicine uses, on the other hand, the harmless, safe, and scalable collection, storing, and interchange of clinical data will aid in the development of possible disease diagnoses and treatment alternatives. A blockchain might be used to store a digital brain as well as to manage neural networks. Only a few firms have accepted that blockchain will play a role in neurotechnology, which is still in its infancy. Conversely, it is unclear how secure storing individual brain data on a blockchain will be. Although the decentralized and open structure of blockchains will almost definitely avoid data from being fiddled with or stolen, many of the traditional issues about huge data gathering remain: that sensitive information might be retailed to third parties for questionable marketing resolutions and that people could be identified circuitously (as with bitcoin) through anonymous identifiers or data designs. As a consequence, people will be able to play a more active part in their own healthcare as a result of this blockchain-based healthcare framework, therefore improving their overall quality of life.

Acknowledgment

The writers are grateful to the administration of Oriental University, Indore, for their assistance.

Conflicts of Interest

There is no potential for a conflict of interest.

Funding

There is no funding issued.

References

[1] Siyal, A. A., Junejo, A. Z., Zawish, M., Ahmed, K., Khalil, A., & Soursou, G. (2019). Applications of blockchain technology in medicine and healthcare: Challenges and future perspectives. *Cryptography*, *3*(1), 3.

[2] Griebel, L., Prokosch, H. U., Köpcke, F., Toddenroth, D., Christoph, J., Leb, I., ... & Sedlmayr, M. (2015). A scoping review of cloud computing in healthcare. *BMC medical informatics and decision making, 15*(1), 1-16.

[3] Bhatti, A., Siyal, A. A., Mehdi, A., Shah, H., Kumar, H., & Bohyo, M. A. (2018, February). Development of cost-effective tele-monitoring system for remote area patients. In *2018 International Conference on Engineering and Emerging Technologies (ICEET)* (pp. 1-7). IEEE.

[4] Zhang, P., White, J., Schmidt, D. C., Lenz, G., & Rosenbloom, S. T. (2018). FHIRChain: applying blockchain to securely and scalably share clinical data. *Computational and structural biotechnology journal, 16*, 267-278.

[5] Zhang, J., Xue, N., & Huang, X. (2016). A secure system for pervasive social network-based healthcare. *Ieee Access, 4*, 9239-9250.

[6] Kuo, T. T., Kim, H. E., & Ohno-Machado, L. (2017). Blockchain distributed ledger technologies for biomedical and health care applications. *Journal of the American Medical Informatics Association, 24*(6), 1211-1220.

[7] Griggs, K. N., Ossipova, O., Kohlios, C. P., Baccarini, A. N., Howson, E. A., & Hayajneh, T. (2018). Healthcare blockchain system using smart contracts for secure automated remote patient monitoring. *Journal of medical systems, 42*(7), 1-7.

[8] Chen, Y., Ding, S., Xu, Z., Zheng, H., & Yang, S. (2019). Blockchain-based medical records secure storage and medical service framework. *Journal of medical systems, 43*(1), 1-9.

[9] Wang, S., Wang, J., Wang, X., Qiu, T., Yuan, Y., Ouyang, L., ... & Wang, F. Y. (2018). Blockchain-powered parallel healthcare systems based on the ACP approach. *IEEE Transactions on Computational Social Systems, 5*(4), 942-950.

[10] Nakamoto, S. (2008). Bitcoin: A peer-to-peer electronic cash system. *Decentralized Business Review*, 21260.

[11] A. Jeffries. Blockchain is meaningless. https://www.theverge.com/2018/3/7/17091766/ blockchain-bitcoin-ethereum-cryptocurrency-meaning, Mar. 2018.

[12] Walch, A. (2017). The Path of the Blockchain Lexicon (and the Law) 36 Review of Banking & Financial Law 713. *University College London, 239.*

[13] Bogoeva, A. (2018). *Blockchain Technology in Healthcare: Opportunities and Challenges* (Doctoral dissertation, Master Thesis, University of Mannheim).

[14] ISO/TC 307 - Blockchain and distributed ledger technologies. https://www.iso.org/committee/6266604/x/catalogue/.

[15] Seebacher, S., & Schüritz, R. (2017, May). Blockchain technology as an enabler of service systems: A structured literature review. In *International conference on exploring services science* (pp. 12-23). Springer, Cham.

[16] Sultan, K., Ruhi, U., & Lakhani, R. (2018). Conceptualizing blockchains: Characteristics & applications. *arXiv preprint arXiv:1806.03693.*

[17] Kruijff, J. D., & Weigand, H. (2017, June). Understanding the blockchain using enterprise ontology. In *International Conference on Advanced Information Systems Engineering* (pp. 29-43). Springer, Cham.

[18] Z. v. Naumann. The Evolution of the Cryptographic Hash Function in Blockchains. https://medium.com/shokone/hash-no-not-that-kind-the-crypto-kind-2e8bf616aa24, Oct. 2017.

[19] IBM Knowledge Center - Symmetric cryptography. https://www.ibm.com/support/knowledgecenter/en/SSB23S_1.1.0.14/gtps7/s7symm.html.

[20] IBM Knowledge Center - Public key cryptography. https://www.ibm.com/support/knowledgecenter/en/SSB23S_1.1.0.14/gtps7/s7pkey.html.

[21] DiffieHellman key exchange. https://en.wikipedia.org/w/index.php?title=Diffie%E2%80%93Hellman_key_exchange&oldid=858357713, Sept. 2018. Page Version ID: 858357713.

[22] Sun, J., Yan, J., & Zhang, K. Z. (2016). Blockchain-based sharing services: What blockchain technology can contribute to smart cities. *Financial Innovation*, *2*(1), 1-9.

[23] Kruijff, J. D., & Weigand, H. (2017, June). Understanding the blockchain using enterprise ontology. In *International Conference on Advanced Information Systems Engineering* (pp. 29-43). Springer, Cham.

[24] Mougayar, W. (2016). *The business blockchain: promise, practice, and application of the next Internet technology*. John Wiley & Sons.

[25] Gervais, A., Karame, G. O., Wüst, K., Glykantzis, V., Ritzdorf, H., & Capkun, S. (2016, October). On the security and performance of proof of work blockchains. In *Proceedings of the 2016 ACM SIGSAC conference on computer and communications security* (pp. 3-16).

[26] Narayanan, A., Bonneau, J., Felten, E., Miller, A., & Goldfeder, S. (2016). *Bitcoin and cryptocurrency technologies: a comprehensive introduction*. Princeton University Press.

[27] Bade, P. V. (2019). *Pro-active market opportunity identification as a key element in the development of innovation strategy* (Doctoral dissertation, Wien).

[28] Kuo, T. T., Kim, H. E., & Ohno-Machado, L. (2017). Blockchain distributed ledger technologies for biomedical and health care applications. *Journal of the American Medical Informatics Association*, *24*(6), 1211-1220.

[29] Xia, Q. I., Sifah, E. B., Asamoah, K. O., Gao, J., Du, X., & Guizani, M. (2017). MeDShare: Trust-less medical data sharing among cloud service providers via blockchain. *IEEE access*, *5*, 14757-14767.

[30] Heston, T. (2017). A case study in blockchain healthcare innovation.

[31] How Blockchain Will Revolutionise Clinical Trials, June 2018. Available online: https://pharmaphorum. com/views-and-analysis/how-blockchain-will-revolutionise-clinical-trials-clinical-trials/ (accessed on 20 November 2018).

[32] Moe Alsumidaie, Blockchain Concepts Emerge in Clinical Trials, Applied Clinical Trials, May 2018. Available online: http://www.appliedclinicaltrialsonline.com/blockchain-concepts-emerge-clinical-trials (accessed on 15 October 2018).

[33] Benchoufi, M., Porcher, R., & Ravaud, P. (2017). Blockchain protocols in clinical trials: Transparency and traceability of consent. *F1000Research*, *6*.

[34] Clauson, K. A., Breeden, E. A., Davidson, C., & Mackey, T. K. (2018). Leveraging Blockchain Technology to Enhance Supply Chain Management in Healthcare:: An exploration of challenges and opportunities in the health supply chain. *Blockchain in healthcare today*.

[35] Mauri, R. Blockchain for Fraud Prevention: Industry Use Cases. July 2017. Available online: https://www.ibm.com/blogs/blockchain/2017/07/blockchain-for-fraud-prevention-industry-use-cases/ (accessed on 16 October 2018).

[36] Swan, M. (2015). Blockchain thinking: The brain as a decentralized autonomous corporation [commentary]. *IEEE Technology and Society Magazine*, *34*(4), 41-52.

[37] Taylor, P. Applying Blockchain Technology to Medicine Traceability; April 2016. Available online: https://www.securingindustry.com/pharmaceuticals/applying-blockchain-technology-to-medicinetraceability/s40/a2766/ (accessed on 16 October 2018).

[38] Plotnikov, V., & Kuznetsova, V. (2018). The prospects for the use of digital technology "blockchain" in the pharmaceutical market. In *MATEC web of conferences* (Vol. 193, p. 02029). EDP Sciences.

[39] Sylim, P., Liu, F., Marcelo, A., & Fontelo, P. (2018). Blockchain technology for detecting falsified and substandard drugs in distribution: pharmaceutical supply chain intervention. *JMIR research protocols*, *7*(9), e10163.

[40] Guzman Trujllo, C. G. (2018). *The role of blockchain in the pharmaceutical industry supply chain as a tool for reducing the flow of counterfeit drugs* (Doctoral dissertation, Dublin Business School).

[41] Fernández-Caramés, T. M., & Fraga-Lamas, P. (2018). A Review on the Use of Blockchain for the Internet of Things. *Ieee Access*, *6*, 32979-33001.

[42] Investopedia "Blockchains". Available online: https://www.investopedia.com/terms/1/51-attack.asp (accessed on 20 October 2018).

[43] Hertig, A. Blockchain's Once-Feared 51 Percent Attack Is Now Becoming Regular. June 2018. Available online: https://www.coindesk.com/blockchains-feared-51-attack-now-becoming-regular/ (accessed on 20 October 2018).

[44] Esposito, C., De Santis, A., Tortora, G., Chang, H., & Choo, K. K. R. (2018). Blockchain: A panacea for healthcare cloud-based data security and privacy?. *IEEE Cloud Computing*, *5*(1), 31-37.

[45] McKinlay, J. Blockchain: Background Challenges and Legal Issues; DLA Piper Publications: London, UK, 2016.

[46] Kamel Boulos, M. N., Wilson, J. T., & Clauson, K. A. (2018). Geospatial blockchain: promises, challenges, and scenarios in health and healthcare. *International Journal of Health Geographics*, *17*(1), 1-10.

[47] Mackey, T. K., Kuo, T. T., Gummadi, B., Clauson, K. A., Church, G., Grishin, D., ... & Palombini, M. (2019). 'Fit-for-purpose?'–challenges and opportunities for applications of blockchain technology in the future of healthcare. *BMC medicine*, *17*(1), 1-17.

Author Biography

Deepika Bairagee

Ms. Deepika Bairagee, B. Pharm, M. Pharm (Quality Assurance), is an Assistant Professor at the Oriental College of Pharmacy and Research, Oriental University, Indore, India. She has five years of teaching experience and two years of research experience. She has spoken at more than 20 national and international conferences and seminars, presenting over 20 research articles. She has over 20 publications in national and international journals. She is the author of over 18 books. She has over 50 abstracts that have been published at national and international conferences. Young Researcher, Young Achievers, and Excellent Researcher were among the honors bestowed upon her. Proteomics and Metabolomics are two areas of research that she is currently interested in.

4

Patient Monitoring using Blockchain

P. Jayasree[1], AVSSS Gupta[1], GSN Koteswara Rao[2]*, Hajeera Fatima[1], Rekha Naresh Babu[3], and Roja Rani Budha[2,4]

[1]Joginpally B.R. Pharmacy College, Hyderabad, Telangana, India
[2]Shobhaben Pratapbhai Patel School of Pharmacy & Technology Management, SVKM's NMIMS, V.L. Mehta Road, Vile Parle (W), Mumbai- 400056, India
[3]Nirmala College of Pharmacy, Mangalagiri, Guntur, Andhra Pradesh, India
[4]Department of Pharmacology, Institute of Pharmaceutical Technology, Sri Padmavati Mahila Visvavidyalayam, Tirupati, Andhra Pradesh, India
*Corresponding Author: Email: drgsnkrao@gmail.com

Abstract

The healthcare industry has undergone revolutionary changes as technology has advanced in recent years. The Internet of Things, Cloud Computing, Blockchain technology, lab-on-a-chip, non-invasive and minimally invasive operations, and other advancements have made it easier to treat a variety of debilitating ailments These new technologies have had a significant impact on both research and the healthcare business. Miniaturized healthcare sensors powered by IoT can be used for clinical tests and self-health tracking. They aid professionals in remote regions in making early diagnoses and treatment recommendations without having direct contact with users. Access control mechanisms and uneven security rules have made it difficult to meet the data's security standards. The patient's vital signs can be monitored using blockchain-based smart contracts and an enterprise-distributed ledger infrastructure. This offers global access to patient medical information at any moment, as well as an immutable and thorough history log. When compared to existing patient monitoring systems, the proposed approach provides more benefits. The blockchain system provides greater monitoring, increased connectivity, and higher data security when compared to traditional patient monitoring systems. Despite the abundance of medical facilities, fatal diseases such as heart disease, cancer, influenza, and pneumonia have increased significantly and claim many lives. A large number of doctors, therapists, nurses, and other personnel constantly monitor and observe patients' health. Patients with chronic diseases are regularly monitored and observed. In recent years, various healthcare monitoring systems have been introduced, and they are used to collect, process, and analyze data retrieved from sensing devices. These healthcare systems are also responsible for tracking and monitoring patients' vital signs. However, when connecting different departments of a hospital in order to effectively share medical data to provide better healthcare services to patients, the issue of legal interoperability arises. No such thing as a centralized system exists. A blockchain can address these problems using its decentralized architecture. Blockchain technology can be used to make his or her medical records unalterable and immutable. Any access or adjustment effort may be instantly labeled and identified across the blockchain. This is useful not just for patient integrity, but it also identifies any criminal activities, such as wholesale fraud or record adulteration. Furthermore, approved medicinal service record sharing and review will be greatly simplified. When a patient comes in, the majority of the patient's suppliers are usually notified immediately. Medication bugs, hypersensitivities, and drug solutions can be accommodated in overall blockchain records relatively quickly using appropriate patient-caring algorithms, removing the need for time-consuming pharmaceutical compromise forms. The use of blockchain technology will thus encourage improved access to care, medical record management, prompt clinical information confirmation, increased security, and more effective care planning for the effective delivery of healthcare services to patients through the management and sharing of medical data. Blockchain is transforming traditional healthcare practices into a more reliable means of effective diagnosis and treatment through safe and secure data sharing. In the future, blockchain could be a technology that can help with personalized, authentic, and secure healthcare by combining all of a patient's real-time clinical data and presenting it in an up-to-date secure healthcare setup.

Keywords: Blockchain, sensors, healthcare, decentralized, patient monitoring.

4.1 Introduction

Blockchain is a technology that lessens the need for a single, centralized authority while still enabling secure and "trustless" interactions between parties. Through the use of game theory and cryptography, it offers consensus, immutability, and decentralization [1]. The foundations for a variety of application domains, such as cryptocurrencies and decentralized applications, are provided by this technology (DApps) [2].

When we visit a hospital care unit, the patient monitoring system is one of the first medical devices we see. It provides doctors and nurses with information about the patient's physiological signals so they can deliver prompt and effective care. The majority of patient monitoring products on the market provide the four physiological signals that are most crucial for health: heart rate, oxygen saturation, body temperature, and electrocardiogram (ECG) activity [3, 4]. The patient should only need to make minimal adjustments during the physiological signal measurement process in order to get reliable results [5].

Infusion pumps, bedside monitors, and other devices that help doctors monitor and diagnose patients effectively are included in modern ICU/CCU equipment. What if there is no doctor available and a patient is dying? What happens if a medical expert is actually on the scene but is not permitted to administer any medication without a prescription from a licensed physician? These conditions raise the patient's chance of dying. India's mortality rate is rising as a result of ambulances being late in getting to hospitals during prime hours [6]. Such occurrences are commonplace in India on a daily basis. In addition, it should be noted that the majority of the time, it takes 40–50 kilometers to travel from the site to the closest hospital. This is quite scary, especially when the patient's condition is steadily getting worse. As the patient is being accompanied by an attendant, the doctor cannot see the patient's vital signs and must rely on the attendant's report in order to administer the medication. In this scenario, a misunderstanding between the doctor and the attendant might lead to a fatality. In these situations, the patient's first hour or so is extremely important because they need to receive immediate medical attention. Therefore, it is crucial to transfer the patient's life to safe hands as soon as possible. Numerous research initiatives in the past had a significant impact on improving and developing telemedicine solutions [7], diagnosing patients from a distance, and monitoring their health status in real time. A smart, portable technology that can provide quick, virtual access to a doctor for emergency cases in real time is urgently needed. The development of an IoT-based patient monitoring system that enables a doctor to view and diagnose a patient from a distance is therefore urgently needed. Automation of telehealth and telemedicine operations and services is made efficient and reliable by combining blockchain technology with smart contracts. Automation of telehealth and telemedicine operations and services is made efficient and reliable by combining blockchain technology with smart contracts. A self-executing program that runs on the blockchain platform is known as a smart contract. It replaces the function of intermediaries in the current healthcare systems and automates business processes. To build trust, the predefined rules among the involved organizations are translated into smart contract functions [8].

4.2 Blockchain Technology

The blockchain technology was devised by an unidentified person "Satoshi Nakamoto" in October 2008. He proposed a peer-to-peer, non-intermediated, electronic cash system introducing the first digital currency named as Bitcoin. This Distributed Ledger Technology (DLT) is a time-stamped chain of transactional blocks, sealed with a cryptographic hash function and digital signature implementing trustless protocol [9, 10]. Bitcoin was the first application of blockchain technology implemented in 2009 [10, 11].

4.2.1 Applications of blockchain

There may be numerous uses for blockchain, including in the fields of finance, power, healthcare, real estate, tourism, social networking, marketplace, mathematics, transportation, entertainment, and the protection of human rights.

4.2.1.1 Blockchain in healthcare

The use of blockchain technology in computing and healthcare is also relatively new. With its features and properties, this technology has great potential to address major issues in the healthcare sector's various subsectors [12].

The pace of development is accelerating at ever-increasing rates in the area of healthcare. Today, there is a need for high-quality medical facilities that are supported by cutting-edge and modern technology. Here, blockchain would be instrumental in revolutionizing the healthcare industry. In addition, the structure of the healthcare system is changing in favor of a patient-centered strategy that emphasizes the access to the right resources for healthcare. Healthcare organizations can better provide adequate patient care and top-notch medical facilities thanks to the blockchain. Using this technology, the time-consuming, repetitive process of health information exchange, which contributes to high healthcare costs, can be resolved quickly. Citizens can participate in health research programs using blockchain technology. In addition, improved research and data sharing on public well-being will improve care for various communities. The management of the entire healthcare system and organizations is done through a centralized database [13, 14].

A blockchain-based system has employed various smart contracts to swiftly and securely transfer the crypto-currency to the wallet of patients as an incentive for sharing their health data. The Ethereum-based system presented enables real-time patient's health monitoring and successfully maintains a time-stamped log of medication taken by the patients. Although efforts have been made to adapt blockchain for a variety of industries, including healthcare, insurance, manufacturing, e-voting, energy, and many more, the technology was primarily applied in the financial industry as the technology that enabled Bitcoin to operate [15]. The healthcare sector is particularly difficult because of its intricate system of influential stakeholders and the need to disrupt it with new ideas. Public health management, remote monitoring, electronic health records (EHR), medical data management, data security, and drug development are a few examples of the applications of blockchain that may be used to address healthcare issues. Surprisingly, by letting patients own their data and decide with whom it is shared, blockchain can allay worries about data ownership and sharing [16] and others.

Blockchain offers exceptional opportunities to harness the power of other emerging technologies and has the potential to address important healthcare issues. A transformation will be possible with the assistance of researchers and practitioners from different fields toward improving and innovating methods for viewing the healthcare industry, despite interoperability challenges such as the lack of an existing standard for developing blockchain-based healthcare applications [17, 18]. Blockchain's ability to solve many complex issues that the healthcare industry currently encounters shall allow for this [19, 20].

4.2.2 The benefits of blockchain for healthcare systems are as follows [21]

(1) Decentralization: Blockchain provides a decentralized health data management back-bone, meaning that all users (doctors, patients, and others) can access the same health records.

(2) Improved data security and privacy: The immutability of blockchain can improve the security of health data, which, once saved to the blockchain, cannot be corrupted or altered.

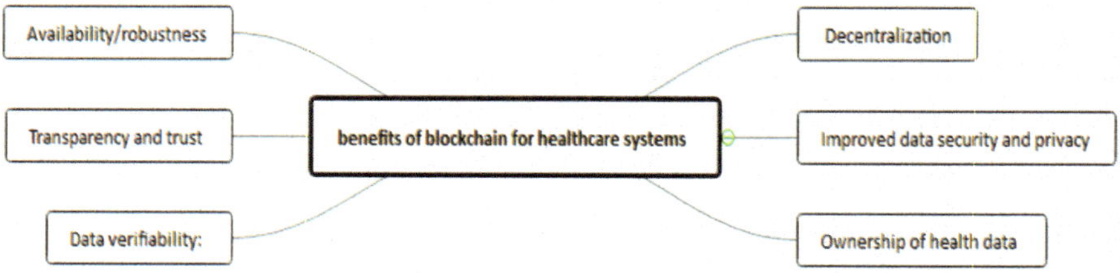

Figure 4.1 Benefits of blockchain for healthcare systems.

(3) Ownership of health data: Blockchain helps patients to own their health data and control how their data are used through strong cryptographic protocols and well-defined smart contracts.
(4) Availability/robustness: The availability of patients' health data that are stored on blockchain is resilient against data losses, data corruption, and some security attacks.
(5) Transparency and trust: Blockchain, being open and transparent, establishes a sense of trust in distributed healthcare systems.
(6) Data verifiability: Even without accessing the plaintext of records that are stored on blockchain, the integrity and validity of those records can be verified.

A data structure known as a blockchain can be used to store health records and ensure decentralization (the transfer of power from local to central governments), transparency, and security. You can think of it as records that are stored as blocks but are not under the control of a single authority. This type of storage is frequently referred to as a "digital ledger." Every transaction in this ledger is authenticated and authorized by the owner's digital signature. As a result, the data in the digital ledger is very secure. The distributed ledger technology serves as the foundation for the blockchain or a more developed iteration of the distributed ledger. Several advantages of blockchain in healthcare system is shown in Figure 4.1.

4.3 Patient Monitoring System (PMS)

Continuous or repetition of observations or measurements of the patients' physiological parameter and the function of life support equipment, for the purpose of guiding management decisions, including when to make therapeutic interventions, and evaluation of those interventions.

4.3.1 Use of PMS

A patient monitor not only alerts doctors and medical staff about potentially life-threatening events, but also provides physiologic input data used to control directly connected life-support devices.

PMS is used in:

- Patients whose physiological regulatory systems are unstable. An individual whose respiratory system has been suppressed by a drug overdose or anesthesia is an example.
- Patients whose condition may be life-threatening. Before a person can notice rising stress signs, it may give warnings, alerts, and recommendations. For instance, a patient with symptoms of an acute myocardial infarction (heart attack).
- Patients who are at high risk of developing a condition that could be fatal. Examples include people who have recently undergone open heart surgery or premature infants with underdeveloped hearts and lungs.
- Patients whose physiological conditions are critical. For instance, those suffering from multiple injuries or septic shock.
- Smart biosensors may identify hazardous substances like lead and mercury and send out alerts.

Patient monitoring systems can be viewed from two perspectives based on the location of the patient – hospitalized monitoring and remote monitoring.

Patients are admitted into hospitals for hospitalized monitoring, and all the sensors are added to the patients' beds. These amenities are now present in the majority of contemporary hospitals. By using IoT devices, it makes it possible to monitor patients continuously around-the-clock [22]. This is very beneficial for critically ill patients, such as those in the ICU or CCU, who require meticulous and ongoing monitoring.

People who are not admitted to hospitals are subject to remote monitoring. The treatment of patients is greatly aided by ongoing health monitoring. It enables remote patient monitoring at all times, enabling doctors to detect various diseases and attacks early on and take precautions [23, 24].

As the world moves toward remote monitoring, real-time, and quick disease detection, remote healthcare is an emerging research area. There are many subcategories of remote healthcare (such as telehealth and mobile health), all of which refer to using technology to monitor patients outside of a hospital setting. The benefits of patient monitoring from a distance include the ability to continuously monitor patients, the ability to detect illnesses early and in real time, the reduction of hospital costs and hospitalizations, the ability to obtain more accurate readings while allowing patients to go about their daily lives as usual, the improvement of healthcare service efficiency by using communication technology, and emergency medical care and service for patients.

4.4 Data Sharing between Telemedicine and Traditional Care

Patients who live in rural locations far from local medical facilities or in places with a dearth of medical personnel typically have access to care through telemedicine. Patients who want to receive convenient medical care are increasingly using it today [25]. Connected patients can get fast treatment for minor but urgent conditions on demand and save time by avoiding waiting at the doctor's office [26]. Many businesses now provide 24/7 continuous access to treatment, and a wide variety of user-friendly apps have been developed for patients to monitor, manage, and report their health utilizing technology [25]. This is due to the increased accessibility of smart mobile and telemedicine devices. For instance, the Apple Health [26] app enables users to connect to vitals monitoring devices and keep the data on their iPhones. The supplier can then be informed of these records as necessary. When compared to traditional physical health treatments, telemedicine services typically include more sophisticated technology and are considerably more widespread. It is typical for clinicians from several networks or areas to treat patients which results in reduction of continuity of care. Primary care physicians may not have access to health information gathered during telemedicine care episodes, leading to an incomplete medical history and a potential risk to the standard of treatment as a whole [27]. Blockchain technology has the ability to break down the communication gap between these providers by doing away with the necessity for a third-party authority and enabling direct interactions between involved individuals. Blockchain technology must be integrated into current, diverse health systems and clinical data standards in order to overcome the difficult data sharing dilemma.

4.5 IoT-Blockchain in Remote Patient Monitoring (RPM)

IoT-blockchain refers to Internet of Things (IoT)-based systems that utilize blockchains. The scalability and dependability of IoT systems can be improved via IoT-blockchain [29]. It also makes IoT devices more interoperable. Blockchain has the ability to process and store heterogeneous data while also preserving data anonymity and integrity. Autonomous interaction in IoT-based systems is a smart contract feature [28]. IoT-blockchain is a practical remedy for RPM as a result.

General RPM system framework: In order to connect patients and doctors in the IoT-Blockchain based RPM system, a blockchain network is often required. This network will be used for all data transfers. Every peer in this network will have access to the same data, which is a feature of distributed ledger technology.

4.6 Framework RPM System with IoT and Blockchain

4.6.1 Components of the framework

The system has three different user types: patients, physicians, and hospitals. According to this framework, every patient is connected to a certain hospital that handles all of their medical issues. In this part, the components of the suggested framework are briefly discussed [19].

- **Patients**: Each patient will be added as a node to the network. Various IoT devices will be placed on their bodies to collect health data. On the patient's smartphone, a mobile app will collect data from the sensors and process it before sending it to the network. As a result, the mobile app can be thought of as a virtual patient in our system.
- **Doctors**: Registered individuals who monitor and treat patients in the system are known as doctors.
- **Hospitals**: Hospitals are the system's healthcare providers. The hospital administration will assign a doctor to each patient so that the assigned doctor has access to the patient's health data in the system.
- **Blockchain network:** A blockchain network will be included in the system to connect all of the system's entities. To be added to this network, all nodes in this network must be verified. Because the data must be accessible to all, the network will be peer-to-peer, and the blockchain will be permissioned. Permissioned blockchain ensures that the network is free of malicious nodes. As there is no rouge node in the system, the PBFT consensus algorithm should be used to ensure the validity of any transaction in the network. Healthcare data will not be directly stored in the blockchain; rather, data storage and access will be stored as blockchain transactions. Patients' processed data should be saved in a database. To ensure secure data access, all users should have

digital signatures. For real-time monitoring, each transaction must be associated with multiple smart contracts. They will be triggered based on the data values and the peers' actions [20].

- **Cloud storage:** As time passes, the amount of healthcare data will grow because monitoring data is constantly collected and must be stored in the system. If we store the data on a blockchain ledger, the devices at the user's end will require a massive amount of storage space. Furthermore, if we want to store data in the blockchain, a node's disconnection may result in data unavailability. As a result, cloud storage can be used to store the actual data, while the blockchain network stores the link to the data in the cloud server as part of the transaction [29].

4.7 Conclusion

Patients and doctors are benefiting greatly from the digitalization of healthcare. The following are the benefits of using blockchain technologies for personal health monitoring. First, they enable the rapid and low-cost integration of health data into a single chain, providing a doctor or patient with comprehensive information about his or her health status. Second, the technology itself ensures that this data is kept private and secure. Third, in addition to data from official sources, personal observations enter the chain in the form of messages and patient complaints, which can be tracked over time and cannot be changed, allowing for a complete picture of the health status and making the best treatment decision.

References

[1] Nakamoto, S.: 'Bitcoin: A peer-to-peer electronic cash system, 2008.

[2] Johnston, D.; Yilmaz, S. O.; Kandah, J.; Bentenitis, N.; Hashemi, F.; Gross, R.; Wilkinson, S.; Mason, S.; 'The general theory of decentralized applications, dapps', *GitHub*, 2014, 9.

[3] Enderle, J.; Blanchard, S.; Bronzino, J.; Introduction to Biomedical Engineering. *Elesevier* 2005, 505-548.

[4] Shahriyar, R.; Bari, M., F.; Kundu, G.; Ahamed, S. I,; Akbar, M. M,; Intelligent Mobile Health Monitoring System (IMHMS). *Journal of Control and Automation*,2009, 2, 3.

[5] Franklin, S. W.; Rajan, S. E.; Personal Area Network for Biomedical Monitoring Systems Using Human Body as a Transmission Medium, *Journal of Bio-Science and BioTechnology*. 2010, 2.

[6] Athavan, K.; Balasubramanian, G.; Jagadeeshwaran, S.; and Dinesh, N.; Automatic ambulance rescue system. *Int J Adv Technol Eng Res*. 2012, 86-92.

[7] Bourouis, A.; Feham, M.; ubiquitous mobile health monitoring. 2011, 3(3), 74-82.

[8] Chacko, A.; Hayajneh, T.; Security and privacy issues with IoT in healthcare. EAI Endorsed Transactions on Pervasive Health and Technology, 2018, 4(14).

[9] Zheng, Z.; Shaoan, X.; Hongning, D.; Xiangping, C.; Huaimin, W.; An overview of blockchain technology: Architecture, consensus, and future trends. In 2017 IEEE International Congress on Big Data (BigData Congress).2017, 557-564.

[10] Kuo, T. Ting.; Hyeon, E. K.; Lucila, O. M.; Blockchain distributed ledger technologies for biomedical and health care applications. *Journal of the American Medical Informatics Association*. 2017, 6, 1211-1220.

[11] Daniel, J.; Arman, S.; Mohammed, A.; Saman, S.; Ben, A.; Blockchain Technology, Cognitive Computing, and Healthcare Innovations. *Journal of Advances in Information Technology*.2017 8, 34-39.

[12] Mettler, Matthias, Blockchain technology in healthcare: The revolution starts here. In 2016 IEEE 18th International Conference on e-Health Networking, Applications and Services (Healthcom), 2016, 1-3.

[13] Chelladurai, U.; Pandian, S.; A novel blockchain based electronic health record automation system for healthcare, *J. Ambient Intell. Humanized Comput*. 2021, 1-6.

[14] Zhang, P.; Schmidt, D. C.; White, J.; Lenz, G.; Blockchain technology use cases in healthcare, in: Advances in Computers, *Elsevier*, 2018 , 111, 1-41.

[15] Sadiku, M.; Eze, K.; Musa, S. "Blockchain technology in healthcare.*International Journal of Advances in Scientific Research and Engineering*.2018, 4, 154-159.

[16] Tandon, A.; Dhir, A. N.; Islam, Mantym, A.; Blockchain in healthcare: A systematic literature review, synthesizing framework and future research agenda. *Computers in Industry*. 2020, 122, 103-290.

[17] P. J. P. A. T. C. Gaynor, M.; Tuttle, N, J.; Adoption of blockchain in health care. *Journal of medical Internet research*, 2020, 150-155.

[18] Agbo, C. C.; Mahmoud, Q. H.; Eklund, J. M. Blockchain Technology in Healthcare: A Systematic Review. *Healthcare*. 2019, 7, 56.

[19] Senthamilarasi, C.; Jansi Rani, J.; Vidhya, B.; and Aritha, H.; 2018. A smart patient health monitoring system using IoT. *International Journal of Pure and Applied Mathematics*. 2018, 119, 59-70.

[20] Alexandru, A.; Nicolae, B.; Elena, Ş.; Paul, C. H.; and Andrei, Z.; An IoT based system for remote patient monitoring. In Procedings of the 17th International Carpathian Control Conference (ICCC). 2016, 1-6.

[21] Muhammad, T.; Muhammad, S.; Shakoor, M.; and Muhammad, S.; A lightweight authentication and authorization framework for blockchain-enabled IoT network in health-informatics. *Sustainability*.2020, 12, 17-21.

[22] 10 Pros and Cons of Telemedicine | eVisit® Telehealth Solutions. (n.d.). Retrieved March 01, 2018, from https://evisit.com/10-pros-and-cons-of-telemedicine/

[23] Sood, S.; Mbarika, V.; Jugoo, S.; Dookhy, R.; Doarn, C. R.; Prakash, N.; and Merrell, R. C.; What is telemedicine? A collection of 104 peer-reviewed perspectives and theoretical underpinnings. *Telemedicine and e-Health*, 2007, 13, (5), 573-590.

[24] What is telemedicine? - Definition from WhatIs.com. (n.d.). Retrieved March 01, 2018, from http://searchhealthit.techtarget.com/definition/telemedicine

[25] IOS - Health. (n.d.). Retrieved March 01, 2018, from https://www.apple.com/ios/health/

[26] Zhang, P.; White, J.; Schmidt, D. C.; Lenz, G.; and Rosenbloom, S. T.; ‘FHIRChain: Applying Blockchain to Securely and Scalably Share Clinical Data, *Elsevier*.2019, 168-175.

[27] Hong, N. D,; Zibin Z,; and Yan, Z,; Blockchain for Internet of Things: A Survey. *Internet of Things Journal*.2019, 6, 8076-8094.

[28] Ana, R,; Cristian, M,; Jaime, C,; Enrique, S,; and Manuel, D,; On blockchain and its integration with IoT. Challenges and opportunities. *Future Generation Computer Systems*.2018, 88, 173-190.

[29] Hoe, T. Y.; Ming F. N.; Soh, P.; Seng, K. C.; Ali, C.; and Jamal, A.; IoT Based Real-Time Remote Patient Monitoring System. 16th IEEE International Colloquium on Signal Processing Its Applications (CSPA).2020, 176-179.

5

Potential of AI in the Advancement of the Pharmaceutical Industry

Akanksha Sharma[1*], Aditi Singh[2], Ashish Verma[3], Rishabha Malviya[4], and Pavan Kumar Arya Padarthi[5]

[1]Monad College of Pharmacy, Monad University, India
[2]Ashoka Institute of Pharmacy, Ashoka Engineering Chauraha, India
[3]School of Pharmacy, Monad University, India
[4]Department of Pharmacy, School of Medical and Allied Sciences, Galgotias University, India
[5]Department of Computer Science in Artificial Intelligence and Robotics, University of Hertfordshire, United Kingdom
*Corresponding Author: Monad College of Pharmacy, Monad University, N.H. 9, Delhi Hapur Road, Kastla, Kasmabad, Pilkhuwa, Uttar Pradesh, 245304, India, Email: akankshasona012@gmail.com,
Contact: +91-8009218455.

Abstract

Artificial intelligence (AI) has revolutionized all sectors of industries all over the world and it has the potential to improve healthcare as well. It is used to examine patients' data while they visit the hospital, prescribed medication, lab tests, and procedures performed. AI applications help in the management of the huge amounts of data generated in the medical field and reveal novel information which would otherwise be hidden in large medical data. AI is a machine learning system that responds to and analyzes data in real time, allowing researchers to acquire data more efficiently. These technologies are also used to find new drugs for healthcare management and patient treatment. Diseases like neurology, cancer, diabetes, and cardiology mainly use AI. Furthermore, the more data AI responds to, the smarter it becomes, propelling the pharmaceutical sector forward. This chapter describes the role of AI in the healthcare and pharma industry. It also focuses on the various applications of AI in the pharma industry which enhances its efficacy. AI applications in the pharma industry must be adopted for further use in the future.

Keywords: Artificial intelligence, pharma industry, healthcare, disease, medication.

5.1 Introduction and History

Artificial intelligence (AI) is a branch of computer science involved in problem-solving via symbolic programming. It has evolved into a problem-solving science with widespread applicability in business, healthcare, and engineering. This artificial intelligence's major goal is to find useful information processing problems and provide an abstract description of how to solve them. It is a field concerned with the creation and implementation of an algorithm for data processing, interpretation, and learning. Artificial intelligence covers a large spectrum of machine learning and statistical technology, pattern recognition, clustering, and similarity-based algorithms. It is a fast-developing technique that has applications in many fields of life and business. The pharmaceutical business has recently discovered new and imaginative methods to employ this sophisticated technology to assist in tackling some of the industry's most pressing issues. Artificial intelligence in the pharmaceutical sector suggests the utilization of automated algorithms in the completion of work that previously needs intelligence. In the last five years, AI has transformed how researchers discover novel therapies, combat disease, and more in the biotech and pharmaceutical industries [1].

AI is a discipline of computer science that is completely concerned with problem-solving and the development of industries capable of doing activities that would otherwise necessitate the use of intelligence and human operators. Machine learning, chatbots, deep learning, self-modifying graph networks, and non-linear grid systems are just a few of the well-known technologies that belong under the AI umbrella. Algorithms are rules that help in estimating or performing problem-solving activities with the utilization of computing tools. Neural networks, AutoQSAR, Deep Signal for genomics, and DeepChem packages from Schrodinger software are examples of surprisingly evolving technologies. The neural network generates and assesses a variety of models to find the best experimental data. Technology can save money and time while also providing a greater understanding of the interactions between various formulation and process parameters [2].

Artificial intelligence is a rapidly growing sector in practically every field. It is not restricted to a single field; it can be used in different sectors of research, technology, and health. The field of artificial intelligence emphasizes how computers evaluate data and emulate the human mental process. Because medication development entails large R&DR&D expenses and a high level of uncertainty in terms of time consumption, artificial intelligence may be one of the most promising options for overcoming these drawbacks. Because there is so much data available, there is a danger that some important elements will be overlooked. Algorithms like deep learning, machine learning, and other expert systems are being utilized to overcome these problems. Delays in drug development, failure in clinical trials, and marketing failure can all be decreased with the successful use of AI in the pharmaceutical business. This overview includes information on the evolution of AI, its subfields, its overall implementation, and its use in the pharmaceutical industry, as well as insights into AI's obstacles and limitations [3].

The year 1956 is commonly regarded as the birth year of AI, as Dartmouth College hosted the renowned conference in that year. However, the previous year, 1955, witnessed the development of the first AI system, Logic Theorist, which was created by Allen Newell and Herbert A. Simon. This technique was used to prove over 40 of Alfred N. Whitehead's and Bertrand Russell's Principia Mathematica theorems. The system's creators, however, were unable to publish. Professor Stephen Hawking, a theoretical physicist, claimed in an interview with the BBC that human efforts to make robots that can think is a tremendous threat to the human race's survival and that the race to produce a perfect AI could lead to the human race's extinction in the future. Professor Hawking issued this caution in response to a question about updating the technology he uses to communicate. They employ AI of a fundamental sort in their technologies. The world, on the other hand, has not taken Professor Stephen Hawking's warning seriously. Innumerable AI studies are being done all around the world. A lot of money is being put into developing a system that can work significantly more efficiently and in a period that a human being can. AI is used in every industry, whether it is in an educational institution, a manufacturing enterprise, a government office, or a research group [4].

AI can assist by revolutionizing the present medication research process and drastically altering how we identify novel disease insights. Technology can more effectively access current research and information, allowing the pharmaceutical business to be more efficient in its procedures. AI can boost pharmaceutical inventions and decrease attrition by supplementing the work of professionals in this field. Scientific data is frequently messy "unstructured" data, which is more difficult to annotate and absorb. It means both industry and academic researchers will have to wait for a longer period to get the data access than they need to create new. Increasing a researcher's access to evidence must make their decision-making more précised and also discover new disease insights.

However, machine learning and AI technologies can make a major difference by allowing scientists to analyze the knowledge of all scientists more swiftly and effectively than ever before. It allows researchers to compare, absorb, and connect data by annotating and structuring it with cutting-edge algorithms. This allows researchers to quickly find relevant material and ask far more in-depth and broad queries about the scientific literature. It also enables the unification of unstructured and structured data in a single format. AI and machine learning can also have an impact on the research and development process in other ways. Better approaches to forecasting chemical attributes and reducing the number of molecules that must be synthesized is a possibility.

Another area where AI and machine learning are being used is proteomic, genomic,genomic and metabolic data to get better disease biomarkers and surrogate measures of therapy efficacy. The time it takes to analyze photographs of cancer or brain scans in neurological disorders can be drastically reduced. Machine learning and AI will be utilized to analyze data from real-world results, data from wearable technology, and data from other sensors.

Table 5.1 Summary of AI application in different fields of health.

S.no	Sector	Function
1.	**Diagnosis**	AI can identify abnormalities with the use of medical images like CT scanners, magnetic resonance imaging, X-rays, and ultrasounds more precisely [6].
2.	**Electronic Health Records**	They assist in the analysis of data obtained from the past to the present, which helps in the improvement of various sorts of treatments and drug usage for disease [7].
3.	**Drug Interactions and Discovery**	Algorithms were capable of extracting information on drug interactions as well as contraindications through research records with the help of AI [8].
4.	**Radiology**	Artificial intelligence can perform X-rays and computed tomography more quickly and precisely [9].
5.	**Psychological Conditions**	The new AI development technologies can be used to detect psychological disorders in children by utilizing eye tracking technology [10].

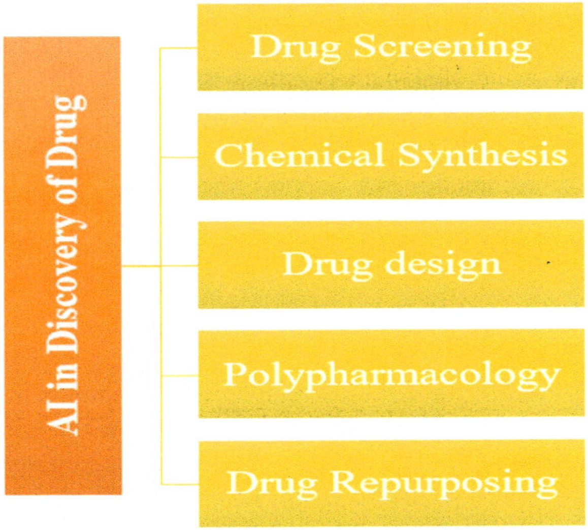

Figure 5.1 The schematic diagram represents the summary of the utilization of AI in drug discovery.

Precision therapy and better patient stratification for clinical trials are also supported by this modern innovation, which should lead to a higher rate of success based on improved clinical trial effectiveness because it is better to choose the most appropriate patient population [5]. Table 5.1 summarizes the AI application in different health sectors and Fig. 5.1 shows the summary of utilization of AI in drug discovery.

5.2 Opportunities in the Pharmaceutical Industry for Artificial Intelligence

5.2.1 Role of AI in drug development

AI can differentiate lead and hit compounds, enabling faster therapeutic target validation and structure design optimization. AI has various advantages but it also has significant data challenges like data scale, diversity, progress, and ambiguity. Drug research datasets of pharmaceutical companies contain data of millions of compounds and traditional machine learning algorithms may be unable to handle them. A computer model, based on quantitative structure-activity relationship (QSAR), can easily determine a huge number of compounds or physicochemical characteristics like log Dlog D or log Plog P, though these models are far from predicting difficult biological aspects like side effects and effectiveness of chemicals. QSAR-based models face challenges like sets of small training, a mistake in training sets experimental data, and a shortage of experimental validations. Recently emerging AI techniques like deep learning (DL) and relevant models are utilized to evaluate the effectiveness and safety of therapeutic drugs.

QSAR modeling techniques like Support Vector Machines, Linear Discriminant Analysis, Random Forest, and Decision Trees have been utilized to determine new API candidates that can be used to speed up the analysis of QSAR [11].

Improved profile analysis, quicker removal of non-lead substances, and therapeutic compound selection at a cheaper cost are all possible with different in silico approaches for virtual screening of compounds from virtual chemical spaces, as well as ligand and structure-based technologies. Drug design technologies like coulomb matrices and molecular fingerprint recognition are used to analyze the chemical, physical, and toxicological features of a lead ingredient [11, 12].

Because of increased chemical space, the gap between drug discovery and development is widening as the search for new therapeutic compounds becomes more time-consuming and challenging. Thus, strategies based on artificial intelligence basics are beneficial in different drug development stages, including discovering and verifying targets of the drug, modeling medicines, and increasing their druggable qualities. It also plays a crucial part in clinical trial design for patients, hence optimizing the decision-making process.

SPIDER is an artificial intelligence approach for assessing the role of natural ingredients and their application in drug development. It was built to primarily forecast the targets for pharmacological compounds such as β -Lapachone, and thus it proved that β -Lapachone causes reversible and allosteric inhibition of 5-Lipoxygenase. A more advanced technique known as read across structure-activity relationship (RASAR) is being utilized to identify the toxicity of unknown chemicals. It is a valuable tool that is being developed on the premise of establishing and identifying the link between molecular structure and toxicity-causing features. This is done with the use of a database for compounds that is available [13].

5.2.2 Drug screening using artificial intelligence

The development of creative AI approaches and increased computer capacity would be used to change drug development and research processes. The pharmaceutical business is experiencing a reduction in the efficiency of its medication enhancement projects as well as an increase in R&D costs. In recent years, the pharmaceutical business has seen a dramatic enhancement in the digitalization of information; efficiently getting, evaluating, and applying this information to address complicated clinical concerns has become a current challenge. With improved computerization, AI can deal with huge amounts of data. Machine learning algorithms are integrated to boost efficiency and production [14].

5.2.3 Prediction of physicochemical characteristics

Using a neural network called ResNet, artificial intelligence can determine physicochemical parameters (solubility, dissociation constant, and partition coefficient) of various medications. This network was more precise in forecasting the molecule's solubility than other non-AI-based models, as indicated by enhanced yield and decreased polysaccharides extraction time obtained from various sources. This demonstrated that artificial intelligence (AI) may be integrated into the medication development process to increase efficiency [14, 15].

Hydrophobicity/hydrophilicity is one of the most useful qualities since it has a significant impact on drug behavior in the body. One of the first and most extensively modeled properties is this one. It is generally represented in terms of the octanol-water partition coefficient (logP) logarithm. The logP value can be used as a rough early ADME screen to rule out potential drug development candidates as soon as feasible. Many computer models for estimating log P have been created in response to this increased interest. These strategies seek to establish a link between a compound's molecular and structural features and its log P value. There are two basic strategies for promoting this task. One of the most frequently used programs, CLOGP, pioneered question-based techniques by storing values for fragments as well as correction factors for fragment interactions in a database. The approach divides molecules into fragments, and the logP value is calculated by adding the fragment values and the correction interaction values [16].

5.2.4 Prediction of bioactivity

Machine learning (ML) is a field of artificial intelligence in which computers learn from the data, recognize patterns, and make judgments without having been explicitly programmed. Machine learning technologies are generally of two types, i.e., supervised and unsupervised. In the former, a function to translate input from output is learned from input–output pairings so that the machine learning model can anticipate future cases. Patterns are previously learned directly from unlabeled data. It is usual to employ supervised algorithms to forecast biological activity. Linear relationships between dependent and independent variables are learned in logistic regression (LgR) and linear regression (LR). When the dependent variable is categorical, LgR is utilized for linear classification. The Bayes theorem and the feature independence criterion are the foundation of Naive Bayes (NB) probabilistic classification technology. Random forests (RFs) are tree-like decision rule models in which every node signifies a feature, every branch describes a decision, and every leaf describes a result. Bagging is used by RFs to construct alternative training models and sets, and predictions are made via majority voting. Support-vector machines (SVMs) are developed to map data into a high-dimensional space by locating a lower-dimensional hyperplane that divides data by utilizing nonlinear kernels. K-nearest neighbors (KNNs) is an instance-based technique that classifies data based on its k-nearest neighbors' similarity. The most common use of partial least squares (PLS) regression is to determine a dependent variable collection from an independent variable. ML is widely utilized in various domains, including chemoinformatics, due to its excellent accuracy and cost-effectiveness. The quantitative structure-activity relationship (QSAR) model optimization is done to increase the prediction of numerous substances' biological activity frequently [17].

The major research area in chemoinformatics is the biological activity of chemical prediction. The utilization of artificial intelligence for this type of activity is crucial while identifying the molecules with desirable qualities. When compared to a random sample, the aim is to choose a compound subset from other samples that are under contemplation and more likely to be bioactive. DrugBank, PubChem BioAssay, ChEBI, MoleculeNet databases, ChemSpider, and T3DB: the toxic exposome database are examples of huge datasets from public domain sources that are suitable for activity prediction. Compounds with desirable biological activity have been discovered using machine learning approaches like as SVMs, RFs, and deep neural networks (DNNs) [17, 18].

5.2.5 Prediction of ADMET using AI

Optimizing pharmacokinetic factors like absorption, distribution, metabolism, excretion, and toxicity (ADMET) is the main problem in medication discovery. As a result, early assessment of a compound's ADMET characteristics is required to efficiently guide subsequent drug discovery procedures. For decades, due to the bioactivity accumulation and strong machine learning algorithms, in silico ADMET property estimation has captivated the interest of both the pharmaceutical industry and academia.

Potential drugs firstly enter the circulatory system to become active inside the body, so absorption is the first hurdle they must overcome. The relationship between drug absorption and other characteristics is complicated. Membrane permeability and Human Intestinal Absorption (HIA) are two examples of qualities that are not only being actively explored but are also closely linked to absorption [19].

To be effective, a medicine must be delivered to the desired location of action after being given or absorbed into the bloodstream. This property of the drug is known as distribution. Many researchers are attempting to estimate the distribution rate of possible medications as well as distribution-related qualities such as plasma protein binding (PPB) rate, the permeability of the blood-brain barrier (BBB), and inhibition of P-glycoprotein (P-gp) by using AI.

Metabolism is a biotransformation process involving many metabolic enzymes. The medicine is converted into another chemical form that can be activated or excreted, or interfere with the metabolic mechanism that regulates the excretion or activation of another medication.

Another major issue in drug development is biotransformation. The pharmacokinetic parameters like half-life and intrinsic clearance explain this

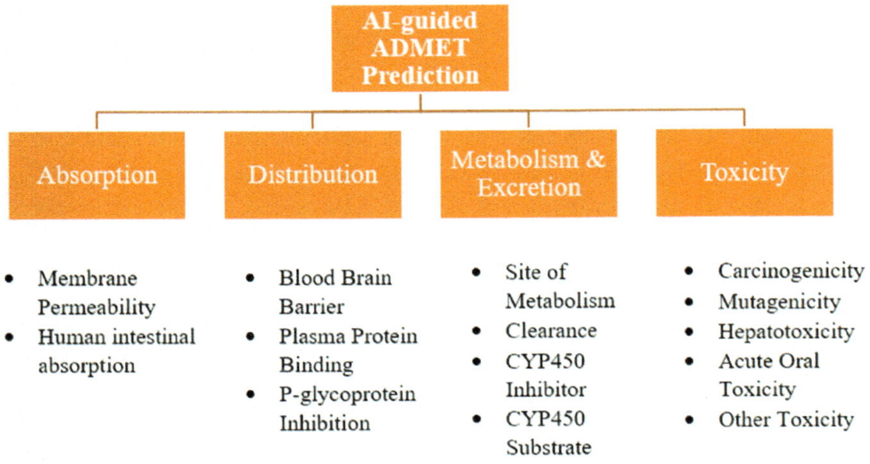

Figure 5.2 Schematic diagram of AI-guided prediction of ADMET.

property of the drug, which is known as metabolic stability. As a result, in silico methods are being used to half-life and forecast intrinsic clearance to lower the expense of tests. “MetStabOn” is an online tool used for the prediction of metabolic stability. They began gathering data from ChEMBL, which has roughly 60–2500 molecules from diverse species such as humans, rats, and mice. They used molecular 2D descriptors to create classification and regression models — the former being trained to evaluate clearance and half-life values directly and the latter being trained to estimate data level [19, 20]. Figure 5.2 shows the schematic diagram of AI-guided ADMET prediction.

5.2.6 Prediction of toxicity

The utilization of artificial intelligence and machine learning helps to increase the safety of drugs which is act as a promising prospect. These algorithms offer data-driven methods for safety and toxicity assessments, allowing for the detection of trends that might otherwise go unnoticed. Logical regression, support vector machines, and random forests are examples of traditional machine learning approaches that can create interpretable models with a modest level of complexity. These approaches are better to utilize when the purpose is to investigate how predictors influence the risk or incidence of an adverse occurrence. Deep neural networks, often known as “artificial intelligence,” are a new class of technologies that allow for more complicated models to be generated at the cost of much more input. These algorithms have the advantage of automatically detecting non-linear patterns in data without needing significant operator intervention. Convolutional and recurrent neural networks are two common examples that are employed in medication safety research. These models are used in pre-clinical toxicity studies of the drug; it helps to mimic patient variety and to aid in the selection of the main compound and trial design. It can also aid in post-marking surveillance to perform comparative efficacy studies, discover drug–drug interactions, and help in making a clinical decision. The field of AI-assisted medication safety and toxicity science is still in its early stages and more research is required to assess its potential therapeutic impact [21].

Artificial intelligence has a wide range of applications in drug toxicity prediction, including carcinogenicity, mutagenicity, hepatotoxicity, and acute oral toxicity.

A model for predicting organ-specific chemical carcinogenicity was recently constructed by utilizing a Bayesian-like technique and MNA (multilevel neighborhoods of atoms) descriptors. This model of QSAR identifies a substance that causes cancer in certain organs. In the future, more comprehensive forecasts could be a key direction for the prediction of drug toxicity model development.

For the construction of predictive compound mutagenicity models, the Ames mutagenicity benchmark dataset is the most often used training dataset. In 2009, this dataset was created. It compiled the results of Ames testing from the VITIC, CCRIS, and GeneTox databases in one place. The benchmark dataset includes 6512 chemicals, from which 3009 are negative (non-mutagenic) and 2503 are positive (mutagenic) [22, 23].

The most common reason for drug development failure and withdrawal is drug-induced liver injury (DILI). Currently, several models for predicting hepatotoxicity of compounds have been described, the majority of which are built using machine learning methods. For example, a Bayesian approach-based hepatotoxicity prediction model and ECFP molecular fingerprinting have been developed. A training set of 295 compounds was utilized to train the model and 237 test compounds set was utilized to test them. In the test set, the model shows a 60% accuracy rate.

Using a regression model (deepAOT-R), molecular graph encoding convolutional neural networks (MGECNN) architecture and a multiclassification model (deepAOT-C) for prediction of acute oral toxicity have been constructed. The test dataset includes 1673 substances; the regression model's R^2 and mean absolute error (MAE) were found to be 0.864 and 0.195, respectively, while the multiclassification model's accuracy was found to be 95.5% [23, 24].

5.3 AI in Drug Molecule Designing

5.3.1 Prediction of target protein structure

In the computational determination of protein structure, there are two distinct circumstances. The most common method used is comparative modeling, which indicates that a novel structure is built on a protein structure scaffold and predicted to be similar to the query structure due to analogy or homology arising from convergent evolution. However, finding a suitable template for comparison modeling is frequently impossible. In such circumstances, structure prediction must be performed from scratch. Prediction is based solely on protein-like biases collected from a known structure of protein database and proper protein conformational space search technique. Despite CABS algorithm's success in the recent CASP6 experiment, de novo structure identification endures a difficult endeavor that is limited to very small proteins having a simple topology. Furthermore, the resulting structures have a limited resolution. There are exceptions to this rule, but they still appear to be more of a "proof of principle" than a standard computing methodology [25].

5.3.2 Predicting drug–protein interactions

Therapeutic (chemical substance) and protein interactions must be identified in the drug development early stages. It is, however, impractical to examine every interaction between these things empirically. Computational approaches have recently acquired a lot of attention because of their effectiveness in identifying possible drug–target interactions (DTI) for biologists and biochemists. DTIs are computed, which creates a heterogeneous graph of medications, proteins, illnesses, and side effects [26].

In drug development, hybrid QM/Molecular mechanics (MM) approaches are effective in the protein–ligand (drug) interactions prediction. For simulated systems, these techniques take quantum effects at the atomic level (in the case of MM/QM), resulting in much-improved accuracy than traditional MM approaches. MM approaches are only applied to simple energy functions which are based on atomic coordinates; QM-based approaches need more time rather than the MM approaches. The use of AI approaches in QM computations implies a choice between MM model's advantageous time–cost and QM accuracy. AI approaches have been trained to imitate the QM energies from atomic coordinates and they can exceed the MM models in terms of speed calculation.

DL is used to determine the small molecules' potential energies, thus replacing the computational demanding quantum chemistry estimations with a quick ML technique. AI is mostly used in atomic simulations and electrical properties prediction. Potential energy produced from quantum chemistry is estimated and used to train DNNs for huge datasets by using DFT (density functional theory) potential energies. For instance, in a study of 2 million elpasolite crystals, the accuracy of ML models is improved with the increasing size of the sample, reaching 0.1 eV/atom for DFT formation energies trained on 10,000 structures. The model was then utilized to assess compositional alternatives for various attributes [27].

5.3.3 AI in de novo drug design

The main purpose of de novo drug design is to find new drug molecules which can meet several important optimization criteria at the same time, such as selectivity, activity, physicochemical, and ADMET qualities. It is a non-trivial problem to optimally meet such a diverse set of needs because of a sheer number of viable solutions, which makes the search procedure long and expensive even when conducted in silico. As a result, having an effective solution that allows for chemical space navigation as well as the production of relevant ideas is critical. To meet these demands, scientists have recently turned their attention to artificial intelligence (AI)-based generative models which can generate promising small compounds. In the drive to develop more efficient ways for the production of chemicals, many neural network topologies have been developed, as well as different types of AI training strategies. Recurrent neural networks (RNNs) and variational autoencoders (VAEs) with long short-term memory (LSTM) cells, generative adversarial networks, and conditional RNNs are successful while synthesizing molecules by using molecular graphs as data representation of molecules [28].

REINVENT 2.0 is a tool for designing tiny compounds from scratch. It handles both goal-directed and distribution-learning situations. The goal-directed scenario use cases which employ a generative model as a search space, reinforcement learning as a search algorithm, and a flexible scoring function as a score objective that can integrate scores from various elements to generate a result. Individual component calculations can be carried out in parallel. The diversity filter penalizes duplication and promotes diversity in identifying solutions, which also influences scores by encouraging exploration. For each use case, comprehensive logging is implemented. The facility to transmit the logs to a remote REST endpoint is also provided, allowing the program to be hidden behind a web interface [28, 29].

5.4 AI in Diagnosis

The disease diagnosis is critical while determining the best course of therapy and ensuring the health of patients. Evaluation of medical data is a complicated and intellectually demanding activity and human error obstructs proper diagnosis. Medical specialists encounter new obstacles every day, with frequent interruptions and changing responsibilities in the healthcare system, which is dynamic with environmental changes. As a result of this variety, disease diagnosis frequently becomes a secondary problem for healthcare professionals. Furthermore, interpretation of medical data has a cognitively demanding endeavor. This applies not only to experienced professionals but also to those professionals who have limited or less experience like junior assistant physicians. Diagnostics is a very complex procedure because medical specialists' availability time is frequently restricted. After all, these diseases may get increased and patient dynamics can also get changed with time. Artificial intelligence use can help to increase diagnostic accuracy and efficiency [30].

Artificial intelligence is a broad term that includes different types of research disciplines including robotics and natural language processing. Recent practical applications such as disease diagnostics and healthcare are focused on a specified task and are being developed by utilizing machine learning. Medical data use algorithms to produce predictions and get improved with time by constantly managing updated and novel data. Algorithms gather data from various sorts of input and knowledge, as well as through years of experience. As a result, AI-enabled computers can analyze more information than humans, potentially outperforming them in some medical activities [31]. Figure 5.3 shows the schematic diagram for the diagnosis of disease by the use of AI.

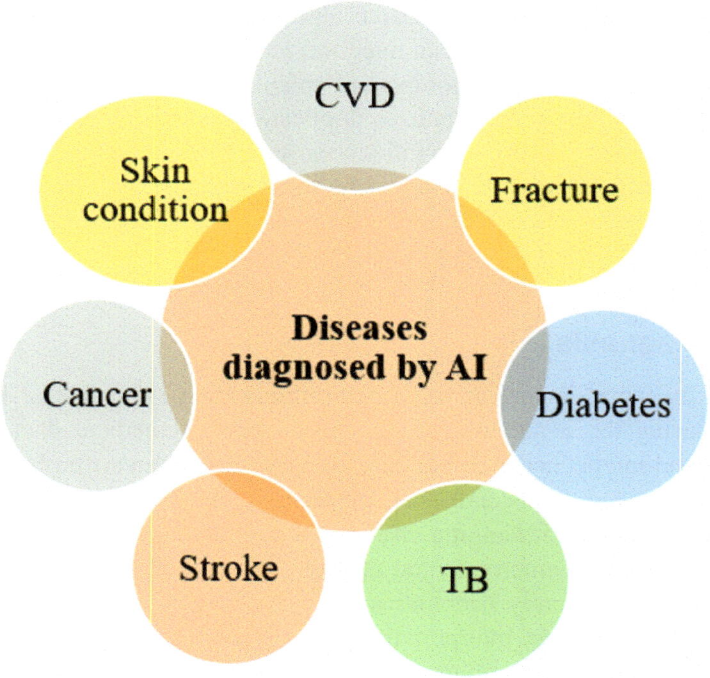

Figure 5.3 A schematic diagram shows the AI utilization in the diagnosis of various diseases.

Different diseases are diagnosed and treated by the utilization of AI which is summarized below.

5.4.1 Cardiovascular disease (CVD)

Rapid economic transition in emerging countries leads to unhealthy lifestyles and environmental changes. Population ageing can raise cardiovascular risk factors and CVD incidence. Patients and society as a whole have been hit hard by CVD. As a result, initiatives for enhancing CVD diagnosis and therapy must be developed in the future. AI can tackle this problem right now. Supervised learning not only plays a significant role in various biological networks operation but it also plays a main role in artificial neural networks operation. As a result, supervised learning can be used in medical diagnosis and therapy, and it has significant therapeutic implications. Unsupervised learning algorithms are also used to solve problems including diagnosis, prediction, and treatment of CVD and cardiovascular imaging evaluation [32].

5.4.1.1 Precision medicine

With the support of AI, it is most likely to adopt a proper medical plan that customizes healthcare for every patient. Clinicians should learn how to use AI technology and gain experience in AI utilization to improve the diagnosis and therapy of cardiovascular disease by analyzing big data. It will help in the transition of the era of precision medicine. Precision medicine, which will tailor treatment to every patient, is most likely to be realized with AI assistance. AI is not expected to be able to take over the clinicians' functions [33].

5.4.1.2 Cardiac imaging analysis

Yan et al. have summarized in their review that Samad et al. found deep learning has accurately predicted survival with more precision after examining echocardiography in numerous situations. Intravascular ultrasound (for lumen's border detection and media-adventitia), optical coherence tomography (for three layers of the coronary artery classification), cardiac single-photon emission computed tomography (for myocardial ischemia diagnosis and to increase the myocardial perfusion imaging diagnosis precision), and magnetic resonance imaging (MRI) (for effective and fast visualization of cardiac segmentation in short-axis MRI) are some of the AI applications in cardiac imaging analysis. Cardiovascular imaging is the most important benchmark for CVD diagnosis [32, 34].

5.4.2 Cancer

Cancer is a disease that is aggressive and has a low median survival rate. Due to the high recurrence and fatality rates, the treatment process is extensive and expensive. To improve the patient's survival percentage, accurate early cancer detection and prognostic prediction are critical. Many scientists have been encouraged to use computational methods like multivariate statistical analysis to analyze disease prognosis, as a result of advances in computer engineering and statistics over the years. The precision of these analyses is more accurate than empirical predictions. In recent years, AI, mainly deep learning and machine learning, has gained popularity in cancer clinical research and the prediction of cancer performance has risen to new heights.

When AI is combined with powerful bioinformatics tools, diagnostic, prognostic, and predictive accuracy can be considerably improved. Machine learning (ML) is a more specialized notion that is becoming more popular. ML is an AI subset that is utilized to build predictive models which help in learning logical patterns from large amounts of historical data to forecast a patient's survival rate. Machine learning utilization help to improve prognosis which has been widely used. Prognosis is a crucial clinical skill, especially for doctors who take care of cancer patients. Cancer susceptibility, recurrence, and survival forecasts have all been demonstrated to improve with machine learning methods. In terms of patient clinical care, ML can produce positive effects. This aspect has prompted bioinformatics and biomedical researchers to create more efficient machine learning methods which can categorize tumor patients into lower or higher-risk recurrence groups for better management of diagnosis [35, 36].

5.4.2.1 Solid tumor diagnosis

Traditional tumor temporal monitoring is limited to predefined metrics such as tumor longest diameter determined by established parameters of World Health Organization (WHO) and Response Evaluation Criteria in Solid Tumors (RECIST) principles and also in estimating tumor burden and determination of the response of treatment. However, AI-based monitoring captures a huge number of discriminative features across images over time that human readers are unable to discern. Although the seemingly disparate components of computer-aided monitoring (computer-aided registration of temporal images, diagnosis, and segmentation) are active areas of research, the topic is still in its infancy, with applications yet to emerge.

Medical imaging can also be useful in determining the intratumor features of lung cancer. Intratumor heterogeneity (ITH) is a prevalent trait in solid tumor malignancies, according to sequencing studies including independent, multiple samples from the same tumor. A tumor is made up of billions of cancer cells that are all independent. At each cell division, DNA damage at low levels, or alterations in epigenetic regulation are integrated, resulting in minor modifications genome of cancer cells which grow with time. Clonal expansion produces a subclone of cancer with all cells of cancer that share a specific and common ancestor. Genomic ITH is described as the presence of several subclones of cancer within the same tumor and has been related to deprived prognosis in non–small cell lung cancer (NSCLC) [37, 38].

The utilization of a deep convolutional neural network (DCNN) to analyze sonographic imaging records obtained from clinical ultrasounds has recently been shown to increase accuracy in the diagnosis of thyroid cancer. When compared to a competent radiologists group, DCNN model had shown better specificity and identical sensitivity in identifying the patients having thyroid cancer. The DCNN model's superior technical performance needs further examination through randomized clinical trials [39].

5.4.2.2 Non-solid tumor diagnosis

Brain cancer and brain tumor is the worst condition on the diseases list. According to the survival statistics, 34% of men and 36% of women persist for 5 years after being diagnosed with a malignant central nervous system (CNS) brain tumor. As a result, tumor early detection saves a lot of lives and AI can make the process more precise and suitable. "Liquid Biopsy" is a revolutionary non-invasive method for detecting brain cancers in their early stages at the lowest cost and with the least risk factor. It is a method to examine non-solid biological tissue, such as plasma, blood, and cerebrospinal fluid. Kar et al. utilize "k-means clustering" in image processing. An artificial intelligence visual perception for "CTC" recognition uses the technologies such as "Convolutional Neural Network" (CNN) for the discovery of ctDNA and the "Support-vector Machine" (SVM) algorithm for ctDNA. "ctDNA" can reveal information about malignant cell growth factors, tumor types, and location [40].

The identification rate of nodules is improved via an AI-based system of automatic lung nodule detection. It is crucial to assess the AI systems' therapeutic value by contrasting AI-assisted nodule determination with genuine radiography results. Zhang et al. detected the lung nodule by using artificial intelligence-assisted CT image data. Participants who had a chest CT scan during November and December 2019 were included in this study retrospectively. 15 radiologists and 14 residents are assisted in the finalization of radiology reports during the real-world radiologist observation. One resident and one radiologist used an AI method to discover and quantify the identified lung nodules. The type and amount of lung nodules were determined by a reading panel using these two approaches. In 860 participants (57±7 years), it was recognized that 111 patients have less than 1 non-solid nodule [41].

5.4.3 Fractures

In the 1960s, AI was firstly used in pathology report evaluation obtained from radiographic images which assist humans. A technique was discovered to change images into numerical data, that was saved on a computer system and analyzed statistically. In the 1980s, traditional computer-assisted detection (CAD) systems were introduced into clinical radiography to determine human programmed patterns in images and alert physicians to areas that required additional attention. Advances in computing power allow for the creation of powerful AI and CAD applications. Newer AI systems claim to have higher accuracies and more effective training procedures. However, the performance of these data-driven algorithms is dependent on the vast volumes of training data availability [42].

Fracture interpretation errors signify around 24% of harmful diagnostic errors encountered in emergency rooms, according to researchers. In addition, during the evening and midnight hours, inconsistencies in the radiological diagnosis of fractures are more likely to occur. To identify leg, torso, pelvis, lumbar spine, and rib cage fractures, the AI algorithm was trained on a huge X-ray dataset from several institutions. According to Guermazi, artificial intelligence (AI) can aid radiologists and other professionals to improve diagnostic performance and efficiency. Furthermore, the technology can improve the hospital's or clinic's patient experience [43].

The FDA has approved an artificial intelligence system that can assist clinicians in detecting wrist fractures in adults. During evaluations of posterior-anterior and medial-lateral X-ray images of the wrist, Imagen OsteoDetect employs machine learning techniques to recognize symptoms of distal radius fracture. To aid professionals in their diagnoses, the program highlights the site of a fracture on the image. The program can be used in a variety of contexts, including primary care, emergency departments, urgent care clinics, and specialist care like orthopedics. OsteoDetect is a complementary tool that should not be used in place of a clinician's radiograph assessment or clinical judgment [44].

Vertebral fractures (VFs) can cause serious issues including significant functional loss and higher death risk and a delayed diagnosis can make the prognosis even worse. For the examination of VFs, plain thoracolumbar radiography (PTLR) is an important technique. As a result, eliminating VF diagnostic mistakes on PTLR is critical. DCNN utilization to identify images has been acknowledged as a potentially helpful diagnostic method; nevertheless, the accuracy of VF detection has not been completely examined. 300 patients' PTLR images were utilized to train a DCNN (150 patients without VFs and 150 patients with VFs).

The model's diagnostic accuracy, specificity, and sensitivity were determined and compared with orthopedic residents, and spine and orthopedic surgeons. The specificity, accuracy, and sensitivity of the DCNN were 86.0% [95% confidence interval (CI) 82.0–90.0%], 84.7% (95% CI 78.8–90.5%), and 87.3% (95% CI 81.9–92.7%). The models' sensitivity and accuracy were found to be comparable to that of orthopedic doctors. The DCNN has been helping doctors to detect VFs early and manage patients effectively, reducing the need for invasive procedures and improving quality of life [45].

5.4.4 Tuberculosis

With the rapid growth in information technology and enhanced focus on interdisciplinary practices, AI has become a novel topic of research for medical practitioners in recent years. In 1956, the phrase "artificial intelligence" was first used in the Dartmouth Summer Research Project which is based on AI. AI has demonstrated some astonishing successes in performing human-level tasks after 50 years of study and development, particularly following earlier discoveries on convolutional neural networks. In 2012, ImageNet Large Scale Visual Recognition Challenge (ILSVRC), AlexNet, a neural network model, attained great success. AI has also proved its ability to handle medical tasks in a variety of other studies and challenges. The TB bacillus morphology is relatively simple in comparison to complex cells and tissues shape. It resembles a thin rod-shaped structure having a length of around 4 m and a diameter of 0.5–1.0 m. After acid-fast staining, the waxy lipid of bacilli's cell wall appears purple-red, contrasting sharply with the blue background. The bacilli detection with such morphology and color after dying is unique for the diagnosis of tuberculosis.

Although TB-AI has a high sensitivity for recognizing bacilli, it is still poor at separating pathogenic bacilli from contaminant bacilli. Differentiating pathogenic bacilli from contaminating bacilli requires recognition of morphological alterations generated by particular histological reactions, like granuloma, inflammation, and caseous necrosis. The TB-AI, framework offers high sensitivity and moderate specificity for recognizing acid-fast stained tuberculosis bacilli automatically. It has the potential to relieve pathologists from tedious tasks like looking for bacilli under a microscope while also decreasing the risk of a false diagnosis. In practice, pathologists must validate positive TB-AI results, whereas negative results must be evaluated to ensure that the digital slides are qualified [46]. Table 5.2 [46] summarizes the characteristics of diabetes care that uses Machine Learning and Artificial Intelligence.

Qin et al. have described the AI utilization to read chest radiographs for tuberculosis diagnosis. Deep learning neural networks have been used in the determination of chest radiography (CXR) to screen pulmonary tuberculosis (TB) patients. There has been no published research that compares different systems of deep learning and population. They performed a retrospective evaluation to determine the efficacious properties of deep learning systems

Table 5.2 Characteristics of diabetes care using Machine Learning and Artificial Intelligence.

S. No.	Area	Description
1.	Diabetes prediction	Algorithms have been used to evaluate the risk of diabetes occurrence based on genetic and clinical data. Certain algorithms can warn physicians about the risk of a missed diabetes diagnosis based on electronic health record data.
2.	Glycemic control	It mostly concerns the artificial pancreas system. A vast number of research have attempted to automate insulin infusion rates based on continuous glucose monitoring (CGM) data and also to recommend insulin bolus doses using various AI algorithms.
3.	Complication and diagnosis	By directly recognizing and classifying phases based on images generated by fundus cameras, an AI/ML technique is revolutionizing retinopathy detection in diabetologists' clinics.
4.	Prediction of glycemic events	Based on CGM data, it is possible to predict impending hypoglycemia or hyperglycemia. This method is already in commercial use.
5.	Prediction of complications	Using baseline clinical and biochemical data, predict the risk of retinopathy, neuropathy, nephropathy, or a cardiovascular event.

(qXR, CAD4TB, and Lunit INSIGHT) in Nepal and Cameroon, for the determination of tuberculosis-associated abnormalities from chest radiographs of outpatients. An Xpert MTB/RIF assay and CXR results are evaluated by the 2 groups of radiologists, which are obtained from the 1196 participants involved in the study. Xpert was utilized as the reference standard. qXR (0.94, 95% CI: 0.92–0.97), Lunit (0.94, 95% CI: 0.93–0.96), and CAD4TB (0.92, 95% CI: 0.90–0.95) all had similar areas under the curve.

Except for one, the deep learning system's specificities were significantly higher than the radiologists' sensitivity. Utilization of DL devices to read CXRs could decrease the number of Xpert MTB/RIF examinations needed by 66% population while maintaining 95% or greater sensitivity. The use of a universal cutoff score obtained from varied results at each site highlights the importance of selecting scores based on a population being screened. Where human resources are limited and automated technique is available, these deep learning techniques help in the evaluation of TB [47].

Jamal et al. have described the AI- and ML-based estimation of susceptible and resistant mutations in TB. The current study is related to a computational platform that employs AI and ML techniques to predict the resistance of medications like rifampicin, pyrazinamide, isoniazid, and fluoroquinolones in the genes katG, rpoB, pncA, inhA, gyrB, and gyrA. Several sequence and structural properties were used to depict single nucleotide changes, indicating the impact of the mutation on the target protein transcribed by every gene. To create the prediction models, they used machine learning techniques such as support vector machine, naive Bayes, k nearest neighbor, and artificial neural network. The classification models had an 85% average accuracy across all genes analyzed and their utility was determined by testing them on an unknown dataset. Furthermore, molecular dynamics and molecular docking simulations were executed for wild-type and predicted the resistance-causing mutant protein and anti-TB medication complexes which help in the evaluation of their impact on protein structure and confirm the reported phenotype.

It was also observed that for inhA, rpoB, katG, pncA, gyrB, and gyrA, the models were extremely accurate, with average accuracies of 88.86%, 88.0%, 87.30%, 85.22%, 78.88%, and 86.88%, respectively. The drug's interaction patterns bound the wild-type, and mutant proteins demonstrated that mutations destabilize catalase-peroxidase (katG) and pyrazinamidase (pncA) effects up to a large extent but have a modestly lower effect in gyrase B (gyrB) and gyrase A (gyrA) [48].

5.4.5 Diabetes

AI and ML is being utilized to determine the diabetes risk by using genetic data in the diagnosis of diabetes using EHR data, prediction of comorbidities like retinopathy and nephropathy, and also in diabetic retinopathy diagnosis. In a country like India, where diabetes occurrence is expected to be 8–10%, with fewer cases in rural areas as compared to urban areas, AI/ML applications would be even more effective. However, according to the CARRS study, in the city of Delhi, prevalence of diabetes is 27%, and 46% or more of the population has prediabetes. Three additional major cities have reported similar levels of frequency. Another study found that the age group of 30–34 years has the highest incidence of diabetes.

Diabetes at such a young age and in such a large number of people would put a great strain on the healthcare system. Health is being hampered by a lack of resources and particularly trained doctors. AI/ML applications in diabetes may be able to aid to close this enormous gap. Another concern in India is uniformity of care (or minimal standard care). A substantial percentage of cases are managed by primary healthcare clinicians and these practices are not audited properly which shows that the average of HbA1c diabetics in India remains around 9% [49].

In the management of diabetes, digital therapies have proven to be a reliable intervention. Patients are more empowered to cope with their diabetes on their own and clinical decision support benefits both healthcare providers and patients. The use of artificial intelligence enables continuous and painless remote monitoring of a patient's symptoms and biomarkers. Furthermore, patient engagement in diabetes care is boosted by social media and online groups. In the case of diabetes, technological advancements have aided in resource optimization. With a decrease in postprandial and fasting glucose levels, glycosylated hemoglobin, and glucose excursions, these smart technical improvements have resulted in better glycemic management. In diabetes care, AI will initiate a paradigm shift, moving away from traditional management tactics toward data-driven precision care [50].

The studies cover a wide range of novel approaches aimed at improving diabetes treatment in four areas: automated retinal screening, patient self-management devices, predictive population risk stratification, and clinical decision support. Numerous AI-powered retinal imaging devices, glucose sensors, predictive modeling programs, smartphone apps, insulin pumps, and other decision-support methods are now available and many more are on the way. Artificial intelligence technologies have the property to revolutionize diabetes and assist millions of people with diabetes in achieving improved blood glucose control, reducing diabetes comorbidities and consequences, and also hypoglycemic episodes. For a person with diabetes (PWDs), their physicians, caretakers, and family, AI applications provide increased efficiency, accuracy, ease of use, and satisfaction [51].

5.4.6 Stroke

Artificial intelligence has a huge range of applications in acute stroke imaging, involving hemorrhagic and ischemic subtypes. The acute stroke must be identified quickly to begin treatment and limit mortality and morbidity. Artificial intelligence can assist with infarct or hemorrhage detection, classification, segmentation, detection of vascular occlusion, Alberta Stroke Program Early CT Score prognostication, and grading, among other components of the stroke therapy paradigm. Using artificial intelligence technologies like convolutional neural networks offers the promising performance of these imaging-based tasks accurately and effectively. Commercially available solutions that provide automated data on different acute stroke triage pathway components are being increasingly incorporated into ordinary clinical trials and practices. These devices provide quick and effective analysis, which aims to improve stroke care delivery at clinics while also reducing clinical workflow turnaround times. Softwares like Aidoc, Avicenna.AI, Brainomix, Rapid.AI, and Viz.AI are used in the detection of stroke [52].

AI algorithms are currently being utilized to assess high-risk groups for the risk of stroke. Han et al. used ML to design a classification model for the prediction of short-term stroke possibilities in patients with atrial fibrillation, which exhibited superior predictive qualities to the traditional CHA2DS2-VASc score (CNN: AUC=0.702; CHA2DS2-VASc: AUC=0.524). CNNs help to predict the risk in deep CNN features context and offer perceptiveness to neural networks featuring engineering process. Lekadir et al. demonstrate the feasibility of CNNs which help in the automatic characterization of the carotid plaque composition (fibrous cap, calcium, and lipid core) found in ultrasound, which is linked to the ischemic stroke risk stratification.

Machine learning is utilized to determine the results in patients having an acute ischemic stroke. Machine learning is utilized to determine clinical results before reperfusion therapy; therefore, mechanical thrombectomy should be considered. Machine learning models (random forests: AUC, 0.870.01; support vector machine: AUC, 0.89 ± 0.01) had considerably outperformed previous scores of prediction in the determination of patients' retrospective cohort with anterior circulation large vessel occlusions which were treated with mechanical thrombectomy, including the Houston Intra-Arterial Therapy 2 score (AUC, 0.82 ± 0.00), the Houston Intra-Arterial Therapy score (AUC, 0.80 ± 0.00), Totaled Health Risks in Vascular Events score (AUC, 0.81 ± 0.00), the Stroke Prognostication Using Age and National Institutes of Health Stroke Scale index (AUC, 0.80 ± 0.00), and the Pittsburgh Response to Endovascular Therapy Score [53].

Large vessel occlusion (LVO) strokes are detected using AI techniques such as CNNs and random forest learning (RFL). There are twenty researches identified that employ ML. RFL was extensively employed in the Alberta Stroke Program Early CT Score (ASPECTS), whereas CNNs were generally utilized in the detection of LVO. The sensitivity of image feature evaluation was higher with CNN than RFL, at 85% vs. 68%. However, the performance measures for AI algorithms use different criteria, making an ideal objective comparison. Brainomix (biggest AI validation for ASPECTS, CNNs are utilized in the detection of automatic LVOs), iSchemaView (thrombectomy has the highest number of perfusion research for validation), General Electric, and Viz.ai are contemporary software platforms that use ML (utilizes CNNs for the automatic LVOs detection, then automatically stimulates the emergency stroke treatment systems) [54].

5.4.7 Skin disease

Dermatology is changing at a rapid pace as well. With the introduction of improved technology and invention, the method used for the diagnosis and therapy of dermatological disorders has altered dramatically. Computer algorithms have been used to assist dermatologists in disease diagnosis, particularly in the case of malignant melanoma. Machine learning has huge clinical, dermoscopic, and dermatopathological image databases; dermatology has taken the lead in implementing AI in the medical area. Skin cancer, atopic dermatitis, and psoriasis are just a few of the dermatology conditions where AI is slowly gaining traction.

5.4.7.1 Skin cancer

Scientists are investigating the utilization of AI to enhance or supplement recent nonmelanoma and melanoma skin cancer screening techniques (NMSC). Nasr–Esfahani *et al.* were the first to train a melanoma recognition neural network, with sensitivity and specificity of 0.81 and 0.80, respectively. Research on deep learning of skin cancers was released in 2017 at Stanford

University. They utilized a single CNN that was trained to evaluate end-to-end images directly. To train a CNN, 129,450 clinical images collected from 2032 various disorders are utilized. They examined its function against 21 board-certified dermatologists on biopsy-proven clinical images with 2 important binary classifications of cases: benign seborrheic keratoses vs. keratinocyte carcinomas and benign nevi versus malignant melanomas. The first case denotes the identification of the most common cancer, whereas the second identification involved the representation of the deadliest skin cancer [55].

5.4.7.2 Atopic dermatitis

Gustafson et al.'s goal in 2017 was to find patients having atopic dermatitis for enclosure genome-associated research. They explained an ML-based phenotypic algorithm. They used the EHR to combine coded data with the information acquired from lasso logistic regression encounter notes. Their algorithm gets more sensitivity and higher predictive value which improves the previous algorithm's low sensitivity. These outcomes show how machine learning and natural language processing can aid with EHR-based phenotyping.

De Guzman et al. created an ANN for the identification of atopic dermatitis and unaltered skin by utilizing image information directly. Multiple hidden node level models that are more robust and resistant to overfitting have been discovered. A small size sample was utilized because this model was developed to be to identified as the best of AI methods. Contextual data could be introduced to AI programs to help them to make better decisions in the current study [55, 56].

5.4.7.3 Psoriasis

Shrivastava et al. created nine alternative types of psoriasis risk assessment systems (pRAS) by combining essential elements in different ways. Three classifiers (Decision Tree (DT), SVM, NN) and three feature selection technologies like Fisher discriminant ratio (FDR), principal component analysis (PCA), and mutual information (MI) are used in these nine pRAS systems. The nine systems were used in two important experiments, i.e., selecting the optimal system combination based on accuracy classification and determining system consistency. The combination of FDR and SVM was identified as the optimal pRAS system, yielding a classification accuracy of 99.84% utilizing cross-validation methodology, utilizing the database employed in research, which comprised 670 psoriasis images. Furthermore, employing the cross-validation technique, the SVM-FDR system delivers 99.99% dependability.

They compared the pRAS system efficacy with manually and automatically segmented lesions [57].

5.5 Challenges to the Adoption of Artificial Intelligence in Pharma

Fully automated drug research has been dreamed of by scientists since the beginning of the computer era. Despite advancements in high-performance computation, robotics, good chemical synthesis, and other fields, in many areas, including biological screening, genome sequencing, and proteomics, the productivity of pharmaceutical development and research has significantly declined rapidly [58]. For instance, every new medication approval cost more than $2.5 billion in 2016, compared to $1 billion in 2013 [59].

Most of these techniques have now been regarded as revolutionary in the past, but they have failed to produce meaningful speed and cost savings in pharmaceutical research and development processes, leading to distrust of novel technology [60]. The originality of the one molecule that was examined in mice was questioned after additional validation of various compounds by utilizing a simple open-source system [61].

The development of a blockbuster medicine for a major ailment, produced exclusively with AI systems, would be the best proof of AI's impact on the pharmaceutical industry: from establishing a novel target, and generating a novel drug to identifying the relevant patients using a companion artificial intelligence biomarker and execution in all clinical trial phases. This type of validation approach, on the other hand, would take a few years and 10 million dollars for serious disorders like cancer or fibrosis. However, the first molecules that in silico medicine plans to put into clinical trials in 2021 were synthesized in 2019 by utilizing earlier algorithms and the targets were discovered in 2018. Different key obstacles to AI-powered discovery of drugs is that therapies developed by using artificial intelligence will take 5–6 years and millions of dollars to get authorization from FDA and the pharmaceutical industry [62].

Another problem is that advanced AI systems are costly to validate and develop, and for commercial organizations, publishing the earlier accomplishments in peer-reviewed journals causes a critical intellectual property loss. Because these records are essential for system's subsequent training, AI-complete success is dependent on the huge amount of data availability.

Records from different database providers can contribute to a company's costs. The record must be consistent and of high quality to confirm prediction accuracy. Other obstacles to widespread AI adoption in the pharmaceutical industry involve a shortage of experienced employees to manage AI-based platforms, inadequate funding for small businesses, anxiety of AI replacing humans and resulting in job losses, skepticism regarding AI-generated data, and the black box phenomena [63].

5.5.1 Main obstacles related to AI in Pharma industry

Despite pharma's experience with AI and deep learning's revolution in other industries, the current impact of the AI wave has been limited in our organization with five possible explanations:

1. Data management
2. Unifying problem
3. Lack of insufficient skillsets
4. Traditional approach related to science
5. Lack of expenditure

For data management, availability, and security, AI plans rely on strict data governance as well as data integration Pharma giants. For biochemical investigations, you could have hundreds of different instruments, patient data, clinical data, sequencing, analytical chemistry, genomics data, gene expression, and wearable sensors — all of which rely on a different database; even single trials can include cell source data and medication information. Candidate information, protocol details, raw data, and data that have been processed, as well as intermediate and final data outcomes, and information externally, academic collaborations, and corporate consortia, are providing more data. The importance of data governance and integration cannot be overstated. This is a significant challenge; because of the variety of data, the sector is thriving [64].

Automation of data management is a required position before evaluating data, but not by itself. AAI solutions rely on strict data governance for availability, management, and security, as well as data integration Pharma giants. For biochemical investigations, you could have hundreds of different instruments. Patient data, clinical data, genomics data, analytical chemistry, gene expression, sequencing, and wearable sensors are each utilized [65].

In a different database event, single trials can include cell source data and medication information.

The importance of data governance and integration cannot be overstated. This is a significant challenge; because of the variety of data, the sector is thriving. Prior to reviewing data, automation of data management is necessary.

5.5.2 Unifying problem

The pharmaceutical industry that aims to rapidly create novel drugs to increase patients' lives does not correspond to a single artificial intelligence challenge. Instead, artificial intelligence is helping to identify better screens and targets, improve modeling, prioritize safety indications, increase enrollment of patients in clinical trials, and solve a variety of other issues. Unlike Amazon's and Netflix's recommender engines, which contribute 35% and 75% of their respective profits, the pharma industry cannot emphasize a single solution but handle other major challenges, thereby decentralizing resources [66].

5.5.3 Insufficient skillsets

Data science bridges the technical gap between obtaining records from databases, cleaning them, applying existing machine learning technologies, and visualizing outcomes. Data scientists require domain knowledge in addition to machine learning mathematics, statistics, and programming relating expertise. The pharmaceutical sector, which is filled with PhDs, has a variety of scientific knowledge, but this combination of abilities is exceptional [67].

5.5.4 Scientific approach

To truly benefit from AI, the present pharmaceutical paradigm must shift from an expert-driven scientific process to a data-driven collaboration between AI and researchers. The scientific method is used in every stage of research and development, from target identification to optimization and screening to clinical trials. It helps in observing and producing data theories and employs them in the test hypotheses. Human intellect is not well matched for formulating complicated multivariable hypotheses with millions of data points [68].

5.5.5 Absence of investment

Pharma organizations have been sluggish to invest in AI, despite their practice of adapting to new technologies. Few organizations may be strategically awaiting the stabilization of fields. With novel AI–Pharma hybrid frameworks, various industries like Benevolent AI and Insilco Medicine emerges their technology for development. Organizations that delay in following AI strategies may never catch up with the emerging technologies [69].

5.5.6 Some other issues of concern

The major concern about the adoption of these technologies is the loss of jobs that would result, as well as the rigorous laws that would be required for AI implementation. These tools, on the other hand, are just meant to make work simpler, not to entirely replace humans. Pharmaceutical companies must have a clear knowledge of the AI technology's potential in solving problems once it has been installed, as well as the realistic goals that can be met. To fully leverage the AI platform's potential, experienced data researchers and software developers with a strong understanding of AI techniques are required [70].

5.6 Conclusion

Artificial intelligence is a significant part of the development of drug and disease analysis. This chapter describes the AI's role in drug screening, physicochemical properties, and ADMET which helps in drug development and discovery. It also focuses on the few diseases for which diagnoses are possible with AI like cardiovascular disease, cancer, fracture, diabetes, skin disorder, tuberculosis, and stroke. Various AI tools which are commercially available are used in the management of the disease. It can also increase patient compliance. It helps to maintain the privacy and security of the records related to the patient disease. It has a great future in the management of the healthcare sector.

Acknowledgments

For the successful completion of this study, all of the writers of this publication are grateful to their respective Departments/Universities.

Conflict of Interest

Authors declare that there is no conflict of interest.

Funding

Not required.

References

[1] Arvapalli, S., and Sharma, J. (2019) Artificial intelligence in pharma industry: A review. *Int. J. Innov. Pharm. Sci. Res. 7*(10), 37-50.

[2] Sethuraman, N. (2020) Artificial Intelligence: A new paradigm for pharmaceutical applications in formulations development. *Indian J. Pharm. Educ. Res. 54*(4), 843-846.

[3] Shanbhogue, M. H., Thirumaleshwar, S., Tm, P. K., and Kumar, S. H. (2021) Artificial intelligence in pharmaceutical field-A critical review. *Curr. Drug Deliv. 18*(10), 1421-1431.

[4] Vyas, M., Thakur, S., Riyaz, B., Bansal, K. K., Tomar, B., and Mishra, V. (2018) Artificial intelligence: the beginning of a new era in pharmacy profession. *Asian J. Pharm. 12*(2), 72-76.

[5] Hunter, J. (2016) Adopting AI is essential for a sustainable pharma industry. *Drug Discov. World Winter 2017*, 69-71.

[6] C. I. F. N. I. F. B. Digital healthcare s.l.gpbullhound. 2013:91643080.

[7] Eren, A., Subasi, A., and Coskun, O. (2008) A decision support system for telemedicine through the mobile telecommunications platform. *J. Med. Syst. 32*(1), 31-35.

[8] Manne, R. (2021) Machine learning techniques in drug discovery and development. *Int. J. Appl. Res. 7*(4), 21-28.

[9] Salman, M., Ahmed, A. W., Khan, A., Raza, B., and Latif, K. (2017) Artificial intelligence in biomedical domain an overview of AI based innovations in medical. *Int. J. Adv. Comput. Sci. Appl.* 8, 319-327.

[10] Erguzel, T. T., and Ozekes, S. (2014) Artificial intelligence approaches in psychiatric disorders. *Journal of Neurobehavioral Studies* 1, 52-53.

[11] Paul, D., Sanap, G., Shenoy, S., Kalyane, D., Kalia, K., and Tekade, R. K. (2021) Artificial intelligence in drug discovery and development. *Drug Discov. Today 26*(1), 80-93.

[12] Mak, K. K., and Pichika, M. R. (2019) Artificial intelligence in drug development: present status and future prospects. *Drug Discov. Today 24*(3), 773-780.

[13] Borisa, P., Singh, D., and Rathore, K. S. (2020) Impact of artificial intelligence on pharma industry. *Manipal Journal of Pharmaceutical Sciences 6*(1), 54-59.

[14] Patel, V., and Shah, M. (2021) A comprehensive study on artificial intelligence and machine learning in drug discovery and drug development. *Intelligent Medicine*.

[15] Cui, R., and Zhu, F. (2020) Ultrasound modified polysaccharides: A review of structure, physicochemical properties, biological activities and food applications. *Trends Food Sci. Technol. 107*, 491-508.

[16] Soto, A. J., Ponzoni, I., and Vazquez, G. E. (2007) Predicting physicochemical properties for drug design using clustering and neural network learning. In: *Brazilian Symposium on Bioinformatics*, 46-57.

[17] Toccaceli, P., Nouretdinov, I., and Gammerman, A. (2017) Conformal prediction of biological activity of chemical compounds. *Ann. Math. Artif. Intell. 81*(1), 105-123.

[18] Correia, J., Resende, T., Baptista, D., and Rocha, M. (2019). Artificial intelligence in biological activity prediction. In *International Conference on Practical Applications of Computational Biology & Bioinformatics*, Springer, Cham, 164-172.

[19] Kim, H., Kim, E., Lee, I., Bae, B., Park, M., and Nam, H. (2020) artificial intelligence in drug discovery: A comprehensive review of data-driven and machine learning approaches. *Biotechnol. Bioprocess Eng. 25*(6), 895-930.

[20] Podlewska, S., and Kafel, R. (2018) Metstabon—online platform for metabolic stability predictions. *Int. J. Mol. Sci. 19*(4), 1-16.

[21] Basile, A. O., Yahi, A., and Tatonetti, N. P. (2019) Artificial intelligence for drug toxicity and safety. *Trends Pharmacol. Sci. 40*(9), 624-635.

[22] Feng, J., Lurati, L., Ouyang, H., Robinson, T., Wang, Y., Yuan, S., and Young, S. S. (2003) Predictive toxicology: benchmarking molecular descriptors and statistical methods. *J. Chem. Inf. Comput. Sci. 43*(5), 1463-1470.

[23] Zhang, L., Zhang, H., Ai, H., Hu, H., Li, S., Zhao, J., and Liu, H. (2018) Applications of machine learning methods in drug toxicity prediction. *Curr. Top. Med. Chem. 18*(12), 987-997.

[24] Xu, Y., Pei, J., and Lai, L. (2017) Deep learning based regression and multiclass models for acute oral toxicity prediction with automatic chemical feature extraction. *J. Chem. Inf. Model 57*(11), 2672-2685.

[25] Latek, D., Ekonomiuk, D., and Kolinski, A. (2007) Protein structure prediction: combining de novo modeling with sparse experimental data. *J. Comput. Chem. 28*(10), 1668-1676.

[26] Manoochehri, H. E., Pillai, A., and Nourani, M. (2019, November). Graph convolutional networks for predicting drug-protein interactions. In *2019 IEEE International Conference on Bioinformatics and Biomedicine (BIBM)* (pp. 1223-1225). IEEE.

[27] Chan, H. S., Shan, H., Dahoun, T., Vogel, H., and Yuan, S. (2019) Advancing drug discovery via artificial intelligence. *Trends Pharmacol. Sci. 40*(8), 592-604.

[28] Blaschke, T., Arús-Pous, J., Chen, H., Margreitter, C., Tyrchan, C., Engkvist, O., Papadopoulos, K., and Patronov, A. (2020) REINVENT 2.0: an AI tool for de novo drug design. *J. Chem. Inf. Model. 60*(12), 5918-5922.

[29] Arús-Pous, J., Johansson, S. V., Prykhodko, O., Bjerrum, E. J., Tyrchan, C., Reymond, J. L., Chen, H., and Engkvist, O. (2019) Randomized SMILES strings improve the quality of molecular generative models. *J. Cheminform. 11*(1), 1-13.

[30] Mirbabaie, M., Stieglitz, S., and Frick, N. R. (2021) Artificial intelligence in disease diagnostics: A critical review and classification on the current state of research guiding future direction. *Health Technol. 11*(4), 693-731.

[31] Mitchell, T., Cohen, W., Hruschka, E., Talukdar, P., Yang, B., Betteridge, J., Carlson, A., Dalvi, B., Gardner, M., Kisiel, B., and Krishnamurthy, J. (20180 Never-ending learning. *Commun. ACM 61*(5), 103-115.

[32] Yan, Y., Zhang, J. W., Zang, G. Y., and Pu, J. (2019) The primary use of artificial intelligence in cardiovascular diseases: what kind of potential role does artificial intelligence play in future medicine?. *J. Geriatr. Cardiol. 16*(8), 585-591.

[33] Krittanawong, C., Zhang, H., Wang, Z., Aydar, M., and Kitai, T. (2017) Artificial intelligence in precision cardiovascular medicine. *J. Am. Coll. Cardiol. 69*(21), 2657-2664.

[34] Samad, M. D., Ulloa, A., Wehner, G. J., Jing, L., Hartzel, D., Good, C. W., Williams, B. A., Haggerty, C. M. and Fornwalt, B. K. (2019) Predicting survival from large echocardiography and electronic health record datasets: optimization with machine learning. *JACC Cardiovasc. Imaging 12*(4), 681-689.

[35] Huang, S., Yang, J., Fong, S., and Zhao, Q. (2020) Artificial intelligence in cancer diagnosis and prognosis: Opportunities and challenges. *Cancer Lett. 471*, 61-71.

[36] Obermeyer, Z., and Emanuel, E. J. (2016) Predicting the future—big data, machine learning, and clinical medicine. *N. Engl. J. Med. 375*(13), 1216-1219.

[37] Bi, W. L., Hosny, A., Schabath, M. B., Giger, M. L., Birkbak, N. J., Mehrtash, A., Allison, T., Arnaout, O., Abbosh, C., Dunn, I. F., and Mak, R. H. (2019) Artificial intelligence in cancer imaging: clinical challenges and applications. *CA Cancer J. Clin. 69*(2), 127-157.

[38] McGranahan, N., and Swanton, C. (2017) Clonal heterogeneity and tumor evolution: past, present, and the future. *Cell 168*(4), 613-628.

[39] Li, X., Zhang, S., Zhang, Q., Wei, X., Pan, Y., Zhao, J., Xin, X., Qin, C., Wang, X., Li, J., and Yang, F. (2019) Diagnosis of thyroid cancer using deep convolutional neural network models applied to sonographic images: a retrospective, multicohort, diagnostic study. *Lancet Oncol. 20*(2), 193-201.

[40] Kar, D., and Halder, S. (2019) Early Detection of Brain Tumor by Using K-Means Clustering, Convolutional Neural Network and Support Vector Machine without any Imaging Test. In *2019 International Conference on Information Technology (ICIT)* (pp. 59-64). IEEE.

[41] Zhang, Y., Jiang, B., Zhang, L., Greuter, M. J., de Boc, G. H., Zhang, H., and Xie, X. (2022) Lung nodule detectability of artificial intelligence-assisted CT image reading in lung cancer screening. *Artificial Intelligence 18*(3), 327-334.

[42] Rainey, C., McConnell, J., Hughes, C., Bond, R., and McFadden, S. (2021) Artificial Intelligence for diagnosis of fractures on plain radiographs: a scoping review of current literature. *Intelligence-Based Medicine* 5.

[43] https://healthitanalytics.com/news/usingartificial-intelligencetoidentifyfractures-on-x-rays

[44] Voelker, R. (2018) Diagnosing fractures with AI. *Jama 320*(1), 23-23.

[45] Murata, K., Endo, K., Aihara, T., Suzuki, H., Sawaji, Y., Matsuoka, Y., Nishimura, H., Takamatsu, T., Konishi, T., Maekawa, A., and Yamauchi, H. (2020) Artificial intelligence for the detection of vertebral fractures on plain spinal radiography. *Sci. Rep. 10*(1), 1-8.

[46] Xiong, Y., Ba, X., Hou, A., Zhang, K., Chen, L., and Li, T. (2018) Automatic detection of mycobacterium tuberculosis using artificial intelligence. *J. Thorac. Dis. 10*(3), 1936-1940.

[47] Qin, Z. Z., Sander, M. S., Rai, B., Titahong, C. N., Sudrungrot, S., Laah, S. N., Adhikari, L. M., Carter, E. J., Puri, L., Codlin, A. J., and Creswell, J. (2019) Using artificial intelligence to read chest radiographs

for tuberculosis detection: A multi-site evaluation of the diagnostic accuracy of three deep learning systems. *Sci. Rep. 9*(1), 1-10.

[48] Jamal, S., Khubaib, M., Gangwar, R., Grover, S., Grover, A., and Hasnain, S. E. (2020) Artificial Intelligence and Machine learning based prediction of resistant and susceptible mutations in Mycobacterium tuberculosis. *Sci. Rep. 10*(1), 1-16.

[49] Singla, R., Singla, A., Gupta, Y., and Kalra, S. (2019) Artificial intelligence/machine learning in diabetes care. *Indian J. Endocrinol. Metab. 23*(4), 495-497.

[50] Ellahham, S. (2020) Artificial intelligence: the future for diabetes care. *Am. J. Med. 133*(8), 895-900.

[51] Dankwa-Mullan, I., Rivo, M., Sepulveda, M., Park, Y., Snowdon, J., and Rhee, K. (2019) Transforming diabetes care through artificial intelligence: the future is here. *Popul. Health Manag. 22*(3), 229-242.

[52] Soun, J. E., Chow, D. S., Nagamine, M., Takhtawala, R. S., Filippi, C. G., Yu, W., and Chang, P. D. (2021) Artificial intelligence and acute stroke imaging. *Am. J. Neuroradiol. 42*(1), 2-11.

[53] Ding, L., Liu, C., Li, Z., and Wang, Y. (2020) Incorporating artificial intelligence into stroke care and research. *Stroke*, *51*(12), 351-354.

[54] Murray, N. M., Unberath, M., Hager, G. D., and Hui, F. K. (2020) Artificial intelligence to diagnose ischemic stroke and identify large vessel occlusions: a systematic review. *J. Neurointerv. Surg. 12*(2), 156-164.

[55] De, A., Sarda, A., Gupta, S., and Das, S. (2020) Use of artificial intelligence in dermatology. *Indian J. Dermatol. 65*(5), 352-357.

[56] De Guzman, L. C., Maglaque, R. P. C., Torres, V. M. B., Zapido, S. P. A., and Cordel, M. O., 2015, December. Design and evaluation of a multi-model, multi-level artificial neural network for eczema skin lesion detection. In *2015 3rd International conference on artificial intelligence, modelling and simulation (AIMS)* (pp. 42-47). IEEE.

[57] Shrivastava, V. K., Londhe, N. D., Sonawane, R. S., and Suri, J. S. (2017) A novel and robust Bayesian approach for segmentation of psoriasis lesions and its risk stratification. *Comput. Methods Programs Biomed. 150*, 9-22.

[58] Scannell, J. W., Blanckley, A., Boldon, H., and Warrington, B. (2012) Diagnosing the decline in pharmaceutical R&D efficiency. *Nat. Rev. Drug Discov.* 11, 191–200.

[59] DiMasi, J. A., Grabowski, H. G., and Hansen, R. W. (2016) Innovation in the pharmaceutical industry: New estimates of R&D costs. *J. Health Econ.* 47, 20–33.

[60] Zhavoronkov, A., Ivanenkov, Y. A., Aliper, A., Veselov, M. S., Aladinskiy, V. A., Aladinskaya, A. V., Terentiev, V. A., Polykovskiy, D. A., Kuznetsov, M. D., Asadulaev, A., and Volkov, Y. (2019) Deep learning enables rapid identification of potent DDR1 kinase inhibitors. *Nat. Biotechnol. 37*(9), 1038-1040.
[61] Walters, W. P., and Murcko, M. (2020) Assessing the impact of generative AI on medicinal chemistry. *Nat. Biotechnol.* 38, 143–145.
[62] Paul, S. M., Mytelka, D. S., Dunwiddie, C. T., Persinger, C. C., Munos, B. H., Lindborg, S. R., and Schacht, A. L. (2010) How to improve R&D productivity: the pharmaceutical industry's grand challenge. *Nat. Rev. Drug Discov. 9*(3), 203-214.
[63] Lamberti, M. J. (2019) A study on the application and use of artificial intelligence to support drug development. *Clin. Ther.* 41, 1414-1426.
[64] https://hbr.org/2017/06/if-your-company-isnt-goodat-analytics-its-not-ready-for-ai
[65] Kaitin, K. I. (2019) Artificial intelligence and patient-centric approaches to advance pharmaceutical innovation. *Clin. Ther. 41*(8), 1406-1407.
[66] www.mckinsey.com/industries/retail/our-insights/how-retailers-can-keep-up-with-consumers
[67] https://hbr.org/2016/11/what-artificial-intelligencecan-and-cant-do-right-now
[68] https://renci.org/wp-content/uploads/2015/11/SCi-Discovery-BigData-FINAL-11.23.15.pdf
[69] https://hbr.org/2018/12/why-companies-that-waitto-adopt-ai-may-never-catch-up
[70] Davenport T. H., and Ronanki R. (2018) Artificial intelligence for the real world. *Harvard Bus. Rev.* 96, 108-116.

Author Biography

Ms. Akanksha Sharma (Assistant Professor)

Akanksha Sharma is an Assistant Professor at Monad College of Pharmacy, Monad University, Hapur. She has completed B. Pharm from Kashi Institute of Pharmacy, Varanasi in 2018. She has completed M. Pharm (Pharmaceutics) from Galgotias University in 2020. She has published research and review papers, mostly in the Scopus indexed journal. She is a good motivator and provides guidance to students for being a good Pharmacy Professional, Researcher, and to be more human.

Mr. Ashish Verma

Ashish Verma is student at School of pharmacy, Monad University, Hapur. He has completed B. Pharm from Kashi Institute of Pharmacy, Varanasi in 2018. He always works with students at ground level to understand along with utilization of different basic concepts of pharmacy in real life. He is a good motivator and provides guidance to students for being a good Pharmacy Professional, Researcher, and to be more human.

Dr. Rishabha Malviya

Dr. Rishabha Malviya is presently working as an Associate Professor at Galgotias University in the Department of Pharmacy,

School of Medical and Allied Sciences Greater Noida, UP, India. He completed his Ph.D. at Galgotias University, India. He completed his M. Pharm in Pharmaceutics (2008-2010) and B. Pharm (2004-2008) from U.P technical university, Lucknow, India. He has published more than 115 articles in different international and national journals. He has published 2 books and 4 book chapters, and also has some patents. He has guided 23 M. Pharm students for their respective project work. He was qualified in Gate with 94.36 percentile in 2008-2009 and also received Faculty Appreciation Award from Meerut Institute of Engineering and Technology and Appreciation Letter from Rexcin Pharmaceuticals Private Limited. He is serving as editorial board member and reviewer of various international and national journals. He is also serving as a consultant/advisor to industry for process optimization and formulation. development.

Dr. Rishabha Malviya

Aditi Singh is an Assistant Professor at Ashoka Institute of Pharmacy. She has completed B. Pharm from Kashi Institute of Pharmacy, Varanasi in 2018. She received gold medal in M. Pharm (2020) from Amity university, Lucknow. She also worked as an assistant professor with Future Group of Institution Bareilly for one year. She is a good motivator and provides guidance to students for being a good Pharmacy Professional, Researcher and to be more human.

6

Use of Artificial Intelligence and Robotics: Making the Drug Development Process Easier

Aditi Singh[1], Ashish Verma[2], Akanksha Sharma[3*], Rishabha Malviya[4], and Mahendran Sekar[5]

[1]Ashoka Institute of Pharmacy, India
[2]School of Pharmacy, Monad University, India
[3]Monad College of Pharmacy, Monad University, India
[4]Department of Pharmacy, School of Medical and Allied Sciences, Galgotias University, India
[5]Department of Pharmaceutical Chemistry, Faculty of Pharmacy and Health Sciences, Royal College of Medicine Perak, Universiti Kuala Lumpur, Malaysia
*Corresponding Author: Monad College of Pharmacy, Monad University, N.H. 9, Delhi Hapur Road, Kastla, Kasmabad, Pilkhuwa, Uttar Pradesh, 245304, India, Email: akankshasona012@gmail.com, Contact: +91-8009218455, ORCID Id: 0000-0002-5325-427X.

Abstract

Robotics is a field of engineering that deals with conception, design, manufacture, and robot operation. Robotics aims to develop intelligent devices that can aid humans in several ways. Medical robots help in surgery, ease hospital logistics, and allow clinical staff to focus more on patients. Robotics is rapidly being used in the pharmaceutical sector to automate specific operations in drug development. This may include drug screening, manufacturing, and anti-counterfeiting tasks. It can help to speed up drug discovery by combining Machine Learning and Artificial Intelligence. The ability to investigate and discover new medication candidates has substantially improved as a result of these technical applications of modern disruptive technologies. Automation technology may increase the speed of the production process while also making it safer and more efficient, all while lowering the cost of labor. This chapter deliberates about Artificial Intelligence and robotics role in formulation discovery and development. It also describes the various tools and techniques that help in the discovery and development of drugs along with the future perspective.

Keywords: Robotics, drug discovery, machine learning, drug development, artificial intelligence.

6.1 Introduction and History of AI in Drug Development

AI aids in the designing of rational drugs [1]. It chooses the most appropriate treatment for a patient, such as personalized medicines that help in decision making, and generates medical data which is utilized in future drug discovery. AI is anticipated in the development of pharmaceuticals [2]. Artificial intelligence can differentiate between lead and hit compounds, enabling quicker structural design optimization and therapeutic target validation [3, 4]. The quantitative structure-activity relationship (QSAR) is a computational model that predicts a huge number of compounds or simple physicochemical properties like log P or log D in a short amount of time [5, 6].

Physicochemical properties of a medication like solubility, degree of ionization, partition coefficient (logP), and intrinsic permeability have an indirect effect on its pharmacokinetic qualities which ultimately target the family of receptors, and must be considered while discovering a novel drug [7]. Physicochemical qualities are envisaged by utilizing different types of AI-based methods.

For instance, machine learning makes advantage of massive datasets which are generated during compound optimization [8]. Molecular descriptors like SMILES strings have properties to determine power, electron density surrounding molecule, and atom coordination in 3D; these aid in algorithms of drug design to produce viable compounds using DNN and forecast their attributes [9].

Table 6.1 represents the various tools utilized in the process of drug discovery [10].

6.1.1 History behind AI

Alan Turing initially proposed the idea of the utilization of computers that represent human intelligence and behavior in 1950 [18]. McCarthy used

Table 6.1 Various tools are utilized in drug discovery procedures.

S. No.	Tools	Description
1.	DeepChem	Drug discovery, using a python-oriented AI tool to select a suitable candidate [11]
2.	DeepTox	A software that is capable of predicting toxicity [12]
3.	DeepNeural NetQSAR	Tools used in the identification of a compound's molecular activity [13]
4.	PotentialNet	Used in the prediction of drug binding [14]
5.	Hit Dexter	Study the molecular response to biochemical assay [15]
6.	Chemputer	Tools used in chemical synthesis [16]
7.	AlphaFold	Used to predict the 2D structure of drugs [17]

the term artificial intelligence (AI) in 1956, describing it as "the science and technology of creating machine intelligence," even though it had been introduced six years before. Turing proposed that computers are programmed to mimic human behavior and intelligence. He created a simple test (later identified as the "Turing test") to assess the computers that are subjected to determine human intelligence; this is mentioned in his textbook "Computers and Intelligence" [19].

Over the past five decades, AI has changed dramatically. Predictive models could be used for diagnostic techniques, therapeutic response prognosis, and potentially integrated healthcare in the future [20]. Early AI research focuses on creating machines that could make inferences or conclusions that are previously made by humans. In 1961, General Motors introduced the very first industrial robotic arm (Unimate) that handled computerized diecasting during the assembly process [21]. Shakey is considered "the very first electronic person," who developed the model in 1966. This would be the first model of a mobile robot that understood the commands and was created at Stanford Research Institute [22].

"AI Winter" covers the majority of the time, denoting a time of lower interest and funding; as a result, lesser notable developments took place. Joseph Weizenbaum introduced Eliza in 1964. Eliza was skilled to chat by utilizing sequence matching and displacement methods that simulate human conversation using natural language processing (NLPNLP) (superficial communication). In the early 1970s, MYCIN, an AI system "backward chaining," was developed. MYCIN might compile a series of probable bacterial pathogens and then suggest antibiotic therapy based on input data filled by the physician with the help of patient information [23].

DeepQA performed the analysis of unstructured content using natural language processing (NLP) and multiple examinations to generate reasonable answers. DeepQA technology could be used to deliver evidence-based medicine replies by extracting data from an electronic medical record of patients and another electronic source. The development and discovery of drugs are understood as a four-stage plan, which resembles a marathon-like structure in which various competing molecules begin their race but only a few reach the end line.

The rate of failure in discovering new medications for Alzheimer's disease management and a diagnosis reached 99.6% between 2002 and 2012. Furthermore, around 38% of novel compounds passed in clinical trials in Phase II and Phase III moved to market. Various AI methods are used in every stage of drug research, including detection and confirmation of molecular targets as well as the discovery of new drugs—synthesis of hit and lead chemicals, and optimization of hit and lead compounds prediction of ADME-Tox, and drug-like substances clinical trials, for instance [24].

6.1.2 AI platforms for target identification

Target identification performance improves with large amounts of omics data and computational approaches. Many efforts have been undertaken to address these issues.

6.1.2.1 DisGeNET

To decrease the variability, accessibility, and genetic information segmentation, DisGeNET gathers the genes associated with disease and variations from a variety of GWAS catalogs, repositories, animal models, and publications. There are 210,498 variant disease associations (VDA) and 628,685 gene-disease associations (GDAGDA) in the dataset [25].

6.1.2.2 LinkedOmics

It aspires to deliver an analytical and comprehensive platform for a huge amount of cancer-related data and clinical information [26].

6.1.2.3 DepMap portal

This model helps scientists to find molecular and genetic cancer dependencies from datasets that are attained from the Broad Institute's Cancer Dependency Map project. The DepMap portal's datasets are separated into three categories: genetic reliance, drug sensitivity, and cellular models [27, 28].

6.1.2.4 Therapeutic target database

The TTD (therapeutic target database) is a database that contains data on recognized beneficial proteins, nucleic acid, diseases, pathways, and medications for the targets in literature [29].

6.1.2.5 Positivity in AI

Artificial intelligence (AI) will forever alter the pharmaceutical industry and the method by which medications are discovered. However, to make effective drug research utilizing AI, one must first learn how to train algorithms with the required domain knowledge This creates the ideal environment for AI and medical research. Chemists can collaborate closely because the former will be able to support the huge amount of data analysis. The latter can be used to train machines, set algorithms, or optimize the data for a specific purpose—a more efficient and precise drug development process.

6.2 Introduction and History of Robotics in Healthcare, Drug Discovery, or Development

In today's world, robots play a significant role in engineering applications. Medical robot in research and development has altered the way medical procedures, particularly surgical operations, are performed, thanks to technological advancements. This remarkable improvement can be ascribed not only to technological advancements such as sensors, actuators, and control systems but also to the imaging system for the development of clinical purposes, like magnetic imaging. Robots are automation that may be programmed to do simple or sophisticated activities, either with or without human support. The expensive cost of robotic systems, the enormous amount of space they take to operate, the necessity for periodic maintenance, and the requirement of properly trained operators like clinical personnel and physicians before usage are just a few of the drawbacks. In the year 1954, George Devol introduced the first robot, "UNIMATE." It is utilized in manufacturing and production [30].

Robots were first used in the medical field in the early 1980s. The practice of medicine is about to be transformed by robots. The development in the design and use of robots in medicine is powered by artificial intelligence, miniaturization, and computer power. When an industrial robot and computed tomography navigation were combined to implant a probe into the brain to obtain a biopsy specimen 34 years ago, medical robots were born. Following that, a variety of robots capable of performing urological procedures including total hip arthroplasty were developed. Mechanical robots were originally used in areas of medicine in the 1980s, but the technology did not reach its full potential until the 1990s.

Mechanical robots have been beneficial in the accurate cannulae aligning that helps in brain biopsies since 1985 when the Puma 560 was introduced [31]. Specialized camera-guided robotic surgical systems such as Minerva,

Neuro-Mate, and the Robot-Assisted Microsurgery system were introduced into settings of brain surgery. The National Aeronautics and Space Administration in the United States investigated the concept of remote surgery, or telesurgery, in the 1970s.

The introduction of robotic systems has had a significant impact on a few major fields of medicine like Renaissance® System, which was initiated in 2011 and had confirmed to enhance the accuracy by 85% to 100% and is widely recognized for utilization in spinal surgeries. In 2015, MAKO, the most popular orthopedic operations robotic system was launched. Robotics tools that are used in the medical field are summarized below with their significant role.

6.2.1 Decade I (first generations): 1990–2000

In 1985, a robot was utilized in a clinical procedure for the first time. An industrial robot was employed to accomplish a brain biopsy by utilizing CT imagingCT imaging and movement preprogramming. Because of safety concerns, the employment of industrial robots to conduct sensitive procedures like brain biopsy was canceled [32].

6.2.1.1 neuromate®

In stereotactic operations, the neuromate robot enables consistent, quick, and precise targeting. The neuromate stereotactic robot is a platform that may be used for a variety of operational neurosurgery techniques [33, 34].

6.2.1.2 ROBODOC® Surgical System

ROBODOC surgical system was the first effective system that was used in a few preoperatively scheduled surgical actions. The ROBODOC® operating system is separated into 2 parts: ROBODOC®, which act as a robotic arm in surgery, and Orthodoc, which acts as a 3D computer modeling station [35].

6.2.1.3 AESOP™ robotic surgical system

The AESOP (Automatic Endoscopic System for Optimal Positioning) Robotic Surgical System, invented by the company named Computer Motion Inc. in the United States, is a first-of-its-kind robotic system for laparoscopic operations. AESOP employs a voice detection system to control a seven-degree-of-freedom robotic arm. It helps to manage the endoscope directly with simple vocal commands [36, 37].

6.2.1.4 CyberKnife® system

The very first robotic system that was developed for stereotactic body radiotherapy and stereotactic radiosurgery therapy was CyberKnife® Robotic Radiosurgery System. Accuracy Inc. in the United States created this system as a frameless image-guided radiosurgery system [38].

6.2.1.5 ZEUS® robotic surgical system

Computer Motion Inc., USA, created Zenith Robotic Surgical Method (ZRSS) as a revolutionary system for doing laparoscopic operations. The ZEUS Robotic Surgical System (ZRSS) was a clinical robot discovered by an American robotics company, Computer Motion, to help in surgery [36].

6.2.1.6 CASPAR®

The CASPAR® (Computer-Assisted Surgical Planning and Robotics) device is a robotic system used in knee and hip surgery, created by CASPAR in Germany [39].

6.2.2 Decade II (middle generations): 2000–2010

6.2.2.1 AcuBot

AcuBot was created with the aim of displacing operating room technicians and surgeons from hazardous operations using CT imaging or fluoroscopy. This will help staff in lowering their radiation exposure. The shape of AcuBot, specifically the S-arm, allows the system to move freely, allowing treatments to be conducted from anywhere on the body using different modalities of imaging [40, 41].

6.2.2.2 PathFinder™

This is the world's largest first robot that is image-guided, which helps in surgery. PathFinder^{TM} is a stereotactic system that includes a camera and a 6-DOF arm. PathFinder^{TM} also has a submillimeter precision capability, which aids in needle guidance during biopsies [42].

6.2.2.3 InnoMotion

The goal of developing this system was to make it compatible and functional with MRI while delivering. It is a precise and repeatable instrument positioned within a magnetic field [43].

6.2.3 Decade III (new generations): 2010–Present

6.2.3.1 ROSA ONE®

In this system, both spine and brain applications are available. The dual-functioning robot can improve the use of robotic platforms for surgeries resulting in the decreased acquisition, repair, and service costs across the institution, streamlining the robotic learning curve. In the case of spine surgical navigation, the robotic system helps surgeons to do invasive procedures in thoracolumbar spine surgeries [44, 45].

6.2.3.2 PRECEYES Surgical System

A new system was developed in the Netherlands, by Preceyes B.V., utilized as robotic assistance during the time of eye surgeries. The use of PRECEYES allows surgeons to manipulate the devices more easily inward the eyes. The device is meant to be like an intraocular equipment—it cannot alter the approach of the procedure in which the process is carried out [46].

6.2.3.3 Ion^{TM} robotic-assisted platform

Intuitive Surgical Inc., USA, invented the Ion^{TM} robotic-assisted platform for nonsurgical biopsy and bronchoscopy treatments. The catheter, controllers, and HD screens for visualization are fitted in a single console. The catheter is developed, which has a 3.5 mm external diameter and a 2.0 mm internal diameter working channel with flexibility and feasibility [47].

6.3 Application of Robotics in the Healthcare Sector

Table 6.2 represents the application of robotics in the healthcare sector.

6.4 AI in Research and Development

Artificial intelligence has the property to improve the chances of drug development systems by bringing major improvements in a variety of fields

Table 6.2 Application of robotics in the healthcare sector.

S. No.	Robot	Application	Year	Reference
1.	MINERVA	Used in the biopsy of brain	1985	[48]
2.	ROBODOC	Used in hip replacement surgery	1992	[49]
3.	ZEUS	Used to do an endoscopy	1998	[50]
4.	Telelap ALF-X	Used to do laparoscopy	2011	[51]
5.	CASPAR	Used to do knee and hip surgery	1997	[52]

like R&D areas, including identification of novel targets, knowledge of targeted-disease relationships, selection of drug candidates, protein structure estimations, molecular compound modeling, understanding disease causes, developing new diagnostic and predictive biomarkers, analyzing biometric data from portable tech, imaging, personalized medicine, clinical trial development, execution, and analysis. Because of the rising importance of digital innovation for data gathering and site monitoring, the influence of the COVID-19 outbreak on clinical study performance may enhance the artificial intelligence application in the execution of clinical trials [53].

In general, medicine is operated by connecting with disorder targets such as proteins, genes, and nucleic acids [54]. AI is mainly utilized in target identification during the research stage. The initial step in drug development is to search for targets that play a role in disease [54]. The most essential part of the procedure is to select the target. It determines the effectiveness of the entire research program; failing to find proper target results in the failure of the research. Machine learning has been proven to speed up the identification of therapeutic targets in recent studies [55]. Based on existing knowledge of the

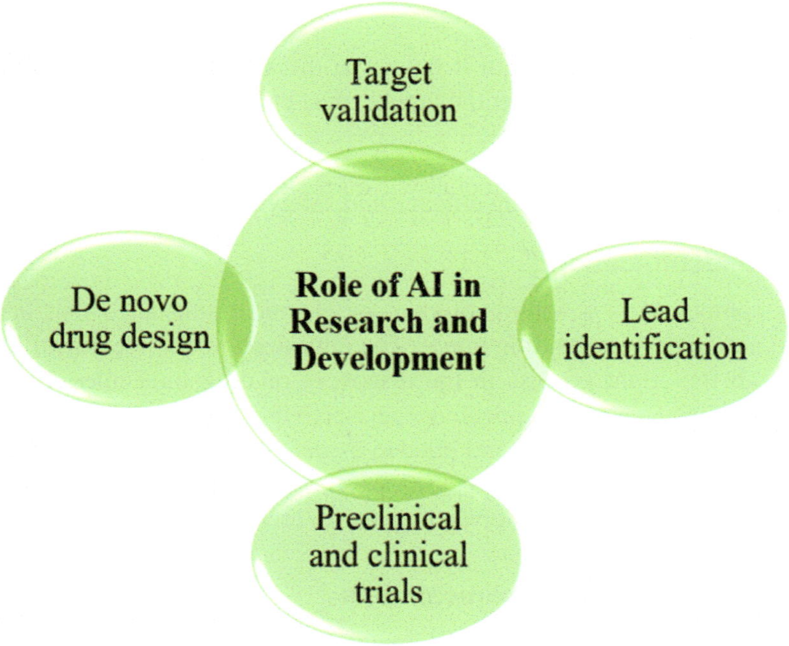

Figure 6.1 Schematic diagram to show the AI importance in research and development.

qualities of already recognized targets, provide a categorization system that categorizes numerous possible targets as treatable/non-treatable. Figure 6.1 summarizes the AI's role in research and development.

6.4.1 Target validation

A good target contains two important attributes. First, it is crucial to the disease's prognosis. Second, it has surface cavities that seem to be in the right form and size for a proposed medicine to bind with [54]. Several recent studies have recommended automating various aspects of target validation.

Target validation is a multicomponent technique for establishing a possible target's involvement in human disease. Proteins that are not associated with disease and, as a result, are not targeted in the drug development procedure should be ruled out as soon as feasible. Enhanced target validation accuracy and consistency come at a cost, but recent investment in target validation could save huge losses by lowering clinical trial attrition due to lack of efficacy. Target validation requires excellent animal and cellular models of disease, validation tools, and reagents, and the ability to transfer these reagents into in vitro and in vivo cells [56]. Google creates a machine learning algorithm that can forecast the recognized target structure better than the experienced field specialists [57].

AI has a huge potential when it comes to the selection of targets and assessing compound effects. Potential targets must be validated in physiologically relevant in vitro tests after being discovered in silico. Target validation with hiPSC-derived models is excellent because they provide scalable and predictive tools for assessing drug efficacy and safety in high throughput.

6.4.2 Lead identification

The lead compound is a natural product or chemical substance that has biological action against the drug target. The optimization and identification of lead is an important process in the discovery of drug molecules. Lead optimization aims to enhance selectivity and activity, and decrease adverse effects by boosting non-bonded and bonded associations with the active site of identified pharmacological targets [58]. Lead is a chemical substance that has a great binding capacity at a given target with low toxicity.

6.4.3 Preclinical trials and clinical trials

Once one target has been discovered, many lead compounds have been chosen, and the effectiveness and safety of the lead compounds are examined in animal studies, generally called preclinical trials or preclinical research. The most significant issue in preclinical study is that medication compounds may behave differently in animals than they do in humans [59]. A more integrated view of the linkage between proteins and genes as well as disease, and the effect of influencing such targets on the disease, can enhance the AI application in drug discovery. However, the field must progress beyond "target–disease" connections to include quantitative and conditional features [60].

6.4.4 De novo drug design

A de novo system of drug design could accelerate the process of finding and optimizing leads, providing for the quick discovery of therapeutically effective compounds. It utilizes machine learning to anticipate new pharmacological compounds with desired properties based on prior information. During the previous decade, the concept has gotten a lot of attention, and several researchers have presented a variety of de novo design methodologies [61].

6.5 Pharmaceutical Product Developments

The use of AI and robotics in pharmaceutical product development are described below. Figure 6.2 summarizes the various pharmaceutical products that are developed by the utilization of AI and robotics.

6.5.1 Nanorobots drug delivery

Drugs are used to manage and treat diseases by therapeutic delivery. It is crucial to develop an efficacious method for therapeutic delivery. When a medicine enters the body, it must first pass through various histological and physicochemical barriers (for example, the blood–retinal barrier, blood–brain barrier, tissue-resident phagocytes as a cellular barrier, and extrinsic and intrinsic gastrointestinal barriers) before reaching its target tissue. Because of the presence of blood flow hemodynamics and pressure of the interstitial fluid, some drugs may have to face difficulties in moving via the circulatory system, cells, or tissues. While going through the digestive tract, such drugs may lose their pharmacokinetic and pharmacodynamic potency [62].

As a result, the choice of delivering a vehicle that is tailored for the illness site and has regulated medication release becomes a critical goal. As depicted in numerous science fiction scenarios, nanorobots foresee a fascinating world

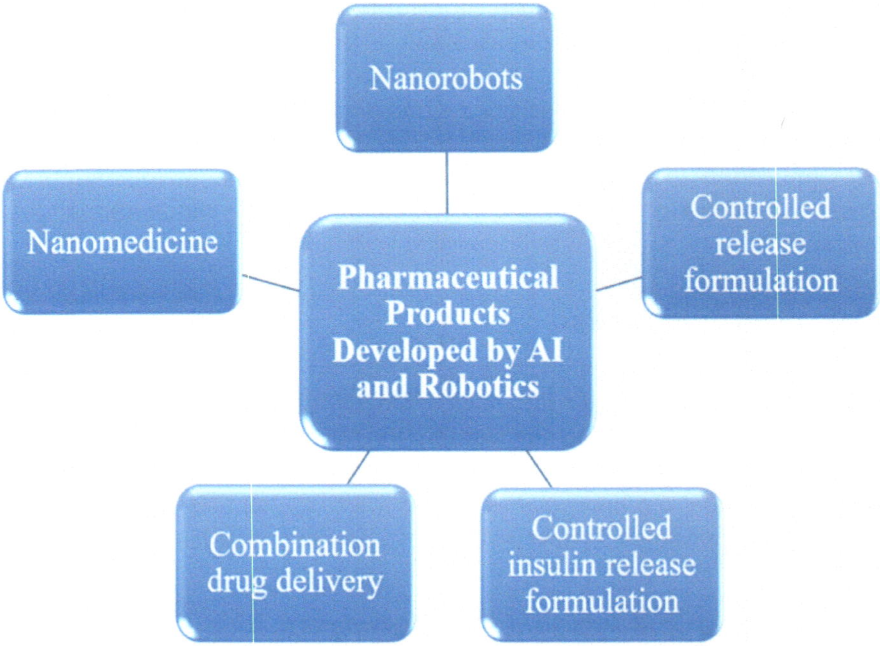

Figure 6.2 The schematic diagram summarizes the various pharmaceutical products that are developed by the utilization of AI and robotics.

for future therapies. Nanorobots are small synthetic tools having the ability to move, perceive, and operate at micro or nanoscale accuracy to do certain duties repeatedly in a closely regulated way, according to their definition. At least one dimension of a nanorobot is in the micrometer (1000 m = 1 mm) or nanometer range (1000 nm = 1 m) [62, 63].

Traditional drug delivery systems differ from robotic approaches at the micro/nanoscale in terms of targeting, sensing, designing, power, and control to conduct vast parallel tasks simultaneously. Nanorobot research for drug discovery has progressed from simple moving beads to complex nanostructures developed in a complicated way. Chemical fuel (like H_2O_2), biomolecular fuel (like enzymes), electromagnetic energy, or light—all are used to power nanorobots. These tiny robots' mobility allows them to go through inaccessible locations including necrotic tumor cores, viscous fluids like the retina vitreous chamber in the eye, and small passageways into micro-capillaries. As a result, these small synthetic robots are programmed to deliver a therapeutic payload to illness sites that are nearly hard to access with current tools that are autonomous or untethered [62, 64].

Prevailing delivery of a drug by micro and nanocarriers rely on systemic circulation and navigation is needed for localized distribution and penetration in tissue beyond passive transport. Drug delivery vehicles should have some specific features, such as propelling force, controlled navigation, cargo towing, and penetration and release in tissue, to ensure precise delivery of therapeutic drugs and to selected disease areas. While current medication delivery methods are unable to achieve these requirements, micro and nanorobots provide a novel and appealing class for the delivery of vehicles. The motor-like micro or nanorobots can deliver therapeutic medications directly to disease locations, boosting the effectiveness of therapeutics and decreasing systemic side effects of very hazardous medications [65].

Many new systems are used in the development of the drug. The early stage witnesses the development of micro/nanorobots for drug delivery, and intracellular delivery, in which nanorobots enter the cellular membranes and deliver different medications straight into the cells. The quick internalization and ultrasound-powered gold nanowire motors movement inside the living cells have been used to speed up intracellular siRNA delivery. When compared to their static nanowire counterparts, these siRNA-loaded nanowires were demonstrated to enter swiftly into diverse cell lines and to greatly enhance effectiveness and gene silencing speed. Magnetic helical micro swimmers were utilized to transport pDNA to embryonic kidney cells of humans with pinpoint accuracy. The wireless pDNA-loaded motors were guided toward the cells when they made contact with the cell and simultaneously discharge their genetic cargo [65, 66]. To improve the accumulation of drugs on smaller targets like individual cells, this approach was tested by utilizing live bacteria. Various coordinated nanorobot teams will move toward the target in the group or individual, then gather and meet at a certain point for the release of pharmaceutical payloads [67].

Drug delivery system (DDS) works directly on the human body's target sites. It can administer medications to precise places while also managing the amount and frequency. Nanorobotics technology can be utilized to implement drug delivery systems for articular disorders, dental, cancer, diabetes, and other diseases like neoplasms, diabetes, hepatitis, pulmonary, and dentistry treatment. One of the benefits of this technology is that it can diagnose and cure diseases with minimal harm to healthy cells, minimizing the chance of side effects and direct reconstructive and healing treatment at subcellular and cellular levels [68]. Figure 6.3 describes the few nanorobots which help in drug delivery and therapies.

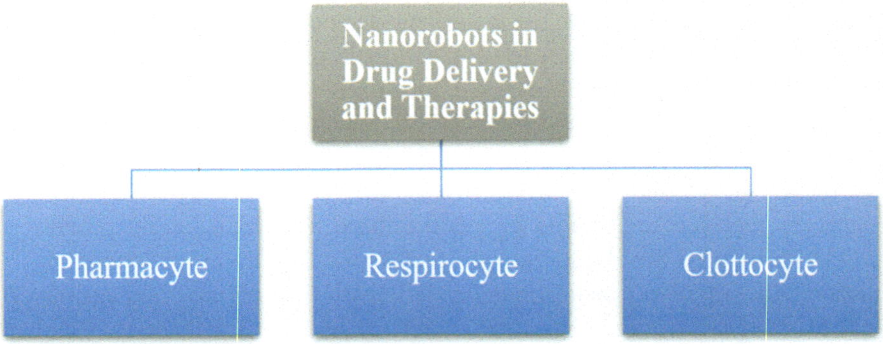

Figure 6.3 Schematic diagram of a few nanorobots which help in the delivery of drugs and therapies.

According to their applications, certain nanorobots in drug delivery and therapies are discussed below.

6.5.1.1 Pharmacyte

Medical nanorobots are nanorobots with a size of 1–2 μm and the ability to transport up to 1 μm^3 of certain medicine in tanks. Mechanical systems for sorting pumps are used to control them. The weight is expelled in the cytosol or extracellular fluid, depending on the condition (the cell cytoplasm aqueous component). They are equipped with chemotactic sensors or molecular markers which ensure pinpoint accuracy in targeting. The onboard power supply is oxygen and glucose collected from local surroundings like intestinal fluid, blood, and cytosol. The nanorobots can be recovered or removed via centrifuge nanapheresis when they complete their missions [68, 69, 70].

Pharmacytes, also known as nanorobotic DDSs (drug delivery systems), are computer-controlled, self-powered systems that are able for digitally precise conveyance time and targeted drug delivery inside the body of the human. Nanorobots cannot get endocytosed always; they can employ transmembrane mechanical nanoinjectors to evade entering a target cell. The manufacturing, designing, and therapeutic employment of pharmacytes show great progress in nanomedicine application. It is used in the future engineering field of clinical nanorobotics [71].

Pharmacytes' "phagocytic flag" targets the cells having biological compounds able of eliciting a response by the body's natural scavenging or defense systems. On the surface of apoptotic cells, for example, new recognition molecules are expressed. Lipid phosphatidylserine is ordinarily limited to the inner side of the plasma membrane but arises outside by following apoptosis, which is one such molecule in T cells. Phagocytic cells can recognize and remove cells that have this molecule on their surface. Phosphatidylserine or other chemicals with a similar effect seeded on the outer wall of a target cell can cause macrophages to engage in phagocytic behavior after wrongly identifying the target cell as apoptotic. T-cell recognition is also enabled by loading B7 costimulatory molecules on the target cell membrane surface, permitting an immunologic response via the immunological synapse. Human cancerous cells and cysts have an apoptotic response which is induced by cytotoxic T cells; thus, these tagging activities should function well against them [72].

6.5.1.2 Respirocyte

It is made up of 18 billion structural atoms that are all perfectly aligned. For maximum strength, it is built by using a diamondoid honeycomb framework. Internal tankage volumes are separated by thick diamond bulkheads. An equatorial circle has twelve pumping stations evenly spaced. Respirocytes use molecular sorting rotors to exchange gases. The tips of the rotors are uniquely designed to collect specific types of molecules. In tanks, gas molecules are closely packed.

There are three types of rotors in each respirocyte. First, before being introduced to the body, oxygen is collected in the lungs or produced, and then released as it travels throughout the body. Another absorbs carbon dioxide (CO_2) from the circulation system and then discharges it through the lungs. To provide energy to the respirocyte, the respirocyte collects glucose from the blood and utilizes it in a method related to cell respiration. An onboard chemomechanical turbine or fuel cell produces electricity by mixing glucose present in the bloodstream with oxygen from internal storage. 0.3 picowatts of electricity are generated by each power plant. One power plant is 42 nm x 42 nm x 175 nm in size, and it contains 100 million atoms weighing 10–18 kg. For regulating gas output and input activities, tank capacity management, and particular procedures, external data is required, necessitating the employment of a variety of sensors. One example is, making a concentration sensor out of a sorting rotor. The respirocyte would only require about 1000 activities every second [73].

Respirocytes would be capable to transport 236% more oxygen to tissues per unit volume than RBCs. Detectors for gas concentration determination are present outside of every device which notifies the nanorobot regarding oxygen loading and discharge of CO_2 at the tissues and lungs, respectively. It is designed by using a nanocomputer with other sensors, as well as externally applied acoustic signals. Transfusable blood substitutes and partial anemia treatment, with prenatal and neonatal lung diseases, are among the most common uses of a respirocyte. It can also be used to improve cardiovascular operations, tumor therapies, asphyxia prevention, sports, artificial breathing, combat, and other diagnostics. Once respirocytes have lost their physical integrity, they will be recognized as a foreign body that is consumed by the macrophages [74].

6.5.1.3 Clottocytes

Hemostasis is the clotting of blood caused by damage of platelets in the endothelial cells of blood arteries. When exposed collagen from wounded blood vessels collides with platelets, it activates them. Normal blood clotting takes 2 to 5 minutes. Nanotechnologies can reduce blood loss and clotting time has been established. Blood clots have been documented to form in some people occasionally. Corticosteroids and other drugs are used to treat this disease. Hormonal secretions, platelet/ blood damage to the lungs, and allergic reactions are some of the side effects of corticosteroid medication [75].

The hypothetically constructed clottocyte is a mechanical platelet or clottocyte capable of hemostasis in a second. It is a circular, serum oxyglucose-powered nanorobot with a compactly folded fiber mesh that measures around 2 m in diameter. The clottocyte has more potency, i.e., 100–1000 times more than that of the mechanism of natural hemostatic. The fiber mesh should be biodegradable and when it gets released, a soluble coating covering will disintegrate as it came into contact with the plasma, exposing a sticky mesh. To govern the coordinated release of mesh from surrounding clottocytes, as well as the multidevice activation radius within the population of local clottocyte, reliable communication methods would be required. As clottocyte rich blood moves toward the injured blood vessel, the clottocyte's onboard sensors quickly show to bleed out of the body and a change in partial pressure can be noticed.

At human body temperature, oxygen molecules of the air permeate the serum. An acoustic pulse is sent to nearby clottocytes. This information would be disseminated quickly. This allows a carefully regulated device-enablement cascade to spread quickly. By sticking with antigens on blood cells, the specific blood group would capture the blood cells in fiber mesh. Every mesh would encircle the mesh present next to it, attracting red blood cells and quickly stopping the bleeding [75, 76].

6.5.2 Controlled-release formulations

In the development of sustained-release formulations, the use of ANNs and logic algorithms aid in the analysis of the formulation component's effects on the release mechanism in the optimization of medicine formulations. To determine the impact of components of tablets on release characteristics, controlled-release clopidogrel formulations were developed by using a fuzzy logic algorithm and ANN. There was a great agreement between experimental data and ANN-based predictions following the controlled-release formulations and complex dosage forms development via utilizing pharmacokinetics simulations and artificial neural networks.

Based on the individual component's content and the nature of co-surfactants, ANNs and GAs are utilized to forecast the colloidal delivery system's phase behavior. Using GA and a supervised ANN, the key chemical descriptors were picked, and a correlation was found between the chosen descriptors and the weight ratio of the phase behavior and system components. According to the findings, molecular volume, chemical composition, lipophilic–hydrophilic balancelipophilic-hydrophilic balance, length of the hydrocarbon chain, and co-surfactants volume all have their significant role. The colloidal delivery system's phase behavior was accurately predicted by the genetic neural network model, suggesting that this method could be utilized to evaluate co-surfactants in pharmaceutical formulations [77].

6.5.3 Pharmaceutical product R&D

Two basic phases of R&D have been established to simplify the research and development process: the early and late phases of research development. Research and development early phase is defined as the translation of a concept into a design and the prototype creation that is tested by utilizing the hypothesized mechanism of action established during the early stage of research.

Simple, lab-scale manufacturing methods are utilized for early product evaluation. In addition to product-specific attributes, comprehensive design of the product and the accurate realization of the prototype with a scalable method is considered an important early phase difficulty. Especially in the case of new pharmacological compounds and consumer items, early efficacy and safety validation are essential. The capability to create huge numbers of anticipated pharmaceutical goods at a defined quality may open up more testing and research options in late-stage development, thus the stability of the actual manufacturing procedure and adaptability development are more desirable [78].

6.5.4 Controlled insulin release

An article printed in the Science Robotics journal describes a system of robotics used in diabetic therapy. The device is one-of-a-kind in the field and comprises a small implantable robot that acts as an infusion system placed into the abdominal cavity which is interfaced with the intestine. A magnetic capsule is docked with the implantable robot which may aid in a refill of the insulin reservoir. The research was done in collaboration with the BioRobotics Institute of Scuola Superiore Sant'Anna, University of Pisa, and Azienda Ospedaliero-Universitaria Pisana (AOUP), and it expands therapy possibilities for an illness that affects millions of people throughout the world. The system suggests traditional treatment strategies as an option. This would eliminate the need for access ports, syringes, and needles while also considering enhancing the quality of the patient's life, particularly those who take insulin numerous times each day.

The intestine is interfaced with the robot, which is surgically inserted in the abdominal cavity. The robot is implanted functions as a precise insulin infusion device, having characteristics similar to a pump capable of exact insulin release. Every 1–2 weeks, when the reservoir is nearly empty, the patient is urged to take a magnetic pill. The pill travels passively through the digestive system until it reaches the implant, where it is attached magnetically. Before the capsule is normally expelled, a unique process allows the insulin to be transported to the reservoir [79].

The employment of synthetic biology techniques to construct cells and external electric fields to regulate them in a new emergent therapeutic approach known as electro-genetics has recently indicated their potential in biomedical tools. In this method, electric fields are utilized to modify cell activity or expression of protein for therapeutic purposes, such as the release of insulin from modified pancreatic beta cells. Glucose sensing and secretion of insulin were decoupled in these modified cells, which were transplanted into the pancreas of diabetes patients (mice models). Insulin is only released in response to an electromagnetic stimulus received from outside body parts. Only these altered cells respond to the stimuli by releasing insulin into vesicles that had previously collected insulin. Redox chemicals were given to *E. coli* and linked with a redox-sensitive genetic circuit that could offer a synthesis of protein that was spatiotemporally controlled by the applied potential. It is the first time that electrode-controlled genetic processes have been successfully applied to bacteria. These novel findings mark the beginning of a revolution in which electrodes may be used to deliver or transport physical/chemical inputs into cells to regulate desired cellular and genetic metabolism results [80].

For administration of insulin intraperitoneally, the robot is implanted in the abdomen extraperitoneal area surgically which is interfaced in the intestine. It is similar to a pump that has pinpoint precision in the delivery of insulin. When the reservoir of the pump is emptied, an ingestible pill will be tasked with replenishing it by connecting and transferring medicine from the pill to the robot's reservoir via a specialized system. The pills are generally swallowed and travel in a loop through the intestines to a "docking" place. A magnetic device is used to grab the capsule and the reservoir filling. At this stage, the magnetic mechanism is turned off and the empty capsule resumes its normal expulsion way. The combination of the control algorithm and the glucose sensor pump will administer the insulin at a particular time with appropriate amounts necessary for proper glycemic control, making it the first-ever implantable artificial pancreas. The tool's name is PILLSID (PILl-refiLled implanted System for Intraperitoneal Delivery), and it can be verified in a preclinical setting. The preclinical results are extremely promising and significant, both technologically and clinically. This approach could open the way for the first fully implantable artificial pancreas development, as well as in the treatment of other acute and chronic disorders affecting intraperitoneal organs [81].

6.5.5 Combination drug delivery

Several pharmaceutical combinations have been discovered, granted, and marketed to cure tough diseases like tuberculosis and cancer due to their synergistic effect, which allows for a faster recovery. For instance, therapy of cancer needs a combination of six or seven therapies, which needs high-throughput screening of a large number of molecules, which is a time taking procedure. ANN is a network-based modeling and logistic regression, used to test drug combinations, and the overall dosage regimen can be improved. Researchers devised a quadratic phenotypic optimization stage for optimal combination therapy detection, which help in the bortezomib-resistant multiple myeloma treatment by utilizing a 114 FDA-approved drugs library. According to this model, the best two-drug combination was mitomycin C

(MitoC) and decitabine (Dec), while the best three-drug combination was MitoC, mechlorethamine, and Dec [82].

If evidence of the synergism or antagonistic effects of medications given simultaneously is available, combination drug administration shows more effectiveness. Use of Master Regulator Inference Algorithm successfully predicts 56% synergism. For the same objective, RF and other approaches like a combination of network-based Laplacian regularized least square synergistic medication. A synergistic drug combination model was employed in a study to predict synergistic anticancer treatment combinations using RF. The authors successfully predicted the 28 synergistic anticancer combinations by using this model, which was created using gene expression profiles and multiple networks. They've identified three such pairings, though the rest could be significant as well. Similarly, using a dataset of 1540 antimalarial medication molecules, a machine learning approach dubbed Combination Synergy Estimation was used to forecast probable synergistic antimalarial combos [82, 83, 84].

6.5.6 Nanomedicine

Nanomedicine is a branch of molecular nanotechnology (MNT) concerned with the development of small biomechanical devices such as nanomachines and nanorobots. Nanometers, or one-millionth of a meter, are the unit of measurement for these devices. Nanomedicine encompasses three intertwined and more prevailing molecular techniques.

1. Nanoscale-structured materials and technologies are required for advanced biosensors and diagnostics, smart pharmaceuticals, targeted drug delivery, and immune-isolation therapy.
2. BiotechnologyBiotechnology, through genomes, proteomics, and artificially produced microorganisms, provides the benefits of molecular medicine.
3. Due to medical nanorobots and molecular machine systems, in vivo chromosomal replacement and individual cell surgery, as well as effective augmentation and development in natural physiological function, will be achievable.

Nanomedicine has the potential to revolutionize how people maintain their health and treat illness. It was realized that in vivo nanorobots would be able to travel straight toward the affected cells or target cells and fix whatever ailment is there at the cellular level without causing additional stress, suffering, or disfigurement [85].

Hypothesis-driven foundational nanomedicine research must be reproducible to support translational outcomes. Standards in the nanomedicine field have been developed to enhance experimental and documentation protocols to ensure reproducibility. Researchers may build on and compare their findings to previous studies, which is crucial for understanding design principles and underlying mechanisms in nanomedicine. This has the potential to expand the application of machine learning in research and forecasting results.

Nanomedicine research must be compared with literature, which needs not only reporting requirements but also proper controls, such as recent best clinical practices. Translational success needs to determine which criteria are most relevant for accurate comparison of nanomedicine studies and this should be a constant debate among nanomedicine researchers. This will necessitate arguing whether half-life, uptake, binding affinity, and endosomal escape efficiency, all are used to forecast translation as well as discovering new techniques to analyze and compare data to arrive at useful conclusions [86].

6.6 AI Tools for Drug Discovery Phase

6.6.1 Deep Chem

New methods for creating gold-standard datasets have been developed, which are particularly useful for DTI (drug target interaction) estimation. MoleculeNet is a platform developed by Wu et al. that serves as a standard for the machine learning approach utilized in molecular systems. QM7/QM7b, QM9, ESOL PDBbind, QM8, FreeSolv, and lipophilicity for regression data and MUV, BACE, PCBA, HIV, Tox21, ClinTox, BBBP, ToxCast, and SIDER for classification data are among the 700,000 chemicals in MoleculeNet's curated dataset. On the data, which was split into validation/training/test subsets, physical chemistry, quantum mechanics, biophysics, and physiology were all investigated. MoleculeNet also contained an open source which is implemented in a variety of well-known molecular featurization and ML technologies, as well as assessment measures.

MoleculeNet is now completely integrated into the open-source DeepChem framework. Aside from these gold-standard sets, attempts have been made to construct purpose-specific datasets, with the aid of the ZINC database which is served as a common resource. Because of the rising availability of open access to experimental information in repositories including

ChEMBL, ZINC, and PubChem, the data resources for VS research have altered substantially when compared to 10 years ago. New datasets created from these sources, like MUV and DUD, as well as new algorithmic methods, are exceedingly promising in terms of enhancing the potential of computational drug development [87].

DeepChem is an open-source application that uses deep learning in drug development. Drug development databases are extremely expensive and even if they are available, they are difficult to use because of ethical reasons. In an experiment, the author discovered that one-shot learning combined with DeepChem helps in the discovery of the drug. AI has already been employed by several research groups and companies to find therapeutic suggestions for COVID-19. COVID-19 medicines manufactured by AI are currently undergoing clinical testing and the approval process [88].

The important prerequisites for introducing machine learning into the process of drug discovery completely depend on reproducibility and traceability. For sharing machine learning models which predict critical pharma-relevant parameters, a modular and extensible software pipeline is being developed. The ATOM Modeling PipeLine prolongs the capabilities of DeepChem open-source library by supporting a range of machine learning and molecular featurization methodologies. DeepChem enables the creation of various machine learning models that aid in the prediction of tiny molecule properties. Although DeepChem Uncertainty Quantification (UQ) analysis may aid to detect model inaccuracies, the efficiency of UQ in filtering predictions may vary substantially, which depends on the dataset and model type [89].

6.6.2 Deep Neural Net QSAR

Neural networks were widely used in the 1990s to investigate quantitative structure-activity relationships. There are a lot of practical difficulties, which were overtaken by the more robust systems such as Random Forest (RF) and Support-vector Machine (SVM), that arose in the early year of the 2000s (like slowly working for huge tasks, difficulty in training, prone to over-fitting, etc.). Over the last 10 years, neural networks have a renaissance in the machine learning field as a result of new tactics for decreasing over-fitting, more effective training algorithms programs, and advances in hardware of the computer. On a collection of huge heterogeneous QSAR datasets gathered from the effort of Merck's drug discovery, Deep Neural Nets (DNNs), i.e., neurDNNs, may typically produce superior prospective predictions than RF. While it is still computationally expensive to train DNNs, Graphical Processing Units (GPUs) are used for this purpose [90].

Quantitative structure-activity relationship approaches are extensively utilized in the development process of drugs. QSAR model is a classification or regression type of model which uses information gathered from a molecule's chemical structure to predict its biological activity. These approaches are frequently utilized to select a list of probable compounds for further laboratory testing, as well as to help scientists comprehend how alterations in structure affect the biological function of the molecule. As a result, in the drug development process, generating accurate and interpretable QSAR models are crucial. Deep neural networks that are advanced have shown great results in a range of research fields like the pharmaceutical industry, for solving regression and classification problems [91].

The deep learning method has been getting the interest of the academic community with enormously successful performance in the development of QSAR models. It can choose features automatically from raw, high-dimensional, and heterogeneous chemical data, which is perhaps the most significant aspect differing from typical machine learning techniques. However, it also perfectly fits the modeling need for large-scale chemical molecule data. In a study, there is an artificial neural network to predict 19 different chemical and biological parameters of a compound. Another intriguing study uses massively multi-task neural networks to synthesize data from diverse biological sources to predict medication activity.

Ammar et al. proposed a particularly successful toolbox based on a similarity search that uses a Bayesian belief network (BBN) to identify new activities of molecules. Networks roots represent fragments, which are essential components of a compound, while leaves represent biological activity classes generated from training datasets on the one hand and the target compound on the other.

In addition, Chakravarti et al. used various types of Long Short-Term Memory (LSTM) neural networks to generate high-quality interpretable QSARs, which were trained directly using either classic SMILES codes or a novel linear molecular notation established as part of this research. Mustapha et al. introduced an extreme gradient boosting (Xgboost) algorithm to predict biological activity which is based on the compounds' molecular structure quantitative description. When compared to other machine learning algorithms, the system performed exceptionally well on seven separate datasets. More recently, a model combining Adaboost, Bagging, and Random Forest was created to improve the prediction performance of novel bioactive compounds in highly heterogeneous datasets [92].

6.6.3 DeepTox

Deep learning is based on cutting-edge ANN techniques and topologies, as well as the recent availability of supercomputers and large datasets. It encounters several distributed input representation levels and the higher levels represent the more abstract ideas. Due to the hierarchy of chemical properties construction, Mayr et al. suggested that deep learning offers a methodology for earlier prediction of toxicity. Furthermore, deep learning allows the determination of all harmful effects as well as highly informative chemical features in a single neural network.

The DeepTox pipeline was created to use deep learning for the prediction of toxicity. The chemical representations of the substances are first normalized using DeepTox. It then generates a vast number of chemical descriptors, which are fed into machine learning algorithms. DeepTox then trains, analyzes, and combines the best models into ensembles in the next stage. Finally, DeepTox forecasts new chemical toxicity in the Tox21 Data Challenge; DeepTox surpassed all other computational approaches. Deep learning beat a variety of other computer systems in toxicity prediction, including support-vector machines, naive Bayes, and random forests, according to the researchers [93, 94].

Advanced AI system algorithms look for similarities between chemicals or use input information to forecast toxicity. The Tox21 Data Challenge, sponsored by the National Institutes of Health, the Environmental Protection Agency (EPA), and the US Food and Drug Administration (FDA), looked into a variety of computational algorithms for toxicity prediction of chemicals and medicines. DeepTox, a machine learning algorithm, performs better than all other approaches by identifying dynamic and static features within molecules. Chemical descriptors, like molecular weight (MW) and Van de Graaff factor (VDF), were able to precisely predict the toxicity of molecules based on predefined features of 2500 toxicophore [95].

DeepTox is a computer toxicity model based on the deep learning approach that produced the best results rather than other computational techniques. Chemical descriptors for DeepTox models were obtained from a huge number of molecular descriptors assessed by utilizing off-the-shelf tools and JCompoundMapper. Numerous studies show the use of deep learning in the prediction of chemical properties. Lusci et al. determined the deep learning algorithms for predicting drug solubility in water. In this research, recursive neural network approaches were utilized to transform chemical structures into graphs [96].

6.6.4 Graph neural networks

Graph neural networks (GNNGNN) have been proposed as a viable modeling technique for predicting molecular properties, with multiple types of research demonstrating that GNN can outperform a standard descriptor-based approach. In research, based on 11 public datasets covering different property endpoints, the capacity and computational effectiveness of prediction models developed by using 8 machine learning algorithms, which include four descriptor-based models (XGBoost, SVM, DNN, and RF) and four graph-based models (GAT, GCN, Attentive FP, and MPNN), were extensively examined and compared.

The outcome reveals that descriptor-based models beat the graph-based models in terms of computational accuracy and efficiency prediction. SVM delivers better outcomes in most regression problems. Both XGBoost and RF can make reliable predictions for classification tasks and few graph-based models like GCN and Attentive FP produces impressive results for a percentage of large or multi-tasking datasets. In terms of processing cost, RF and XGBoost are the two most effective algorithms, and require less time to train a model even for a huge dataset. The SHAP approaches can efficiently investigate the knowledge of established domains for descriptor-based models through model interpretations [97].

In scientific applications such as physics, biomedical science, and computational chemistry, GNNs have demonstrated outstanding performance. GNNs have shown promise in essential tasks such as hit-finding and liability screening (i.e., predicting the binding affinity and toxicity of candidate therapeutic compounds, respectively) in early-phase drug development. There is currently a no drug discovery benchmark that addresses real-world issues concerning model reliability under distributional shifts. As a result, Han et al. introduced the CardioTox, a data benchmark that is compiled from 9K+ drug-like compounds from ChEMBL, NCATS, and FDA validation databases and is based on a real-world drug discovery challenge.

They produce additional chemical annotations and provide unique metrics to measure the models against real-world norms around the responsible deployment of GNN to assess model reliability. Overconfident mispredictions are often far from training data, according to the study. As a result, they have created distance-aware GNNs: GNN-SNGP (Spectral-normalized Neural Gaussian Processes). GNN-SNGPs aid in improving distance awareness, lowering overconfident mispredictions and producing more calibrated forecasts without sacrificing accuracy [98].

6.6.5 PotentialNet

The drug development process is a multiparameter optimization problem with enormous time scales. By using feature learning rather than feature engineering, the deep neural networks show their ability to outperform both knowledge-based and classic physics-based machine learning models which help in the prediction of molecular properties that are an essential part of the discovery of the drug.

The purpose of these models was to achieve best-in-class performance in terms of protein-ligand binding affinity. The fact that these deep neural networks set novel benchmarks in many ligand-based functions add to their effectiveness. Simultaneously, the Regression Enrichment Factor EF(R) is being created as a metric for evaluating the early chemical data computational model enrichment. A cross-validation technique based on structural homology clustering is devised, allowing for more accurate quantification of model generalizability, a crucial distinction between the goals of utilizing machine learning for the discovery of drugs and regular tasks of machine learning [99].

The Stanford Pande Lab and Merck Research Laboratories recently wrapped off year-long cooperation to systematically determine the performance of machine learning models in a pharmaceutical scenario. PotentialNet surpassed Random Forests in predicting a wide variety of chemical attributes important for drug development and discovery. They proved that PotentialNet gained a median of 0.16 $\Delta R2$ above Random Forests after temporally separating 31 test datasets including over two million chemical data points. The improved performance is due to many major technological advancements over old cheminformatic approaches, including the better expressivity of a graph convolution, the capacity to learn rather than hard code chemical characteristics, and the network's ability to transfer learning. This developed method can accelerate drug development and discovery [100].

6.7 AI in Drug Discovery Process

AI follows various phases in the drug discovery process which are described below. Figure 6.4 summarizes the drug discovery process.

6.7.1 Drug screening

In chemoinformatics, artificial intelligence has become a valuable resource. Several machine learning techniques for activity prediction have recently evolved, and they have quickly become an essential method for extracting

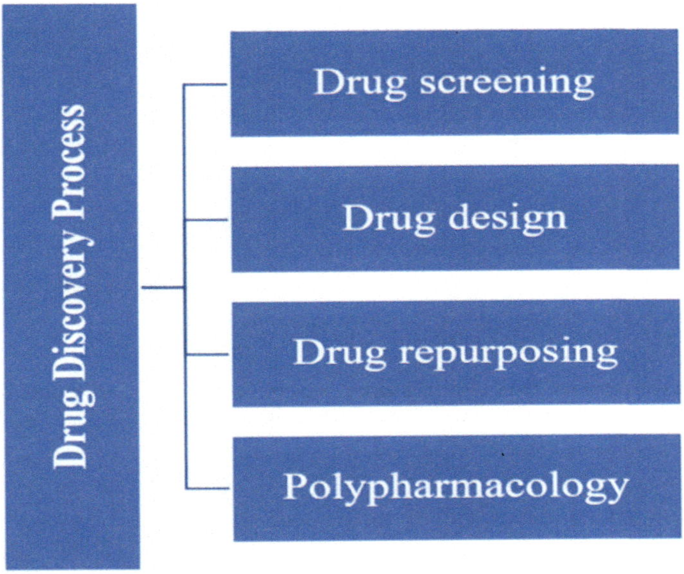

Figure 6.4 Schematic diagram shows the drug discovery process.

chemical information from massive compound data. These methods enable compound discovery to be automated to locate biologically active compounds with important features. ML is widely utilized in various domains, including chemoinformatics, due to its excellent accuracy and cost-effectiveness. The field's evolution has been hastened by recent computational advancements and the development of datasets for the storing of molecular structures and attributes. Combinations and diverse methodologies from classical machine learning, as well as complicated deep learning architectures, were applied by the researchers.

A common technique is to improve the biological activity prediction of multiple compounds by optimizing quantitative structure-activity relationship models. The prediction of chemical biological activity is an important area of research in chemoinformatics. The use of artificial intelligence for this type of activity is crucial for identifying molecules with desirable qualities. In comparison to a random sample, the goal is to select a subset of compounds from all those considered that have a higher probability of being bioactive. For successful utilization of machine learning in property prediction, it needs to access large datasets. Utilizing machine learning technologies like SVMs, RFs, and deep neural networks, compounds with desirable biological activity have been found (DNNs) [101].

Chemical compounds are heavily regulated in terms of their use and manufacturing. Chemical toxicity and adverse consequences resulting from chemical exposure are important regulatory considerations for a variety of businesses, including chemical, pharmaceutical, and food, because they can cause direct damage to animals, plants, humans, or the environment. Simultaneously, there is an increase in demand to employ silica computational models instead of traditional in vivo toxicity testing on testing animals (e.g., European Union REACH/3R principles, US government Tox21 and ToxCast, and so on). This is due to a variety of factors, including time efficiency and increased economic, as well as robustness and superior reliability to in vivo tests, particularly when the artificial intelligence (AI)-based models get introduced [102].

Commercially available chemicals do not have their toxicity data. HTS investigations, such as the US Environmental Protection Agency's (EPA) ToxCast program in partnership with the federal Tox21 research program, produce biological data that can be utilized to construct models for anticipating potential toxicity. Forecasting physicochemical properties and also exposure potential is essential. Experimental datasets obtained from EPI Suite get reanalyzed via modern cheminformatics methodologies utilization, which help to discover new QSPR models which are capable of generating computationally effective, open, and transparent HTS property predictions in support of environmental modeling activities. The six physicochemical parameters were determined by utilizing EPI Suite datasets like octanol-water partition coefficient (logP), boiling point (BP), water solubility (logS), melting point (MP), bioconcentration factor (logBCF), and vapor pressure (logVP). The new models may be used to quickly estimate physicochemical characteristics in an open-source HTS approach to feed chemical fate and toxicity prediction models in the environment [103].

6.7.2 Drug design

In the late 1980s and early 1990s, the emergence of high-powered computer capabilities ushered a novel era of computational design of drugs. A mechanism for analyzing de novo, emergent 3D data on protein therapeutic targets and delivering new compounds for synthesis was developed. Computer-aided drug creation was praised for its capability to create unique and customized molecular scaffolds with unrivalled selectivity and potency. Small compounds would be developed to interact with key residues in binding sites, leaving the medicinal chemist's designs irrational and biased. Hundreds, if not thousands, of molecules would not be required [104].

Machine learning records must be balanced and FAIR (findable, accessible, interoperable, and reusable; often referred to as "fully AI ready") and ALCOA (findable, accessible, interoperable, and reusable) (legible, attributable, original, contemporaneous, and accurate). It is a well-known contradiction that roughly 80% of research time on ML is consumed on the collection of data, processing, and cleaning, yet only 20% of the time is spent on algorithms. Tools like Kernel-based methodologies for drug–drug interactions, OSCAR for chemical text mining, CHEMDNER for identifying the drug name and chemical compound, and ChemSpot and tmChem for identifying chemicals in patents or ML to recognize similarities in sentences are useful in evidence-based medication, which aid to save time during the process of data collection.

Common vector space illustration is used for the classification and recognition of patterns, and it facilitates the sorting of biological data into machine learning for the discovery of the drug. It is not appropriate always, particularly in situations requiring small compounds and vectors of various sizes. The Simplified Molecular-Input Line-Entry System (SMILES) illustrates the various types of atoms and their connections. Extended-connectivity fingerprints indicate a molecule's topology and can be used for structural activities. Nuclear charges and their locations are displayed in the Coulomb matrix. Symmetry functions depict the structural features such as angles and distances; grid feature displays structural information of the drug with their receptor as well as intermolecular forces, making it applicable to predict affinities of binding. Weave featurization summarizes (in vector form) the information about atoms pairs, like their distance, structure of the ring, and graph convolution, which represents (in vector form) the valence, sort, and hybridization of atoms surrounding every center.

Better techniques to depict molecular structures are kernel functions, labeled graphs, trees, fingerprints, and molecular holograms. Fingerprints are 100 to 1000-bit strings that are encoded as binary vectors (1/0). They encrypt the yes or no options for certain molecular features, such as the presence of a side chain [105].

6.7.3 Drug repurposing

Drug repurposing (known as drug repositioning, redirecting, reprofiling, and drug rediscovery) is a policy for discovering new therapeutic uses for authorized drugs in medical indications other than those for which they were approved originally. Medication repurposing has various advantages over new drug development, including the opportunity to accelerate the discovery process and skip safety testing during clinical development and testing. Drug repurposing allows for the avoidance of safety testing in preclinical models and humans if the safety study for the original indication has been completed. It is used to indicate the compatibility of the dose with the novel usage, potentially cutting overall development costs.

In recent years, several computer algorithms for a more systematic drug repurposing procedure have been created. For in silico drug repurposing, common data sources involve electronic health records, gene expression response profiles or genome-wide association analyses, route maps, chemical structures, target binding assays, and other phenotypic profiling data. Because of its capacity to anticipate the binding conformation of small-molecule ligands to the proper target-binding site, molecular docking is a commonly utilized in silico approach in structure-based drug design. The downside of molecular docking is that many target proteins' 3D structures have yet to be discovered, which is essential to implement docking simulations. Furthermore, the precision of docking-based techniques is reduced when the number of proteins known as ligands is insufficient [106].

Drug research and development is a long and money-consuming process. To circumvent these limitations, computers are employed to develop drugs, a technique known as in silico drug design. To undertake docking studies, a variety of instruments and software are available, and the parameters allow the drug and target structure to be changed to reach the desired outcome. CADD is an area that merges molecular biology, immunology, biochemistry, nanotechnology, and computer science. Various publicly accessible databases require storing protein and genetic data in the form of a sequence. Some databases store medication and structural information that is utilized for docking and biosimulation research. The target for the therapeutic molecule should be done on the structural form and which provide genetic information of an organism. This is a time-saving approach because the outcomes are delivered within a few minutes of the input being entered, and they are rather dependable [107].

6.7.4 Polypharmacology

Polypharmacology is a relatively new branch of pharmacological science that investigates these occurrences. Polypharmacology's purpose is to find tiny chemical molecules that have off-target functions. Polypharmacology was offered as a powerful and feasible alternative paradigm for designing adaptable medicinal compounds to meet urgent medical needs, and it has progressed in that direction. Higher efficacy, lower resistance, and a better safety profile are all benefits of medications that can regulate many biological targets at the same time, which can be accomplished with polypharmacological monotherapies or combination therapies. Drug repurposing and drug resistance are two areas where polypharmacology comes in handy.

Sildenafil (Viagra) was originally discovered to treat hypertension and ischemic heart disease before becoming an important factor in the treatment of erectile dysfunction. Poziotinib and ceritinib have recently been repurposed to cure EGFR exon-20 insertions in NSCLC patients and ALK-negative in patients with lung cancer. PROTAC (proteolysis targeting chimera), BsMAb (bispecific monoclonal antibody), and Chimeric antigen receptor T cell are only a few examples of multi-targeted medicines that have benefited from the polypharmacology approach (CAR-T) [108].

Li et al. demonstrated how to use KinomeX, an artificial intelligence-powered at the online stage that utilizes deep neural networks to determine polypharmacology in kinases based on their chemical structures. DNN, which was trained to utilize over 14,000 bioactivity data points obtained from over 300 kinases, is used in this platform. As a result, it can be used to look into a drug's overall selectivity for the kinase family and specific kinase subfamilies, which can help with the development of new chemical modifiers. In this research, NVP-BHG712 was used as a model molecule to anticipate its principal targets and off-targets with reasonable accuracy [109].

6.8 Future of Robotics and AI

In the medical field, expediting supply delivery and cleaning, robots are revolutionizing surgery and freeing up time for doctors to spend with patients. Robots are now utilized in clinical settings to assist health personnel and improve patient care, in addition to operating rooms. During the COVID-19 pandemic, hospitals and clinics began using robots for a far broader range of jobs to help decrease pathogen exposure. It has become evident that health robotics' operational savings and risk reduction give benefits in a variety of areas.

However, AI has advanced to the point that it can now automate many of a physician's laborious, repetitive procedures, for example, it shortens the time it takes to evaluate a bacterial swab and provide an appropriate antibiotic. This frees up time and mental resources for the physician to focus on higher-level tasks like patient education and clinical assessment. The possibilities for AI technology in healthcare are diverse and fascinating. Insurance verification, skin cancer diagnosis, test result analysis, and medical record data analysis are all areas where AI applications are being investigated by healthcare providers.

6.9 Conclusion

Robotics and AI are in huge demand in the development and design of the drug. Nowadays, AI and robotics are used in the field of research and development, which help in the management of time, cost-effectiveness, and uses technologies that give accuracy in the outcomes. There is a vast variety of AI tools that are used in the drug discovery phase which is discussed in detail in the chapter such as DeepChem, Deep Neural Net QSAR, DeepTox, and Neural Graph Fingerprints and PotentialNet. AI also helps in the process of drug discovery through drug screening, designing, repurposing, and polypharmacology. The chapter also focuses on the various pharmaceutical product development which is utilized in the treatment of various diseases such as nanorobots, controlled insulin release, combination drug delivery, and nanomedicine. Robotics and AI have a great future ahead because it helps in the research field.

Acknowledgments

For the successful completion of this study, all of the writers of this publication are grateful to their respective Departments/Universities.

References

[1] Paul, D., Sanap, G., Shenoy, S., Kalyane, D., Kalia, K. and Tekade, R. K., 2021. Artificial intelligence in drug discovery and development. *Drug Discovery Today*, *26*(1), p.80.

[2] Blasiak, A., Khong, J. and Kee, T., 2020. CURATE. AI: optimizing personalized medicine with artificial intelligence. *SLAS TECHNOLOGY: Translating Life Sciences Innovation*, *25*(2), pp.95-105.

[3] Mak K.-K., Pichika M. R. Artificial intelligence in drug development: present status and future prospects. *Drug Discovery Today.* 2019;24:773–780.

[4] Sellwood, M. A., Ahmed, M., Segler, M. H. and Brown, N., 2018. Artificial intelligence in drug discovery. *Future medicinal chemistry*, *10*(17), pp.2025-2028.
[5] Zhu H. Big data and artificial intelligence modeling for drug discovery. *Annu. Rev. Pharmacol. Toxicol.* 2020;60:573–589.
[6] Ciallella H. L., Zhu H. Advancing computational toxicology in the big data era by artificial intelligence: data-driven and mechanism-driven modeling for chemical toxicity. *Chem. Res. Toxicol.* 2019;32:536–547.
[7] Zang, Q., Mansouri, K., Williams, A. J., Judson, R. S., Allen, D. G., Casey, W. M. and Kleinstreuer, N. C., 2017. In silico prediction of physicochemical properties of environmental chemicals using molecular fingerprints and machine learning. *Journal of chemical information and modeling*, *57*(1), pp.36-49.
[8] Yang, X., Wang, Y., Byrne, R., Schneider, G. and Yang, S., 2019. Concepts of artificial intelligence for computer-assisted drug discovery. *Chemical reviews*, *119*(18), pp.10520-10594.
[9] Hessler, G. and Baringhaus, K. H., 2018. Artificial intelligence in drug design. *Molecules*, *23*(10), p.2520.
[10] Ramesh, A. N., Kambhampati, C., Monson, J. R. and Drew, P. J., 2004. Artificial intelligence in medicine. *Annals of the Royal College of Surgeons of England*, *86*(5), p.334.
[11] https://github.com/deepchem/deepchem
[12] http://www.bioinf.jku.at/research/DeepTox
[13] https://github.com/Merck/DeepNeuralNet-QSAR
[14] https://pubs.acs.org/doi/full/10.1021/acscentsci.8b00507
[15] http://hitdexter2.zbh.uni-hamburg.de/
[16] https://zenodo.org/record/1481731
[17] https://deepmind.com/blog/alphafold
[18] http://refhub.elsevier.com/S0016-5107(20)34466-7/sref1_
[19] http://refhub.elsevier.com/S0016-5107(20)34466-7/sref2_
[20] http://refhub.elsevier.com/S0016-5107(20)34466-7/sref7
[21] http://refhub.elsevier.com/S0016-5107(20)34466-7/sref8
[22] http://refhub.elsevier.com/S0016-5107(20)34466-7/sref10
[23] http://refhub.elsevier.com/S0016-5107(20)34466-7/sref14
[24] http://refhub.elsevier.com/S0016-5107(20)34466-7/sref16
[25] Piñero, J., Ramírez-Anguita, J. M., Saüch-Pitarch, J., Ronzano, F., Centeno, E., Sanz, F. and Furlong, L. I., 2020. The DisGeNET knowledge platform for disease genomics: 2019 update. *Nucleic acids research*, *48*(D1), pp.D845-D855.

[26] Vasaikar, S. V., P. Straub, J. Wang, and B. Zhang (2018) LinkedOmics: analyzing multi-omics data within and across 32 cancer types. Nucleic Acids Res. 46: D956-D963.

[27] Meyers, R. M., Bryan, J. G., McFarland, J. M., Weir, B. A., Sizemore, A. E., Xu, H., Dharia, N. V., Montgomery, P. G., Cowley, G. S., Pantel, S. and Goodale, A., 2017. Computational correction of copy number effect improves specificity of CRISPR–Cas9 essentiality screens in cancer cells. *Nature genetics*, *49*(12), pp.1779-1784.

[28] Tsherniak, A., F. Vazquez, P. G. Montgomery, B. A. Weir, G. Kryukov, G. S. Cowley, S. Gill, W. F. Harrington, S. Pantel, J. M. Krill-Burger, R. M. Meyers, L. Ali, A. Goodale, Y. Lee, G. Jiang, J. Hsiao, W. F. J. Gerath, S. Howell, E. Merkel, M. Ghandi, L. A. Garraway, D. E. Root, T. R. Golub, J. S. Boehm, and W. C. Hahn (2017) Defining a cancer dependency map. Cell. 170: 564-576.e16.

[29] Wang, Y., S. Zhang, F. Li, Y. Zhou, Y. Zhang, Z. Wang, R. Zhang, J. Zhu, Y. Ren, Y. Tan, C. Qin, Y. Li, X. Li, Y. Chen, and F. Zhu (2020) Therapeutic target database 2020: enriched resource for facilitating research and early development of targeted therapeutics. Nucleic Acids Res. 48: D1031-D1041.

[30] Camarillo, D. B., Krummel, T. M. and Salisbury Jr, J. K., 2004. Robotic technology in surgery: past, present, and future. *The American Journal of Surgery*, *188*(4), pp.2-15.

[31] A robot with improved absolute positioning accuracy for CT guided stereotactic brain surgery.*Kwoh YS, Hou J, Jonckheere EA, Hayati SIEEE Trans Biomed Eng. 1988 Feb; 35(2):153-60.*

[32] Beasley, R. A., 2012. Medical robots: current systems and research directions. *Journal of Robotics, 2012.*

[33] Song, E. K. and Seon, J. K., 2012. Computer assisted orthopedic surgery in TKA. *Recent Advances in Hip and Knee Arthroplasty.*

[34] http://surgrob.blogspot.com/2008/12/integrated-surgical-systems-inc.html

[35] M. Hoeckelmann, I. Rudas, P. Fiorini, F. Kirchner, and T. Haidegger, "Current capabilities and development potential in surgical robotics," *International Journal of Advanced Robotic Systems*, vol. 12, no. 5, p. 61, 2015.

[36] F. Pugin, P. Bucher, and P. Morel, "History of robotic surgery: from AESOP® and ZEUS® to da Vinci®," *Journal of Visceral Surgery*, vol. 148, no. 5, pp. e3–e8, 2011.

[37] M. Hoeckelmann, I. Rudas, P. Fiorini, F. Kirchner, and T. Haidegger, "Current capabilities and development potential in surgical robotics," *International Journal of Advanced Robotic Systems*, vol. 12, no. 5, p. 61, 2015.
[38] I. Gibbs, "Frameless image-guided intracranial and extracranial radiosurgery using the Cyberknife^{TM} robotic system," *Cancer/Radiothérapie*, vol. 10, no. 5, pp. 283–287, 2006.
[39] W. Siebert, S. Mai, R. Kober, and P. Heeckt, "Technique and first clinical results of robot-assisted total knee replacement," *The Knee*, vol. 9, no. 3, pp. 173–180, 2002.
[40] K. Cleary, A. Melzer, V. Watson, G. Kronreif, and D. Stoianovici, "Interventional robotic systems: applications and technology state of the art," *Minimally Invasive Therapy & Allied Technologies*, vol. 15, no. 2, pp. 101–113, 2006.
[41] D. Stoianovici, K. Cleary, A. Patriciu et al., "Acubot: a robot for radiological interventions," *IEEE Transactions on Robotics and Automation*, vol. 19, no. 5, pp. 927–930, 2003.
[42] M. Bucolo, A. Buscarino, A. Spinosa, G. Stella, and L. Fortuna, "Human machine models for remote control of ultrasound scan equipment," in *Proceedings of the IEEE International Conference on Human-Machine Systems (ICHMS)*, pp. 1–6, Rome, Italy, April 2020.
[43] J. Kettenbach and G. Kronreif, "Robotic systems for percutaneous needle-guided interventions," *Minimally Invasive Therapy & Allied Technologies*, vol. 24, no. 1, pp. 45–53, 2014.
[44] M. Lefranc and J. Peltier, "Evaluation of the ROSA^{TM} Spine robot for minimally invasive surgical procedures," *Expert Review of Medical Devices*, vol. 13, no. 10, pp. 899–906, 2016.
[45] https://www.zimmerbiomet.com/en/products-and-solutions/zb-edge/robotics/rosa-brain.html
[46] D. Maberley, M. Beelen, J. Smit et al., "A comparison of robotic and manual surgery for internal limiting membrane peeling," *Graefe's Archive for Clinical and Experimental Ophthalmology*, vol. 258, no. 4, pp. 773–778, 2020.
[47] Dogangil, G., Davies, B. L., & Rodriguez y Baena, F. (2010). A review of medical roboticsfor minimally invasive soft tissue surgery. Proceedings of the Institution of Mechanical Engineers. Part H, Journal of Engineering in Medicine, 224(5), 653–679. doi:10.1243/09544119JEIM591 PMID:20718269

[48] Beasley, R. A. (2012). Medical robots: Current systems and research directions. Journal of Robotics, 2012, 1–14. doi:10.1155/2012/401613
[49] Schulz, A. P., Seide, K., Queitsch, C., von Haugwitz, A., Meiners, J., Kienast, B., & Jürgens, C. et al. (2007). Results of total hip replacement using the Robodoc surgical assistant system: Clinical outcome and evaluation of complications for 97 procedures. International Journal of Medical Robotics and Computer Assisted Surgery, 3(4), 301–306. doi:10.1002/rcs.161 PMID:18000945
[50] Ballantyne, G. H. (2002). Robotic surgery, telerobotic surgery, telepresence, and telementoring. Surgical Endoscopy, 16(10), 1389–1402. doi:10.1007/s00464-001-8283-7 PMID:12140630
[51] Stark, M., Benhidjeb, T., Gidaro, S. and Morales, E. R., 2012. The future of telesurgery: a universal system with haptic sensation. *Journal of the Turkish German Gynecological Association*, *13*(1), p.74.
[52] Gomes, P., 2011. Surgical robotics: Reviewing the past, analysing the present, imagining the future. *Robotics and Computer-Integrated Manufacturing*, *27*(2), pp.261-266.
[53] https://www.zs.com/insights/is-data-science-the-treatment-for-inefficiencies-in-clinical-trial-operations
[54] Deore, A. B., Dhumane, J. R., Wagh, R. and Sonawane, R., 2019. The stages of drug discovery and development process. *Asian Journal of Pharmaceutical Research and Development*, *7*(6), pp.62-67.
[55] Costa, G. G., Cardoso, K. C., Del Bem, L. E., Lima, A. C., Cunha, M. A., de Campos-Leite, L., Vicentini, R., Papes, F., Moreira, R. C., Yunes, J. A. and Campos, F. A., 2010. Transcriptome analysis of the oil-rich seed of the bioenergy crop Jatropha curcas L. *BMC genomics*, *11*(1), pp.1-9.
[56] Winkler, H., 2003. Target validation requirements in the pharmaceutical industry. *Targets*, *2*(3), pp.69-71.
[57] Hutson, M., 2019. AI protein-folding algorithms solve structures faster than ever. *Nature*.
[58] Bhatt, T. K. and Nimesh, S. eds., 2021. *The Design and Development of Novel Drugs and Vaccines: Principles and Protocols*. Academic Press.
[59] Pound, P. and Ritskes-Hoitinga, M., 2018. Is it possible to overcome issues of external validity in preclinical animal research? Why most animal models are bound to fail. *Journal of translational medicine*, *16*(1), pp.1-8.
[60] Bender, A. and Cortés-Ciriano, I., 2021. Artificial intelligence in drug discovery: what is realistic, what are illusions? Part 1: ways to make

an impact, and why we are not there yet. *Drug discovery today*, *26*(2), pp.511-524.

[61] Schneider, G. and Clark, D. E., 2019. Angew. Chem. *Int. Ed.*, *58*, pp.10792-10803.

[62] Singh, A. V., Ansari, M. H. D., Laux, P. and Luch, A., 2019. Micro-nanorobots: important considerations when developing novel drug delivery platforms. *Expert opinion on drug delivery*, *16*(11), pp.1259-1275.

[63] Li, J., de Ávila, B. E. F., Gao, W., Zhang, L. and Wang, J., 2017. Micro/nanorobots for biomedicine: Delivery, surgery, sensing, and detoxification. *Science Robotics*, *2*(4).

[64] Felfoul, O., Mohammadi, M., Taherkhani, S., De Lanauze, D., Xu, Y. Z., Loghin, D., Essa, S., Jancik, S., Houle, D., Lafleur, M. and Gaboury, L., 2016. Magneto-aerotactic bacteria deliver drug-containing nanoliposomes to tumour hypoxic regions. *Nature nanotechnology*, *11*(11), pp.941-947.

[65] Li, J., de Ávila, B. E. F., Gao, W., Zhang, L. and Wang, J., 2017. Micro/nanorobots for biomedicine: Delivery, surgery, sensing, and detoxification. *Science Robotics*, *2*(4).

[66] Wang, W., Li, S., Mair, L., Ahmed, S., Huang, T. J. and Mallouk, T. E., 2014. Acoustic propulsion of nanorod motors inside living cells. *Angewandte Chemie International Edition*, *53*(12), pp.3201-3204.

[67] Kei Cheang, U., Lee, K., Julius, A. A. and Kim, M. J., 2014. Multiple-robot drug delivery strategy through coordinated teams of microswimmers. *Applied physics letters*, *105*(8), p.083705.

[68] da Silva Luz, G. V., Barros, K. V. G., de Araújo, F. V. C., da Silva, G. B., da Silva, P. A. F., Condori, R. C. I. and Mattos, L., 2016. Nanorobotics in drug delivery systems for treatment of cancer: a review. *J Mat Sci Eng A*, *6*, pp.167-180.

[69] Hussan Reza, K., Asiwarya, G., Radhika, G. and Bardalai, D., 2011. Nanorobots: The future Trend of Drug Delivery and Therapeutics. *International Journal of Pharmaceutical Sciences Review and Research*, *10*(1), pp.60-8.

[70] Freitas Jr, R. A., 2009. Medical Nanorobotics: The Long-Term Goal for Nanomedicine. *Nanomedicine design of particles, sensors, motors, implants, robots and devices. Artech House, Norwood Ma*, pp.367-392.

[71] Tewabe, A., Abate, A., Tamrie, M., Seyfu, A. and Siraj, E. A., 2021. Targeted drug delivery—from magic bullet to nanomedicine: Principles, challenges, and future perspectives. *Journal of Multidisciplinary Healthcare*, *14*, p.1711.

[72] Freitas, R. A., 2006. Pharmacytes: An ideal vehicle for targeted drug delivery. *Journal of Nanoscience and Nanotechnology*, *6*(9-10), pp.2769-2775.

[73] Hariharan, R. and Manohar, J., 2010, December. Nanorobotics as medicament:(Perfect solution for cancer). In *INTERACT-2010* (pp. 4-7). IEEE.

[74] Sandhiya, S., Dkhar, S. A. and Surendiran, A., 2009. Emerging trends of nanomedicine–an overview. *Fundamental & clinical pharmacology*, *23*(3), pp.263-269.

[75] Chaudhari, P. M. and Shekokare, H. L., PHARMACEUTICAL SCIENCES.

[76] Eshaghian-Wilner, M. M. ed., 2009. *Bio-inspired and nanoscale integrated computing* (Vol. 1). John Wiley & Sons.

[77] Hassanzadeh, P., Atyabi, F. and Dinarvand, R., 2019. The significance of artificial intelligence in drug delivery system design. *Advanced drug delivery reviews*, *151*, pp.169-190.

[78] Colombo, S., 2020. Applications of artificial intelligence in drug delivery and pharmaceutical development. In *Artificial Intelligence in Healthcare* (pp. 85-116). Academic Press.

[79] https://www.santannapisa.it/en/news/implantable-robots-and-magnetic-capsules-diabetes-treatment-study-published-science-robotics

[80] Alfonta, L., 2021. Bioelectrochemistry and the Singularity Point "I Robot"?. *Israel Journal of Chemistry*, *61*(1-2), pp.60-67.

[81] https://www.emergency-live.com/news/implantable-robots-and-magnetic-capsules-the-new-frontier-of-insulin-infusion-in-diabetics/

[82] Paul, D., Sanap, G., Shenoy, S., Kalyane, D., Kalia, K. and Tekade, R. K., 2021. Artificial intelligence in drug discovery and development. *Drug Discovery Today*, *26*(1), p.80.

[83] Tsigelny, I. F., 2019. Artificial intelligence in drug combination therapy. *Briefings in bioinformatics*, *20*(4), pp.1434-1448.

[84] Li, X., Xu, Y., Cui, H., Huang, T., Wang, D., Lian, B., Li, W., Qin, G., Chen, L. and Xie, L., 2017. Prediction of synergistic anti-cancer drug combinations based on drug target network and drug induced gene expression profiles. *Artificial intelligence in medicine*, *83*, pp.35-43.

[85] Patel, G. M., Patel, G. C., Patel, R. B., Patel, J. K. and Patel, M., 2006. Nanorobot: a versatile tool in nanomedicine. *Journal of drug targeting*, *14*(2), pp.63-67.

[86] Richardson, J. J. and Caruso, F., 2020. Nanomedicine toward 2040. *Nano letters*, *20*(3), pp.1481-1482.

[87] Rifaioglu, A. S., Atas, H., Martin, M. J., Cetin-Atalay, R., Atalay, V. and Doğan, T., 2019. Recent applications of deep learning and machine intelligence on in silico drug discovery: methods, tools and databases. *Briefings in bioinformatics*, *20*(5), pp.1878-1912.

[88] Arora, K. and Bist, A. S., 2020. Artificial intelligence based drug discovery techniques for covid-19 detection. *Aptisi Transactions On Technopreneurship (ATT)*, *2*(2), pp.120-126.

[89] Minnich, A. J., McLoughlin, K., Tse, M., Deng, J., Weber, A., Murad, N., Madej, B. D., Ramsundar, B., Rush, T., Calad-Thomson, S. and Brase, J., 2020. AMPL: a data-driven modeling pipeline for drug discovery. *Journal of chemical information and modeling*, *60*(4), pp.1955-1968.

[90] Ma, J., Sheridan, R. P., Liaw, A., Dahl, G. E. and Svetnik, V., 2015. Deep neural nets as a method for quantitative structure–activity relationships. *Journal of chemical information and modeling*, *55*(2), pp.263-274.

[91] Xu, Y., 2022. Deep Neural Networks for QSAR. In *Artificial Intelligence in Drug Design* (pp. 233-260). Humana, New York, NY.

[92] Hu, S., Chen, P., Gu, P. and Wang, B., 2020. A deep learning-based chemical system for QSAR prediction. *IEEE journal of biomedical and health informatics*, *24*(10), pp.3020-3028.

[93] Mayr, A., Klambauer, G., Unterthiner, T. and Hochreiter, S., 2016. DeepTox: toxicity prediction using deep learning. *Frontiers in Environmental Science*, *3*, p.80.

[94] Batool, M., Ahmad, B. and Choi, S., 2019. A structure-based drug discovery paradigm. *International journal of molecular sciences*, *20*(11), p.2783.

[95] Yang, X., Wang, Y., Byrne, R., Schneider, G. and Yang, S., 2019. Concepts of artificial intelligence for computer-assisted drug discovery. *Chemical reviews*, *119*(18), pp.10520-10594.

[96] Zhao, L., Ciallella, H. L., Aleksunes, L. M. and Zhu, H., 2020. Advancing computer-aided drug discovery (CADD) by big data and data-driven machine learning modeling. *Drug discovery today*.

[97] Jiang, D., Wu, Z., Hsieh, C. Y., Chen, G., Liao, B., Wang, Z., Shen, C., Cao, D., Wu, J. and Hou, T., 2021. Could graph neural networks learn better molecular representation for drug discovery? A comparison study of descriptor-based and graph-based models. *Journal of cheminformatics*, *13*(1), pp.1-23.

[98] Han, K., Lakshminarayanan, B. and Liu, J., 2021. Reliable Graph Neural Networks for Drug Discovery Under Distributional Shift. *arXiv preprint arXiv:2111.12951.*

[99] Feinberg, E. N., Sur, D., Wu, Z., Husic, B. E., Mai, H., Li, Y., Sun, S., Yang, J., Ramsundar, B. and Pande, V. S., 2018. PotentialNet for molecular property prediction. *ACS central science*, *4*(11), pp.1520-1530.

[100] https://medium.com/@pandelab/step-change-improvement-in-molecular-property-prediction-with-potentialnet-f431ffa32a2c

[101] Correia, J., Resende, T., Baptista, D. and Rocha, M., 2019, June. Artificial intelligence in biological activity prediction. In *International Conference on Practical Applications of Computational Biology & Bioinformatics* (pp. 164-172). Springer, Cham.

[102] Pérez Santín, E., Rodríguez Solana, R., González García, M., García Suárez, M. D. M., Blanco Díaz, G. D., Cima Cabal, M. D., Moreno Rojas, J. M. and López Sánchez, J. I., 2021. Toxicity prediction based on artificial intelligence: A multidisciplinary overview. *Wiley Interdisciplinary Reviews: Computational Molecular Science*, p.e1516.

[103] Zang, Q., Mansouri, K., Williams, A. J., Judson, R. S., Allen, D. G., Casey, W. M. and Kleinstreuer, N. C., 2017. In silico prediction of physicochemical properties of environmental chemicals using molecular fingerprints and machine learning. *Journal of chemical information and modeling*, *57*(1), pp.36-49.

[104] Jordan, A. M., 2018. Artificial intelligence in drug design—the storm before the calm?. *ACS medicinal chemistry letters*, *9*(12), pp.1150-1152.

[105] Arabi, A. A., 2021. Artificial intelligence in drug design: algorithms, applications, challenges and ethics. *Future Drug Discovery*, (0), p.FDD59.

[106] Tanoli, Z., Vähä-Koskela, M. and Aittokallio, T., 2021. Artificial intelligence, machine learning, and drug repurposing in cancer. *Expert opinion on drug discovery*, pp.1-13.

[107] Selvaraj, G., Kaliamurthi, S., Peslherbe, G. H. and Wei, D. Q., Application of Artificial Intelligence in Drug Repurposing: A Mini-Review.

[108] Chaudhari, R., Fong, L. W., Tan, Z., Huang, B. and Zhang, S., 2020. An up-to-date overview of computational polypharmacology in modern drug discovery. *Expert opinion on drug discovery*, *15*(9), pp.1025-1044.
[109] Li, Z., Li, X., Liu, X., Fu, Z., Xiong, Z., Wu, X., Tan, X., Zhao, J., Zhong, F., Wan, X. and Luo, X., 2019. KinomeX: a web application for predicting kinome-wide polypharmacology effect of small molecules. *Bioinformatics*, *35*(24), pp.5354-5356.

Author Biography:

Ms. Akanksha Sharma (Assistant Professor)

Akanksha Sharma is an Assistant Professor at Monad College of Pharmacy, Monad University, Hapur. She has completed B. Pharm from Kashi Institute of Pharmacy, Varanasi in 2018. She has completed M. Pharm (Pharmaceutics) from Galgotias University in 2020. She has published research and review papers, mostly in the Scopus indexed journal. She is a good motivator and provides guidance to students for being a good Pharmacy Professional, Researcher, and to be more human.

Mr. Ashish Verma

Ashish Verma is student at School of pharmacy, Monad University, Hapur. He has completed B. Pharm. from Kashi Institute of Pharmacy, Varanasi in 2018. He always works with students at ground level to understand along with utilization of different basic concepts of pharmacy in real life. He is a good motivator and provides guidance to students for being a good Pharmacy Professional, Researcher, and to be more human.

Rishabha Malviya

Rishabha Malviya is presently working as an Associate Professor at Galgotias University in the Department of Pharmacy, School of Medical and Allied Sciences Greater Noida, UP, India. He completed his Ph.D. from Uttarakhand Technical University, Dehradun, India. He completed his M. Pharm in Pharmaceutics (2008âĂŞ2010) and B. Pharm (2004âĂŞ2008) from U.P technical university, Lucknow, India. He has published more than 115 articles in different international and national journals. He has published 5 books and 14 book chapters and also has some patents. He has guided 25 M. Pharm students for their respective project work. He is serving as editorial board member and reviewer of various international and national journals.

Aditi Singh

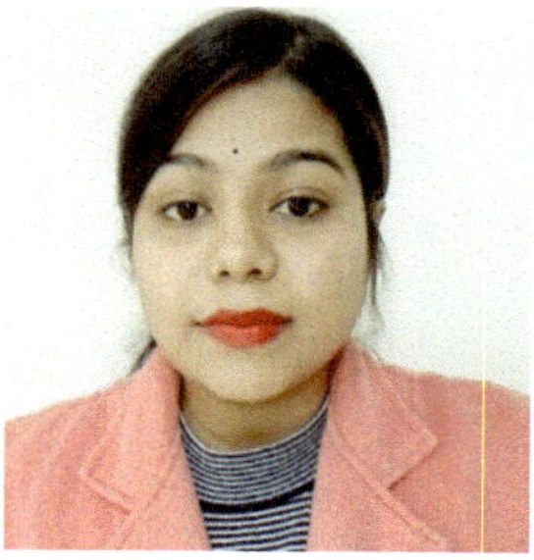

Aditi Singh is an Assistant Professor at Ashoka Institute of Pharmacy. She has completed B. Pharm from Kashi Institute of Pharmacy, Varanasi in 2018. She received gold medal in M. Pharm (2020) from Amity university, Lucknow. She also worked as an assistant professor with Future Group of Institution Bareilly for one year. She is a good motivator and provides guidance to students for being a good Pharmacy Professional, Researcher, and to be more human.

7

Pharmaceutical Packaging: New Impulse through Artificial Intelligence

Smriti Ojha[1*], Anubhav Anand[2], Manoj Saini[3], Sudhanshu Mishra[1], and Kamal Dua[4]

[1]Department of Pharmaceutical Science and Technology,
Madan Mohan Malviya University of Technology, India
[2]Department of Pharmaceutics,
Hygia Institute of Pharmaceutical Education and Research, India
[3]Department of General Medicine,
All India Institute of Medical Science, India
[4]Faculty of Health, Australian Research Centre in Complementary and Integrative Medicine, University of Technology Sydney, Australia
*Corresponding Author: Department of Pharmaceutical Science and Technology, Madan Mohan Malviya University of Technology, Gorakhpur, Uttar Pradesh, India, 273015 EMail: smritiojha23@gmail.com

Abstract

Packaging is an integral component of the pharmaceutical industry. Today, the traditional manufacturing process appears to be risky, as it entails the possibility of human error. Furthermore, in terms of labor costs, it is not very cost-effective. In the healthcare and pharmaceutical industries, artificial intelligence has enormous promise. Machine learning and computer vision are slowly becoming viable alternatives to traditional methods for quality control. Cognitive technology and robotics automation is a world that is both disruptive and transformative. Artificial intelligence and robotic process automation have firmly established themselves in various worldwide businesses, including packaging. Artificial intelligence's expansion in packaging and distribution is no less exciting, given that it is a crucial component and contributor to the rise of intelligent warehouses. Different AI-assisted solutions, including robots, are used in many aspects, from product designing to packaging and distribution.

Keywords: Artificial intelligence, pharmaceutical packaging, robotic packaging, labor cost.

7.1 Introduction

Despite rapid technical advancements, pharma companies still confront many challenges in producing medications and batches. By 2027, the worldwide packaging business will reach $1,652.28 billion, with the pharmaceutical packaging market expected to reach $144.23 billion [1]. Pharmaceutical industries seek new ways to react to the changing market conditions; therefore, they take AI intentionally on their schedule. Bots (robotic process automation) design more valuable processes, make more accurate predictions, and considerably decrease development costs. There are five challenges for pharmaceutical packaging [2]:

a) To ensure the pharmaceutical product's quality
b) To propose safe products
c) To maintain efficiency and upgrade product performance
d) To respond to challenges of the rapidly changing industry
e) To test the limit of artificial intelligence

The primary method remains unchanged in AI packaging, and the formulation parameters are still certified by GMP standards. The only differences are the process development tool and the requisite hardware [3]. Visual inspection during batch manufacturing and packaging, for example, should be undertaken to eliminate human-made errors. Artificial intelligence helps in the development of better medications and therapies. Bots, or robotic process automation, can significantly reduce development costs, design more efficient processes, and improve forecast accuracy. As a result, the packaging business now has more prospects. Machine learning is a crucial component of the "Internet of Things" megatrends like data collecting and Internet security. Artificial intelligence (AI) platforms for the pharmaceutical inspection system use deep learning and machine learning models and reduce false reject rates with reasonable accuracy [4]. These techniques are used for particle inspection, detecting cosmetic defects, and reducing objects' misclassification. AI has shown to be a reliable and successful technology for leading the charge. Increased demand for cartons, consumer goods, and flexible packaging are just a few reasons the packaging sector adopts AI [5]. Today, it is all about giving organizations a competitive edge, and AI and machine learning make growing operations less hazardous and more efficient. Artificial intelligence has enormous promise in the packaging business to provide disruptive experiences. With AI being deployed in a more extensive range of packaging processes, the technology will likely impact the entire supply chain [6]. Various technologies have already been developed to inspect different product surfaces. They are usually made up of steps, each presenting its obstacles. Efficient calibration of multiple sensors, including cameras and lighting systems, is required during the acquisition phase [6, 7]. Figure 7.1 demonstrates various machine learning techniques, and these processes are also valuable for pharmaceutical packaging.

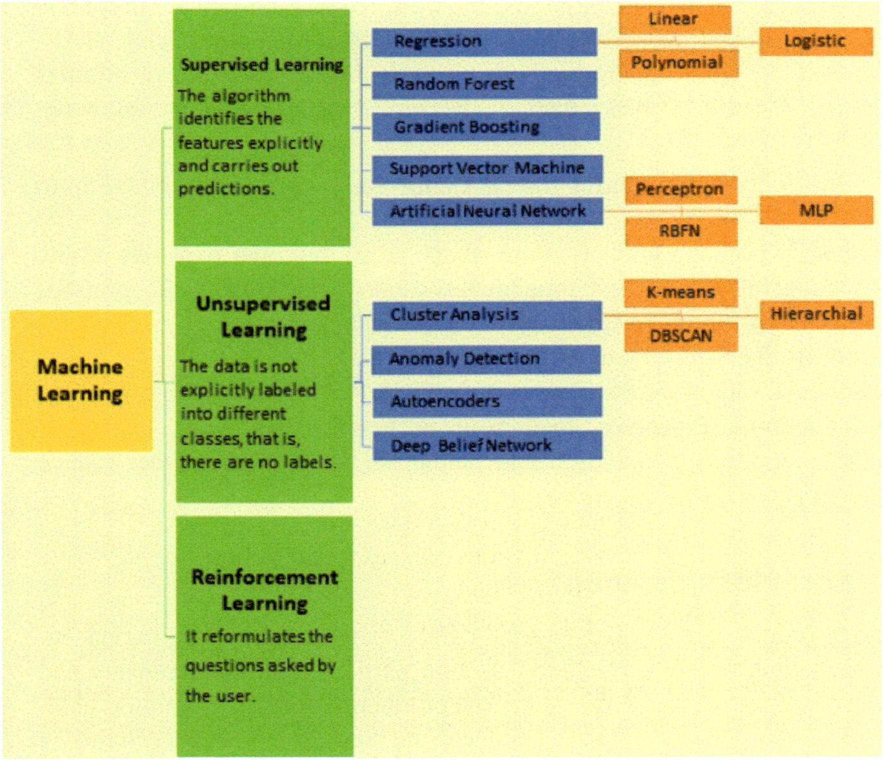

Figure 7.1 Types of machine learning.

7.2 Role of AI in Pharmaceutical Packaging

The typical medicine production process appears to be unsafe today: it involves the chance of human error and is inefficient in terms of verification time. The pharmaceutical sector relies heavily on the packaging. Pharmaceutical packaging had a global market value of US$ 6.2 billion in 2018 and is predicted to increase at a 7.4% annual rate to US$ 8.9 billion by 2023 [8]. Automation in pharma packaging has been around for decades, but it has witnessed a comeback in recent years thanks to new technology. Machine learning and computer vision are slowly becoming viable alternatives to traditional methods for quality control. Artificial intelligence (AI) can improve medicine manufacturing during the packaging stage. AI has proven to be a dependable technology for leading the way in the industry's future evolution, from production to packaging to distribution [9]. The increasing need for eco-friendly packaging, consumer goods, and the circular economy are just a few of the key reasons the packaging sector embraces artificial intelligence (AI). The technology that underpins it (machine learning) improves in minutes rather than decades. AI-based technologies are advantageous in the following terms [10]:

- Time consumption during the packaging stage can be reduced by up to 14%
- Identify package faults (texture, shape, size, improper packing) on the manufacturing line and immediately remove them from the process; drastically minimize labor cost and labor interaction
- Increased detection rate while reducing false reject rates
- Reduced setup time for recipes and parameters or "parameterization"
- Reduction /avoidance of costly re-inspection
- Data monitoring, trending, and predictive solutions to further reduce defects

7.3 Defect Identification

Ensuring product quality and spotting defects is essential in the pharmaceutical packaging process. Detecting foreign particles and contaminants and discovering crushed, defective, or broken products before distribution is challenging for any pharmaceutical manufacturing company, especially in failing traditional vision systems. Manual inspection adds significant labor and administrative costs to the plant when compared to machine inspection since detection requires repetitive and accurate work [11]. Other hazards, such as changes in size, shape, and form, or the discoloration of products, also present huge and often expensive hurdles that have to be overcome. A solution to this widespread problem has been found in AI, used to revolutionize traditional systems pharma manufacturing firms use. In recent years, image processing and machine vision technology have been used to develop defect detection algorithms. For example, the adaptive threshold method is frequently used for simple defect segmentation. Surface defect detection technology also relies heavily on texture analysis technology (*Fast Method of Detecting Packaging Bottle Defects Based on ECA-EfficientDet*, n.d.). AI-based models learn from real-world customers and associated packaging problems to develop optimum packaging choices reducing product damage, shipment damage, shipping cost, and related complaints. Figure 7.2 represents a layout for AI-assisted defect identification.

The CV (computer vision) technique and customized hs can detect faults at any level, necessitating the creation of a CNN that can be utilized for most applications with minor alterations. For example, incomplete foil sealing in bottles is a critical problem, adversely affecting the product's safety and stability. A thermal imaging technology was used to inspect foil sealing integrity in real time. The sensing equipment may collect the electromagnetic radiation profile released by the foil sealing ring through the polymer plastic caps in the specific application of bottle packaging [12]. This allows thermographs of the covered foil that are not achievable with visible light-based imaging methods. The thermal imaging camera is positioned above the conveyor belt, which transfers the capped bottles after the induction sealing step for this inspection application. The information is analyzed in real time

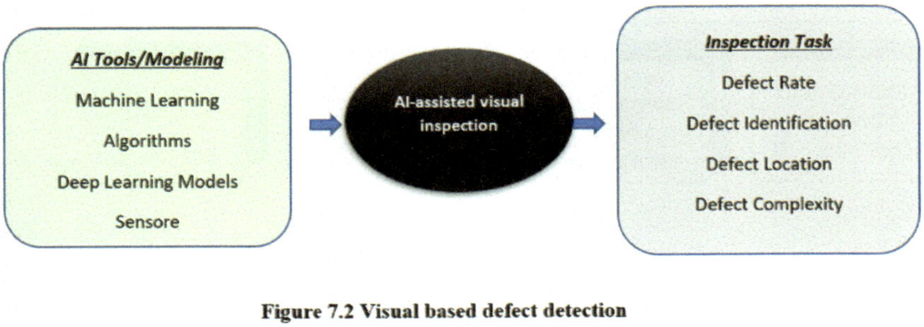

Figure 7.2 Visual-based defect detection.

utilizing high-speed image processing software once the radiation patterns from each bottle's induction sealed foil ring is captured. Pre-determined algorithms and set threshold values for thermal pattern variability enable the detection and discrimination of various flaws that can compromise the integrity of the bottle foil seal [13]. The above example explains how AI is about to transform defect detection by helping concerned manufacturers meet complex inspection requirements while maintaining quality. These machine learning and algorithm-based models are used to develop a vision system for packaging inspection with 100% accuracy. The hierarchy of visual-based image representation includes (Figure 7.3):

- Image compression
- Pre-processing
- Sharpening
- Edge extraction

Liu et al. solve the problems of vial inspection in the pharmaceutical packaging process [14]. To obtain the region of interest (ROI), they employed a threshold technique consisting of a few small patches generated using picture blocking, with better results than other image segmentation methods. The local binary pattern (LBP) descriptors are first extracted in the ROI, followed by the construction of visual dictionaries using k-means clustering in the following computational architecture. At last, they

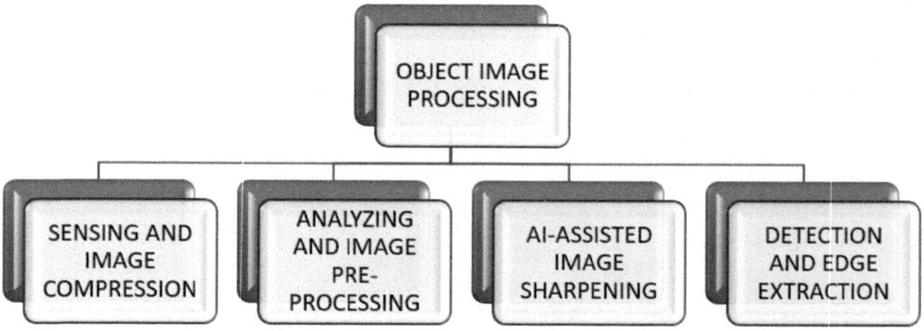

Figure 7.3 Object Representation for AI-assisted image analysis

Figure 7.3 Object representation for AI-assisted image analysis.

use the support vector machine (SVM) classifier to evaluate whether the vials have faults because the visual dictionaries can effectively represent the image [15]. Experiments reveal that the LBP outperforms the others in the feature extraction operation, (with maximum recognition efficiency of roughly 90%) compared to the others, owing to the extraction of accurate texture features [16]. In the pharmaceutical industry, penicillin bottles are commonly used to hold liquid, freeze-dried powder, and other medications. However, faults like wrinkles, tilting, and sunken may arise during the packing process. The solution based on the BP neural network classifier and the SIFT descriptor has been presented to address this challenge. The experimental findings suggest that this method's lowest accuracy is 96%; even if the number of training samples is small, a 99.6% accuracy will be achieved (10 training samples) [17]. Another study's foundation was laid on the specific problem domain of surface defect identification on pharmaceutical solid oral dosage forms. On the recently provided Sensum SODF dataset, Racki *et al.* comprehensively test and compare the suggested convolutional neural network architecture, TriNet. The dataset includes two types of solid oral dosage forms: non-translucent hard-shelled capsules with print and translucent soft-shelled capsules with variously shaped faulty

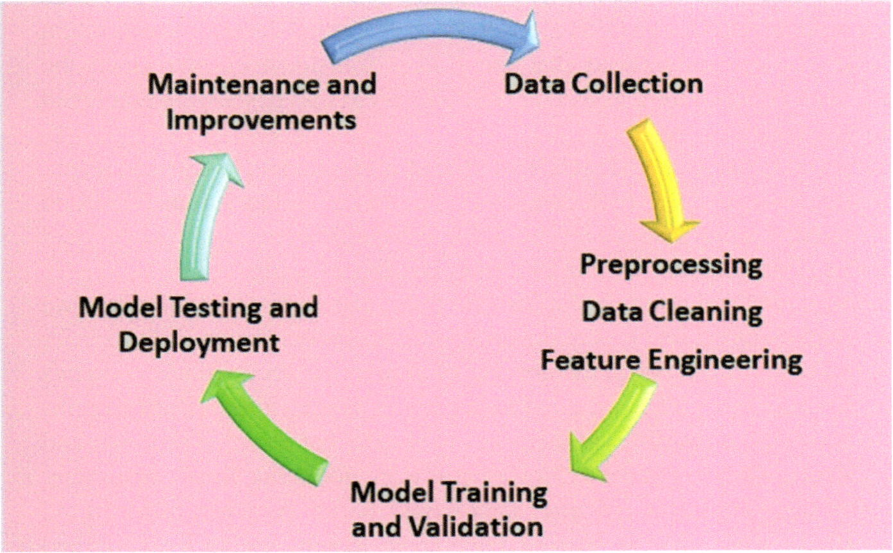

Figure 7.4 The lifecycle of machine learning.

sections hand-annotated by a pharmaceutical product inspection domain expert.

In another study, to swiftly identify printing problems, lower the cost of manual sorting and increase the packaging industry's production efficiency. A multilayer perceptron kernel function SVM training model was prosed using machine vision and machine learning. The faults on the pharmaceutical boxes are split into two groups based on analyzing the factors that influence print quality: form defects and color defects [18]. The classifier determines any faults on the printed packaging box's surface. The result showed the effective detection rate is 98.026%, which is higher (8.3744%) than the traditional pattern recognition technology [19]. Various stages of machine learning are depicted in Figure 7.4.

Sorting goods

In any system, detecting objects is a critical stage. Bahaghighat et al. used object detection, feature extraction, and classification methods in their model to address this problem. They compared template matching (TM) and Haar cascade techniques for object detection. The TM algorithms were ineffective, with the best-case scenario achieving only approximately 50% accuracy, but the Haar cascade achieved an acceptable accuracy of roughly 90%. Following that, various powerful approaches such as the Radon transform, Gabor wavelet, HOG, and ORB algorithms were used in the feature extraction process. The results showed that the Radon transform outperformed the others, with HOG coming in second [13]. The SVM and KNN were employed in the classification stage.

In comparison to SVM, KNN produced a significantly superior result. Finally, the best model, which combined Haar cascade, Radon transform, and KNN, yielded more than 88% [20]. Table 7.1 summarizes some AI-assisted algorithms and software used in pharmaceutical packaging.

Sorting recycled goods is not the first thing that comes to mind when we think about using AI services in the packaging sector (as shown in Table 7.2), but it is a beautiful fit. With the amount of debris that accumulates and ends up in the seas every day, we need to increase our recycling efforts significantly. Sorting commodities is necessary to ensure that recycled products and byproducts are put to good use. However, it is monotonous, time-consuming, and with little value for humans. This would be an excellent match if AI and robotics were used in sorting the goods. Robots are being equipped with artificial intelligence to perform such tasks as the advent of intelligent automation approaches [24].

Table 7.1 Example of AI-assisted software used in pharmaceutical packaging.

	Real-Time System	Experimental System
Tablet surface defects	RNA Systems™ Canadian Optel's CountSafe™ tablet inspection systems	Intelligent laser speckle Classification (*ILSC*) Technique [21]
Tablet color defect	SPINE™	
Tablet porosity	TIE-XR™	THz radiation [21]
Tablet internal fracture	–	X-ray micro-computed tomography (XmCT) [22]
Film coating	–	Terahertz pulsed imaging (TPI)

Table 7.2 AI-assisted sorting and identification of packaging defects.

Methodology	**References**
PET bottle defect inspection method with self-adaptive gamma adjustments to bottle images	[23]
Texture area defect detection algorithm based solely on phase change	[1]
Combined mean squared cyclic detection and entropy partition and proposed an improved random cyclic detection method to determine defective regions on the bottoms of bottles	[2]

7.4 Data Labeling

Investigating and resolving a labeling issue requires time, which may be saved with increased monitoring. Incorrectly labeled products can result in the loss of hard-earned money for enterprises. When we examine how machine learning is applied to business processes, it is clear that it has the potential to be a game-changer by delivering reliable data, analysis, and insights into operations. HALS is a human-augmenting AI-based labeling system in which untrained Deep Learning Models learn from human demonstrations, train themselves, and start to boost human annotation ability [25]. Van der Wal et al. stated, "We run experiments using four different cellular labelling tasks on two visually distinct stains—Hematoxylin and Eosin (H&E) and immunohistochemistry (IHC). Working with seven pathologists from Stanford and the University of California at San Francisco (UCSF), we demonstrate that HALS can reduce the workload of annotators by an average of 90.6% while slightly increasing the effectiveness of the annotated data by 4.34%." Organizations that use machine learning in processes like labeling benefit from more consistent procedures and avoid consumer unhappiness. Labeling using machine learning in the packaging industry could become the norm, resulting in fewer manual errors and increased process efficiency [26]. The pharmaceutical industry must deal with the fact that labels for products marketed in any geographic market must meet the regulatory standards of that country or region. There is a danger that the information on the labels will be inconsistent because there are so many various regulatory standards for the same product around the world. Problems with product labeling or packaging artwork cause over half of all pharmaceutical recall [27].

7.5 Warehouse Automation

Smart warehouses powered by AI are a game-changing notion in various industries today. Deep technology is tightly integrated, and while it has resulted in significant operational benefits, it has also aided firms in keeping their finances in line [28, 29]. As a result of the demand, some RPA bot suppliers have concentrated their efforts on the manufacturing industry, particularly the benefits it may bring to packing. It is a complicated procedure with its own set of difficulties regarding warehouse management. Warehouse systems and automation are inextricably linked; the more streamlined and integrated they are with other devices and processes, the better the results. Warehouses powered by the Internet of Things are known as intelligent warehouses [28].

Packaging is a critical component of modern AI and intelligent warehousing systems. AI systems may gather data from various sources and make packaging recommendations. This necessitates a re-evaluation of packaging standards and the exploration of alternatives to fulfill customer sensitivity and needs [27].

7.6 Optimization of Product Packaging with AI

AI in packaging allows companies to create one-of-a-kind, bright, and distinctive package designs that truly reflect their brand's culture. Furthermore, AI enhances the package inspection procedure. Over time, the way items are marketed to buyers has become as important as, if not more important than, the products themselves. The taglines and colorful images on the cans of aerated drinks are more easily recognized and remembered than the sugary syrup inside. Aside from keeping the products secure from the weather, proper packaging aids in the faster sale of the product due to consumers' typical tendency to associate quality and reliability with aesthetics [29]. Businesses already utilize AI in various digital marketing areas, so incorporating AI into packaging makes sense for the companies.

7.7 AI-assisted Designing for Aesthetic Packaging

Product and package design become more autonomous using generative design technologies. These technologies generate many design iterations for a product's packaging. They promise to reduce product development and design lead times in the future. A generative design tool operates iteratively, which means it first produces a design based on the limitations given, then improves it by following the directions of a human designer [31]. Designers perfect the initial design by selecting the output areas (known as the "feasible region") with successive iterations. AI can be used instead of a human designer to achieve the desired output with the fewest possible iterations [4]. AI can be used instead of a human designer to achieve the desired outcome with the most periodic possible iterations. Machine learning models can pick the outputs, reducing the amount of effort and money spent on package design.

The package design is an essential aspect of the brand's identification. As a result, creating an aesthetically beautiful package design that aligns with the brand's ethos for more precise marketing and increased product sales is critical. The application of AI in packaging, combined with generative design tools, aids organizations in producing accurate designs at a rapid pace [27].

7.8 AI-assisted Selection of Packaging Material

Amazon and other large retailers utilize artificial intelligence to choose the best packaging material, enabling such enterprises to create more environmentally friendly product packaging. Furthermore, such materials are being used to strengthen packaging and make it more damage-resistant to lessen the risk of product damage during delivery [32]. As one may be aware, making the proper material selections in packaging is difficult due to the unlimited options and combinations available. Machine learning algorithms comb through all accessible data. Such technologies examine factors like porosity, stiffness, and elasticity before making material suggestions for different types of products. AI can also be used in packaging in a variety of ways. Machine learning and artificial intelligence (AI) can help companies save packaging time while simultaneously enhancing packaging quality and design [33].

7.9 AI Integrated Approaches Used in Pharmaceutical Packaging

7.9.1 Convolutional neural network approach (CNN pack)

The CNN approach is effectively used to classify various images, face recognition and verification, object detection, and identification. CNN techniques are also employed on numerous workstations with desktops to solve demand storage and computational resource-related queries [34]. The CNN pack method establishes a link between classical signal and picture compression and CNN compression theory, allowing us to further investigate CNN techniques in the frequency domain.

7.9.2 Computer vision approach

This approach may detect problems at any level and necessitate the development of a CNN that, with minor alterations (training and hyperparameter setup), can be employed for most workloads. There may come a time when creating a custom CNN for a particular task is necessary [34]. It is possible to detect medication production difficulties on the manufacturing line using computer vision and machine learning. The customer was able to achieve the following aims by utilizing AI technologies in medicine:

- Identifying medicine with faults (cracks, contamination, blotches)
- Lowering labor costs and enhancing full quality processing
- Real-time detection of flaws and instant warnings regarding violations

7.9.3 Statistical approach

Statistical methods, for example, histogram, matrix analysis and calculations, binary and linear systems, correlation coefficients, and other parametric analyses, were employed to create a suitable statistical approach-based product packaging. This approach helps create spatial relations of image pixels with accuracy, further used for image discrimination. This approach uses computational techniques and data memory and is not adequate for random textures. This is also sensitive to noise, with no automatic threshold selection.

7.9.4 Structural approach

The methods employed for the structural approach are primitive measurements, edge feature study, object skeleton representation, and various morphological operations. This is a simple, easy to operate and implement strategy. This approach is also advantageous in extracting low-level features of the image. Structural analysis also facilitates the buildup of a statistical histogram with variable strengths and is suitable for random textures. This approach is also sensitive to noise and depends on applied statistical methods for structural analysis.

7.9.5 Filter approach

Spatial domain filtration, joint special filtration, frequency, and special frequency analysis build a filter approach. This approach helps extract unique information about objects which is further used for image localization. It also measures unique frequency domains of things that help to outperform space-related translations, rotations, and expansions.

7.9.6 Model-based approach

The fractal model uses partial features of objects to expand images. The random field model combines statistical and spectral methods to predict texture and orientation-related information. The taxes model is used for analysis based on image segmentation. The autoregressive model solves texture-related problems with model-based approaches.

7.10 Critical Features of AI-assisted Packaging

7.10.1 Cloud computing

Data is always available because it is stored online. The certified cloud-based platform for storing photos and data can be used with any cloud-based system and allows operators to control images saved on the server.

7.10.2 Security

Multi-factor authentication and encrypted communication also offer total data protection and access management.

7.10.3 Assistance

Continuous assistance is accessible for all platform capabilities throughout the process, aiding pharmaceutical businesses with various activities, such as a labeling assistant tool that optimizes categorization timing and new recipe creation.

7.10.4 Monitoring

The platform features a range of statistics and visualizations (heat maps, confusion matrix, and more) for model performance evaluation. Pharma companies can track and monitor all processes through real-time reports.

7.10.5 Advantages of AI-assisted Packaging

Companies are leveraging machine learning and algorithms to build more intelligent packaging solutions as part of AI innovation. 3D printing is becoming more common in industrial applications, and not only will designers be affected by these new technologies, but the entire supply chain will also need to adapt. The following are some of the numerous technologies that will have an impact on the packaging industry:

7.10.6 Packaging prototypes in 3D space with the aid of AI

Because AI can be used to design or create prototypes without human labor sources, it is the future of development and design. The AI assist in creating a three-dimensional prototype; if the product requires assembly, one must program this into the appropriate algorithm. It is not as simple as letting an AI wild on CAD files with no guidance.

7.10.7 Designing as per product's needs

Designers are already employing virtual reality and augmented reality headsets to create packaging in some circumstances. AI will be able to visualize an algorithmically produced package appropriate for specific products with higher processing power [35].

7.10.8 Packaging of different shapes and sizes for specific products [36]

Packages can already be altered in structure, but artificial intelligence will expand the options. Artificial intelligence might create containers in various shapes and sizes to accommodate specific products, such as cereal or hot dogs. Specific machine parts must be manufactured with CNC milling when creating packaging in unusual forms [32]. In packaging, customization is necessary because it increases consumer loyalty by making it personal. This personalization also builds trust in the firm that makes the goods because it went to the trouble of customizing packaging [37].

7.10.9 Packaging with RFID tags or QR codes

RFID tags and codes will need to be put into the packaging design to allow smart feature compatibility. This extra feature may raise packing costs, but it should be considered throughout the design phase [38].

7.10.10 AI-driven automation with controlling robots

Machines must be precisely programmed with instructions in the production process, whereas AI-driven automation may do tasks without detailed instructions. AI is also utilized to ensure that products are of high quality. Machines' ability to self-diagnose faults with a system or component before requiring human involvement can increase productivity and reduce downtime [39]. This could lead to producers producing more flexible items in smaller quantities that are customized according to the needs of each consumer [40]. Customization's flexibility would give customers more options while assuring product uniformity across all orders, resulting in higher customer satisfaction [41].

7.10.11 Sensors for temper resistant packaging

This system will assist businesses in preventing the misuse of their products, such as the sale of stolen goods or counterfeit material. The device should also detect when shipments have been dropped in transit, which poses a significant danger of damage [42].

7.10.12 Optimization of production lines and processes

Companies can increase profits by lowering labor expenses and increasing output. When processing data fast and efficiently, AI-enabled machines are more exact than people. According to thorough research, they only take about 20% as much time to learn something new as a human counterpart [43]. In this sense, automation is already taking place. Still, for many people, unnoticed, owing to a lack of understanding about the topic at hand: whether or not artificial intelligence should replace human occupations [44].

7.10.13 Sustainable packaging practices

Artificial intelligence (AI) can forecast demand and consumption and expedite the manufacturing process, thus cutting down on waste throughout the manufacturing process. By improving supply chain and inventory management, optimizing distribution routes, and tracking items throughout transportation, AI will help the packaging sector expedite its shift to sustainable practices. Alternative packaging options can also be generated using AI, which reduces complexity and resource requirements [45].

7.10.14 Preventative maintenance

Machines break down due to normal wear and tear or when they are not appropriately operated. Unplanned maintenance is the leading cause of packaging machine downtime. A lack of human labor at the industrial level can result in wasted hours in a week that cannot be recovered. Artificial intelligence may be able to detect problems before they occur, reducing the need for downtime [46].

7.10.15 Use of augmented reality (AR) and virtual reality (VR)

Virtual reality will soon be a standard feature of many firms' customer experiences and package design processes, as immersive VR devices like the Oculus Rift and HTC Vive become more affordable for small businesses [47]. Major stores such as Target, Walmart, and Home Depot have experimented with introducing VR into many elements of their business. We may expect other retail sectors to follow suit in the coming years as this technology becomes more prevalent in these businesses [48].

7.11 Components for AI-assisted Packaging

AI takes data from sensors, analyzes it, and then adjusts its operation in response to the findings. The idea is to collect a large amount of data, including factors that are not necessarily relevant to the process under control [49]. AI improves system performance by providing more precise inspection and maintenance of the material. The key drivers for AI-assisted packaging are listed below.

7.11.1 Big data

"Big data" will only grow as trillions of sensors are implemented in production and made products. Many gadgets have provided mountains of data to process, both structured (in databases and spreadsheets) and unstructured (in the form of text) (such as text, audio, video, and images) [50]. AI-assisted processing used these data as input to find historical patterns, anticipate more accurately, make real-time modifications, etc.

7.11.2 Processing power

Parallel processing has made it cheaper and faster to manage enormous volumes of data with complicated AI-powered systems thanks to accelerating technologies like cloud computing and graphics processing units. "Deep learning" chips, which are currently a hot topic of research, will push parallel computation even farther in the future [50].

7.11.3 Connected globe

In combination with social media platforms, global industrial supply chains have profoundly altered how people connect and what information they may expect at what times. Increased connectivity via the Internet of Things (IoT) speeds up the dissemination of information and fosters knowledge sharing. Open-source groups building AI Tools/Modeling and sharing applications will make up a growing "collective intelligence."

7.11.4 Software

The popularity of open-source machine learning standards and platforms demonstrates how open-source software and protocols speed the democratization and adoption of AI. An open-source strategy could result in less time spent on ordinary coding, industry standardization, and broader use of developing AI Tools/Modeling.

7.11.5 Algorithms and problem-solving operations

Researchers have made progress in various areas of AI, including "deep learning," which entails layers of neural networks designed to mimic the way the human brain processes information. Another new area of research is "deep reinforcement"—an AI agent learns by trial and error with little or no initial input data, using a reward function.

7.12 Conclusion

Pharmaceutical packaging is an integral part of the industry. The typical manufacturing process looks risky today since it involves the risk of human mistakes. Pharmaceutical companies must take steps when manufacturing and packaging their products to avoid flaws in pharmaceutical products. This entails adhering to standard operating procedures, using quality control measures, and maintaining a monitoring workforce. Pharmaceutical companies can reduce the risk of defects and errors by implementing AI inspection systems and other quality control measures. It protects the companies against financial losses due to defective products or packages.

Acknowledgment

The authors are thankful for all the support and help provided by Madan Mohan Malviya University of Technology, Gorakhpur, Uttar Pradesh, India.

Conflict of Interest

The authors declare no conflict of interest.

Funding

This work received no specific grant from any funding agency.

References

[1] Kondapi, D. (2022, March 16). Pharmaceutical packaging: How automation & digitization have influence. https://www.industr.com/en/pharmaceutical-packaging-how-automation-digitisation-have-influence-2645258

[2] Girshick, R., Donahue, J., Darrell, T., & Malik, J. (2014). RCNN: Regions with CNN features. Proceedings of the Ieee Conference on Computer Vision and Pattern Recognition. http://gwylab.com/pdf/rcnn_chs.pdf

[3] Gross, A. (202 CE, February 13). How AI can keep pharma safe - European Pharmaceutical Manufacturer. European Pharmaceutical Manufacturer. https://pharmaceuticalmanufacturer.media/pharmaceutical-industry-insights/how-ai-can/

[4] Girshick, R., Donahue, J., Darrell, T., & Malik, J. (2013a). Rich feature hierarchies for accurate object detection and semantic segmentation. *Proceedings of the IEEE Computer Society Conference on Computer Vision and Pattern Recognition*, 580–587. https://doi.org/10.48550/arxiv.1311.2524

[5] *[1311.2524] Rich Feature Hierarchies for Accurate Object Detection and Semantic Segmentation*. (n.d.). Retrieved April 19, 2022, from https://arxiv.org/abs/1311.2524

[6] Yousefi, H., Su, H. M., Imani, S. M., Alkhaldi, K., Filipe, C. D., & Didar, T. F. (2019). Intelligent Food Packaging: A Review of Smart Sensing Technologies for Monitoring Food Quality. *ACS Sensors*, 4(4), 808–821. https://doi.org/10.1021/ACSSENSORS.9B00440/ASSET/IMAGES/MEDIUM/SE-2019-00440B_0007.Gif

[7] Zhang, H., Wei, X., Chan-Park, M. B., & Wang, M. (2022). Colorimetric Sensors Based on Multifunctional Polymers for Highly Sensitive Detection of Food Spoilage. *ACS Food Science & Technology*, 2(4), 703–711. https://doi.org/10.1021/ACSFOODSCITECH.2C00019

[8] *Pharmaceutical Trend in 2019: New Impulses Through Artificial Intelligence – Interpack*. (n.d.). Retrieved April 1, 2022, from https://www.interpack.com/en/Discover/TIGHTLY_PACKED_Magazine/PHARMACEUTICS_PACKAGING/News/Pharmaceutical_Trend_in_2019_New_Impulses_through_Artificial_Intelligence

[9] Zhu, Y., Li, G., Wang, R., Tang, S., Su, H., & Cao, K. (2021a). Intelligent fault diagnosis of hydraulic piston pump combining improved LeNet-5 and PSO hyperparameter optimization. *Applied Acoustics*, 183. https://doi.org/10.1016/J.APACOUST.2021.108336

[10] Essid, O., Laga, H., & Samir, C. (2018). Automatic detection and classification of manufacturing defects in metal boxes using deep neural networks. *PLOS ONE*, 13(11), e0203192. https://doi.org/10.1371/JOURNAL.PONE.0203192

[11] Sa, J., Li, Z., Yang, Q., & Chen, X. (2020). Packaging defect detection system based on machine vision and deep learning. *2020 5th International Conference on Computer and Communication Systems, ICCC*

[12] Hajizadeh, S., Núñez, A., & Tax, D. M. J. (2016). Semi-supervised Rail Defect Detection from Imbalanced Image Data. *IFAC-Papers Online*, 49(3), 78–83. https://doi.org/10.1016/J.IFACOL.2016.07.014

[13] Zhong, G., Wang, L. N., Ling, X., & Dong, J. (2016). An overview on data representation learning: From traditional feature learning to recent deep learning. *Journal of Finance and Data Science*, 2(4), 265–278. https://doi.org/10.1016/J.JFDS.2017.05.001

[14] Liu, Y., Chen, S., Tinglong, T., & Zhao, M. (2017a). Defect inspection of medicine vials using LBP features and SVM classifier. *2017 2nd International Conference on Image, Vision and Computing, ICIVC* 2017, 41–45. https://doi.org/10.1109/ICIVC.2017.7984515

[15] *Defect Inspection of Medicine Vials Using LBP Features and SVM Classifier | Semantic Scholar*. (n.d.). Retrieved April 19, 2022, from https://www.semanticscholar.org/paper/Defect-inspection-of-medicine-vials-using-LBP-and-Liu-Chen/436a612c17a470cfd82a8d3a4b10c1658fd8c51a

[16] Liu, Y., Chen, S., Tinglong, T., & Zhao, M. (2017b). Defect inspection of medicine vials using LBP features and SVM classifier. *2017 2nd International Conference on Image, Vision and Computing, ICIVC* 2017, 41–45. https://doi.org/10.1109/ICIVC.2017.7984515

[17] Feng, Y., Tang, T., & Chen, S. (2019). A Method of Penicillin Bottle Defect Inspection Based on BP. Neural Network. *Communications in Computer and Information Science*, 1043, 31–40. https://doi.org/10.1007/978-981-13-9917-6_4/FIGURES/12

[18] Golnabi, H., & Asadpour, A. (2007). Design and application of industrial machine vision systems. *Robotics and Computer-Integrated Manufacturing*, 23(6), 630–637. https://doi.org/10.1016/J.RCIM.2007.02.005

[19] Wu, Y., & Lu, Y. (2019). An intelligent machine vision system for detecting surface defects on packing boxes based on support vector machine. *Measurement and Control (United Kingdom)*, 52(7–8), 1102–1110. https://doi.org/10.1177/0020294019858175

[20] Bahaghighat, M., Akbari, L., & Xin, Q. (2019). A machine learning based approach for counting blister cards within drug packages. *IEEE Access*, 7, 83785–83796. https://doi.org/10.1109/ACCESS.2019.2924445

[21] Orun, A., & Smith, G. (2017). Micro-Structural Analysis of Tablet Surface Layers by Intelligent Laser Speckle Classification (ILSC) Technique: an Application in the Study of both Surface Defects and Subsurface Granule Structures. *Journal of Pharmaceutical Innovation*, 12(4), 296–308. https://doi.org/10.1007/S12247-017-9290-0/FIGURES/10

[22] Yost, E., Chalus, P., Zhang, S., Peter, S., & Narang, A. S. (2019). Quantitative X-Ray Microcomputed Tomography Assessment of Internal Tablet Defects. *Journal of Pharmaceutical Sciences*, 108(5), 1818–1830. https://doi.org/10.1016/J.XPHS.2018.12.024

[23] Sheng, Z., & Wang, G. (2022a). Fast Method of Detecting Packaging Bottle Defects Based on ECA-EfficientDet. *Journal of Sensors*, 2022. https://doi.org/10.1155/2022/9518910

[24] Marques, G., Agarwal, D., & de la Torre Díez, I. (2020). Automated medical diagnosis of COVID-19 through EfficientNet convolutional neural network. *Applied Soft Computing Journal*, 96. https://doi.org/10.1016/J.ASOC.2020.106691

[25] van der Wal, D., Jhun, I., Laklouk, I., Nirschl, J., Richer, L., Rojansky, R., Theparee, T., Wheeler, J., Sander, J., Feng, F., Mohamad, O., Savarese, S., Socher, R., & Esteva, A. (2021). Biological data annotation via a human-augmenting AI-based labeling system. *Npj Digital Medicine* 2021 4:1, 4(1), 1–7. https://doi.org/10.1038/s41746-021-00520-6

[26] Lecun, Y., Bengio, Y., & Hinton, G. (2015). Deep learning. *Nature*, 521(7553), 436–444. https://doi.org/10.1038/nature14539

[27] Gong, Y., Liu, L., Yang, M., & Bourdev, L. (2014a). *Compressing Deep Convolutional Networks using Vector Quantization*. https://doi.org/10.48550/arxiv.1412.6115

[28] Ramachandran, P., Zoph, B., & Le, Q. v. (2017a). *Searching for Activation Functions*. http://arxiv.org/abs/1710.05941

[29] Sheng, Z., & Wang, G. (2022a). Fast Method of Detecting Packaging Bottle Defects Based on ECA-EfficientDet. *Journal of Sensors*, 2022. https://doi.org/10.1155/2022/9518910

[30] Sa, J., Li, Z., Yang, Q., & Chen, X. (2020). Packaging defect detection system based on machine vision and deep learning. *2020 5th International Conference on Computer and Communication Systems, ICCCS* 2020, 404–408. https://doi.org/10.1109/ICCCS49078.2020.9118413

[31] *Introducing Deep Learning with MATLAB - MATLAB & Simulink.* (n.d.). Retrieved April 19, 2022, from https://in.mathworks.com/campaigns/offers/deep-learning-with-matlab.html?ef_id=CjwKCAjwu_mSBhAYEiwA5BBmf-FDPbPb5-IW2xTkFbA8z4pkB160lz8bX8EKOpLYSPq4XiECWAYWGxoCjVgQAvD_BwE:G:s&s_kwcid=AL!8664!3!227584766104!b!!g!!%2Bconvolutional%20%2Bneural%20%2Bnetworks&s_eid=psn_45581054546&q=+convolutional%20+neural%20+networks&gclid=CjwKCAjwu_mSBhAYEiwA5BBmf-FDPbPb5-IW2xTkFbA8z4pkB160lz8bX8EKOpLYSPq4XiECWAYWGxoCjVgQAvD_BwE

[32] Gong, Y., Liu, L., Yang, M., & Bourdev, L. (2014b). *Compressing Deep Convolutional Networks using Vector Quantization.* http://arxiv.org/abs/1412.6115

[33] Gong, Y., Liu, L., Yang, M., & Bourdev, L. (2014a). *Compressing Deep Convolutional Networks using Vector Quantization.* https://doi.org/10.48550/arxiv.1412.6115

[34] Wang, Y., Liu, M., Zheng, P., Yang, H., & Zou, J. (2020). A smart surface inspection system using faster R-CNN in cloud-edge computing environment. *Advanced Engineering Informatics*, 43, 101037. https://doi.org/10.1016/J.AEI.2020.101037

[35] Misra, D. (2019). *Mish: A Self Regularized Non-Monotonic Activation Function.* http://arxiv.org/abs/1908.08681

[36] Sheng, Z., & Wang, G. (2022b). Fast Method of Detecting Packaging Bottle Defects Based on ECA-EfficientDet. *Journal of Sensors*, 2022. https://doi.org/10.1155/2022/9518910

[37] Ramachandran, P., Zoph, B., & Le, Q. v. (2017b). *Searching for Activation Functions.* http://arxiv.org/abs/1710.05941

[38] Tsao, W.-C., & Tu, Y.-H. (2017). 1137 I www.irmbrjournal. *International Review of Management and Business Research*, 6, 3. www.irmbrjournal.com

[39] Kwon, Y. J., Kim, J. G., Seo, J., Lee, D. H., & Kim, D. S. (2007). A tabu search algorithm using the Voronoi diagram for the capacitated vehicle routing problem. *Proceedings - The 2007 International Conference on Computational Science and Its Applications, ICCSA* 2007, 480–485. https://doi.org/10.1109/ICCSA.2007.86

[40] *(15) (PDF) Expert Robots for Automatic Packaging and Processing.* (n.d.). Retrieved April 19, 2022, from https://www.researchgate.net/publication/236201867_Expert_robots_for_automatic-packaging-and-processing

[41] *The QR-code Reorganization in Illegible Snapshots Taken by Mobile Phones | Semantic Scholar*. (n.d.). Retrieved April 19, 2022, from https://www.semanticscholar.org/paper/The-QR-code-reorganization-in-illegible-snapshots-Sun-Sun/72c84093173e5ddd27eeed7d94a206d006176a58

[42] Zhu, Y., Li, G., Wang, R., Tang, S., Su, H., & Cao, K. (2021b). Intelligent fault diagnosis of hydraulic piston pump combining improveLeNet-5 and PSO hyperparameter optimization. *Applied Acoustics*, 183. https://doi.org/10.1016/J.APACOUST.2021.108336

[43] Wang, Z., Zhao, W., Du, W., Li, N., & Wang, J. (2021). Datadriven fault diagnosis method based on the conversion of erosion operation signals into images and convolutional neural network. *Process Safety and Environmental Protection*, 149, 591–601. https://doi.org/10.1016/J.PSEP.2021.03.016

[44] Gao, Z., Zhang, Y., & Li, Y. (2020). Extracting features from infrared images using convolutional neural networks and transfer learning infrared Physics and Technology, 105. https://doi.org/10.1016/J.INFRARED.2020.103237

[45] Krizhevsky, A., Sutskever, I., & Hinton, G. E. (2017). ImageNet classification with deep convolutional neural networks. *Communications of the ACM*, 60(6), 84–90. https://doi.org/10.1145/3065386

[46] LeCun, Y., Bottou, L., Bengio, Y., & Haffner, P. (1998). Gradient-based learning applied to document recognition. *Proceedings of the IEEE*, 86(11), 2278–2323. https://doi.org/10.1109/5.726791

[47] Ramachandran, P., Zoph, B., & Le, Q. v. (2017c). *Searching for Activation Functions*. http://arxiv.org/abs/1710.05941

[48] *Virtual Reality (VR) & Augmented Reality (AR) Technologies for Tourism and Hospitality Industry | Nayyar | International Journal of Engineering & Technology*. (n.d.). Retrieved April 19, 2022, from https://www.sciencepubco.com/index.php/ijet/article/view/11855

[49] Azuma, R., Baillot, Y., Behringer, R., Feiner, S., Julier, S., & MacIntyre, B. (2001). Recent advances in augmented reality. *IEEE Computer Graphics and Applications*, 21(6), 34–47. https://doi.org/10.1109/38.963459

[50] Akçayır, M., & Akçayır, G. (2017). Advantages and challenges associated with augmented reality for education: A systematic review of the literature. *Educational Research Review*, 20, 1–11. https://doi.org/10.1016/J.EDUREV.2016.11.002

Author Biography

Smriti Ojha

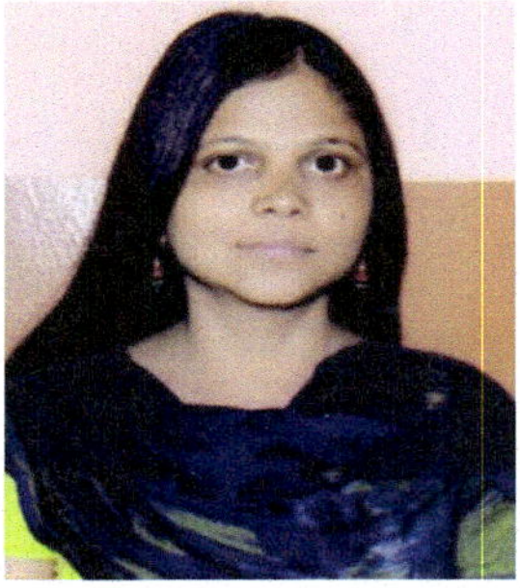

Smriti Ojha is an experienced Professor with a demonstrated history of working in the Pharmaceutical education industry. She earned Doctorate in Pharmaceutical sciences from Dr. A.P.J. Abdul Kalam Technical University, Lucknow. She is actively engaged in research area of Drug Delivery, Pharmaceutics, Pharmaceutical Research, and nanotechnology. Currently she is working in Madan Mohan University of Technology, Gorakhpur, Uttar Pradesh, India. This book chapter is a very important contribution to her interest in different facets of research area and future endeavors.

Sudhanshu Mishra

Sudhanshu Mishra completed his M. Pharm (Pharmaceutics) from Rajiv Gandhi Proudyogiki Vishwavidyalaya and is currently working as a teaching faculty in the Department of Pharmaceutical Science & Technology, Madan Mohan Malaviya University of Technology, Gorakhpur. He has worked on the herbal topical formulation for the treatment of arthritis during his M. Pharm research work and developed an interest in arthritis-related research work. Meanwhile, he is working on various literature work like writing review articles for the different novel approach and technology for targeting chronic diseases. He has been participating in various academic activities like international seminars, conferences, workshops, and oral presentations. This book chapter is one of the important contributions to his interest in technology and the future research area.

Anubhav Anand

Anubhav Anand is a working Professor in the Department of Pharmaceutics at the Hygia Institute of Pharmaceutical Education and Research, Lucknow, Uttar Pradesh, India. He graduated from Meerut Institute of Engineering and Technology, Meerut, UP and cleared GATE 2004 and post-graduation from Babu Banarasi Das National Institute of Technology and Management, Lucknow, UP, India AICTE. He received a Doctorate from the Dr. APJ Abdul Kalam Technical University, Lucknow, India, in 2020. He has an overall teaching experience of more than 15 years. He has worked at various academic institutions like Bharat Institute of Technology Meerut, UP, India, Hygia Institute of Pharmaceutical Education and Research, Lucknow and Babu Banarasi Das University, Lucknow, India. The main area of interest is drug delivery system and nanotechnology.

Manoj Saini

Manoj Saini is a medical graduate student at the All India Institute of Medical Science, Jodhpur, Rajasthan, India. He is currently affiliated to All India Institute of Medical Science, Bhuvneshwar, Odisha, India. He has been participating in various activities like international seminars, conferences, and workshops. He is currently learning and expanding his knowledge and skills in Medical Science.

8

Digital Assistant in the Pharmaceutical Field for Advancing Healthcare Systems

Ashish Verma[1], Akanksha Sharma[2*], Aditi Singh[3], Rishabha Malviya[4], and Shivkanya Fuloria[5]

[1]School of Pharmacy, Monad University, India
[2]Monad College of Pharmacy, Monad University, India
[3]Ashoka Institute of Pharmacy, India
[4]Department of Pharmacy, School of Medical and Allied Sciences, Galgotias University, India
[5]Faculty of Pharmacy, AIMST University, Malaysia
*Correspondence Author: Monad College of Pharmacy, Monad University, N.H. 9, Delhi Hapur Road, Kastla, Kasmabad, Pilkhuwa, Uttar Pradesh, 245304, India, Email: akankshasona012@gmail.com, Contact: +91-8009218455, ORCID Id: 0000-0002-5325-427X.

Abstract

The execution of digital techniques in the medical field can improve public healthcare flexibility and accessibility. It incorporates the availability of open reports about treatment, complications, and recent biomedical research advancements in health. Digital Health Assistants like smartphone or desktop applications provide fast and direct access to medical services through an online network of messaging (WhatsApp, Telegram, WeChat, etc.) to patients. New digital technologies have the property to enhance the capabilities of different therapeutic and diagnostic systems and tools. Digital medical technologies mainly include the Internet of Things, big data, artificial intelligence, blockchain, and telemedicine technologies that assist in the system of healthcare. In several nations, the use of various forms of digital technologies has resulted in improved medical care quality, affordability, efficiency, and accessibility. This chapter describes the various technologies which are used as an assistant in the healthcare system. It also focuses on the different devices that are utilized in patient care. The limitation and challenges related to the digital healthcare system are also summarized in this chapter. Before deploying a digital device in the healthcare sector, proper scientific research is required.

Keywords: Digital technology, artificial intelligence, blockchain, big data, healthcare, Internet of Things.

8.1 Introduction

References of general drug-related information, references of specialist drug information (e.g., pediatrics, infectious diseases, cardiology, psychology, oncology, herbals), applications of diagnostic, calculators of medical, nursing references, and patient monitoring databases are all accessible for the Personal Digital Assistance (PDA). Because of the vast number of programs, as well as issues like memory and cost needs, healthcare practitioners should be judicious in the use of medications that are used during PDA [1]. Healthcare workers require access to up-to-date information at any time and from any location, and a Personal Digital Assistant may be capable to assist their needs. A personal digital assistant is a mobile device that has been widely used in healthcare for a variety of purposes. A PDA, with its appropriate features and software applications, could be the tool that healthcare professionals and students require [2].

Although its leadership function in mobile technology, PDAs are not widely utilized in Sweden today because of their appropriate functionalities shortage and software applications. PDA is a little, portable computer with additional functionalities than a calculator that can gather data in the same way as a personal computer (PC) does. An address book, calendar, schedule, e-mail, and notepad are basic functions of most PDAs. The PDA is useful for rapid data management in clinical and field situations in which data must be synchronized with PC. PDAs are broadly used in healthcare practice—this trend is projected to continue. Although PDA is primarily a useful instrument, it is also allied with challenges such as inadequate technical and security assistance. Healthcare providers require admittance to information numerous times a day, which can be fulfilled by PDA. There are several medical software applications and documents available for PDA, with varying degrees of quality. With great delight, a considerable amount of medical scholars use the PDA for educational reasons and the care of patients [2].

Information and communication technology (ICT) is a critical component of digitized associations which can improve operational efficiency and competitiveness. Advanced digital technology and devices are generally used for value generation and innovation across industries in today's Fourth Industrial Revolution (4IR) era. There is no exception in the healthcare industry. Digital techniques such as artificial intelligence (AI), smart sensors, machine learning, robots, big data analytics, and the Internet of Things (IoT) are being aggressively deployed by hospitals and healthcare providers around the world, particularly in developed economies, to improve care quality and operational efficiency. According to research conducted by Aruba, a Hewlett-Packard Enterprise firm, more than 60% of clinics around the world have integrated IoT in their facilities [3].

Digital Health Assistants like smartphone or desktop applications give clients rapid and direct access to various medical services via an internet messaging network (WhatsApp, WeChat, Telegram, etc.). Symptom Checker is available in an AI-based "self-service" guiding system that evaluates and understands symptoms. Medical advice is available through a live chat with experienced doctors. MyDoc offers video consultations for 7 days in a week, and online video consultations with locally licensed physicians who can offer advice on medical diagnosis, treatment, health recommendations, and prescriptions in the local language. After video consultation with MyDoc, prescription medicine is delivered to the patients' door as needed [4].

Digital techniques like big data, AI, blockchain, Internet of Things, and telemedicine are generally in healthcare management which are described below.

Although the phrase "big data" has become ubiquitous, there is yet to be a common definition for its use. Big data, according to McKinsey, refers to datasets that are having too large a typical software tools. Database helps to acquire, manage, store, and analyze reports. The "3V" definition of big data offered by Gartner is that big data belongs to extreme velocity, volume, and various data assets which necessitate price effectively, novel forms of processing information increase the decision making and insight. According to various definitions, big data also has a fourth dimension: veracity, which refers to data quality, trustworthiness, and authenticity. The European Commission's Directorate-General for Research and Innovation's Health Directorate recommended the following description of big data for health research in the healthcare system—big data refers to large volume, clinical, diverse biological, lifestyle, and environmental data gathered from a person to huge cohorts, about their wellness and health status [5].

Big data is an act of intelligence for Electronic Health Records (EHRs), as it can connect operational, financial, and clinical analytic systems, and can help with evidence-based healthcare. Evidence-based medicine entails a systematic assessment of past clinical records to offer information for decision makers. Big data is useful in detecting disease in HIV patients' clinical genomic studies. However, to achieve the aims of big data analytics, rigorous data management is required. Data sources, data governance, data content, data consistency, data quality, data security and access, data stewardship, and user training all are part of this. Without proper management and control, data-related challenges might occur, such as unreliable, unavailable, missing, or erroneous data. As a result, data management goals are to deliver accurate, authentic, and reliable data that is important for good healthcare for decision-making. As a result, big data proposals must examine all the features of big data processes, including data capture, storage, search, sharing, and analysis [6].

The work of doctors and other professionals in healthcare will be facilitated and enhanced by AI tools but not replaced. AI is poised to assist healthcare workers with a wide range of duties, including administrative tasks, patient outreach, clinical documentation, and also in specialized areas like medical device automation, image analysis, and monitoring of patients. The value of AI-powered techniques in next-generation healthcare technology is being recognized by the healthcare ecosystem. AI has the potential to improve any procedure in healthcare operations and delivery. For example, in the case of price reductions, AI plays a major role in the healthcare system by providing a major motivator for AI employment. AI uses are expected to save the United States $150 billion in healthcare costs by 2026.

The shift from a reactive to a proactive healthcare strategy focused on the management of health rather than treatment of the disease for a substantial portion of these cost savings. As a result, fewer hospitalizations, medical visits, and treatments are expected. AI-based techniques will play a key role in assisting people in maintaining their health through continuous monitoring and coaching, as well as ensuring earlier diagnosis, personalized therapies, and more effective follow-ups. By 2021, the AI-related healthcare market is estimated to reach USD 6.6 billion, representing a 40% compound yearly growth rate [7].

There are differing viewpoints on the most useful AI applications in healthcare. In 2018, Forbes predicted that administrative workflows, robotic surgery, image analysis, clinical decision support, and virtual assistants will be the most important sectors. Accenture published a report in 2018 that covered the same topics as well as connected machines, decrease in dose error, and cyber security in which AI plays an important role. According to a 2019 McKinsey report, linked and cognitive gadgets, targeted and personalized medicine, electroceuticals and robotics-assisted surgery, all are important sectors where AI can grow efficiently in the future [8].

Blockchain is a public digital ledger and decentralized system which records transactions across several computers in such a way that no record can be changed retrospectively without affecting subsequent blocks. Each 'block' in the blockchain is confirmed and linked to the one before it, making a continuous chain. Blockchain delivers a high level of accountability because every transaction is recorded and verified publicly. No one can change the data written in the blockchain after it has been entered. Its purpose is to show that the data is current and unaltered. Data is stored on networks rather than a central database in Blockchain, which improves stability while also exposing its vulnerability to hacking [9].

Blockchain is a new technology that is being used to develop novel solutions in a type of field, like healthcare. In the healthcare system, a blockchain network is used to store and share data of patients across hospitals, pharmacies, diagnostic laboratories, and clinicians. In the medical profession, blockchain applications can properly identify serious and even deadly errors. As a result, it can enhance the security, performance, and transparency of data of medical sharing in the healthcare system. Medical institutions can use this technology to obtain insight and improve medical records analysis. In clinical trials, blockchain plays a critical role in detecting deceit; this technique can increase the efficacy of data for healthcare [10].

It helps to alleviate concerns about data alteration in healthcare by enabling a distinctive data storage pattern with the highest security level. It gives data access variety, interconnection, accountability, and authentication. Records of health data must be maintained confidential and safe for a variety of reasons. Blockchain enables decentralized data protection in healthcare while also avoiding unique dangers. Scholars can utilize this technique to examine a vast amount of previously unknown information about a certain group of people. It is beneficial to the growth of precision medicine if adequate funding for longitudinal research is made to be available [10, 11].

The Internet of Things (IoT) has the property to revolutionize healthcare. The Internet of Things (IoT) connects the Internet with physical devices, allowing data to be received and sent by the Internet. Machine learning, sensors help with real-time analysis, and embedded systems have all grown into and from the Internet of Things concept. It is about the smart clinical idea and other equipment that are connected to the Internet by wired or wireless connections. To do the desired work, smart devices can obtain and share data in everyday life. Smart cities, cars, electronics, entertainment systems, residences, and connected healthcare are all benefiting from IoT applications. IoT deployment in the medical industry relies on a variety of sensors, artificial intelligence, medical devices, diagnostic, and advanced imaging technologies.

The Internet of Things connects all computational, mechanical, and digital techniques to transport data over the Internet without any need for human communication. In today's world, many people die as a result of inaccurate and untimely health information. Through the use of sensors, this technology can instantly alert users to health-related risks. IoT has a strong ability to perform a successful operation and analyze results afterward. The use of IoT aids in the betterment of patient care. IoT allows for real-time monitoring, which saves lives from a variety of ailments such as diabetes, asthma attacks, heart failure, high blood pressure, and so on. Smart medical devices connect to a smartphone to seamlessly communicate essential health records to a physician. These devices also gather information on oxygen levels, weight, blood pressure, sugar levels, etc. [12].

Mobile health [mHealth], eHealth, ambient assisted living, wearable tools, semantic tools, smartphones, and community-based healthcare are just a few of the applications and services of IoT in healthcare that have recently been reviewed. These services have been extensively detailed and can be used to record and monitor health development remotely by professionals of healthcare, enhance chronic conditions self-management, help in primary abnormalities determination, identification of fast-track symptoms, deliver early intervention, and enhance adherence to prescriptions. These functions have the potential to make better use of healthcare possessions while also providing high-quality, low-cost medical treatment [13].

Telemedicine is a health-related service that uses telecommunication and electronic information techniques to provide care. It refers to the entire set of deliverables aimed at assisting patients and their doctors or healthcare professionals. Online consultations with patients, telehealth nursing, control in a remote area, remote psychiatry, and physical rehabilitation are just a few of the applications. It improves healthcare options, improves emergency service performance and quality, decreases diagnosis time, and saves money for both physicians and patients by streamlining clinical processes and lowering hospital transportation costs [14].

Due to travel costs, regular clinic visits are costly, especially in remote locations. People choose telemedicine in the age of the pandemic of Covid-19 when physical communication is risky. Fortunately, when telemedicine facilities are utilized via video conferencing or other virtual techniques, medical visits can be decreased. As a result, telemedicine saves time and money for both the healthcare practitioner and the patient. Furthermore, because of its quick and favorable properties, it can help hospitals and clinics simplify their process. This innovative technique would make it easier to keep track of patients who have been discharged and supervise their recovery. It is adequate to state that telemedicine can produce a great situation. A medical practitioner who uses telemedicine to treat and diagnose patients in a rural location is referred to as a telemedicine practitioner.

Using health applications for planned follow-up visits enhances the efficiency of doctors and patients by increasing the likelihood of follow-up, minimizing missed appointments, and improving patient results. Patients must have a complete medical history with him and use the high-definition audio–video system to show the physician regarding any of their noticeable bruises, rashes, or other indicators that are required for treatment. Practitioners will also require a payment processing and file management system. Doctors and patients can analyze the therapy procedure by using telemedicine technologies. This technology is a supplement to physical consultation and not a replacement for it. For individuals who are unable to visit a doctor, this technology is now a safe option [15].

8.2 Digital Assistants' Role in the Healthcare System

Digital assistants in healthcare are not a novel idea; they have been in improvement since the first conversational robots were introduced. With the increasing world population, healthcare systems are becoming increasingly overburdened. Because of the possible growth in triage processes automation and the supervision possibility in ambulatory care, the installation of digital assistants is boosting the approach to healthcare and enhancing the efficacy of healthcare.

8.2.1 For psychological therapy

Mental healthcare is primarily provided by general practitioners (GPs) or other primary health professionals in most rural and remote regions. Patients have limited access to experienced psychologists or psychiatrists or may wait an inordinate amount of time for treatment. Because of the scarcity of mental health facilities in these locations, primary care practitioners are expected to address more complex psychiatric presentations, often without the assistance of specialists. Patients in regional, rural, and distant locations frequently have difficulty in getting timely mental health treatment, resulting in unfair results when compared to their urban counterparts.

This condition is typically caused by a scarcity of specialized face-to-face psychotherapy facilities in the community. The early progress of digital psychotherapy was an alternate delivery technique for the treatment purpose which offers a way to close this healthcare gap while also avoiding the problems associated with workforce maldistribution. Digital psychotherapy, mainly cognitive behavioral therapy, is equally efficacious as face-to-face psychotherapy, according to multiple randomized controlled trials and a major meta-analysis. Increased understanding of available choices could help people in rural and distant areas to get access to psychological treatment. Patients with mild-to-moderate depressive or anxiety disorders should consider digital psychotherapy as an option [16].

Despite the numerous advantages that digital treatment delivery provides, there are also possible drawbacks. Phone and Internet reception in rural and distant areas may be limited or patchy, there is a limiting approach to sources. The more difficult fact is that neither access to the Internet nor personal gadget is widely available. Furthermore, information technology skills and minimum literacy are necessary that may restrict the utility of delivery for the treatment of individuals who lack these abilities. Another key factor is to consider all presently digital choices based on a primarily Western paradigm that may be inconvenient for particular culturally and linguistically diverse individuals and communities.

Finally, because digital psychotherapy is less organized than face-to-face sessions, it needs some self-motivation to access material and complete courses regularly. Patients who have a high level of avolition or avoidance may need more help from family or professionals to stay engaged. It is also critical that GPs have adequate training to help their patients who are undergoing these treatments. In an ideal world, this would be created by the creator of every online course and would be in the form of recognized training modules that support GPs' continuing professional growth needs. Because of lower face-to-face frequency encounters, greater use of digital psychotherapy has the property to increase caseload capacity which individual practitioners can serve [17].

8.2.2 Symptoms diagnosis and patient triage

CSC (chatbot-based symptom checker) apps have recently become popular in the mobile app industry. A computer program chatbot can engage in human-to-human communication. A CSC app uses chatbots to diagnose medical symptoms and engage in chats with users. Users communicate with a chatbot incorporated in the CSC app to input their symptoms and receive diagnoses. The majority of CSC apps debuted in the last few years, with the invention of AI algorithms for conversational chatbots. According to estimations, some CSC apps (such as Ada, K Health, and HealthTap) have been downloaded over one million times since their release. Despite their popularity, CSC apps have received little attention in the healthcare domain as a consumer-facing diagnostic technology; they can assist medical professionals or healthcare providers in seeking information and reducing diagnostic errors [18].

Computer-aided diagnosis (CAD) systems are sophisticated tools that enable physicians in making the best judgments possible by reducing the risk of clinical cognitive errors. The suggested approach makes use of a large health-related dataset curated via Altibbi firm that comprises various unstructured patient queries written in various Arabic dialects, as well as structured symptoms reported by general practitioners (GPs). The system consists of a combination of machine learning models that have been trained by using two modalities like symptoms of the patient and medical queries.

Experiments were conducted using a variety of feature representation technologies (such as word and statistical embeddings) and machine learning classifiers, such as Stochastic Gradient Descent Classifier (SGD Classifier), Random Forest (RF), Logistic Regression (LR), and Multilayer Perceptron (MLP) variants. In terms of categorization accuracy, the output of combining the two modalities has demonstrated promising predicting capacity, with an accuracy of 84.9%. The acquired outcomes show that the model can determine a diagnosis of various medical illnesses based on given symptoms and patient enquiries, which can help physicians for making the best possible judgments [19].

Because of the possible growth in triage procedures automation and supervision possibility in ambulatory care, the installation of digital assistants enhances access to healthcare and the efficacy of healthcare. Several applications were discovered to be built on third-party frameworks during the research of digital assistants for diagnosis of symptoms and patient triage. Infermedica is a structure that appears as the utmost frequent among the applications. The platform offers an API for patient triage and preliminary medical diagnosis that can be used in various applications such as symptom diagnostic digital assistants and adaptive patient intake forms. Natural language processing and a specialty recommender algorithm that discovers nearby healthcare facilities based on user's locality are among the extra services available for optional implementation in the framework [20].

8.2.3 Digital assistant for treatment monitoring

Self-monitoring upsurges people's awareness regarding their behavior and the factors that cause or surround it. However, paper record (PR) takes time and effort to complete, which is the most popular way of self-monitoring. Furthermore, PRs prevent individuals from receiving instant, real-time external motivation and support. A personalized feedback message is a reasonable next step and it is based on data that feedback can help reinforce motivation for behavior change when it is given in the context of achieving a goal. Through the feedback mechanism, emerging technologies may increase self-monitoring and weight-loss therapy success [21].

The information processing needs behavioral self-management of diabetes. Combining self-monitoring with behavioral self-management intervention using a personal digital assistant (PDA) may increase adherence and patient outcomes. A personalized digital assistant is a little handheld computer. There was only one study that used PDA-based therapies in diabetic individuals. When patients with diabetes employed an electronic monitoring system for diabetes by a handheld electronic diary to document food amounts and blood glucose readings for 6 months, Tsang *et al.* found a substantial decrease in hemoglobin A1c when compared to the standard paper-based tracking technique. According to an earlier symposium held at the Society of Behavioral Medicine and PDA, convenience and potability can improve devotion to self-monitoring, though there is a scarcity of empirical evidence on how PDAs might be integrated into typical behavioral change treatments to improve diabetes adherence [22].

An alternative to paper documentation is a personal digital assistant with nutritional software. This goal is to explain differences in changes in diet till 6 months; between these days patients were randomly allocated to utilize a paper record or a PDA for their self-monitoring in a weight-loss clinical trial treatment. Between 2006 and 2009, self-monitoring adherence as well as changes in diet and weight were analyzed. The participants (n = 192) were 78% male and 84% female, with a mean of 49 years of age and BMI (body mass index) 34.1 kg/m^2. The groups do not vary in terms of intake of energy, % calories from fat, or the food servings numbers for groups studied at the baseline.

Both groups exhibited significant weight, consumption of energy, and % calories from total saturated fatty acids and fat reductions at 6 months ($P < 0.001$), with no differences between groups. In comparison to the paper documentation group, the PDA group extensively enhanced their fruit consumption ($P = 0.02$) and vegetable ($P = 0.04$) while decreasing intake of refined grain ($P = 0.02$). Changes in the percentage of calories from total fat ($P = 0.02$), trans-fatty acids ($P = 0.04$), and monounsaturated fatty acids ($P = 0.002$) revealed interactions between the two groups and self-monitoring. In both groups, frequent self-monitoring was linked with added sugar ($P = 0.01$) and total sugar ($P = 0.02$) intake. The results show that utilization of a PDA for self-monitoring could help people become extra conscious of their behavior and dietary changes [23].

8.3 Electronic Health Record (EHR)

During periods of patient care, an EHR maintains the results of clinical and administrative interactions between a provider (physician, nurse, others) and a patient. As a result, the EMR represents the physicians' practice patterns, job functions, knowledge, and expertise when they construct it [24]. A digitized counterpart of a patient's paper chart is termed an electronic health record (EHR). EHRs are patient-centered, actual records that make content accessible to authenticated users securely and immediately.

When an EHR system does include a patient's treatment and medical history, it is intended to go beyond traditional clinical record which is obtained from a provider's office and can comprise a wider view of patient care. EHRs are an essential characteristic of health.

- The medical history, diagnosis, treatment plans, prescriptions, immunization schedules, radiology pictures, allergies, plus laboratory and test outcomes of a patient are all kept in this file.
- They allow providers to approach evidence-based equipment to make decisions about the care of patients.
- The provider workflow can be streamlined and automated.

EHRs are invented to exchange information with other healthcare practitioners, like laboratories, diagnostic imaging centers, pharmacies, specialists, emergency rooms, schools, and workplace clinics, so they enclose data from all physicians involved in the care of patients [25].

An electronic health record (EHR) is a library of electronically preserved records regarding a person's lifetime health and status, kept in such a way that it may be accessible by numerous legitimate users. A computer-based patient record system includes data management capabilities such as clinical alerts and reminders, information resources for support of healthcare decisions, and aggregate data analysis for research and management.

8.3.1 Benefits of EHR

The benefits of EHR is described below [26]. Table 8.1 describes the benefits of electronic health records.

8.3.2 Ways to differentiate an electronic health record from a paper-based record

An EHR is versatile and flexible. The record can be entered in a form that makes the process of entering data easier and presented in a variety of styles that are appropriate for their analysis. Furthermore, the EHR can incorporate multimedia data like echocardiographic video loops and radiological images, which have not been previously available in the traditional medical record. Documentation in an EHR can become more accessible since it is captured as printed text rather than handwritten and it can also be more organized because the input is structured [27]. Some EHRs created between 1971 and 1992 used hierarchical or relational databases and were built around or alongside hospital accounting and booking systems. COSTAR, PROMIS, TMR, and HELP were created as healthcare systems to assist in the improvement of medical care and research [28, 29].

Table 8.1 Benefits of electronic health record.

S. No	The benefits of Electronic Health Record
1.	EHRs guarantee that patient data can be consulted at any time from any location.
2.	EHRs can be simply saved, take up less room, and be kept for an unlimited period.
3.	When it is in electronic format, the number of data loss is reduced.
4.	EHRs assist in the monitoring of a patient's clinical development and the advancement of patient compliance.
5.	The electronic health record (EHR) provides an overview of a person's clinical events throughout their life.
6.	EHRs are easily adaptable among healthcare workers.
7.	EHRs can be utilized to do research.
8.	EHRs help doctors make smart choices and provide evidence-based care.

8.3.3 Initiatives by the Government of India

In 2013 September, in India, the Ministry of Health and Family Welfare (MoH&FW) announced the first set of electronic health record standards. The EMR Standards Committee, which is part of the Ministry of Health and Family Welfare, made these suggestions [30]. Table 8.2 describes the goals of EHR standards while Figure 8.1 describes the function of EHR.

Table 8.2 Goals of EHR standards [30].

S. No	Goals
1.	Utilizing adopted standards, encourage technological innovation.
2.	Reduce implementation expenses as much as feasible.
3.	Look at overall best practices, lessons learned, policies, and frameworks.
4.	All vendors and stakeholders should be motivated to engage and embrace.

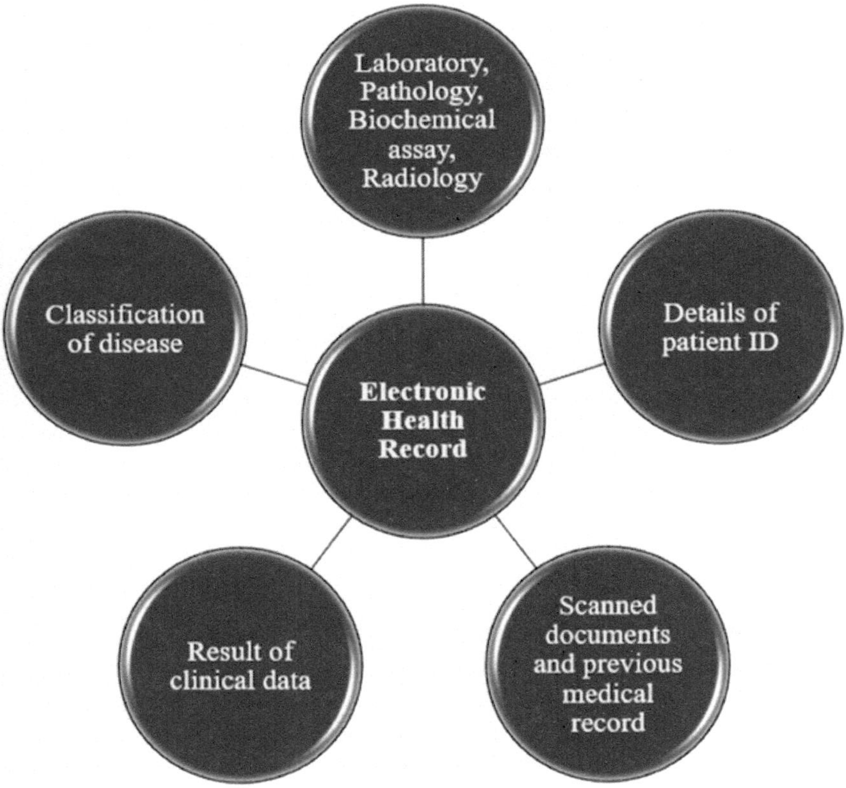

Figure 8.1 Illustration of the function of electronic health records.

8.4 Personal Health Record (PHR)

Individuals keep a Personal Health Record (PHR), which is an electronic, universally accessible, lifelong collection of health information. PHRs have a wide range of advantages, including improved patient–provider relationships; more patient empowerment; reduced healthcare costs; improved safety, efficiency, coordination, and quality of care [31]. PHR is a digitized, globally accessible, and lifelong health information resource managed by individuals. Patients and providers can gain information from PHRs in a variety of ways. PHRs consist of a variety of data, from laboratory results to radiology images and reports on blood pressure, and blood glucose readings are taken at home [32].

PHRs not only record data in a format that the patient can understand, but they also provide a wealth of healthcare information on how to interpret results and what measures should be taken [33]. PHRs can help patients and clinicians communicate more effectively by reducing the amount of information that is lost in verbal communication. PHRs let patients keep track of their medical problems, medications, and health-related activities such as self-care and self-monitoring [34]. An additional alternative is that the PHRs receive information from clinical devices like accelerometers, gyroscopes, wireless scales, wristbands, and smart watches. The Internet of Things refers to the progress of these technologies like IoT [35, 36].

PHR includes various types of information like phone numbers, doctor's names, allergies caused by medications including dosages, dates, and a list of surgeries and illnesses, chronic health problems like high blood pressure, immunization history, and family history.

8.4.1 PHR advantages

Owning a PHR can exactly save a life. In an emergency, it can rapidly provide essential information to first responders, like as illnesses being treated for, medications being taken, allergies related to drugs, and doctor's contact information. The benefits of PHR are summarized in Figure 8.2.

8.4.1.1 Keep track of health and evaluate it

Keep track of improvement toward achieving health objectives, like lowering cholesterol.

8.4.1.2 Make the utmost of physician visits

Prepare questions for the doctor as well as information that you would like to provide, such as recent blood pressure readings.

Figure 8.2 The schematic figure shows the benefits of PHR.

8.4.1.3 Manage health between physician visits

Upload and analyze records from home monitoring tools like blood pressure cuff. Reminder according to physician's instructions from the last visit.

8.4.1.4 Get systematized

Track medications, vaccinations, appointments, and screening or preventive services like mammograms. Researchers suggest that when parents use personal health data for their kids, kids are more likely to have preventive well-child examinations on time [37].

8.5 Medical Practice Management (MPM) Software

A medical practice management system (also known as a PMS) is a software-based information and enterprise management solution for physician offices that provide a collection of core functions to support the operations of a single or several medical practices. EMR (electronic medical records) systems are frequently linked to a practice management system (PMS) [38]. Some knowledge from both systems overlap, such as patient and provider information.

The key distinction between the two is that the EMR system collects clinical charting aspects of a visit, while the practice management application (PMS) is used for administrative and financial purposes. Following a patient visit, the practice management system enters a set of charges relating to the specific service delivered to the patient.

These payments are often associated with a fee and are submitted by using a blend of current procedural terminology (CPTCPT) and International Classification of Diseases (ICDICD) codes. A patient management system (PMSPMS) is a form of medical software that is used to handle daily activities at a hospital, nursing home, or physician's clinic by dealing with the day-to-day operations of medical practice in a physician's office [39].

8.5.1 Applications of patient management system/medical practice management system

- Store a range of patient data, including demographics, insurance plans (primary, secondary, and tertiary), and medicine orders.
- Attach photos, movies, audio files, and Microsoft workplace documents to patient and office documents in a variety of multimedia formats. Set up reminders for patient-related issues, billing, and scheduling, among other things.
- Save notes on patients, billing issues, and more those are date, time, and user-stamped.
- Keep an eye on how patients are referred to your practice.
- Before establishing claim transactions, post any co-payments or credits to the patient's account [40].

8.6 Big Data in Biomedical Research

Biomedical research has begun to take advantage of the opportunities offered by big data. Large-scale databases, numerous data sources, enhanced capacity of storage, and unique computational methods are all used in big data research to enable high-speed data analytics [41]. Big data trends in the biomedical domain enable and allow improvements in areas like brain imaging, whole-genome sequencing, digital phenotyping, and mobile medicine [42]. Big data also allows investigators to derive health perceptions from non-medical data sources, such as data from social media, wearable trackers, and Internet searches [43]. Big data research brings up new avenues for speeding up health-related research and possibly eliciting developments that help patients [44].

Big dataBig data is a novel concept and infrastructure which allows case studies to be transformed into huge, data-driven research. The three fundamental features of big data, generally referred to as the 3Vs: volume, variety, and velocity, are widely regarded as defining qualities of big data. First and foremost, the quantity of data in biomedical informatics fields is expanding at an exponential rate. The diversity of data kinds and structures is the second aspect of big data. The biomedical big data ecosystem consists of many multiple levels of data sources, resulting in a diverse dataset for researchers. The third feature of massive data is velocity, which refers to the speed with which data is processed and generated. The latest generation of sequencing technologies allows for the low-cost synthesis of billions of DNA sequence data each day, because gene sequencing necessitates greater speeds [45].

8.6.1 Applications of big data

Bioinformatics study examines molecular changes in biological systems. With today's customized medicine trends, there is a rising need to store, collect, and evaluate these huge datasets in a reasonable time amount [46, 47]. Big datasets in bioinformatics applications help investigators to obtain and analyze biological data by providing data repositories, efficient data manipulation tools, and computer infrastructure. MapReduce and Hadoop are currently used widely within the field of biomedical sciences [48].

Big data could aid in the transmission of information. Most doctors find it difficult to stay updated on the most recent evidence-based guidelines for clinical practice. Medical literature has been digitized, which has substantially increased access; nonetheless, the vast number of researches makes information translation challenges. It would be extremely difficult for a practitioner to read through all relevant studies and guidelines to establish an effective treatment approach for patients with numerous chronic illnesses even if they had access to them. This issue could be solved by analyzing existing EHRs and creating a dashboard that helps clinicians to make better judgments. In cooperation between IBM's Watson supercomputer and Memorial Sloan-Kettering Cancer Centre, this approach is being utilized to help identify and recommend treatment options for cancer patients [49, 50].

The big data method is different from standard decision-support devices in that it makes recommendations based on real-time data investigation of a patient rather than rule-based decision trees. Data-driven clinical decision support systems may also aid with price savings and appropriate treatment uniformity. Clinicians may receive notifications informing them about diagnostic and treatment decisions made by respected peers encountering alike patient profiles, similar to how purchasers receive messages from Amazon (e.g., this book was also purchased by consumers like you) [50].

8.6.2 Platform for big data (Hadoop cluster)

Hadoop can be utilized to process massive amounts of healthcare records in an environment of the cloud. Rack servers connected with the rack switch top help in the construction of Hadoop clusters. Rack switch uplinks are connected with a second switch set having the same bandwidth. This cluster is put in the cloud so that its workflow can acquire the results it needs from enormous data sources. EHR data was loaded into a cluster and looked up for questions in this situation. The cluster's workflow is like this: HDFS (Hadoop Distributed File System) loads the records into the cluster. MapReduce algorithm is used for data analysis. HDFS saves and writes data to the cluster.

The cluster's results are read via HDFS. To know the number of patients diagnosed with heart disease from huge EHR datasets, Hadoop is used to process and analyze the data efficiently. Hadoop breaks huge data volumes into smaller parts and distributes them while processing over numerous devices, allowing it to generate results quickly. Massive data must be fed into a Hadoop cluster for processing to achieve faster parallel processing. The data will be broken down into smaller chunks by the client, and each chunk will be transferred to a different machine for processing. Each data chunk runs parallelly with various machines to avoid data loss. Hadoop administrators must manually define the number of racks in every slave data node available in the form of the cluster to avoid loss of data and poor performance of the network [51].

Hadoop is made up of two basic parts: storage and processing.

8.6.2.1 Storage

A distributed file system called HDFS (Hadoop Distributed File System) helps in storage. It is a fault-tolerant distributed system of files that are meant to work on commodity hardware. HDFS is a file system that allows high throughput access to records and is well-suited to applications with huge record collections. HDFS is a distributed file system that can store data across thousands of machines. The architecture of HDFS is master/slave. Files of HDFS are divided into fixed-size blocks. The block size can be changed, but it shows defaults at 64 megabytes.

8.6.2.2 Processing (MapReduce)

It is a programming model developed by Google in 2004 to make it easier to construct fault-tolerant algorithms that handle large amounts of data in parallel with large groups of hardware. This works on a large data collection by splitting the problem and datasets into separate sets and running them in parallel.

The two main functions of MapReduce are as follows:

- **Map:** The Map function is used to filter, transform, or parse data and is always called first. Reduce takes the output from Map as its input.
- **Reduce:** Reduce is an optional function that is typically used to summarize data from the Map function [52].

When conducting MapReduce jobs, Hadoop goals to run Map and Reduce tasks on a system where data get processed, avoiding the copying of data across systems. The application demonstrates that MapReduce tasks are beyond efficient when only one huge file is utilized as input rather than a large number of little files. Because little files are spread across multiple machines, copying them to the MapReduce system needs significant overheating. The application claims that a small file slows the execution of the process by 10 to 100 times.

The healthcare industry handles numerous difficulties in processing data to provide great service to all parties included. One of the subjects discussed is the processing of a medical image. Hadoop provides a solution to analyze an increasing number of medical photos from diverse resources and extract the information required to make a proper diagnosis. The Hadoop Image Processing Interface (HIPI) shows how image processing can be done [53].

8.7 Internet of Things (IoT) and their Advantages in Healthcare

kHealth is an IoT-based system of health monitoring that serves as an example of standard IoT healthcare system frameworks. To develop tailored predictive models, kHealth leverages both physiological and personal observations which are sensed by using wearable tools on subscription patients, also public (e.g., CDC and hospital given) and population (Twitter and a weather service) level data. The IoT sensors monitor and transmit data like peak respiratory flow rate, activity level, weight, as well as environmental factors (outdoor air quality index (AQI), humidity, pollen, hydrocarbons, ozone, mold, nitric oxide, carbon dioxide, and carbon monoxide levels) and location to kHealth provider.

In addition to sensor data, kHealth service uses datasets of the public, which provide statistics on disease propensity based on different socioeconomic and demographic characteristics. To assess and determine the patient's condition status, kHealth uses machine learning and other data mining methods which involve Semantic Web technology. In brief, kHealth gathers relevant characteristics from wearable tools and another dataset, then generates personalized health predictive models for its members and approved physicians and researchers [54].

IoT essentially redefines multiple areas such as digital connectivity, adequate security at various levels, quality control, system optimization through devices, management in various sectors at various stages, automobile, building, monitoring, and healthcare. The benefits of IoT in various sectors are boundless, but it has various applications such as reducing errors, enhancing systems management, efficient processes, improving security, utilization of assets in an enhanced manner, improved treatment, faster disease diagnosis, synchronized monitoring and reporting, affordable end-to-end connectivity, absolute alerts assistance and tracking, and medical assistance in a remote area [55].

8.7.1 IoT-based healthcare architecture

The network layer is the perception layer and the application layer contains three core layers that make up IoT architecture for healthcare delivery. Figure 8.3 shows the three core layer of IoT architecture that helps in healthcare delivery.

8.7.1.1 Perception layer: data-collecting sensing systems

The Internet of Things is built on the foundation of perception and identification technologies. Radio frequency identification (RFID), webcams, infrared sensors, medical sensors, GPS, and smart device sensors are examples of sensors that can detect changes in the environment. These sensors provide comprehensive perception via location recognition, object recognition, and geographic recognition as well as the ability to transform this data into digital signals for easier network transmission. Sensor technologies enable real-time monitoring of therapies with the collection of a wide range of physiological characteristics of a patient, allowing diagnoses and high-quality treatment to be delivered quickly [56].

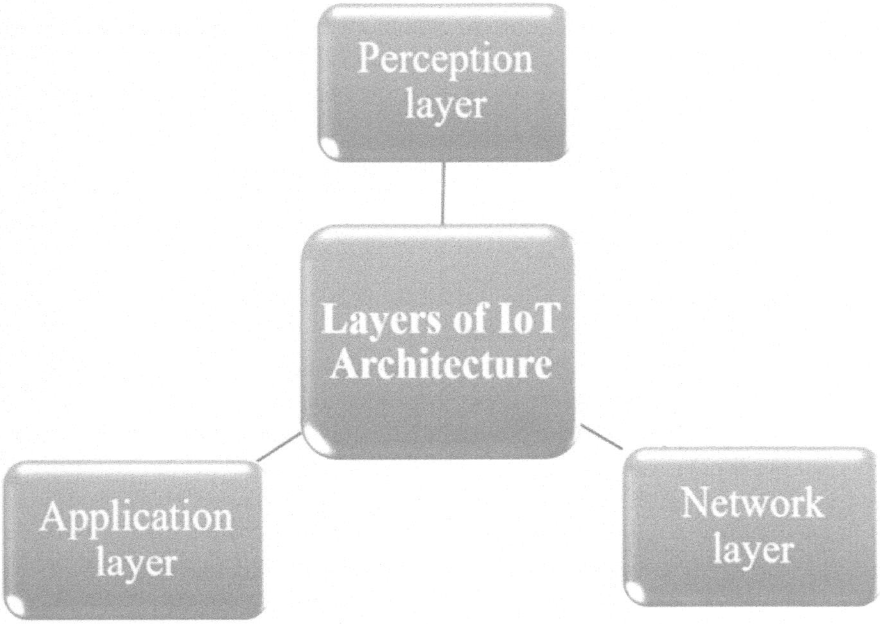

Figure 8.3 Three core layers of IoT architecture help in healthcare delivery.

The perception layer plays a major job to sample data about the environment using various types of perception devices and discern the states of those devices. It obtains useful information by processing data with cooperative accessing methods and then transmitting it to the network layer via access devices such as WSN gateways [57].

8.7.1.2 Network layer: data communication and storage

Perception layer data is transmitted through an existing communication network via the network layer [58]. Different private networks, Internet, wireless, and wired communication networks make up the network layer. It serves as a nerve controller for people and the brain is utilized to transmit and process information from a perceptual layer. The Internet of Things network layer is developed, which is on top of today's Internet infrastructure and mobile telecommunication. Its main use is to send data across a long distance. The network layer, which is often regarded as the most mature element, consists of numerous communication networks and integrated networks based on the Internet. It also has a component that intelligently handles enormous amounts of data.

The IoT information management center includes cloud computing, expert system, platform, and so on, i.e., the network layer not only has network operation competence but also enhances information operation competence. For instance, in a mobile payment system, once the network layer has confirmed the built-in RFID data captured and sent to the Internet using simple equipment, the payment will be made via the network of the bank. The infrastructure of IoT allows delivering common services which are done by the network layer [58].

The essential technique which makes the Internet of Things centered on data realized is the handling and administration technique for perceptual data in the network layer. Data memory, analysis, inquiry, excavation, and interpretation, also the philosophy and technology of data-driven behaviors and decisions are all covered by this technology. Cloud calculative stage will be a key aspect of the network layer and the base of most applications in the application layer as an analysis and memory platform for mass perceptual data. The operator of a communication network plays a critical role in the network layer of industrial chains and the fast growth of cloud calculative platforms will be another aid to the Internet of Things progress [59, 60].

8.7.1.3 Application Layer

High-level features like IoT content retrieval services, access control, and management of data are provided by the application layer [61]. The application layer completes public intelligent storage and analysis of data-related information, realizes information processing and all types of intelligent application exchanging and sharing done with the help of information technology such as cloud computing, database technology, middleware, expert system, and so on. The development of an IoT applications variety is based on the application support layer's data processing, and it employs technology such as virtual reality, multimedia, and human–computer interface to create an intelligent application interface between user and IoT, as well as the implementation and use of all types of intelligent information [62].

8.8 Artificial Intelligence in Biomedical Engineering

AI is often known as the study of "intelligent agents," or any system that can see and understand its environment and take proper action to increase its chances to attain its goals.

8.8.1 AI in living assistance

AI technologies combined with smart robotic systems are leading the path to a better life quality. NNs may be trained to detect expressions of human faces as commands using certain image processing processes. Furthermore, facial expression analysis based on HMIs enables people with impairments to control robot support vehicles and wheelchairs without the use of a sensor or joystick attached to the body [63].

RUDO, an "ambient intelligent system," assists blind individuals in living alongside sighted people and working in specialized industries like electronics and informatics. It consists of many modules which primarily ensure or support while approaching people recognition, alerting other house members regarding any movement inside the flat, children (sighted) supervision, cooperation between blind and sighted person (for example, while studying), and heating control and zonal regulation by a blind person. It offers a single user interface that allows blind people to access different functions. The interface for blind persons aids in computer work, including Braille writing on a normal keyboard and specialized work in electronics and informatics like as programming [64].

Expert systems (ES) is a subset of artificial intelligence that is utilized in different applications, involving medical consultation and earlier help in rehabilitation evaluation and intervention. ES-MRES-MR, a web-based platform, can help doctors to make better decisions when it comes to treating people with brain injuries, strokes, and dementia. A simultaneously produced version for "non-expert" consumers is offered for application and possible commercial manufacturing. This is particularly effective for assisting remote those with permanent impairment of memory who have reached a cognitive training plateau and require the prosthetic system to improve memory for daily independence [65].

8.8.2 AI in biomedical information processing

Because of its great capability of model construction and parallel learning, artificial intelligence is fast-growing and exerts an enhanced impact in the biomedical processing hardware and algorithms field. AI-based biomedical applications include intelligent monitoring of EMG, monitoring of ECG, and monitoring of hearing aids and blood pressure. AI-based classification of algorithms is utilized for automated classification and diagnosis in a broad range of AI-based biomedical applications. When compared to traditional signal processing algorithms, AI-based algorithms aid clinicians in improving the intelligence, diagnosis accuracy, and classification by automatically extracting and analyzing features of a signal while being less affected by subjective factors.

In the past, various AI-based categorization methods have been suggested. Support vector machine (SVM), back propagation neural network (BPNN), long short-term memory network (LSTM), convolutional neural networks (CNN), recurrent neural networks (RNN), probabilistic neural networks (PNN), fuzzy neural networks, and others are examples of neural networks. Many algorithms are appropriate for various applications. CNN and SVM, for example, are commonly employed in signal processing of ECG, while fuzzy classifiers are widely used in monitoring blood pressure [66].

Artificial intelligence is employed in the healthcare industry for a variety of functions, including coordinating bed scheduling, staff rotation, and giving medical information, among other things. As a clinical decision support system, artificial neural network systems are used. Computer-aided interpretation of medical pictures, for example, can be used to scan digital images from computed tomography to highlight salient portions for identifying probable ailments, such as spotting a tumor. One of the most common applications of AI is heart sound analysis. Using AI data mining techniques, diseases such as lung cancer and heart disease can be predicted early [67].

8.8.3 AI in biomedical research

Biomedical research has evolved into a data-centric activity in the last decade, thanks to novel material and experimental procedures linked to data gathering, distribution, and utilization. For example, in the emerging field of precision medicine, "omic" data are now regularly collected alongside clinical, phenotypic, lifestyle, and socio-economic data to create larger-than-ever research cohorts. Artificial intelligence is expected to facilitate the simultaneous calculation of such different arrays of data, advancing precision medicine's promise of more personalized methods for the diagnosis and treatment of individual patients. Artificial intelligence is being used in drug development to analyze huge libraries of potentially therapeutic compounds, automate biomedical literature searches using natural language processing techniques, and anticipate trial dosage in translational medicine.

Machine learning is also being used to create prediction models that could aid doctors in prognostication and tailoring medicine and rehabilitation for particular patients, such as those following a stroke. For example, electronic health records (EHR) allow for use of real-world data to develop knowledge about the consequences of a medical operation (be it a diagnosis, a prognosis, therapy, or a rehabilitation plan). AI may be used to mine EHRs for disease familiarity or people at risk for a specific chronic condition, as well as help health systems organize themselves by assisting with triage and patient management [68].

Since the 1950s, AI scientists have strived to understand the language of humans. Speech recognition, translation, text analysis, and other language-related goals are among the applications covered by NLP (Natural language processing). Statistical and semantic NLP are the two main techniques. Statistical NLP is based on machine learning (in particular, deep learning neural networks) and has recently improved recognition accuracy. It necessitates a vast "corpus," or body of language to learn from. The generation, comprehension, and classification of clinical documentation and published research are the most common uses of NLP in the healthcare industry. NLP systems help to analyze unstructured clinical notes, in the preparation of reports (for example, on radiological examinations), patient dialog transcription, and conversational AI conduction [69].

8.9 AI in Diagnosis and Prediction

Artificial intelligence's application in medicine is currently at the forefront. The predictive and diagnostic analysis of diverse medical images, such as retina photographs and skin lesions, radiologic images, and microscopic pathologic images all of these are the clinical practice areas where artificial intelligence is predicted to have a significant impact. Artificial deep neural networks contain multiple layers of artificial neuronal links stack that simulate neuronal connections of brain and methods specialized for image analysis like convolutional neural network is a type of deep neural network that conceptually imitates visual pathway, are largely responsible for this potential usefulness.

Before implementing artificial intelligence devices in clinical practice, it is necessary to conduct a thorough evaluation of their clinical utility and performance. Demonstrating the technical soundness of artificial intelligence systems for medicine is required to verify their clinical performance and utility. It begins after technical soundness has been statistical and established, and it necessitates a thorough understanding and application of important epidemiologic principles to generate high-level proof that goes beyond basic tool knowledge. Inadequately addressing statistical and epidemiologic concepts can lead to distortion, and in some cases, overestimation, of clinical performance and AI tool utility [70].

As more technologies turn to AI for help, it is no wonder that cancer diagnostic procedures have been slowly integrating approaches to improve the diagnosis of patients with greater precision and accuracy. Another advantage is the system's capacity to manage vast data amounts and isolate information that experts are unable to notice. The effort to improve medical imaging methods began with an examination of how deep learning can improve the diagnosis of cancer by utilizing imaging. Devices that allow for enhanced ability to interpret and scan images faster, ensure great workflow and image quality, or increase the quality of an image by incorporating 3D techniques into the extraction of an image are all part of the effort to improve medical imaging methods. Though imaging modalities appear to be a natural fit for AI, the prospective application of AI to aid with pathology and genetic disease detection appears to be equally promising and deserves equal attention. This may necessitate adjustments to recent medical testing procedures or the development of new ways to view illnesses as they emerge. Overall, improving recent testing or imaging technologies can be transformational [71].

A stroke illness system based on AI that uses EMG biosignals from ordinary life performs both offline and online processing. Deep learning and machine learning-based model management and development of EMG data are included in offline processing. Based on EMG biosignals acquired in real time from everyday living, an online processing function and early prediction and diagnosis of stroke have been developed. The data of EMG biosignals acquired in real time throughout daily walking is updated in the repository in the offline module according to the system's cycle. Machine learning and deep learning technologies are utilized to preprocess gathered EMG biosignals and create a learning model. Learning models with machine learning methods are generated using attribute subset selection from the preprocessed EMG for early identification and prediction of stroke disorders. Before being employed in real-time stroke predictions, ML LSTM-based learning models are generated and delivered to the second module for online processing. At the request of the user or system, the online module measures and gathers real-time EMG biosignals in everyday life. The "preprocessing and normalization" phase cleans up the acquired EMG data by removing any missing or incomplete data. Because each attribute's lowest and maximum values differ, a normalizing step is used based on the measurement unit.

It is possible to ensure that the projected model taught performs optimally and to give analytical data. LSTM-based prediction models and pre-trained machine learning are used in the "Real-Time Stroke Prediction" block. Utilizing the determined EMG optimum characteristics subset, semantic analysis based on machine learning and real-time prediction is done. Currently, the deep-learning LSTM model uses EMG biosignals that have gone through preprocessing blocks to achieve earlier prediction and detection of stroke in real time. The medical staff or hospital receives these forecasts and semantic analysis information. Finally, people are assisted with medical inspections and treatment facilities with emergency alarms and speedy hospital visits as appropriate, based on the physician's diagnosis of the danger of stroke [72].

Deep learning, machine learning,machine learning and cognitive computing are examples of artificial intelligence (AI) approach that may play a crucial role in the cardiovascular (CV) drug evolution to provide accurate CV therapy. AI can make use of huge data and improve medical care. Cardiovascular diseases (CVDs) are complicated in reality and varied in character since they are caused by a variety of environmental (like air pollution), genetic, and behavioral variables (e.g., gut and diet microbiome). Rather than assessing a basic score system or standard risk in CV variables, much more progress needs to be made to properly and effectively forecast outcomes. Picture recognition in CV imaging and pattern recognition in diverse syndromes, both benefit from deep learning AI employing big data. AI can categorize novel phenotypes or genotypes of heart failure (HF) with preserved ejection fraction (HFpEF), and unique diagnostic echocardiographic characteristics which lead to innovative targeted therapy. Furthermore, 2-dimensional speckle-tracking echocardiography (2D-STE) quantitation has not been able to adequately assess left ventricular ejection since left ventricular ejection fraction is commonly calculated by the time-honored "eyeball" method or manually tracing boundaries method, both of which lack precision and reproducibility. As a result, AI could help to increase 2D-STE quantification accuracy and other cardiac imaging techniques.

To enable precision CV medicine, the paradigm is evolving away from traditional statistical methods and toward AI. Instead of physicians initiating ideas, big data are utilized to develop novel hypotheses automatically. Instead of replacing doctors, artificial intelligence will help them to make better clinical decisions [73].

8.10 Blockchain Taxonomy

There are four types of blockchain systems now in use: private, public, consortium, and hybrid blockchains.

8.10.1 Public blockchains

Public blockchains (like Ethereum and Bitcoin) allow a fully decentralized network in which any member can view the content of the blockchain and participate in the consensus process [74, 75].

8.10.2 Private blockchains

Private blockchains are used to track data transactions between different departments or persons and are specialized to single enterprise solutions. To join the network, each participant must first give their approval, after which they will be deemed a known member.

8.10.3 Consortium blockchain

Consortium blockchain is a permissioned network that is exclusively accessible to a certain set of people. It is utilized as a distributed database that is auditable and reliably synced and keeps participant data exchanges recorded.

8.10.4 Hybrid blockchains

Hybrid blockchains bring advantages of both public and private blockchains together. As a result, a public blockchain is used to make the ledger completely available, while a private blockchain runs in the background to manage access toward ledger alterations [75].

8.11 Blockchain Use Cases in Healthcare

8.11.1 Blockchain in remote patient monitoring

Healthcare is a crucial priority for every country's overall development. Doctors provide healthcare to improve or maintain people's health by treatment of disease, diagnosis, prevention, accident, illness, and other physically and mentally unwell people. Nowadays, everyone is compelled to go to the hospital for regular examinations and diagnoses, which is an expensive and time-consuming process. As a result, even the nearest hospital is out of reach for a seriously ill patient. To address this issue, the healthcare industry has implemented RPM, in which patients wear wristwatches (WDs) that capture real-time health data like heart rate, ECG, blood pressure, and temperature. This data aid physicians in their diagnosis, and with the decentralized AI support, they can make health-related recommendations to their patients. Patients were diagnosed remotely by physicians using this method, which improved the patient's quality of care [76, 77].

The most difficult and RPM-targeted application area is obtaining real-time patient information remotely. The current system collects real-time data from WDs and stores it on a centralized cloud server. Each node in a centralized atmosphere is linked to a central entity or single node. In any scenario, if central organizations fail, the likelihood of data loss increases. Take a backup of your data and store it on a centralized cloud server to fix this problem. Another issue was that the system was not protected against various harmful attacks such as confidentiality, integrity, and availability threats [77, 78].

As the use of Internet of Things tools and other remote patient monitoring systems grows, security issues concerning logging and data transfer emerge. To deal with the protected health information (PHI) these tools generate, use blockchain-based smart contracts to provide secure medical sensor management and analysis. A system in which sensors connect with a smart tool that calls smart contracts and writes data of all events held on the blockchain uses an Ethereum protocol based on the private blockchain. By sending messages to medical experts and patients in real time, this smart contract system would facilitate real-time monitoring of the patient and medical interventions while also keeping a record secure of those who initiated these activities. Different security concerns connected with remote patient monitoring would be addressed and notifications would be delivered to all parties included in a HIPAA-compliant way [79].

The majority of traditional RPM topologies have a remote server. A Local Processing Unit (LPU) or a Base Station connects a cloud server to a Body Area Sensor Network (BASN). Even though current designs can handle patient monitoring, because the architecture is centralized, systems are stopped by Denial of Service (DoS) or Ransom assaults. Furthermore, architectures of centralized healthcare will be not able to handle massive volumes of end-to-end communication to keep up with the expected exponential expansion of medical IoT devices. Healthcare professionals and patients must trust third-party cloud service providers for cloud processes to satisfy the high processing and storage needs of remote patient monitoring. Patients are rarely assured accountability and traceability of their medical records while using cloud services. Furthermore, integrating RPM records into electronic health records could compromise the high level of privacy that several patients anticipate [80].

8.11.2 Pharmaceutical supply chain

Decentralized blockchains enable new varieties of distributed applications. The financial industry is particularly interested in employing blockchains to automate and digitalize procedures, particularly when several stakeholders are involved. Many start-ups suppose that the cost savings from automated procedures may be extended to another area as well. Modum.io AG is a start-up that aims to integrate blockchain technology into the pharmaceutical supply chain. Since there are so many participants in the supply chain, blockchain technology can be utilized to automate procedures and save money [81].

Blockchain was identified as an emerging technology in a review of recent and developing techniques to reduce the fake drugs problem, with the ability for tracing and tracking drug reagents and products, detection of counterfeit via information verification of supply chain participants, and incorporate anti-counterfeit tools into the Internet of Things and interoperability between unrelated databases in the supply chain. The blockchain technology used in healthcare research and clinical practice is now generating a lot of attention, and it is being investigated for its potential to enhance the security of health records in the face of rising cyberattacks. Outside of healthcare, other sectors are looking at the possibilities for establishing a trustworthy environment in which people can supply and receive a variety of services [82].

When an industry makes a novel product, it generates a unique hash and assigns it to it. The hash of the product will be used to register it on the blockchain (unique ID). On a blockchain network, the product will be treated as a digital asset, and its hash will be used to trace it at any moment. Depending on the preference of manufacturers, any additional product information is stored off-chain or on-chain. Utilizing a few forms of identification, off-chain data will be blended with on-chain data. In utmost blockchain-based apps, a hash digest of all off-chain data (like SHA-256) is generated and connected to on-chain data. However, storing huge files (such as photos) off-chain and text data on-chain is an optimal option. The maker will register the product on the blockchain, and its ownership will be readily transferred to another participant using a user-friendly mobile app. If a wholesaler wants to buy medications from a manufacturer, the manufacturer will physically transfer the drugs to the wholesaler while also registering a transfer transaction on a blockchain. The wholesaler will repeat the process to transfer pharmaceuticals to distributors and will conduct business with the pharmacy in the same way.

Now imagine that Doctor Alice requires some medications and wants to get them from a pharmacy. Dr. Alice will utilize a smartphone app to look up drugs ID and validate their whole travel from manufacturer to drugstore. If the product is real, a mobile app will display its entire history; however, if the drug is counterfeit, no information will be presented. Dr. Alice will purchase medications once they get certain proof of their originality. Other participants (like family, nurse, and patients) will be able to trace the medications' trip in the same way that the doctor can [83].

According to a survey, one of the most notable businesses that need attention is the pharmaceutical supply chain. Every year, the WHO estimates that $200 billion worth of fraudulent, counterfeit, and substandard pharmaceuticals is sold on the global market. As a result, numerous blockchain healthcare solutions, such as block verify, chronicled, farm trust, and others, have been launched to protect the pharmaceutical supply chain [84].

8.11.3 Health insurance claims

The health insurance claim procedure is handled by insurance companies, healthcare providers, and clearinghouses, according to HIPAA (Health Insurance Portability and Accountability Act). The clearinghouse is in charge of coordinating health insurance claims between insurers and providers.

Permissioned blockchain is an excellent prospect for addressing the concerns of transparency and traceability in a distributed health insurance claim system with various parties exchanging data and cooperating. Unlike a public blockchain, which allows anybody to join and participate secretly, assessed blockchain functions as an entrance for a participant, approving to join the network or conduct transactions [85, 86].

In general, blockchain relies on a shared and distributed database known as a ledger, which is made up of a linked block sequence that stores and secures time-stamped transactions. The insurer may aggregate information from many sources by maintaining all transactions in the ledger, allowing them to make choices on the fly. The smart contract (SC), which is a self-executing script that allows legal contracts or business logic to be implemented on a distributed ledger, is another significant blockchain component. Insurance policies and access control rules can both be automated with SCs.

Permissioned blockchain with certificate authorization, Hyperledger Fabric version 1.0.5 was chosen as blockchain architecture to execute the suggested health insurance claim program. Furthermore, Hyperledger Fabric is a commercial blockchain platform that is built by using templates to define companies and peer nodes [86].

By utilizing smart contracts and highlighting the SWOT analysis of this technique, insurance companies will be able to establish a safe blockchain medium for claim processing in the insurance industry. A smart contract is a computer-assisted trade that PERFORMS the provisions of a contract. The contract's overall goal is to provide easy terms of payment, liens, secrecy, and enforcement, as well as to eliminate unintentional and malicious exclusions. A good level of trust is always established via a contract. Bringing down misrepresentation misery, authorization and mediations expenses, and other transaction costs are all related to monetary objectives. The insurance company's process begins with registering client information, honoring policy claims, policy issuance, keeping client data confidential, detecting wrong claims through the use of a decentralized digital repository, lowering operational costs, and having an organized way to discover any suspicious claim patterns and market trends. Blockchain is an answer to the above-mentioned thorough procedure. It also focuses on the structure of various used cases to have highly accurate access control stated in smart contracts of various endorsers [87].

Monitoring and managing data, as well as providing customer service, are two of the most important responsibilities of healthcare insurance carriers. Insurance firms do not exchange patient data due to legislation and business secrets, but because the data is not incorporated and in synchronization with insurance providers, there is an upsurge in the frequency of healthcare frauds. Health insurance companies are frequently given confusion or incorrect information to force them to pay for bogus claims made by policyholders. Individual policyholders may be eligible for benefits from a variety of insurance companies. According to the National Health Care Anti-Fraud Association (NHCAA), billions of dollars are lost yearly. Building a system to securely monitor and handle insurance activities by combining records from all insurance firms is vital to prevent health insurance fraud [88].

8.12 Telemedicine and Its Advantages

According to the World Health Organization (WHO), "The conveyance of healthcare facilities, where distance is a major problem, by healthcare professionals are solved by using communication and information techniques for the exchange of valid information which helps in the treatment, diagnosis, preventing injuries and disease.

When participants are separated by a significant distance, telemedicine utilizes electronic information and communication technology to offer and support the healthcare system. "Tele" comes from a Greek word that means "distance," and "mederi" comes from a Latin word that means "to heal." Telemedicine has been dubbed "healing by wire" by Time magazine. In the care of a patient, education, administration, research, and public health, telemedicine has a large range of utilization. People in rural and distant places around the world struggle to get timely, high-quality healthcare. People of these places frequently have poor access to quality healthcare, because specialist doctors are more likely to be found in densely populated urban locations. Telemedicine offers the ability to overcome this gap and make healthcare more accessible in rural locations [89].

For diabetes, patients must be monitored frequently to avoid long-term consequences. Diabetes mellitus is becoming more common in younger individuals with hectic job schedules and other obligations. Monitoring of outpatients has traditionally needed frequent trips that are time taking and cause significant disruption to hectic work or home routine. Much could be achieved by using teleconsultation to provide at least some of the essential monitoring. This will reduce the impact of medical intervention on daily living and allow health professionals to perceive patients in their homes more frequently than they already do [90].

In the case of hypertension, patients can now measure their blood pressure and submit findings to their GP over the phone, thanks to the availability of electronic blood pressure monitors. Medication prescriptions might then be based on the transmitted outcomes and arranged as previously said. It is reasonable to assume that taking blood pressure measurements at home and work would result in more representative blood pressure readings and as a result, a reduction in the number of hypertension patients is observed. Patients may initially be overseen via an affordable audiovisual link to check that readings were being precisely recorded [90, 91].

The common thread running across all telemedicine applications is that a patient of some sort (like as a patient or a healthcare provider) seeks advice from someone with more competence in a related subject, even though the parties are separated in location, time, or both. The interaction between the patient and the expert, as well as the sort of data obtained from patient are utilized to classify telemedicine episodes.

Pre-recorded (also known as store-and-forward) or real-time interactions are the most common types of interactions (also called synchronous). In the former, data is collected and stored in some format before being transferred to an expert for interpretation at a later date via proper means. Email is a popular way to forward and store information. In contrast, there is no discernible latency between the information being communicated, collected, and shown in real-time interactions. As a result, persons at the sites can interactively communicate with one another. Videoconferencing is a popular way to communicate in real time.

Data and text, as well as images, audio, and video pictures, can be transmitted between the two sites in a variety of formats. Telemedicine episodes can be characterized by combining the interaction and information which would be communicated. In other applications, like teleradiology, which includes the transfer of digital radiographs between institutions, interaction can be real time or prerecorded; the latter needs an expert to be there to provide an opinion as a picture is being acquired and communicated [92].

8.13 Conclusion

The ability to access medical information immediately provide the potential to enhance the care of the patient. There are various tools and techniques which have these capabilities like AI, IoT, blockchain, big data, and telemedicine. A digital assistant helps in the psychological therapy, diagnosis of symptoms, and patient triage. AI is also used in biomedical engineering for living assistants, biomedical information processing, and biomedical research. Blockchain has efficiency in remote patient monitoring. The manuscript focuses on the use of telemedicine and IoT in public health-public health. In the future, artificial intelligence and the Internet of Things will improve patient care and quality of life. Personal health monitoring will be possible with wearable technologies that go beyond today's fitness bands. Devices will be able to spot symptoms early by the use of big data analytics.

Acknowledgments

For the successful completion of this study, all of the writers of this publication are grateful to their respective Departments/Universities.

Conflict of Interest

There is no conflict of interest.

Funding

No funding is required.

References

[1] Keplar, K. E., Urbanski, C. J., and Kania, D. S. (2005) Update on personal digital assistant applications for the healthcare provider. *Ann. Pharmacother. 39*(5), 892-907.

[2] Lindquist, A., Johansson, P., Petersson, G., Saveman, B. I., and Nilsson, G. (2008) The use of the Personal Digital Assistant (PDA) among personnel and students in health care: A review. *J. Med. Internet Res. 10*(4), 1-15.

[3] Lee, D., and Yoon, S. N. (2021) Application of artificial intelligence-based technologies in the healthcare industry: Opportunities and challenges. *Int. J. Environ. Res. Public Health 18*(1), 1-18.

[4] https://www.prnewswire.com/in/news-releases/allianz-partners-expands-its-digital-health-assistant-to-ten-markets-in-asia-pacific-805482211.html

[5] Pastorino, R., De Vito, C., Migliara, G., Glocker, K., Binenbaum, I., Ricciardi, W., and Boccia, S. (2019) Benefits and challenges of Big Data in healthcare: an overview of the European initiatives. *Eur. J. Public Health 29*(3), 23-27.

[6] Hermon, R., and Williams, P. A. (2014) Big data in healthcare: What is it used for? 40-49.

[7] Bohr, A., and Memarzadeh, K. (2020) The rise of artificial intelligence in healthcare applications. In *Artificial Intelligence in healthcare* (pp. 25-60). Academic Press.

[8] Singhal, S., and Carlton, S. (2019) The era of exponential improvement in healthcare. *McKinsey & Company* 1-16.

[9] Khezr, S., Moniruzzaman, M., Yassine, A., and Benlamri, R. (2019) Blockchain technology in healthcare: A comprehensive review and directions for future research. *Appl. Sci. 9*(9), 1-28.

[10] Haleem, A., Javaid, M., Singh, R. P., Suman, R., and Rab, S. (2021) Blockchain technology applications in healthcare: An overview. *International Journal of Intelligent Networks 2*, 130-139.

[11] Liang, X., Zhao, J., Shetty, S., Liu, J., and Li, D. (2017) Integrating blockchain for data sharing and collaboration in mobile healthcare applications. In *2017 IEEE 28th annual international symposium on personal, indoor, and mobile radiocommunications (PIMRC)* (pp. 1-5). IEEE.

[12] Javaid, M., and Khan, I. H. (2021) Internet of Things (IoT) enabled healthcare helps to take the challenges of COVID-19 Pandemic. *J. Oral Biol. Craniofac. Res. 11*(2), 209-214.

[13] Kelly, J. T., Campbell, K. L., Gong, E., and Scuffham, P. (2020) The Internet of Things: Impact and implications for health care delivery. *J. Med. Internet Res. 22*(11), 1-11.

[14] Weinstein, R. S., Lopez, A. M., Joseph, B. A., Erps, K. A., Holcomb, M., Barker, G. P., and Krupinski, E. A. (2014) Telemedicine, telehealth, and mobile health applications that work: opportunities and barriers. *Am. J. Med. 127*(3), 183-187.

[15] Haleem, A., Javaid, M., Singh, R. P., and Suman, R. (2021) Telemedicine for healthcare: Capabilities, features, barriers, and applications. *Sensors International, 2*, 1-12.

[16] Weightman, M. (2020) Digital psychotherapy as an effective and timely treatment option for depression and anxiety disorders: Implications for rural and remote practice. *J. Int. Med. Res. 48*(6), 1-7.

[17] Batterham, P. J., Sunderland, M., Calear, A. L., Davey, C. G., Christensen, H., Teesson, M., Kay-Lambkin, F., Andrews, G., Mitchell, P. B., Herrman, H., and Butow, P. N. (2015) Developing a roadmap for the translation of e-mental health services for depression. *Aust. N. Z. J. Psychiatry, 49*(9), 776-784.

[18] You, Y., and Gui, X. (2020) Self-Diagnosis through AI-enabled Chatbot-based Symptom Checkers: User Experiences and Design Considerations. *AMIA Annu. Symp. Proc.* 2020, 1354-1363.

[19] Faris, H., Habib, M., Faris, M., Elayan, H., and Alomari, A. (2021) An intelligent multimodal medical diagnosis system based on patients' medical questions and structured symptoms for telemedicine. *Inform. Med. Unlocked, 23*, 1-12.

[20] https://developer.infermedica.com/docs/introductionv

[21] Burke, L. E., Conroy, M. B., Sereika, S. M., Elci, O. U., Styn, M. A., Acharya, S. D., Sevick, M. A., Ewing, L. J., and Glanz, K. (2011) The effect of electronic self-monitoring on weight loss and dietary intake: a randomized behavioral weight loss trial. *Obesity 19*(2), 338-344.

[22] Sevick, M. A., Zickmund, S., Korytkowski, M., Piraino, B., Sereika, S., Mihalko, S., Snetselaar, L., Stumbo, P., Hausmann, L., Ren, D., and Marsh, R. (2008) Design, feasibility, and acceptability of an intervention using personal digital assistant-based self-monitoring in managing type 2 diabetes. *Contemp. Clin. Trials, 29*(3), 396-409.
[23] Acharya, S. D., Elci, O. U., Sereika, S. M., Styn, M. A., and Burke, L. E. (2011) Using a personal digital assistant for self-monitoring influences diet quality in comparison to a standard paper record among overweight/obese adults. *J. Am. Diet. Assoc. 111*(4), 583-588.
[24] Ambinder, E. P. (2005) Electronic health records. *J. Oncol. Pract. 1*(2), 57-63.
[25] https://www.healthit.gov/faq/what-electronic-health-record-her
[26] Bajpai, N., and Wadhwa, M. (2020) India's National Digital Health Mission. 1-28.
[27] Tang, P. C., and McDonald, C. J. (2006) Electronic health record systems. In *Biomedical informatics* (pp. 447-475). Springer, New York, NY.
[28] Pryor, T. (1983) Gardner RM. Clayton PD and Warner HR: The HELP system. *J*. 87-102.
[29] Octo Barnett, G. (1989) The application of computer-based medical-record systems in ambulatory practice. In *Implementing Health Care Information Systems*, 85-99.
[30] Ozair, F. F., Jamshed, N., Sharma, A., and Aggarwal, P. (2015) Ethical issues in electronic health records: A general overview. *Perspect. Clin. Res. 6*(2), 73-76.
[31] Vance, B., Tomblin, B., Studney, J., and Coustasse, A. (2015) Benefits and barriers for adoption of personal health records. Business and Health Administration Association Annual Conference, at the 51st Annual Midwest Business Administration Association International Conference, Chicago, IL, 1-16.
[32] Sharp, L. K., Carvalho, P., Southward, M., Schmidt, M. L., Jabine, L. N., Stolley, M. R., and Gerber, B. S. (2014) Electronic personal health records for childhood cancer survivors: an exploratory study. *J. Adolesc. Young Adult Oncol. 3*(3), 117-122.
[33] Scherger, J. E. (2005) Primary care needs a new model of office practice. *BMJ, 330*(7504), 358-E359.
[34] Fuji, K. T., Abbott, A. A., Galt, K. A., Drincic, A., Kraft, M., and Kasha, T. (2012) Standalone personal health records in the United States: meeting patient desires. *Health Technol. 2*(3), 197-205.

[35] Gubbi, J., Buyya, R., Marusic, S., and Palaniswami, M. (2013) Internet of Things (IoT): A vision, architectural elements, and future directions. *Future Gener. Comput. Syst. 29*(7), 1645-1660.

[36] Li, S., Da Xu, L., and Zhao, S. (2018) 5G Internet of Things: A survey. *J. Ind. Inf. Integr. 10*, 1-9.

[37] https://www.mayoclinic.org/healthy-lifestyle/consumer-health/in-depth/personal-health-record/art-20047273

[38] https://www.limswiki.org/index.php/Medical_practice_management_system

[39] Davey, S., and Davey, A. (2015) Effect of practice management softwares among physicians of developing countries with special reference to Indian scenario by Mixed Method Technique. *J. Family Med. Prim. Care 4*(2), 208-216.

[40] http://www.binaryspectrum.com/industries/healthcare/focusareas/practice_management_software-val.html

[41] Ta, V. D., Liu, C. M., and Nkabinde, G. W. (2016, July) Big data stream computing in healthcare real-time analytics. In *2016 IEEE international conference on cloud computing and big data analysis (ICCCBDA)* (pp. 37-42). IEEE.

[42] Marx, V. (2013) The big challenges of big data. *Nature 498*(7453), 255-260.

[43] Vayena, E., and Gasser, U. (2016) Strictly biomedical? Sketching the ethics of the big data ecosystem in biomedicine. In *The ethics of biomedical big data* (pp. 17-39). Springer, Cham.

[44] Ienca, M., Vayena, E., and Blasimme, A. (2018) Big data and dementia: charting the route ahead for research, ethics, and policy. *Front. Med.* 5, 1-7.

[45] Luo, J., Wu, M., Gopukumar, D., and Zhao, Y. (2016) Big data application in biomedical research and health care: a literature review. *Biomed. Inform. Insights* 8, 1-10.

[46] Schuster, S. C. (2008) Next-generation sequencing transforms today's biology. *Nat. Methods*, *5*(1), 16-18.

[47] Morozova, O., and Marra, M. A. (2008) Applications of next-generation sequencing technologies in functional genomics. *Genomics 92*(5), 255-264.

[48] Taylor, R. C. (2010) An overview of the Hadoop/MapReduce/HBase framework and its current applications in bioinformatics. *BMC Bioinform. 11*(12), 1-6.

[49] Reis, B. Y., Kohane, I. S., and Mandl, K. D. (2009) Longitudinal histories as predictors of future diagnoses of domestic abuse: modelling study. *Bmj. 339*, 849.

[50] Murdoch, T. B., and Detsky, A. S. (2013) The inevitable application of big data to health care. *Jama 309*(13), 1351-1352.

[51] Rallapalli, S., Gondkar, R., and Ketavarapu, U. P. K. (2016) Impact of processing and analyzing healthcare big data on cloud computing environment by implementing hadoop cluster. *Procedia Comput. Sci.* 85, 16-22.

[52] Beakta, R. (2015) Big data and hadoop: A review paper. *Int. J. Comput. Sci. Inf. Technol. 2*(2), 13-15.

[53] Augustine, D. P. (2014) Leveraging big data analytics and Hadoop in developing India's healthcare services. *Int. J. Comput. Appl. 89*(16), 44-50.

[54] Sharma, S., Chen, K., and Sheth, A. (2018) Toward practical privacy-preserving analytics for IoT and cloud-based healthcare systems. *IEEE Internet Comput. 22*(2), 42-51.

[55] Dalal, P., Aggarwal, G., and Tejasvee, S. (2020, April) Internet of Things (IoT) in Healthcare System: IA3 (Idea, Architecture, Advantages and Applications). In *Proceedings of the International Conference on Innovative Computing & Communications (ICICC)*, 1-6.

[56] Ibrahim, A. U., Al-Turjman, F., Sa'id, Z., and Ozsoz, M. (2020) Futuristic CRISPR-based biosensing in the cloud and internet of things era: an overview. *Multimed. Tools Appl.* 1-29.

[57] Duan, R., Chen, X., and Xing, T. (2011, October) A QoS architecture for IOT. In *2011 International Conference on Internet of Things and 4th International Conference on Cyber, Physical and Social Computing* (pp. 717-720). IEEE.

[58] Khattak, H. A., Shah, M. A., Khan, S., Ali, I., and Imran, M. (2019) Perception layer security in Internet of Things. *Future Gener. Comput. Syst. 100*, 144-164.

[59] Yang, Z., Yue, Y., Yang, Y., Peng, Y., Wang, X. and Liu, W. (2011, July) Study and application on the architecture and key technologies for IOT. In *2011 International Conference on Multimedia Technology* (pp. 747-751). IEEE.

[60] Urien, P., Elrharbi, S., Nyamy, D., Chabanne, H., Icart, T., Lecocq, F., Pépin, C., Toumi, K., Bouet, M., Pujolle, G. and Krzanik, P. (2009, November) HIP-Tags architecture implementation for the Internet of

Things. In *2009 First Asian Himalayas International Conference on Internet* (pp. 1-5). IEEE.

[61] Sun, X., and Ansari, N. (2017) Traffic load balancing among brokers at the IoT application layer. *IEEE Trans. Netw. Serv. Manag. 15*(1), 489-502.

[62] Zhong, C. L., Zhu, Z. and Huang, R. G. (2015, August) Study on the IOT architecture and gateway technology. In *2015 14th International Symposium on Distributed Computing and Applications for Business Engineering and Science (DCABES)* (pp. 196-199). IEEE.

[63] Rong, G., Mendez, A., Assi, E. B., Zhao, B., and Sawan, M. (2020) Artificial intelligence in healthcare: review and prediction case studies. *Engineering 6*(3), 291-301.

[64] Hudec, M., and Smutny, Z. (2017) RUDO: A home ambient intelligence system for blind people. *Sensors 17*(8), 1-45.

[65] Man, D. W. K., Tam, S. F., and Hui-Chan, C. W. Y. (2003) Learning to live independently with expert systems in memory rehabilitation. *NeuroRehabilitation 18*(1), 21-29.

[66] Wei, Y., Zhou, J., Wang, Y., Liu, Y., Liu, Q., Luo, J., Wang, C., Ren, F., and Huang, L. (2020) A review of algorithm & hardware design for AI-based biomedical applications. *IEEE transactions on biomedical circuits and systems, 14*(2), pp.145-163.

[67] Shukla, S., Lakhmani, A., and Agarwal, A. K. (2016, April) Approaches of artificial intelligence in biomedical image processing: A leading tool between computer vision & biological vision. In *2016 International Conference on Advances in Computing, Communication, & Automation (ICACCA)(Spring)* (pp. 1-6). IEEE.

[68] Blasimme, A., and Vayena, E. (2019) The ethics of AI in biomedical research, patient care and public health. *Patient Care and Public Health (April 9, 2019).* In *Oxford Handbook of Ethics of Artificial Intelligence, Forthcoming*, 703-718.

[69] Davenport, T., and Kalakota, R. (2019) The potential for artificial intelligence in healthcare. *Future Healthcare Journal 6*(2), 94-98.

[70] Park, S. H., and Han, K. (2018) Methodologic guide for evaluating clinical performance and effect of artificial intelligence technology for medical diagnosis and prediction. *Radiology 286*(3), 800-809.

[71] Yu, C., and Helwig, E. J. (2021) The role of AI technology in prediction, diagnosis and treatment of colorectal cancer. *Artif. Intell. Rev.* 55, 323-343.

[72] Yu, J., Park, S., Kwon, S. H., Ho, C. M. B., Pyo, C. S., and Lee, H. (2020) AI-based stroke disease prediction system using real-time electromyography signals. *Appl. Sci.* 10, 1-19.

[73] Krittanawong, C., Zhang, H., Wang, Z., Aydar, M., and Kitai, T. (2017) Artificial intelligence in precision cardiovascular medicine. *J. Am. Coll. Cardiol. 69*(21), 2657-2664.

[74] Wood, G. (2014) Ethereum: A secure decentralised generalised transaction ledger. *Ethereum Project Yellow Paper 151*(2014), 1-32.

[75] Fekih, R. B., and Lahami, M. (2020, June) Application of blockchain technology in healthcare: A comprehensive study. In *International Conference on Smart Homes and Health Telematics* (pp. 268-276). Springer, Cham.

[76] Siyal, A. A., Junejo, A. Z., Zawish, M., Ahmed, K., Khalil, A., and Soursou, G. (2019) Applications of blockchain technology in medicine and healthcare: Challenges and future perspectives. *Cryptography 3*(1), 1-16.

[77] Hathaliya, J., Sharma, P., Tanwar, S., and Gupta, R. (2019, December) Blockchain-based remote patient monitoring in healthcare 4.0. In *2019 IEEE 9th International Conference on Advanced Computing (IACC)* (pp. 87-91). IEEE.

[78] Gupta, R., Tanwar, S., Kumar, N., and Tyagi, S. (2020) Blockchain-based security attack resilience schemes for autonomous vehicles in industry 4.0: A systematic review. *Comput. Electr. Eng.* 86, 1-15.

[79] Griggs, K. N., Ossipova, O., Kohlios, C. P., Baccarini, A. N., Howson, E. A., and Hayajneh, T. (2018) Healthcare blockchain system using smart contracts for secure automated remote patient monitoring. *J. Med. Syst. 42*(7), 1-7.

[80] Uddin, M. A., Stranieri, A., Gondal, I., and Balasubramanian, V. (2019, October.) A decentralized patient agent controlled blockchain for remote patient monitoring. In *2019 International Conference on Wireless and Mobile Computing, Networking and Communications (WiMob)* (pp. 1-8). IEEE.

[81] Bocek, T., Rodrigues, B. B., Strasser, T., and Stiller, B. (2017, May) Blockchains everywhere-a use-case of blockchains in the pharma supply-chain. In *2017 IFIP/IEEE symposium on integrated network and service management (IM)* (pp. 772-777). IEEE.

[82] Sylim, P., Liu, F., Marcelo, A., and Fontelo, P. (2018) Blockchain technology for detecting falsified and substandard drugs in distribution: pharmaceutical supply chain intervention. *Jmir Res. Protoc. 7*(9), 1-13.

[83] Haq, I., and Esuka, O. M. (2018) Blockchain technology in pharmaceutical industry to prevent counterfeit drugs. *Int. J. Comput. Appl. 180*(25), 8-12.

[84] Jamil, F., Hang, L., Kim, K., and Kim, D. (2019) A novel medical blockchain model for drug supply chain integrity management in a smart hospital. *Electronics 8*(5), 1-32.

[85] Xu, X., Weber, I., Staples, M., Zhu, L., Bosch, J., Bass, L., Pautasso, C., and Rimba, P. (2017, April) A taxonomy of blockchain-based systems for architecture design. In *2017 IEEE international conference on software architecture (ICSA)* (pp. 243-252). IEEE.

[86] He, X., Alqahtani, S., and Gamble, R. (2018, July) Toward privacy-assured health insurance claims. In *2018 IEEE International Conference on Internet of Things (iThings) and IEEE Green Computing and Communications (GreenCom) and IEEE Cyber, Physical and Social Computing (CPSCom) and IEEE Smart Data (SmartData)* (pp. 1634-1641). IEEE.

[87] Thenmozhi, M., Dhanalakshmi, R., Geetha, S. and Valli, R. (2021) Implementing blockchain technologies for health insurance claim processing in hospitals. *Mater. Today: Proc.* 1-4.

[88] Saldamli, G., Reddy, V., Bojja, K. S., Gururaja, M. K., Doddaveerappa, Y., and Tawalbeh, L. (2020, April) Health care insurance fraud detection using blockchain. In *2020 Seventh International Conference on Software Defined Systems (SDS)* (pp. 145-152). IEEE.

[89] Dasgupta, A., and Deb, S. (2008) Telemedicine: A new horizon in public health in India. *Indian J. Community Med. 33*(1), 3-8.

[90] Hjelm, N. M. (2005) Benefits and drawbacks of telemedicine. *J. Telemed. Telecare 11*(2), 60-70.

[91] Zhang, Y., Bai, J., Zhou, X., Dai, B., Cui, Z., Lin, J., Ding, C., Zhang, P., Yu, B., Ye, L., and Shen, D. (1997) First trial of home ECG and blood pressure telemonitoring system in Macau. *Telemed. J. 3*(1), 67-72.

[92] Craig, J., and Petterson, V. (2005) Introduction to the practice of telemedicine. *J. Telemed. Telecare 11*(1), 3-9.

Author Biography

Ms. Akanksha Sharma (Assistant Professor)

Akanksha Sharma is an Assistant Professor at Monad College of Pharmacy, Monad University, Hapur. She has completed B. Pharm from Kashi Institute of Pharmacy, Varanasi in 2018. She has completed M. Pharm (Pharmaceutics) from Galgotias University in 2020. She has also published research and review papers mostly in the Scopus indexed journal. She is a good motivator and provides guidance to students for being a good Pharmacy Professional, Researcher, and to be more human.

Mr. Ashish Verma

Ashish Verma is student at School of pharmacy, Monad University, Hapur. He has completed B. Pharm from Kashi Institute of Pharmacy, Varanasi, in 2018. He always works with students at ground level to understand along with utilization of different basic concepts of pharmacy in real life. He is a good motivator and provides guidance to students for being a good Pharmacy Professional, Researcher, and to be more human.

Rishabha Malviya

Rishabha Malviya is presently working as an Associate Professor at Galgotias University in the Department of Pharmacy, School of Medical and Allied Sciences Greater Noida, UP, India. He completed his Ph.D. at Galgotias University, India. He completed his M. Pharm in Pharmaceutics (2008âĂŞ2010) and B. Pharm (2004âĂŞ2008) from U.P technical university, Lucknow, India. He has published more than 115 articles in different international and national journals. He has published 2 books and 4 book chapters and also has some patents. He has guided 23 M. Pharm students for their respective project work. He was qualified in Gate with 94.36 percentile in 2008âĂŞ2009 and also received Faculty Appreciation Award from Meerut Institute of Engineering and Technology and Appreciation Letter from Rexcin Pharmaceuticals Private Limited. He is serving as an editorial board member and reviewer of various international and national journals. He is also serving as a consultant/advisor to industry for process optimization and formulation.

Aditi Singh

Aditi Singh is an Assistant Professor at Ashoka Institute of Pharmacy. She has completed B. Pharm from Kashi Institute of Pharmacy, Varanasi in 2018. She received gold medal in M. Pharm (2020) from Amity university, Lucknow.

She also worked as an assistant professor with Future Group of Institution Bareilly for one year. She is a good motivator and provides guidance to students for being a good Pharmacy Professional, Researcher, and to be more human.

9

Deep Learning Techniques and Drug Release

Shilpa Singh[1], Shilpa Rawat[1*], Rishabha Malviya[1], Sonali Sundram[1], and Sunita Dahiya[2]

[1]Department of Pharmacy, School of Medical and Allied Science, Galgotias University, Greater Noida, India
[2]Department of Pharmaceutical Sciences, School of Pharmacy, University of Puerto Rico, USA
*Corresponding Author: Department of Pharmacy School of Medical and Allied Science, Galgotias University, Greater Noida, Uttar Pradesh, India
Email Id: Shilpirawat38216@gmail.com.

Abstract

Pharmaceutical formulation development appears to be heavily reliant on the labor-intensive, time-consuming, and expensive traditional trial-and-error method based on the specific experiences of pharmaceutical scientists, despite advances in technology. Deep learning (DL) has recently gained popularity due to its significant ability to perform automatic feature extraction in a wide range of challenging domains, which has led to its widespread application. A problem in pharmaceutical formulation development, drug release prediction, is the subject of the current study, which investigates how DL can be applied to the problem. Several different neural network architectures were constructed and trained in this study, resulting in accurate drug release profile predictions consistent with experimental results. It is demonstrated by the ease with which these widely applicable DL models can be recognized with only a small number of datasets that statistics strategies have great potential in highly developed pharmaceutical formulation development.

Keywords: Deep learning, pharmaceutical formulation, drug release, artificial intelligence, machine learning, deep neural networks, convolutional neural networks.

9.1 Introduction

Deep learning (DL) techniques that use deep artificial neural networks have sped up progress in computer vision, speech recognition, and natural language processing. With these important advances, DL is getting closer to one of its primary goals: artificial intelligence. DL has the advantage of being able to learn features automatically using a broad technique [1].

A multilayer stack of simple neural networks with nonlinear input–output mappings, such as deep neural networks (DNNs), convolutional neural networks (CNNs), recurrent or recursive neural networks (RNNs), and other deep networks with more than one hidden layer and more neurons in each layer, is typically used to perform this procedure. DL architectures can handle large amounts of data with little human intervention. These useful methodologies have also been applied to chemo- and bioinformatics for a variety of tasks, including predicting aqueous solubility, structure-activity relationship analysis, and predicting the sequence specificity of DNA/RNA binding proteins [2]. DL is an independent learning process that has already been widely implemented in various fields of research, commerce, and government [3]. DL, as opposed to standard machine learning (ML) algorithms that require field knowledge to build derived features, may move from limited approximations to more abstract levels autonomously. Furthermore, because DL is more sensitive to irrelevant and specific minute fluctuations, these methods achieve higher accuracy than traditional ML methods. Most of the time, deep convolutional networks (DCNs) based on visual neuroscience are excellent at processing images and videos and voice and audio[4–7]. Drugs are often created by discovering biomaterial targets on which the drug may work, like a protein whose activity could be altered by a chemical to have therapeutic efficacy. The cure of some complicated or concurrent disorders often necessitates the use of many medications, which might raise the risk of adverse reactions. As a result, drug–target recognition, compound–protein identification, as well as drug–drug interaction identification are critical for drug research and development (R&D) [8]. Because developing new drug molecules is expensive and requires extensive research, producing enhanced pharma preparations for current and very popular pharmaceuticals appears to be a viable option for the pharma business. The pharmacologic activities, effectiveness, or care of lively compounds could all be improved with the good construction of drug delivery systems (DDSs). Advanced materials used as pharma excipients in the development of DDSs could aid in the resolution of issues relating to the required drug release at the specified dissolving speed or the specified location [9]. Artificial intelligence (AI) is a branch of computer engineering that focuses on the development of machine intelligence that mimics human behavior. Computer learning is a recent AI application that is also built on the notion of allowing the machine to learn for itself by providing access to information [10]. ML approaches to estimate aqueous solubility is one of the first uses of DL in pharma studies [11]. Figure 9.1 depicts the role of AI in pharmaceutical sciences. ML processes are frequently employed in different domains of biomedicine, from biomarker creation to drug discovery as well, and computational biology technologies are widely utilized.

DL is a broad category of ML techniques that have shown the potential to increase the available abstraction using massive, heterogeneous, high-dimensional datasets. That's the type of information about biology

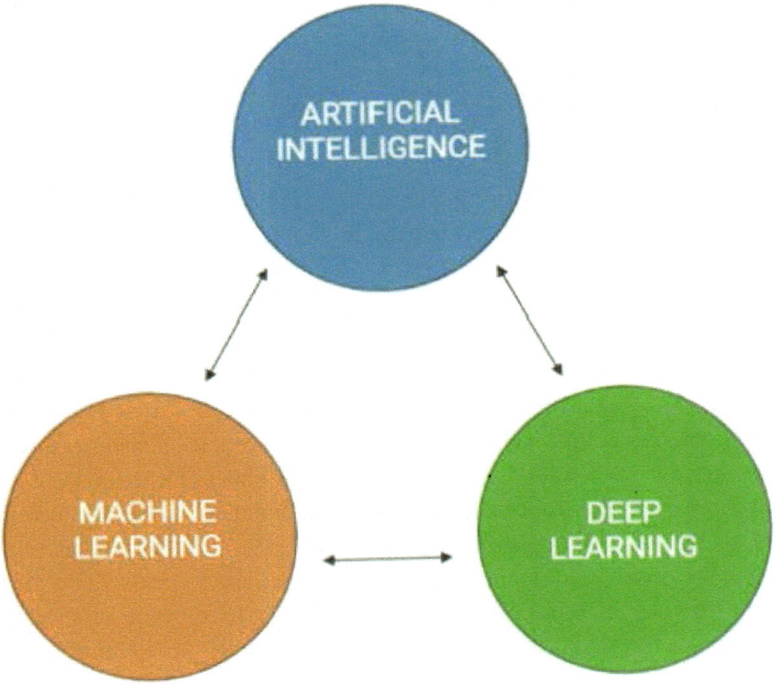

Figure 9.1 A comparison of the relationships among AI, deep learning, and machine learning.

that is currently available [12]. ML and DL (a subset of ML) have made enormous technical advances in the last 40 years, causing huge shifts in various sectors. It has also evolved into a strong instrument suitable for automation procedures in construction companies but lags behind the other industries in terms of efficiency and results [13]. DL is the latest type of ML that concentrates on learning from hierarchical feature data structures.

The rapid advancement in computer processing capacity in recent times has paved the way for establishing true approaches for solving very complicated and non-linear issues. ML is currently applied in most areas of study as well as in daily life, including online browsing, spam filtering, fraud detection, and stock trading, to name a few [14]. DL does have the capacity to detect unimportant or specific minute deviations, allowing these algorithms to achieve greater precision than some other ML methods [15]. Furthermore, a DL system forecasts drug release through polylactide–coglycolide microspheres in the field of drug formulations [16]. The relationship between AI, machine learning, and deep learning is given in Figure 9.1.

9.2 Drug Development

In the pharmacy, active medication molecules must be formed into appropriate formulations and dosing schedules. The R&D effectiveness of new molecular entities (NMEs), as determined by the amount of NMEs brought to market by the pharma industry per billion US dollars spent on R&D, has steadily declined in recent years [17]. Novel dosage forms are becoming more common in the pharmacy sector as new molecular entities (NME) output remains stagnant. The development of innovative preparations takes far less time and money than the development of NMEs. Using DDSs can also improve the medicinal activities of NMEs, such as pharmacokinetics and pharmacodynamics. Since the 1950s, the current pharmaceutical industries have evolved for more than 60 years, strongly related to pharmaceutical formulations and drug delivery technologies [18]. The commencement of contemporary pharmaceutics was marked by this event. In general, current pharmaceutics can be divided into two generations [19, 20]. DL has become more popular in pharmaceutical research over the last 5 years. The first of these studies, published in 2013, compared DL to certain other ML algorithms for predicting medication solubility in water. According to the findings, DL outperformed all other methodologies. Additional pharmacological uses of DL have now been revealed. For example, to decrease medication toxicity, a DCN is formed to forecast molecule epoxidation sensitivity [21]. DL has also been used to forecast drug-induced liver harm successfully [22]. Furthermore, in limited data drug development, multitasking DL, as well as one-shot learning techniques, performed better than single-task learning [23, 24].

9.3 Basics of Machine Learning

ML is a subset of AI that tries to describe systems by using data to train computer methods. For example, using data from many prior tests on the stability of active pharmaceutical industry formulations, ML might be able to forecast the stability of specific drug preparation. The latest innovations in ML techniques, as well as the widespread availability of faster processing hardware and the emergence of user-friendly ML tools, have considerably improved access to strong ML models. Such trends have resulted in a surge in actual ML and AI applications, particularly in the pharmaceutical and healthcare industries. The use of ML in various fields has resulted in better cancer diagnosis [25–27], the development of novel anti-fibrotic drugs [28, 29] molecules, as well as the creation of self-driving labs [30, 31]. There are two types of ML: unsupervised and supervised. Guiding an algorithm for solving a predetermined task is referred to as "supervised learning [32]." The learning data in unsupervised learning contain unlabeled data. There are no designated outputs for such inputs. Clustering is the most common approach to unsupervised learning. Clustering can be used to anticipate a data pattern. Clustering can be done in a variety of ways, including hierarchical and statistical clustering [33]. Would this freshly manufactured medicine be digested by the gut microbiota? "For example, The ML program needs to have access to tagged data to create a response. In the preceding scenario, the ML algorithm would be given a list of medications, together with their chemical characteristics, that were classified as sensitive or not sensitive to gut microbial metabolism." The program would next examine the chemical properties of the freshly produced drug and the list of labeled pharmaceuticals for commonalities [34]. Without even being explicitly taught how to do it in detail, ML models attempt to handle certain problems. On the contrary, ML approaches to develop predictive methods using existing data relating to the job at hand. Inferences in models in guided ML methods use training datasets, wherein the datasets are marked with the "actual" result. This permits models for the connection between outputs and inputs to be inferred on this testing dataset, which must then be confirmed on independent test and/or validating data sources to avoid

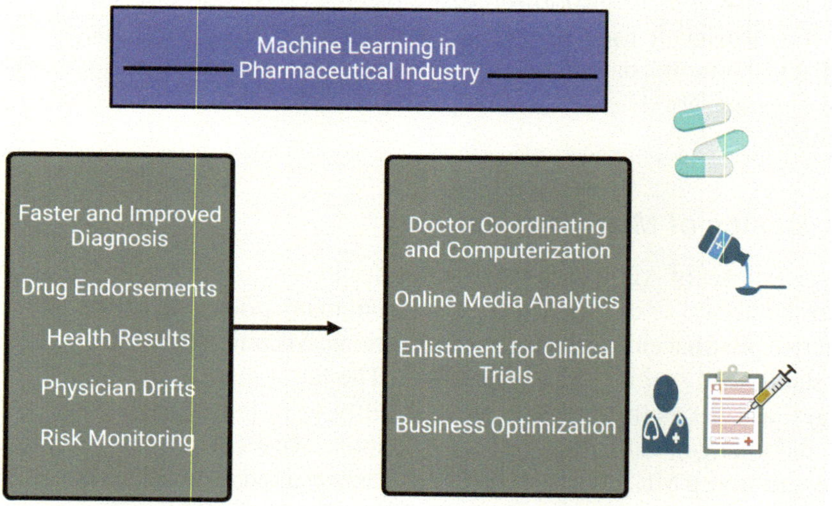

Figure 9.2 Application of machine learning in the pharmaceutical industry.

overfitting to the training set of information distributions. Unmonitored ML approaches, however, are taught on unlabeled sets. Cluster and anomalous detection techniques are great examples [35]. New strategies for designing new materials as well as structural transporters for multi-agent delivery methods could be created. Many strategies for drug development and discovery have been developed using ML [36]. A well-designed ML technique may significantly boost research, improve formulas, conserve money, maintain consistent quality, as well as collect and store specialized information and experience from specialists in a well-defined topic [16]. There are various applications of machine learning in the pharmaceutical industry as shown in Figure 9.2.

9.4 Deep Learning

It's worth noting that the phrase "DL" has nothing to do with the system's intelligence and its ability to replicate the mind in any significant sense. This merely means that it will be made up of numerous levels of asymmetric processing elements as well as its straight links. DL is just linear algebra with a dash of multivariable calculus as well as probability tossed in for good measure [37]. DL is a current reincarnation of the ANN from the late 1980s and early 1990s, so it employs complex, multi-level DNNs to develop systems that can recognize features from large volumes of unlabeled or tagged training data. The scale and scope of the systems used in DL vary significantly from those used in classic artificial neural networks [38]. DL approaches are effective at handling big datasets of medication combinations. In the realm of bioinformatics, these strategies exhibit better results than ML. DL approaches can construct abstract representations from massive amounts of data. CNN, RNN, and autoencoders are three DL architectures that are commonly employed in drug combo research [39].

McCulloch and Pitts presented the first artificial neuron (AN) structure in 1943 as a computer model of neurological function. So perceptrons, a two-layer neural network employed in basic tasks, were succeeded by some other version, the back-propagation method, which has been utilized for fast multiplayer network training since the late 1960s. AN could be coupled to create an ANN [40]. DL strategies, in particular, could be utilized to replace correlation strategies in monitored applications—where the primary objective is to correctly estimate one or more tags or consequences that come with each data point—as well as in unaccompanied, or "exploratory" applications—where the primary objective is to summarize, describe, or identify interesting patterns from the data created by clustering [41].

9.5 The Evolvement of Deep Learning

Machines can learn to complete tasks using DL approaches. DL is a type of ML that teaches itself to describe an issue as a pyramid of ideas. The deepest levels of human brain functioning influenced the DL. Complex models are subsets of DL models. Models with much more complexity (i.e., a bigger number of variables as well as hyperparameters) have such a large amount of independence, which gives us more flexibility to match the data. The majority of DL techniques are dependent on ANN principles [42]. DL theory and techniques have advanced at a breakneck pace in recent years, ushering in a new age of AI and an entirely new approach to creating smart intrusion prevention technologies. RNNs that have been around for centuries and whose true capacity alone has barely started to be recognized as CNNs have also lately provided a substantial growth in the realm of DL due to growing computation power [43]. DL is known for its ability to approximate nearly any functionality or is progressively demonstrating predicting precision that exceeds that of human analysts. DL models, however, aren't without flaws:

they frequently display large variations and might even slip in local loss minimum throughout learning. Ensemble approaches, which aggregate the outputs of numerous DL models to create more generalization than a single product, have been demonstrated to provide greater generalizability than just a single model [44].

9.5.1 Deep learning techniques

Various neural networks are designed specifically for real-time uses. Autoencoders are used in this form of learning [45].

9.5.2 Artificial neural networks

ANNs are at the heart of DL, a subfield of ML. An ANN is a computational platform made of a set of interrelated nodes (AN) that mimic the mind's neuronal features. ANNs "learn" in the same way people do: by interacting with it and replying to a variety of stimuli in their immediate surroundings [46]. ANNs are of special importance because of their adaptable design, which enables them to be used for several scenarios across all three kinds of ML. ANNs are mathematical models of linked processing elements termed "artificial neurons" that are motivated by the idea of processing information in biological systems. Every link between neurons produces impulses that may be strengthened or dampened by a load that is also continually modified during the learning experience, similar to synapses in the brain. Messages are only received by following neurons if an activation function determines that a specific threshold has been reached. Neurons are often arranged into networks with multiple levels. In most cases, an input layer takes data input (e.g., object photographs from an online store) and an output layer creates the final result (e.g., categorization of products) [47]. The fact that ANNs do not require rule-based, well-structured experimental methods and can also map functions utilizing prior or incomplete information is one of their most useful features. With inexact input data, ANNs may discriminate between linear and nonlinear architectures. As a result, ANN is also referred to as "expertise multidimensional modeling" [48]. While ANNs are radical abstractions of biological equivalents, they are designed to tackle complicated issues by using the functional data of network servers rather than replicating the properties of natural systems. The attractiveness of ANNs stems from their illustrious background. Nonlinearity, high parallelism, solidity, defect and error tolerance, cleverness, as well as the ability to handle inaccurate and fluid data are all handling characteristics [49, 50].

9.5.3 Deep neural networks

DL, particularly DNNs, is a computing approach that is influenced by nature that has been used in a variety of domains such as computer vision and image recognition [51]. DNNs are used in DL approaches to model greater data representations. DNNs are multilayered networks of linked as well as interactive artificial neurons that can conduct a wide range of data manipulations. These have several hidden layers of neurons, the amount of which can be adjusted to change the number of information abstractions. In the fields of physics and voice, signals, picture, video, as well as text analytics and recognition, DL has improved state-of-the-art efficiency by even more than 30%, whereas the previous decade failed to achieve 12% gains [52]. DNNs' hierarchical nature provides an opportunity to learn characteristics at numerous levels; each one corresponds to a different degree of abstractions. The earliest levels teach basic characteristics, which are subsequently collected in the deeper layers to build higher-level ideas [53]. The fully connected neural network (DNN) is perhaps the most basic design of DL models, consisting of a sequence of layers of neurons that are each linked to all neurons in the preceding layer. The fundamental designs are expanded upon in more advanced models [54].

9.5.4 Convolutional neural networks

CNN is one of the most well-known architectures in DL and it is used in a variety of applications including image speech recognition, and also natural language processing (NLP). The contemporary CNN arose from Fukushima's invention of the recognition in the 1980s, which was motivated by Hubel and Wiesel's studies on the input patch in a cat's visual cortex. Regional neuron types assume responsibility for detecting specific regions in the sensory space while processing visual information, and CNN replicates this behavior by generating two major characteristics in the convolution layer: sparse connection and weight sharing [55]. Every level in a CNN consists of a sequence of layers that are slid through the preceding layer's result to retrieve local information across various portions of the input [48].

9.5.5 Autoencoders

An autoencoder (AE) is made up of hidden units that encode a latent dominating architecture with a smaller size concerning the input signal. A complete link among neurons inside the input, hidden, as well as output layers, distinguishes the design. There have been many variations produced, one of which has the benefit of not requiring labeled data when employing unlabeled data [56]. An AE is a characteristic of extracting technique that depends on unsupervised neural networks that learn the optimum parameters to rebuild its result as closely as possible to its inputs. Its capacity to produce stronger as well as non-linear generalizations than principal component analyzing is one of its appealing properties. Backpropagation is used to do this, as well as the target values are set to be equivalent to the inputs. To put it another way, it's attempting to learn approximately close to the identity function [57]. Learning the latent area to represent a certain attribute and then exploring it, it's been used to construct molecules [58].

9.5.6 Generative adversarial networks

In a competitive strategy, generative adversarial networks (GANs) use two networks. One network must produce information, while another must detect whether a given data point is a network-generated fake or a genuine one from the use of information. The producing network learns to build high-quality imitations of the set of information by fighting with others [59]. It has been used to solve the issue of inverted molecular design [60].

9.5.7 Recurrent neural networks

RNNs have become more essential in domains such as computer vision, NLP, semantic comprehension, voice recognition, language processing, translations, image descriptions, as well as personal activity recognition in recent times [61–63].

The following are the stages involved in training an RNN model:

1. Create a network architecture and use random weights and biases to start the simulation.
2. Calculate the anticipated output using forward propagation.
3. Determine the outputs layer's error.
4. Using an optimization strategy, do a backward propagation to modify the weights.
5. Steps 2–4 are repeated for as many epochs (or iterations) as necessary until the loss function values are judged minimal [64].

9.5.8 Restricted Boltzmann machine

Restricted Boltzmann machine (RBM) is a modeling approach that could generate a probability distribution across a collection of inputs. The term "restricted" refers to the prohibition of interconnections among nodes in the same tier. RBMs are being used to train each layer of a major network one at a time. The RBM is made up of two layers of neurons: a transparent layer for the input vector as well as a hidden layer for the input vector h. There are no intralayer interconnections between the neurons in the visible layer and the neurons in the hidden layer [65].

9.5.9 Dynamic neural network

In 2002, dynamic neural networks were used for the first time to anticipate drug release characteristics from a controlled release formulation. Drug release patterns are modeled as series data curves, with each time point influencing subsequent projections. The recurrence network of Elman has been used. Because information is stored and expanded in real time in dynamically neural networks, it is believed to be beneficial in time-dependent procedures such as drug release predictions and drug stability difficulties. As a consequence, the research team has effectively used dynamic neural networks to generate design space for matrix tablet formulation as well as compare the findings to static network results. The case study that follows includes previously unreleased information which may be valuable to read as a guideline in selecting and developing a suitable network for the topic under consideration. This study's goal was to create an ANN model for optimizing matrix tablet mechanical features and also drug release profiles. The network's inputs have been the proportion of matrix-forming materials but also compressing force, whereas the network's outputs are mechanical qualities (porosity and tensile strength) of tablets, and also drug release profiles [66]. Transfers learning is a way of starting a new activity with the representations learned from a prior one. In "NPL," this job is most typically Image Net-based supervised learning and Internet-scale language modeling in "Computer Vision" [67].

9.5.10 Recurrent neural networks

Recurrent neural networks with sequence history information have made a breakthrough in sequential data such as text and music. Pharmaceutical formulation data consists of formulation compositions and manufacturing techniques that are not visually or sequentially represented. As a result, the fully connected deep feed-forward neural network is an excellent choice for predicting pharmaceutical formulations. In an oral disintegrating pill prediction study, DNNs beat ANNs with one convolution layer [68]. Using the maximum dissimilarity approach with the small group filter and representative starting set selection, the representative validation set was selected from the tiny and unbalanced oral disintegrating tablet data (MD-FIS) [69]. Additional comparisons of DL with other ML algorithms are required to identify beneficial combinations [70].

9.6 Deep Learning in Bioinformatics

The number of papers linked with bioinformatics and computational biology has rapidly increased, as well as DL has been employed in a variety of applications, including protein disease prediction. It results in a quick technique that was similar to certain other ML techniques for testing datasets depending on the area under the curve (AUC) as well as recollection stats. It didn't outperform the other disordered approaches, but it did have the benefit of being quick. Depending on 35,000 unattached docking complexes created by RosettaDock and evaluated on 25 docking complexes, not in the training dataset, DL was also utilized to improve docked protein complexes [71].

9.7 Dissolution and Release of Drug

Fick's law may be used to explain the release of the drug in the easiest of situations, such that, regardless of the liquid flow, dissolution is directed by diffuse in the path of the pharmaceutical concentration gradient as well as chemical possibility gradients. Figure 9.3 depicts the drug dissolution and release process. Fick's law stands true if the following criteria are satisfied: the composition is diffusion-controlled; the drug's diffusion coefficient is consistent; the ideal sink requirement is fulfilled, along with the polymer membrane just outside of the drug carrier doesn't dissolve all through the launch period; the components' geometry is unaffected [72]. The emphasis of formulations researchers is generally on dissolution profiles, which are at the core of the process. Before going on to bioequivalence (BE) research, systematic in vitro dissolution experiments are done regularly. One of the most common strategies for solving solubility issues is to change the particle size of the drug constituent. Modulating the size is more crucial than lowering it for the appropriate profile in vitro as well as in vivo [73]. Many factors must

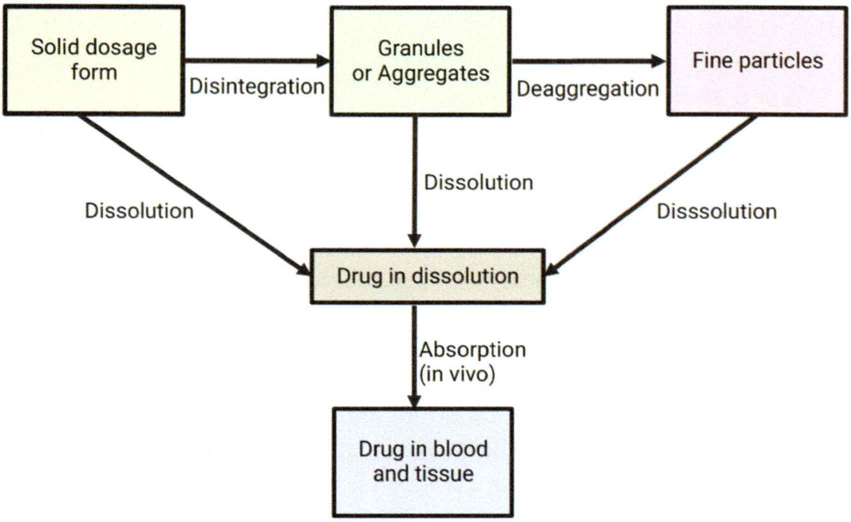

Figure 9.3 Drug dissolution and drug release process.

be considered while structuring embedded DDSs, including amount modification, quarry delivery, comfortable release, as well as an intelligent control system [74]. Certain drug molecules adhere to polymers, reducing their releasing capability, which is one cause of diffusion modification. Models are available, based on whether the thermodynamic equilibrium among binding as well as free drugs is maintained [75]. Combining molecular robots with DL architecture to build optimum drug delivery pathways to specified locations is a future strategy. One technique might be to dispatch molecular bots on "training runs" to their precise destination, so that once inside the patients with the pharmaceuticals, they "know" just where to distribute it [46]. For modeling the release of diclofenac sodium from polyethene oxide-controlled release matrix tablets, dynamically neural pathways competent for modeling dissolution rate and much more exact predictions of drug release profile (as opposed to MLP and static networks) were used [76]. On-demand dosage or rate of drug release, targeted delivery, and pharmacological stability should all be considered when creating smart delivery systems. Suitable algorithms must be used to govern the quantity and time of drug release in self-monitoring delivery methods. Intelligent DDSs are being developed using digital technologies, wireless connectivity, as well as ANNs, which may be effective in overcoming the limits of traditional treatment procedures. ANNs were also utilized to create the best sustained-release forms formulations and forecast their dissolving patterns [77].

9.7.1 In vitro studies

Preclinical in vitro experiments: substances that have been screened up to this point are examined in a cell stack. Petri dish investigations take place in the in vitro stage. The efficacy of the medicine is evaluated in this stage by examining the molecule that interacts with the target.

Among the most important analytical methodologies in the pharma industry is in vitro dissolution analysis. For example, it is widely used in research and development, as well as routine quality control (QC), for purposes such as improving formulations, predicting product performance in vivo, assessing stability, batch-to-batch variation, and creating response surfaces and in vivo–in vitro interactions. For the optimization of drug release as well as the identification of relevant process factors, many forms of ANNs were investigated [78].

If using ML algorithms, greater information is often preferable. In comparison to other scientific fields, data collecting in pharmaceutical formulation development is sluggish and costly. In vitro, drug release investigations may take up to 3 months to process, but thorough in vivo research is costly and constrained by ethical constraints. Data mining from the existing literature is a trend lately in chemistry and biology. Published scientific research is a publicly available set of information, and several articles increasingly leverage formulation information from prior publications to train ML models [79]. In studies evaluating the impact of numerous aspects like formulations and compressing parameters on tablet physiochemical characteristics, such a model (ANN) gave greater fitting and forecasting capabilities in the creation of solid dosage forms. That was a valuable tool for the creation of micro emulsion-based drug carriers that required minimal research effort. Innovation could save cash and effort while also providing greater expert knowledge in the relationships between various reformulation parameters [80].

9.7.2 In vivo studies

Animal research: Inside this stage, substances that have passed the in vitro stage of evolution are collected as well as examined on animals or mice. The conclusions drawn in such animal experiments are much more accurate than those found in 2D in vitro cellular structure simulations. Failing at this phase is also increased because of the variation in the structure of the cell model in animals, as well as the outcomes from in vitro experiments might not even correspond with those of in vivo [81].

If combined with multi-modal and/or multi-scale modeling, traditional and new DL architecture may be used to teach molecular shuttle to autonomously detect their location in vivo. The number of molecular shuttles might grow, laying the groundwork for an autonomous swarming to go to many locations and discharge their pharmaceutical cargo [46].

9.8 Application of Deep Learning in Pharmaceutical Formulation

Due to its high potential for automated feature extraction, DL has been widely used in a variety of difficult industries. The goal of this study is to use DL techniques to predict pharmaceutical formulations and drug releases. An automated dataset selection technique was developed to select representative data as validation and test datasets. Six different ML approaches were pitted against DL. Both DNNs and ML models outperform other models in terms of accuracy, with the latter displaying good predictions of pharmaceutical formulations and drug releases [82]. DL has grown in popularity in pharmaceutical research over the last eight years. According to Laski et al. (2013), the first of these experiments compared DL to other ML methods for predicting drug water solubility. Table 9.1 depicts recent progress of deep and machine learning in formulation design. According to the data, DL outperformed all other approaches. As a result, new DL applications in the pharmaceutical

Table 9.1 Recent progress of deep and machine learning in formulation design.

S. No	Deep and ML Approaches	Formulations	References
1	Hybrid expert system with ANNs	Formulations for hard gelatin capsules	[89]
2	Expert system (SeDeM Diagram)	Tablets that dissolve in the mouth	[90, 91]
3	Expert system with ANNs	Tablets for osmotic pumps	[92, 93]
4	Ontology-based expert system	Tablets with an immediate effect	[94]
5	ME expert 2.0	Formulations for microemulsions	[95]
6	Fuzzy logic-based expert system	Freeze-dried formulations	[96]
7	Cubist and random forest	Formulations containing cyclodextrin	[97, 98]

industry have been documented [83]. Hughes et al. (2015) developed a DCN that can predict the epoxidation reactivity of compounds to medicine toxicity [84]. According to Xu (2015) et al., DL has also been successfully used to predict drug-induced liver harm [85]. It was reported by Ma et al. (2015). On quantitative structure-activity relationships (QSAR) datasets, DNNs were said to be capable of producing better predictions than other ML algorithms [86]. Furthermore, when it came to drug discovery with small datasets, multitask DL and one-shot learning strategies outperformed single-task learning [23]. Furthermore, using DL to investigate ever-expanding databases in drug development allows us to not only learn from the past but also forecast future drug reprogramming [87, 52, 88]. Various types of deep learning applications in the pharmaceutical industry are given in Figure 9.4.

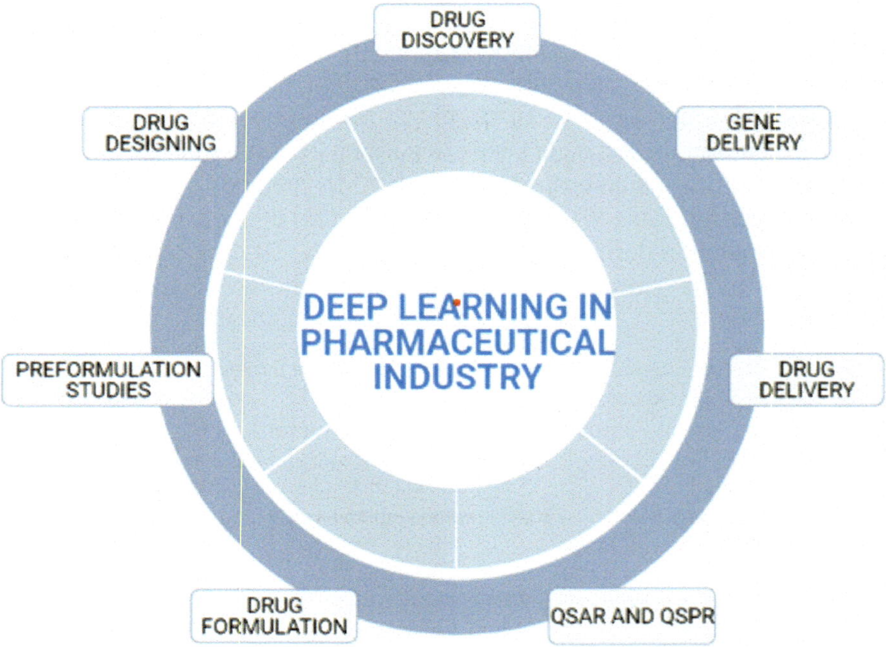

Figure 9.4 Application of deep learning in the pharmaceutical industry.

9.9 Application of Deep Learning Releasing of Drug

Recent applications of DL models and architectures include DNN in bioinformatics, CNN in drug discovery and QSAR measurements, and long short-term memory (LSTM) in computational biology and pharmaceutical research. Larger datasets are required for DL methods to predict drug release from pharmaceutical formulations. Unfortunately, the experimental data in a pharmaceutical formulation is limited, making it difficult to make reliable predictions of drug release and penetration profiles. As a result, to speed up the training of DL models, the size of the data used must be as large as possible. Salma et al. created piroxicam topical films in 2021 by combining CTS and XG and their derivatives. The primary objectives were to improve in vitro drug release and ex vivo permeability to achieve sustained drug release from topical films. In addition, a perfect formulation for achieving a sustained drug release rate was created. The in vitro drug release and penetration characteristics of PX from topical films were estimated using DL and ML algorithms. The purpose of this research was to find the best computational technique for forecasting drug release and permeation patterns. Because testing alternative formulations experimentally are difficult and time-consuming, this prediction model could be used to save money during the early stages of medication development [99]. DL is a general-purpose learning technology that extracts characteristics from raw data automatically. The ability of DL to automatically change the concentration and release time of pharmaceuticals could be used to increase productivity, effectiveness, and therapeutic response [68]. DL technology enables the creation of smart medicine delivery systems (e.g., Janus micro- or nano-particles capable of delivery of multiple drugs). A microchip implant with electronic components, wireless communication devices, and a power supply has been implanted for programmed drug administration (Microchips, Inc.). A programmable remote control regulates drug release in this DL technique. This device contains implantable microchips, a chip containing pharmacological doses, and a titanium case containing an electronics battery that powers the chip.

Computational intelligence technology enables the development of intelligent pharmaceutical delivery systems (e.g., Janus micro- or nanoparticles capable of delivery of multiple drugs). A microchip implant with electronic components, wireless communication devices, and a power source was implanted for controlled medication administration (Microchips, Inc.). In this DL technique, the drug release is controlled by a programmable controller. Microchips with drug dosages have been implanted in this device.

The exterior layer of the microchip is made up of a titanium shell that is supported by an electrical battery that allows the chip to function [100]. Biocompatible microcontrollers have been used to dispense medications and manage insulin supplies in osteoporotic patients. The successful integration of drug sensors, insulin delivery systems, statistical models, and optimization techniques is advantageous in this context. The digital delivery system, as well as the drug-specific target system, can change the dosage or rate of drug delivery, according to the DL concept. In auto-delivery devices, proper algorithms should be used to control the volume and timing of drug release. DL, wireless connections, and artificial networks give controlled delivery systems more flexibility. The devices receive commands from third-party sources, collect data, and manage medication releases [101]. As a result, ANNs have been proposed as trustworthy tools for capturing cause-and-effect relationships and predicting in vitro and in vivo data correlations, as well as applications in genome sequencing, bioinformatics, statistical modeling, pharmaceutical product development, absorption and bioavailability prediction, and behavioral patterns [102–105]. IVIVC and pattern recognition can be used to perform bioavailability interpolation and complex correlations [106]. Data obtained after the formation of IVIVC using a modified DL technique as a non-linear modeling tool for predicting sustained release paracetamol matrix tablet formulations was shown to be similar to those seen in vivo. This demonstrates the suitability of DL analysis for predicting drug behavior in vivo, as well as its ability to apply sophisticated relationships between dependent and independent parameters, compensate for variances in drug release kinetics under various conditions, and accurately estimate drug actions in vivo [107].

The use of controlled-release formulations in combination with DL and fuzzy inference system algorithms to generate sustained-release formulations aids in the investigation of the effect of dosage forms on release qualities [108]. Following the development of complex pharmaceutical formulations and the design of controlled-release formulations using pharmacokinetics models and DL, a strong link was established between experimental data and DL-based predictions [107], [109–110]. Pharmacokinetic simulations and ANNs were used to develop controlled-release formulations with appropriate dissolution profiles and bioavailability, as well as predict in vitro and in vivo behavior, and good agreement was found between ANN-predicted and experimental findings, indicating the utility of ANN models for the development of formulations with appropriate physicochemical properties. Pharmacokinetic simulations and ANNs were used to develop controlled-release formulations with appropriate in-vitro solubility and bioavailability, as well as to forecast their in-vitro or in-vivo activities. A positive relationship was found between ANN-predicted and study observations, demonstrating that ANN models can be used to generate formulations with adequate physical and chemical properties [111].

DL models for controlled-release particle dissolving profiles, such as beads, pellets, and microspheres, have also been developed. Using ideal situations, the neural network for predicting the experimental matrix was built. According to dissolution experiments, alginate beads can transport papain to the small intestine in pH ranges comparable to the human gastrointestinal system. After accelerated and long-term stability tests, the shelf-life of papain encapsulated in alginate was significantly improved, demonstrating the technique's potential for developing sustainable beads susceptible to site-specific drug administration [77]. The release rate of matrix-controlled release theophylline capsules was predicted using a DL neural network. High $f2$ values (>60) confirmed that the DL-predicted release profile was comparable to those observed in the trials [112]. The in vitro release pattern was correctly predicted by DL. To assess the impact of preparative parameters during the solvent evaporation process for the creation of acrylic microspheres for controlled release, an ANN model was developed [113]. An experiment was carried out to estimate drug release in the case of topically applied iontophoresis. It was carried out to assess the efficacy of a DL method and the viability of this model-smart learning program for drug release prediction [114]. As a modeling tool, DL has been used to predict drug release patterns from hydrodynamically balanced systems. Based on its chemical structure and formulation descriptions, DL aided incorrectly in predicting the release profiles of various medications and identifying the significant variables impacting the drug's release [115]. The differences in the delayed and rapid release of paracetamol from multilayer dosage form suppositories were studied using a DL technique, as well as compartment-based modeling and simulation [97]. High-accuracy release profiles from test formulations were predicted using networks with multilevel inverters. Compaction power and polymer fraction were discovered to be the most influential parameters in drug release profiles. To model the release of diclofenac sodium from polyethene oxide controlled release matrix tablets, networks capable of modeling solubility and dissolution rates, as well as a more precise prognostication of drug release kinetics, were used [116].

9.10 Predictive Models for Drug Release of Deep Learning

In a DL-based drug release and permeability prediction model, the fundamental issue stems from the difficulty of developing a model that accurately simulates drug kinetics. DL provides a huge number of algorithmic patterns that can be used to anticipate drug permeability release [117]. Three DL models, classified into three subcategories, predict the drug release and permeation profile: (1) (DNN) long-term, (2) CNN, and (3) short-term (LSTM). These advanced models were created using Keras, a Python-based neural network library. This DL program is based on Tensor Flow or Theano and serves as a wrapper for them. The Lenovo Legion Y7000's 17th and 19th generation CPU systems, with 16 GB of memory and the professional quality NVIDIA GeForce GTX 1060 (6 GB) graphics, are in charge of this program. This DL program was first released on March 27, 2015, and it is expected to be stable by June 17, 2020. An Approach to Data Training: The dataset was divided into two parts to assess the accuracy of the computer models' predictions. 70% of the set of data has been used as a training dataset, with the remaining 30% being used as a testing dataset. The training set has been used to learn the mathematical algorithms and adjust the variables, whereas the test set was used to determine prediction accuracy on an unknown dataset. Larger datasets are required for DL methods to predict drug release and permeability from pharmaceutical formulations. In contrast, the scientific findings in drug formulations are sparse, making accurate forecasting of the release of drugs and systemic absorption profiles difficult. However, because there isn't much data on how drugs are released and absorbed in pharmaceutical formulations, making reliable predictions about how the drugs will work is difficult. As a result, to make DL model training as efficient as possible, the amount of data used must be as large as possible [118].

9.11 Deep Learning Models for Prediction of Drug Release and Permeation

These are some of the major challenges in using DL models to predict drug release from pharmaceutical dosage forms, owing to a lack of accurate scientific results, as testing diverse formulations scientifically is time-consuming and labor-intensive. On the contrary, DL methods require large datasets to forecast the release of the drug and systemic absorption characteristics. GAN was used to optimize the amount of the information set and to develop the formulations for this purpose. The large dataset necessitates the use of a GAN application. GAN is an ML technique that learns to generate new information with the same set of statistics as a training dataset. The training of DL models was significantly improved after using this neural technique for data improvement. On the other hand, DNN after training differs from experimental data. The scatter plot model was built using the seaborne Python plugin. The high correlation between DNN's anticipated information and experimental data shows that DNN accurately forecasts drug release and systemic absorption, with the majority of DNN's predicted data being very similar to real data. As a result of the findings, it was discovered that augmenting the data with GAN improved DNN performance. Apart from previous studies that concentrated solely on the use of ML-based approaches to predict drug release and diffusion rates, this new research goes beyond that. DNN was the most accurate model for demonstrating how formulation physicochemical properties affect drug release and permeation kinetics [119].

9.12 Conclusions

DL is a type of self-directed learning that is commonly used in research, business, and government. These beneficial techniques are also used in cheminformatics and bioinformatics. Identifying biomaterial targets for drugs is a common practice in drug development. R&D relies heavily on target recognition, compound protein identification, and drug–drug interactions. A subfield of AI is the development of ML that mimics human behavior. From biomarker development to drug discovery, ML is widely used in biomedicine. Intelligent DDSs make use of digital, wireless, and AI technologies. When designing smart delivery systems, on-demand drug release, targeted delivery, and pharmacological stability should all be taken into account. Finally, we have highlighted that Robots and DL architecture could be used in the future to create optimal drug delivery pathways. When combined with multi-modal and/or multi-scale modeling, DL architecture can teach molecular shuttles to self-locate in vivo. An autonomous swarm of molecular shuttles could travel to multiple locations and deliver pharmaceutical cargo. Electronic components, wireless communication devices, and a power source are all contained on a microchip. To release drugs, DL techniques employ programmable controllers. The interoperability of drug sensors, insulin delivery systems, and optimization techniques is advantageous in this situation. It was found that there was a substantial correlation between experimental data and ANN predictions. The ANN-predicted and study observations had a positive correlation. Controlled-release particle dissolving profiles have also been developed using DL models. From hydrodynamically balanced systems, DL predicted drug release patterns (DL). GAN uses the same statistics as a training dataset to generate new data, whereas DL methods require large datasets to predict drug release and systemic absorption. The DNN model accurately depicted how formulation properties influence drug release and permeation kinetics.

Acknowledgment

Authors are thankful to all co-authors to make their contributions in completing this chapter.

Conflict of Interest

There is no conflict of interest.

Funding

No funding is required.

References

[1] Yusuf, A., Sebastien, B., Samira, E., Charlie, G., Brendan, L., Eric, M., Cosmic, P., and Alfredo, S. (2016). Deep Learning. Chapter 1, Introduction.

[2] Xu, Y., Dai, Z., Chen, F., Gao, S., Pei, J., and Lai, L. (2015) Deep learning for drug-induced liver injury. *J. Chem. Inf. Model.*. 55, 2085–2093.

[3] Bengio, Y., Courville, A., and Vincent, P. (2013) Representation learning: a review and new perspectives. *IEEE Transactions on Pattern Analysis and Machine Intelligence*. 35, 1798–1828.

[4] LeCun, Y., Bengio, Y., and Hinton, G. (2015) Deep learning. *Nature*. 521, 436–444.

[5] Schmidhuber, J. (2015). Deep learning in neural networks: an overview. *Neural. Netw*. 61, 85–117.

[6] Krizhevsky, A., Sutskever, I., and Hinton. G.E. (2012) Imagenet classification with deep convolutional neural networks. *Advances in Neural Information Processing Systems*. 25.

[7] Hinton, G., Deng, L., Yu, D., Dahl, G.E., Mohamed, A.R., Jaitly, N., Senior, A., Vanhoucke, V., Nguyen, P., Sainath, T.N., and Kingsbury, B. (2012) Deep neural networks for acoustic modeling in speech recognition: the shared views of four research groups. *IEEE Signal Processing Magazine*. 29, 82–97.

[8] Jin, S., Zeng, X., Xia, F., Huang, W., and Liu, X. (2021) Application of deep learning methods in biological networks. *Briefings in Bioinformatics*. 22, 1902–1917.

[9] Winnicka, K. (2021). Advanced materials in drug release and drug delivery systems. *Materials*. 14, 1042.

[10] Kalaiselvi, T., & Padmapriya, S. T. (2021). Brain tumor diagnostic system—a deep learning application. *Machine Vision Inspection Systems, Volume 2: Machine Learning-Based Approaches*, 69-90.

[11] Lusci, A., Pollastri, G., and Baldi, Pierre. (2013) Deep architectures and deep learning in chemoinformatics: the prediction of aqueous solubility for drug-like molecules. *J. Chem. Inform. Model.*. 53, 1563–1575.

[12] Mamoshina, P., Vieira, A., Putin, E., and Zhavoronkov, A. (2016) Applications of deep learning in biomedicine. *Mol. Pharm.* 13, 1445–1454.

[13] Xu, Y., Zhou, Y., Sekula, P., and Ding, L. (2021) Machine learning in construction: from shallow to deep learning. *Dev. Built. Environ.* 6, 100045.

[14] Kim, I.-W., Oh, J.M. (2017) Deep learning: from chemoinformatics to precision medicine. *J. Pharm. Invest.* 47, 317–323.

[15] Schmidhuber, J (2015). Deep learning in neural networks: an overview. *Neura.l Netw.* 61, 85–117.

[16] Zawbaa, H.M., Szlęk, J., Grosan, C., Jachowicz, R., and Mendyk, A. (2016) Computational intelligence modeling of the macromolecules release from PLGA microspheres—focus on feature selection. *PLoS. One*. 11, e0157610.

[17] Scannell, J.W., Blanckley, A., Boldon, H., and Warrington, B. (2012) Diagnosing the decline in pharmaceutical R&D efficiency. *Nat. Rev. Drug. Discov.* 11, 191–200.

[18] Lee, P. I., & Li, J. X. (2010). Evolution of oral controlled release dosage forms. *Oral controlled release formulation design and drug delivery. John Wiley & Sons, Inc*, 21-31.

[19] Park, K. (2015) Drug delivery of the future: chasing the invisible gorilla. *J. Control. Release*. 240, 2–8.

[20] Park, K. (2014) Controlled drug delivery systems: Past forward and future back. *J. Control. Release*. 190, 3–8

[21] Yang, Y., Ye, Z., Su, Y., Zhao, Q., Li, X., and Ouyang, D. (2019). Deep learning for in vitro prediction of pharmaceutical formulations. *Acta pharmaceutica sinica B*, *9*(1), 177-185.

[22] Xu, Y., Dai, Z., Chen, F., Gao, S., Pei, J., and Lai, L. (2015). Deep learning for drug-induced liver injury. *Journal of chemical information and modeling*, *55*(10), 2085-2093.

[23] Ramsundar, B., Liu, B., Wu, Z., Verras, A., Tudor, M., Sheridan, R. P., & Pande, V. (2017). Is multitask deep learning practical for pharma?. *Journal of chemical information and modeling*, *57*(8), 2068-2076.

[24] Altae-Tran, H., Ramsundar, B., Pappu, A. S., & Pande, V. (2017). Low data drug discovery with one-shot learning. *ACS central science*, *3*(4), 283-293.

[25] Hosny, A., Parmar, C., Quackenbush, J., Schwartz, L. H., & Aerts, H. J. (2018). Artificial intelligence in radiology. *Nature Reviews Cancer*, *18*(8), 500-510.

[26] Wu, N., Phang, J., Park, J., Shen, Y., Huang, Z., Zorin, M., & Geras, K. J. (2019). Deep neural networks improve radiologists' performance in breast cancer screening. *IEEE transactions on medical imaging*, *39*(4), 1184-1194.

[27] McKinney, S. M., Sieniek, M., Godbole, V., Godwin, J., Antropova, N., Ashrafian, H., & Shetty, S. (2020). International evaluation of an AI system for breast cancer screening. *Nature*, *577*(7788), 89-94.

[28] Zhavoronkov, A., Ivanenkov, Y. A., Aliper, A., Veselov, M. S., Aladinskiy, V. A., Aladinskaya, A. V., ... & Aspuru-Guzik, A. (2019). Deep learning enables rapid identification of potent DDR1 kinase inhibitors. *Nature biotechnology*, *37*(9), 1038-1040.

[29] Stokes, J. M., Yang, K., Swanson, K., Jin, W., Cubillos-Ruiz, A., Donghia, N. M., & Collins, J. J. (2020). A deep learning approach to antibiotic discovery. *Cell*, *180*(4), 688-702.

[30] Langner, S., Häse, F., Perea, J. D., Stubhan, T., Hauch, J., Roch, L. M., & Brabec, C. J. (2020). Beyond ternary OPV: high-throughput experimentation and self-driving laboratories optimize multicomponent systems. *Advanced Materials*, *32*(14), 1907801.

[31] MacLeod, B. P., Parlane, F. G., Morrissey, T. D., Häse, F., Roch, L. M., Dettelbach, K. E., & Berlinguette, C. P. (2020). Self-driving laboratory for accelerated discovery of thin-film materials. *Science Advances*, *6*(20), eaaz8867.

[32] McCoubrey, L. E., Elbadawi, M., Orlu, M., Gaisford, S., & Basit, A. W. (2021). Harnessing machine learning for development of microbiome therapeutics. *Gut Microbes*, *13*(1), 1872323.
[33] Rafi, T. H. (2021). A Brief Review on Spiking Neural Network-A Biological Inspiration.
[34] McCoubrey, L. E., Elbadawi, M., Orlu, M., Gaisford, S., & Basit, A. W. (2021). Harnessing machine learning for development of microbiome therapeutics. *Gut Microbes*, *13*(1), 1872323.
[35] Schmidt, B., & Hildebrandt, A. (2021). Deep learning in next-generation sequencing. *Drug Discovery Today*, *26*(1), 173-180.
[36] Das, S. C., & Prakash, A. (2021). A Systematic Review on Drug Delivery Systems Based on Their Mechanism of Drug Release and Their Applications. *International Journal for Research in Applied Sciences and Biotechnology*, *8*(3), 55-63.
[37] Cohen, S. (2021). The basics of machine learning: strategies and techniques. In *Artificial Intelligence and Deep Learning in Pathology* (pp. 13-40). Elsevier.
[38] Vamathevan, J., Clark, D., Czodrowski, P., Dunham, I., Ferran, E., Lee, G., & Zhao, S. (2019). Applications of machine learning in drug discovery and development. *Nature reviews Drug discovery*, *18*(6), 463-477.
[39] Kumar, V., & Dogra, N. (2021). A comprehensive review on deep synergistic drug prediction techniques for cancer. *Archives of Computational Methods in Engineering*, 1-19.
[40] Lavecchia, A. (2019). Deep learning in drug discovery: opportunities, challenges and future prospects. *Drug discovery today*, *24*(10), 2017-2032.
[41] Ching, T., Himmelstein, D. S., Beaulieu-Jones, B. K., Kalinin, A. A., Do, B. T., Way, G. P., & Greene, C. S. (2018). Opportunities and obstacles for deep learning in biology and medicine. *Journal of the Royal Society Interface*, *15*(141), 20170387.
[42] Piroozmand, F., Mohammadipanah, F., & Sajedi, H. (2020). Spectrum of deep learning algorithms in drug discovery. *Chemical Biology & Drug Design*, *96*(3), 886-901.
[43] Yin, C., Zhu, Y., Fei, J., & He, X. (2017). A deep learning approach for intrusion detection using recurrent neural networks. *Ieee Access*, *5*, 21954-21961.

[44] Ju, C., Bibaut, A., & van der Laan, M. (2018). The relative performance of ensemble methods with deep convolutional neural networks for image classification. *Journal of Applied Statistics, 45*(15), 2800-2818.

[45] Shetty, D., Varma, J., Navi, S., & Ahmed, M. (2020). Diving deep into deep learning: history, evolution, types and applications. *The International Journal on Media Management, 9*, 2278-3075. Shetty, D., Varma, J., Navi, S., & Ahmed, M. (2020). Diving deep into deep learning: history, evolution, types and applications. *The International Journal on Media Management, 9*, 2278-3075.

[46] Akay, A., & Hess, H. (2019). Deep learning: current and emerging applications in medicine and technology. *IEEE journal of biomedical and health informatics, 23*(3), 906-920.

[47] Janiesch, C., Zschech, P., & Heinrich, K. (2021). Machine learning and deep learning. *Electronic Markets, 31*(3), 685-695.

[48] Kathiresan, K., Pattanayek, S., & Umamaheswari, (2020) E. Stimulus of artificial neural network in drug discovery, development and research. *International Journal of Pharmacy and Industrial Research*, 10(01):45-50.

[49] Sadeeq, M. A., & Abdulazeez, A. M. (2020, December). Neural networks architectures design, and applications: A review. In *2020 International Conference on Advanced Science and Engineering (ICOASE)* (pp. 199-204). IEEE.

[50] Schmidhuber, J. (2015). Deep learning in neural networks: An overview. *Neural networks, 61*, 85-117.

[51] Hock, S. C., Siang, T. K., & Wah, C. L. (2021). Continuous manufacturing versus batch manufacturing: benefits, opportunities and challenges for manufacturers and regulators. *Generics and Biosimilars Initiative Journal, 10*(1), 1-14.

[52] Aliper, A., Plis, S., Artemov, A., Ulloa, A., Mamoshina, P., & Zhavoronkov, A. (2016). Deep learning applications for predicting pharmacological properties of drugs and drug repurposing using transcriptomic data. *Molecular pharmaceutics, 13*(7), 2524-2530.

[53] Ahmad, J., Farman, H., & Jan, Z. (2019). Deep learning methods and applications. In *Deep learning: convergence to big data analytics* (pp. 31-42). Springer, Singapore.

[54] Cao, Y., Geddes, T. A., Yang, J. Y. H., & Yang, P. (2020). Ensemble deep learning in bioinformatics. *Nature Machine Intelligence, 2*(9), 500-508.

[55] Jing, Y., Bian, Y., Hu, Z., Wang, L., & Xie, X. Q. S. (2018). Deep learning for drug design: an artificial intelligence paradigm for drug discovery in the big data era. *The AAPS Journal*, *20*(3), 1-10.

[56] Manco, L., Maffei, N., Strolin, S., Vichi, S., Bottazzi, L., & Strigari, L. (2021). Basic of machine learning and deep learning in imaging for medical physicists. *Physica Medica*, *83*, 194-205.

[57] Shone, N., Ngoc, T. N., Phai, V. D., & Shi, Q. (2018). A deep learning approach to network intrusion detection. *IEEE transactions on emerging topics in computational intelligence*, *2*(1), 41-50.

[58] Gómez-Bombarelli, R., Wei, J. N., Duvenaud, D., Hernández-Lobato, J. M., Sánchez-Lengeling, B., Sheberla, D., & Aspuru-Guzik, A. (2018). Automatic chemical design using a data-driven continuous representation of molecules. *ACS central science*, *4*(2), 268-276.

[59] Goodfellow, I., Pouget-Abadie, J., Mirza, M., Xu, B., Warde-Farley, D., Ozair, S., ... & Bengio, Y. (2014). Generative adversarial nets. *Advances in neural information processing systems*, *27*.

[60] Sanchez-Lengeling, B., Outeiral, C., Guimaraes, G. L., & Aspuru-Guzik, A. (2017). Optimizing distributions over molecular space. *An objective-reinforced generative adversarial network for inverse-design chemistry (ORGANIC)*.

[61] Peng, X., Wang, L., Wang, X., & Qiao, Y. (2016). Bag of visual words and fusion methods for action recognition: Comprehensive study and good practice. *Computer Vision and Image Understanding*, *150*, 109-125.

[62] Liu, A. A., Su, Y. T., Jia, P. P., Gao, Z., Hao, T., & Yang, Z. X. (2014). Multiple/single-view human action recognition via part-induced multitask structural learning. *IEEE transactions on cybernetics*, *45*(6), 1194-1208.

[63] Keerthana, V., Mohaideen, S. S., Vigneshwaran, L. V., & Kumar, M. S. (2022). Role of artificial intelligence in drug development. *International Journal of Research in Pharmaceutical Sciences and Technology*, *3*(1), Awaiting-Awaiting.

[64] Baştanlar, Y., & Özuysal, M. (2014). Introduction to machine learning. *miRNomics: MicroRNA biology and computational analysis*, 105-128.

[65] Wani, M. A., Bhat, F. A., Afzal, S., & Khan, A. I. (2020). Unsupervised deep learning architectures. In *Advances in Deep Learning* (pp. 77-94). Springer, Singapore.

[66] Ibrić, S., Djuriš, J., Parojčić, J., & Djurić, Z. (2012). Artificial neural networks in evaluation and optimization of modified release solid dosage forms. *Pharmaceutics*, *4*(4), 531-550.

[67] Shorten, C., Khoshgoftaar, T. M., & Furht, B. (2021). Deep learning applications for COVID-19. *Journal of Big Data*, *8*(1), 1-54.

[68] Bengio, Y., Simard, P., & Frasconi, P. (1994). Learning long-term dependencies with gradient descent is difficult. *IEEE transactions on neural networks*, *5*(2), 157-166.

[69] Saleem, M., Valle, H. E., Brown, S., Winters, V. I., & Mahmood, A. (2018). The hiperwall tiled-display wall system for big-data research. *Journal of Big Data*, *5*(1), 1-45.

[70] Han, R., Yang, Y., Li, X., & Ouyang, D. (2018). Predicting oral disintegrating tablet formulations by neural network techniques. *Asian journal of pharmaceutical sciences*, *13*(4), 336-342.

[71] Ekins, S. (2016). The next era: deep learning in pharmaceutical research. *Pharmaceutical research*, *33*(11), 2594-2603.

[72] Wang, W., Ye, Z., Gao, H., & Ouyang, D. (2021). Computational pharmaceutics-A new paradigm of drug delivery. *Journal of Controlled Release*, *338*, 119-136.

[73] Simões, M. F., Silva, G., Pinto, A. C., Fonseca, M., Silva, N. E., Pinto, R. M., & Simões, S. (2020). Artificial neural networks applied to quality-by-design: From formulation development to clinical outcome. *European Journal of Pharmaceutics and Biopharmaceutics*, 152, 282-295.

[74] Waheed, A., Kumar, A., and Bindu, H. (2020). Assessing the role of artificial intelligence in the design of drug delivery systems. *International Journal of Medical Science and Diagnosis Research (IJMSDR)*, 4(12):22-27.

[75] Grassi, M., & Grassi, G. (2014). Application of mathematical modeling in sustained release delivery systems. *Expert opinion on drug delivery*, *11*(8), 1299-1321.

[76] Chen, G., Li, J., Zhang, S., Song, C., Li, G., Sun, Z., ... & You, J. (2012). A sensitive and efficient method to systematically detect two biophenols in medicinal herb, herbal products and rat plasma based on thorough study of derivatization and its convenient application to pharmacokinetics with semi-automated device. *Journal of Chromatography A*, *1249*, 190-200.

[77] Hassanzadeh, P., Atyabi, F., & Dinarvand, R. (2019). The significance of artificial intelligence in drug delivery system design. *Advanced drug delivery reviews*, *151*, 169-190.

[78] Nagy, B., Petra, D., Galata, D. L., Démuth, B., Borbás, E., Marosi, G., ... & Farkas, A. (2019). Application of artificial neural networks for Process Analytical Technology-based dissolution testing. *International Journal of Pharmaceutics*, *567*, 118464.

[79] Bannigan, P., Aldeghi, M., Bao, Z., Häse, F., Aspuru-Guzik, A., & Allen, C. (2021). Machine learning directed drug formulation development. *Advanced Drug Delivery Reviews*, *175*, 113806.

[80] Sethuraman, N. (2020). Artificial Intelligence: A New Paradigm for Pharmaceutical Applications in Formulations Development. *Indian Journal of Pharmaceutical Education and Research*, *54*(4), 843-846.

[81] Manne, R. (2021). Machine learning techniques in drug discovery and development. *International Journal of Applied Research*, *7*(4), 21-28.

[82] Yang, Y., Ye, Z., Su, Y., Zhao, Q., Li, X., & Ouyang, D. (2019). Deep learning for in vitro prediction of pharmaceutical formulations. *Acta pharmaceutica sinica B*, *9*(1), 177-185.

[83] Lusci, A., Pollastri, G., & Baldi, P. (2013). Deep architectures and deep learning in chemoinformatics: the prediction of aqueous solubility for drug-like molecules. *Journal of chemical information and modeling*, *53*(7), 1563-1575.

[84] Hughes, T. B., Miller, G. P., & Swamidass, S. J. (2015). Modeling epoxidation of drug-like molecules with a deep machine learning network. *ACS central science*, *1*(4), 168-180.

[85] Xu, Y., Dai, Z., Chen, F., Gao, S., Pei, J., & Lai, L. (2015). Deep learning for drug-induced liver injury. *Journal of chemical information and modeling*, *55*(10), 2085-2093.

[86] Ma, J., Sheridan, R. P., Liaw, A., Dahl, G. E., & Svetnik, V. (2015). Deep neural nets as a method for quantitative structure–activity relationships. *Journal of chemical information and modeling*, *55*(2), 263-274.

[87] Vanhaelen, Q., Mamoshina, P., Aliper, A. M., Artemov, A., Lezhnina, K., Ozerov, I., ... & Zhavoronkov, A. (2017). Design of efficient computational workflows for in silico drug repurposing. *Drug Discovery Today*, *22*(2), 210-222.

[88] Wilson, W. I., Peng, Y., & Augsburger, L. L. (2005). Generalization of a prototype intelligent hybrid system for hard gelatin capsule formulation development. *AAPS PharmSciTech*, *6*(3), E449-E457.

[89] Aguilar-Díaz, J. E., García-Montoya, E., Suñe-Negre, J. M., Pérez-Lozano, P., Miñarro, M., & Ticó, J. R. (2012). Predicting orally disintegrating tablets formulations of ibuprophen tablets: an application of the new SeDeM-ODT expert system. *European journal of pharmaceutics and biopharmaceutics*, *80*(3), 638-648.

[90] Aguilar, J. E., Montoya, E. G., Lozano, P. P., Negre, J. M. S., Carmona, M. M., & Grau, J. R. T. (2013). New SeDeM-ODT expert system: An expert system for formulation of orodispersible tablets obtained by direct compression. In *Formulation tools for pharmaceutical development* (pp. 137-154). Woodhead Publishing.

[91] Zhang, Z. H. (2013). Expert system for the development and formulation of push–pull osmotic pump tablets containing poorly water-soluble drugs. In *Formulation tools for pharmaceutical development* (pp. 73-108). Woodhead Publishing.

[92] Zhang, Z. H., Dong, H. Y., Peng, B., Liu, H. F., Li, C. L., & Liang, M. (2011). Design of an expert system for the development and formulation of push–pull osmotic pump tablets containing poorly water-soluble drugs. *International journal of pharmaceutics*, *410*(1-2), 41-47.

[93] Chalortham, N., Ruangrajitpakorn, T., Supnithi, T., & Leesawat, P. (2013). Oxpirt: ontology-based expert system for production of a generic immediate release tablet. In *Formulation tools for pharmaceutical development* (pp. 203-228). Woodhead Publishing.

[94] Mendyk, A., Szlęk, J., & Jachowicz, R. (2013). ME_expert 2.0: a heuristic decision support system for microemulsions formulation development. In *Formulation tools for pharmaceutical development* (pp. 39-71). Woodhead Publishing.

[95] Trnka, H., Wu, J. X., Van De Weert, M., Grohganz, H., & Rantanen, J. (2013). Fuzzy logic-based expert system for evaluating cake quality of freeze-dried formulations. *Journal of Pharmaceutical Sciences*, *102*(12), 4364-4374.

[96] Merzlikine, A., Abramov, Y. A., Kowsz, S. J., Thomas, V. H., & Mano, T. (2011). Development of machine learning models of β-cyclodextrin and sulfobutylether-β-cyclodextrin complexation free energies. *International journal of pharmaceutics*, *418*(2), 207-216.

[97] Salma, H., Melha, Y. M., Sonia, L., Hamza, H., & Salim, N. (2021). Efficient prediction of in vitro piroxicam release and diffusion from topical films based on biopolymers using deep learning models and generative adversarial networks. *Journal of pharmaceutical sciences*, *110*(6), 2531-2543.

[98] Prescott, J. H., Lipka, S., Baldwin, S., Sheppard, N. F., Maloney, J. M., Coppeta, J., & Santini, J. T. (2006). Chronic, programmed polypeptide delivery from an implanted, multireservoir microchip device. *Nature biotechnology*, *24*(4), 437-438.

[99] Farra, R., Sheppard Jr, N. F., McCabe, L., Neer, R. M., Anderson, J. M., Santini Jr, J. T., . & Langer, R. (2012). First-in-human testing of a wirelessly controlled drug delivery microchip. *Science translational medicine*, *4*(122), 122ra21-122ra21.

[100] De Matas, M., Shao, Q., Richardson, C. H., & Chrystyn, H. (2008). Evaluation of in vitro in vivo correlations for dry powder inhaler delivery using artificial neural networks. *European Journal of Pharmaceutical Sciences*, *33*(1), 80-90.

[101] Brier, M. E., Zurada, J. M., & Aronoff, G. R. (1995). Neural network predicted peak and trough gentamicin concentrations. *Pharmaceutical research*, *12*(3), 406-412.

[102] Veng-Pedersen, P., & Modi, N. B. (1993). Application of neural networks to pharmacodynamics. *Journal of pharmaceutical sciences*, *82*(9), 918-926.

[103] Gobburu, J. V., & Shelver, W. H. (1995). Quantitative structure–pharmacokinetic relationships (QSPR) of beta blockers derived using neural networks. *Journal of pharmaceutical sciences*, *84*(7), 862-865.

[104] Dowell, J. A., Hussain, A., Devane, J., & Young, D. (1999). Artificial neural networks applied to the in vitro—in vivo correlation of an extended-release formulation: Initial trials and experience. *Journal of pharmaceutical sciences*, *88*(1), 154-160.

[105] Parojčić, J., Ibrić, S., Djurić, Z., Jovanović, M., & Corrigan, O. I. (2007). An investigation into the usefulness of generalized regression neural network analysis in the development of level A in vitro–in vivo correlation. *European journal of pharmaceutical sciences*, *30*(3-4), 264-272.

[106] Tan, C., & Degim, İ. T. (2012). Development of sustained release formulation of an antithrombotic drug and application of fuzzy logic. *Pharmaceutical Development and Technology*, *17*(2), 242-250.

[107] Chen, Y., McCall, T. W., Baichwal, A. R., & Meyer, M. C. (1999). The application of an artificial neural network and pharmacokinetic simulations in the design of controlled-release dosage forms. *Journal of controlled release*, *59*(1), 33-41.

[108] Aktas, E., Eroglu, H., Kockan, U., & Oner, L. (2013). Systematic development of pH-independent controlled release tablets of carvedilol

using central composite design and artificial neural networks. *Drug development and industrial pharmacy*, *39*(8), 1207-1216.

[109] Chansanroj, K., Petrović, J., Ibrić, S., & Betz, G. (2011). Drug release control and system understanding of sucrose esters matrix tablets by artificial neural networks. *European journal of pharmaceutical sciences*, *44*(3), 321-331.

[110] Peh, K. K., Lim, C. P., Quek, S. S., & Khoh, K. H. (2000). Use of artificial neural networks to predict drug dissolution profiles and evaluation of network performance using similarity factor. *Pharmaceutical research*, *17*(11), 1384-1389.

[111] Asadi, H., Rostamizadeh, K., Salari, D., & Hamidi, M. (2011). Preparation of biodegradable nanoparticles of tri-block PLA–PEG–PLA copolymer and determination of factors controlling the particle size using artificial neural network. *Journal of microencapsulation*, *28*(5), 406-416.

[112] Lim, C. P., San Quek, S., & Peh, K. K. (2003). Prediction of drug release profiles using an intelligent learning system: an experimental study in transdermal iontophoresis. *Journal of pharmaceutical and biomedical analysis*, *31*(1), 159-168.

[113] Mendyk, A., Jachowicz, R., & Dorożyński, P. (2006). Artificial neural networks in the modelling of drugs release profiles from hydrodynamically balanced system. *Acta Poloniae Pharmaceutica. Drug Research*, *63*(1).

[114] Belič, A., Grabnar, I., Karba, R., & Mrhar, A. (2003). Pathways of paracetamol absorption from layered excipient suppositories: artificial intelligence approach. *European journal of drug metabolism and pharmacokinetics*, *28*(1), 31-40.

[115] Petrović, J., Ibrić, S., Betz, G., Parojčić, J., & Đurić, Z. (2009). Application of dynamic neural networks in the modeling of drug release from polyethylene oxide matrix tablets. *European journal of pharmaceutical sciences*, *38*(2), 172-180.

[116] Maltarollo, V. G., Gertrudes, J. C., Oliveira, P. R., & Honorio, K. M. (2015). Applying machine learning techniques for ADME-Tox prediction: a review. *Expert opinion on drug metabolism & toxicology*, *11*(2), 259-271.

[117] Lefnaoui, S., Rebouh, S., Bouhedda, M., & Yahoum, M. M. (2020). Artificial neural network for modeling formulation and drug permeation of topical patches containing diclofenac sodium. *Drug Delivery and Translational Research*, *10*(1), 168-184.

[118] Lefnaoui, S., Rebouh, S., Bouhedda, M., Yahoum, M. M., & Hanini, S. (2018, November). Artificial neural network modeling of sustained antihypertensive drug delivery using polyelectrolyte complex based on carboxymethyl-kappa-carrageenan and chitosan as prospective carriers. In *2018 International conference on applied smart systems (ICASS)* (pp. 1-8). IEEE.

[119] Simon, L., & Fernandes, M. (2004). Neural network-based prediction and optimization of estradiol release from ethylene–vinyl acetate membranes. *Computers & chemical engineering*, *28*(11), 2407-2419.

10

Tissue Response Study using Deep Learning Techniques

Akanksha Pandey[1], Rishabha Malviya[1], Sonali Sundram[1*], and Karteek Telikicherla[2]

[1]Department of Pharmacy, School of Medical and Allied Science, Galgotias University, India
[2]Whitbread, United Kingdom
*Corresponding Author: Department of Pharmacy, School of Medical and Allied Science, Galgotias University Greater Noida, Uttar Pradesh, India, Email ID: sonaliaim13@gmail.com, Mob. No. : +91-7903471348.

Abstract

An "immune-profile" investigates the relationship between immune responses and the development and recurrence of human tumors. In this case, several biomarkers are used to specify distinct precomputed tomographic scanning of the immunity cellular mass. Research interests include a system that can quickly and accurately identify different types of immunity cells. Radiology enables noninvasive monitoring of the same location over time, revealing additional tumor features not visible on static images at a single timepoint. Patients were divided into two groups based on their mortality risk: higher and lower.

Radiographic characteristics independent of tumor volume can be identified using image-based neural network algorithms. With the addition of more timepoints, the mortality behavior and prognosis estimate utilizing CNN and RNN networks improved. Non-invasive tumor phenotype monitoring that could be used to develop predictions regarding individualized therapy can all be hurt by factors including viability, anticipation, and pathologic response.

Keywords: Immune responses, tumors, deep learning, CNN networks, RNN networks, biomarkers.

10.1 Introduction

Staining IHC-biological slides has the benefit of detecting proteins in the cellular segment, and is thus frequently available to examine the allocation and specification of the specialized cells into living tissue, such as malignant and immunity cells. Malignancies, for example, frequently, have immune cell penetrates, which might also limit tumor development or promote tumor proliferation [1]. Several bio-markers are employed to specify distinct as precomputed tomographic scanning of the immunity cellular mass in this case, as well as the total population of every form is compared to the patients' clinical outcomes. An "immune-profile" explores the relationship within both the immunity responses as well as the development and recurring of human tumors as such an emergent research issue of considerable interest in pathological sciences and immunological sciences. An immunological profiles research, on the other hand, necessitates the human observer manually counting the quantity of distinct immune cells within specified lymph node areas that can comprise hundreds or even thousands of cells. This is a time-consuming and tiresome procedure, and the outcomes are subjected to within-individual variation. A system that can quickly and accurately identify distinct kinds of immunity cells is of major research and therapeutic interest to eliminate the monotony of manual calculations.

Pulmonary malignancy is among the most common malignancies globally, and it is the foremost source of death from malignancy in both industrial and developing countries [2]. The majority of these individuals have non–small cell lung carcinoma (NSCLC), which has a five-year survival rate of only 18% [3, 4]. Even though current medical advances result in a significant rise in the level of mortality rates, such progress is less significant in lung cancer because the majority of symptoms and identified individuals have advanced illness [5]. Nonsurgical methods, including radiation, chemotherapy, targeted therapy, or immunotherapies, are frequently used to treat delayed tumors. That emphasizes the critical importance of employing follow-up radiography to evaluate the therapeutic response and track tumor radiographic changes over time [5]. Clinical response evaluation criteria like RECIST [6] use simple size-based parameters like axial diameter of lesions to examine time-series data.

Artificial intelligence (AI) makes it possible to examine radiographic tumor characteristics quantitatively rather than qualitatively, a technique known as "radiomics" [7]. Various research has shown that non-invasively describing tumor characteristics has more prediction performance than standard clinical assessments [8–11]. Early machine learning techniques entailed deriving artificial characteristics for visual data characterization, including effectiveness in recognizing indicators for outcome evaluation and medical response projection [12–16]. Current advances in deep learning (DL) [7] have shown that image data without human feature definition can be done successfully [17]. Convolutional neural networks (CNNs) are used to automate the collection of visual characteristics as well as the detection of nonlinear correlations in massive information. Through transfer learning, CNNs, which have been learned on thousands of pictorial data, could be employed in medical imaging [18]. In oncology, this has been proved in terms of tumor determination and mounting [18]. Artificial intelligence advancements can be used in the clinic to improve the quality of healthcare by supporting precise and timely outcome support [7, 12].

The bulk of quantifiable scanning research has concentrated on developing diagnostic indicators for a particular timepoint [19, 20]. However, because the tumor is a dynamic living tissue involving contributions from vascular and stems cells that may react, the phenotype may not even be fully represented at a specific point in time [21, 22]. Post treatment computed tomography scans from normal clinical follow-up could be useful for tracking alterations in phenotypic features following radiotherapy. These radiotherapies had already been used in modern technology and the DL approach in the categorization of videos as well as language Processing to accommodate observational studies [23]. Furthermore, just a few research within imaging have been using these advances in computational methodologies [24].

In this research, we combine pre-treatment and follow-up CT imaging using AI inside the deepest sense training, particularly CNNs and RNNs, to forecast mortality as well as another final factor that affect computed tomographic scanning in patients with NSCLC. Two datasets were studied, each encompassing individuals with such a third stage pulmonary malignancy diagnosis who were considered with different therapeutic regimes. We constructed and tested DL prototypes in sufferer's receiving authoritative chemo and radiation therapy in the first dataset. Another additional dataset includes patients receiving chemotherapy, and radiation surgical intervention was used to test the network's generality as well as further pathological validation. Without a volumetric segmentation process, just single-click seed points were required for tumor localization, indicating the simplicity with which a huge proportion of images at many timepoints can be incorporated in deep learning analysis. Response evaluation in clinical trials, personalized medicine practices, and personalized clinical care can all benefit from CT imaging-based patient survival forecasts. These studies have important implications for such clinical application of AI-based image indicators because these could be used non-invasively, frequently, at such a cheap cost, also with minimal human input.

Among all, the most difficult question in medical imaging assessment is recognizing the picture element of tissues or abrasions from background diagnostic pictures such as computed tomography or magnetic resonance imaging scans to offer essential information on the shapes and sizes of these tissues. Using available technologies, several scientists have suggested numerous auto-segmentations techniques. Traditional techniques, outer perimeter recognition filtration, as well as quantitative simulation have been used, after which, for a long period, machine learning (ML) advances to acquiring handcrafted features dominated. The top focus for creating any such scheme was always developing as well as retrieving these characteristics, as well as the complexities of such research methods were viewed as a significant barrier to implementation. Learning techniques first appeared in the 2000s as a consequence of device breakthroughs, and those quickly showed great functionality in image analysis tasks. Because of their hopeful expertise, learning methods had already emerged as the leading preference for image classification, especially healthcare segmentation. The segmentation process based on deep learning methodologies has now gotten preference, emphasizing the importance of this technology. To the best of my knowledge, hardly a comprehensive study of medical image processing using the deep learning method has already been released. For example, [25] and [26] seem to be two comprehensive study articles on medical image analysis. In a study, Shen et al. wrapped numerous sorts of health image recognition, but they failed to respond to the scientific attributes of medical image segmentations (MIS) [26]. A few other factors [25] include medical imaging techniques using computed tomography, including categorization, identification, as well as certification, making it a medical image analysis review rather than a specialized MIS analysis. Because of the extensive scope of this page, the intricacies of networks, capabilities, and flaws abound. Figure 10.1 basically represents the method of treatment providing using advanced and recent invented diagnosis approaches which we are going to study in the chapter.

This prompted us to write this post to provide an overview of current methods. This survey focuses on machine learning approaches used in contemporary medical picture segmentation research, examines their structures

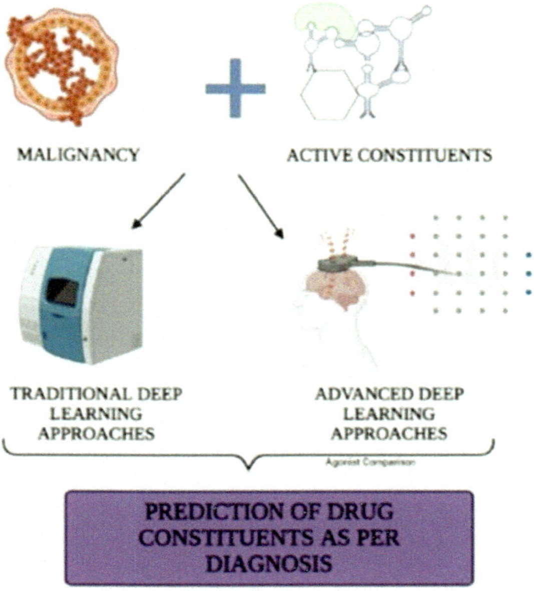

Figure 10.1 Representing the way of providing treatment by the method advanced diagnosis approach.

and methodologies in greater depth, and assesses their strengths and drawbacks. Methodologies (network structures [NS]), training methodologies, and problems are the three primary aspects of computed tomographic scanning of this article.

The NS section describes the most common NS used for picture segmentation, as well as their benefits and drawbacks. It is intended to cover the structure's evolving sequence. Here, we attempt to discuss the most important constructed computed tomographic scanning that has a considerable advantage over its predecessors. The Training Techniques section delves into the most cutting-edge methods for training DNN models. The Challenges section discusses a variety of issues that can arise when utilizing deep learning algorithms to segment medical images. These difficulties are primarily connected to network design, information, and pedagogy. This segment also proposes potential solutions based on the literature to address each of the issues relating to network architecture, data, and training.

In most cases, an IHC detection assay is used to highlight a tissue slide, with a constellation of differentiation (CD) polypeptide indicators indicating immunity cells and the nucleus marker Hematoxylin (HTX) recognizing nuclei. A CCD colour photographic camera attached to a microscope, or maybe a detector, is then used to image the stained slide. The obtained RGB colour picture combines the expressions of the immunity cell layer and universal cell nuclei biomarkers. Various methods for detecting these cells have already been proposed by the authors. The majority of the solutions rely on image processing techniques to collect the symmetrical data of cellular appearance attributes. Pavin et al., for example, suggested a reiterative supporting methodology to group and clump non-convex intuitive spherical symmetry alongside an object's radial line and exhibited its usefulness in the recognition of nuclei with a round edible form [27]. Xin et al. [28] improved the detection of overlapping cells by combining the shifted Gaussian kernel at the center of the voting region with Pavin's technique. Cell identification has also been studied using machine learning approaches in journals. To detect cell-like patches, Arteta et al. [29] suggested a standard statistical matching approach learned from structured SVM. All three approaches, however, are partial to nuclei detection instead of plasma membrane detection. Because the most common immunity cell markers are membrane markers, such as CD-3 and CD-8 for universal T-cells and cytotoxic T-cells, individually, the pigment seems like a ring rather than a blob. Mualla et al. [30] developed another machine learning-based approach for untouched cellular imaging that has the qualities of retaining adequate disparity of cellular borders utilizing SIFT, Random Forests, and Hierarchical Clustering (HC). SIFT main points are divided into tissues and backgrounds in this study, and all main points inside every cell are associated via HC. The procedure has been tested on a huge dataset and proved to be reliable and stable. However, extending it to identify inflammatory responses in IHC labeled imaging is not straightforward.

Niazi et al. recently introduced an automated CD8 cytotoxic T-cell counting approach in [31], in which normalized multi-scale Gaussian difference is utilized to detect potential locations, and colour and intensity information is being used to merge the outcomes. Because of the wide range of cell shapes and sizes, this image processing and rule-based technique may be susceptible to failure. Meanwhile, DL approaches like CNNs [32] have shown tremendous promise in detecting mitotic cells in histology data labeled with Hematoxylin and Eosin [33]. Even as challenging mitotic cell identification issue struggles with enormous physical variance and high complexity, this provides an excellent resource of motivation for designing a novel learning-based immunity cellular recognition technique. CNN, as a powerful pixel classifier, analyzes the image into multiple segments centered at every frame and assigns a classifying tag to every smear. The benefit of CNNs is that the quality signifiers are instinctively understood as kernel matrices in the convolution levels, thus generating intricate attributes for immune cells requires less effort.

10.2 Research Methodologies

The approach of our algorithm is presented through Figure 10.2 by demonstrating the general structure basically representing the methods used in the separation. Several biomarkers are assigned with single or maybe other categories of immunity cells in the study of malignant tissues. CD3 is, for example, a universal marker (UM) for all T-cells, but CD-8 selectively marks the layers of cytotoxic T-cells. The IHC picture is initially not mixed into Hematoxylin and T-cell marker networks to detect T-cells. The pixels in the T-cell network are then identified as highlights or background utilizing CNNs, which produces a possibility plan as a result. Ultimately, we use non-max suppression to get the T-cell centroids from the probability map.

10.2.1 Colour separation

Unmixing every frame of RGB images into various pharmacologically relevant networks equivalent to various stained colours is possible using several strategies described in the literature. Ruifrok et al. created an un-mixing algorithm (UMA) [34] to unmix the RGB picture with up to triple pigments in the transformed optical density space, which is the most extensively operating technique in the computerized pathological area. The approach suggests that

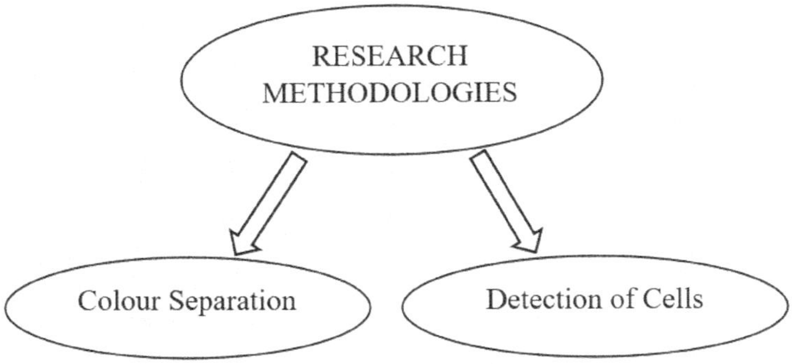

Figure 10.2 Approaches of research methodologies.

every image of the colour mixture an R3 is a straightaway sequence of the clean stained colours and resolves a linear system to derive appropriate combo masses b RM provided the standard colour vectors xi R3 of the pure stains. The linear system is given by the equation $a = Xb$, where $X = [x1,...,$ $xM]$, M 3 is the standard colour vector. The majority of the work with in journal [35] would be for multi-spectral picture un-mixing, which isn't really suitable to RGB images. To our understanding, no method has yet been documented in the literature that can successfully separate over and above three primary stains from such RGB images. Due to the tiny quantity of marks present on every frame, we modified Ruifrok's technique by introducing the L1 norm constraint for b in this study. We get the following benefits from the sparse constraint:

1) The linear system is no longer defective, allowing over three colours to be unmixed.
2) Because of the sparsity regularization, background sound is considerably reduced in the undifferentiated streams, resulting in a higher information noise ratio.

10.2.2 Detection of cells

Due to the huge diversity of information generated by a range of challenges, including various categories of tissue, tissue sector cuts, inorganic coloring artefacts, computed tomographic scanning , as well as scanning focusing difficulties, detecting immune cells accurately is a difficult process. Sparse colour unmixing is utilized to separate an RGB image I into immune cell identifiers and nucleus indicator channels, which are indicated as Idab and Ihtx, correspondingly. The detectors are then trained using Idab as the input picture.

10.3 Materials and Procedures

10.3.1 Cohorts of patients

For this study, we employed two separate accomplices, Dataset A (D-A) and Dataset B (D-B), comprising a combination of two hundred sixty sufferers with the third stage NSCLC. D-A included one hundred seventy-nine sufferers who received final radiation treatment and chemotherapy with drugs (carboplatin/paclitaxel or cisplatin/etoposide (chemoRT)) at Brigham and WFCC between 2003 and 2014 and had a minimum of one checkout CT scanning. Again, for delta analysis of the baseline and checkout CT scanning at one, three, and six months following radiotherapy, we evaluated an aggregate of five hundred eighty-one computed tomographic scanning (average of 3.2; range 2–4 scans/patient, one hundred twenty-five diminution computed tomographic scanning from positron emission tomography, and four hundred fifty-six diagnostic computed tomographic scanning). The computed tomographic scanning and positron emission tomography tests were performed with noose up of iodized contrast, and the contrast used in chest computed tomographic scanning is determined by the individual and according to clinical recommendations. Not that all participants got radiological examinations at any timepoint to give a fair portrayal of clinical circumstances. This study excluded patients who had surgery before or after starting therapy. The study's major goal was to estimate persistence and predictive variables for third-stage sufferers who were cured using final radiotherapy. Training/tuning (n = 107) and test (n = 72) were randomly assigned to Dataset A. The final radiation therapy cohort was evaluated for overall survival as well as three additional clinical objectives, including distant metastases, loco regional recurrence, and progression. Between 2001 and 2013, 89 patients with stage III NSCLC treated with neo adjuvant radiation and chemotherapy before surgical resection at our institution were included in dataset B, which included an additional test (trimodality). The application of a wide range of industry-standard treatment processes on dataset B offered additional validation. A total of 178 CT pictures were taken before surgery at two separate points in time: before and after radiation therapy, both before surgery. Patients having distant metastases or a gap of more than 120 days between chemo radiotherapy and resection, as well as those with no survival analysis, were excluded from the study. There were no histopathological exclusions in any group. The estimation of pathophysiologic responses, evaluated during a surgical procedure, was always the target point of the extensive test group of trimodality participants. Predicated to surgical pathological findings, every remaining tumor was categorized as either responder [36].

10.3.2 Image pre-processing and CT acquisition

Computed tomographic scanning was collected at the organization utilizing a GE "Light speed" computed tomography scanning during therapy, preparation, and checkout scans, following established imaging procedures. A chunk of the pictures is from positron emission tomography-computed tomographic scanning procurements and the follow-up scans had varying axial spacing.

During preparation and the one-, three-, and six-month follow-up computed tomography scanning results post conclusive radiotherapy, the tumor imaging region's input is determined there at the center of the specified key point. In 3D Slicer 4.8.1, the seed points were specified individually [36]. The CT voxels then extrapolated to $1*11*1$ mm^3 utilizing linear and closest neighbor interpolation due to the heterogeneity in layer widths and in-plane resolution. This was important to interpret the radiological information to a homogenous resolution to provide a steady input for the suggested design. Because the sliced widths were limited to 5 mm, the 2D provided impression was acquired at a slicing that was no more than 2 mm away from such a non-interpolated layer. Most complicated interpolated techniques, which entail and may be reliant on multiple constraints and need a retentive computation period, were avoided by using linear interpolation. The fine-scale was chosen to keep things simple.

Providing contributions toward the model, three axial segments of 50×50 mm^2 are centered on the chosen cluster center being employed. These are 5 mm away from each other, with the cluster center on the very same primary layer as the center slice. The CT scans' highest layer thickness was 5 mm. Through using pre-trained models ResNet CNNs, which was focused on original/actual RGB imaging, a transferable teaching method was used. The three axial slices were sent into the CNN network as input. Three 2D slices provide information for the group to get information from while keeping the amount of characteristics smaller than a complete 3D method. This minimizes GPU recollection utilization as well as preparation time while also limiting overfitting. On the training data, picture augmentation was conducted, which included illustration orientation, transcription, as well as rotating distortion, which is a common good practice that has been found to boost execution [37]. The pre-treatment and checkout pictures received the same augmentation, resulting in the network generating a planning for the complete input arrays of pictures. The distortion was measured in millimeters and had no effect on the tumor's or surrounding tissues' shape.

10.3.3 The structure of a neural network

Python 2.7, Keras 2.0.8, and Tensorflow 1.3.0 were used to build the network (Python 2.7, Keras 2.0.8, Tensor flow 1.3.0). A foundation upon which to construct ResNet CNN was trained using the ImageNet dataset, which comprises over 14 million original images. A CNN was defined for each timepoint scan, resulting in three CNNs for input with three timepoint scans. The network model's outcome was therefore supplied into convolution layer with time-domain-aware GRU. Because of its capacity to discover from illustrations missing individuals screening at critical periods, RNN algorithms were used to ensure that the network could manage missing scans [38, 39]. Because no scans were available at the time, this timepoint was excluded from which was before the network's throughput. To decrease prediction error, averaged nearly, as well as connected layer upon layer, were also implemented just after GRU, with bulk standardization [40] as well as drop-outs [41]. It, after every convolution layer, it enables the finished softmax layerâĂŹs binary classification outcome. The suggested framework assessed a design without any need for obey images by using only the primary treatment impression and replacing the repeated as well as normal convolution with such a total surface.

The process of passing on information is known as knowledge transfer. The ResNet [31] CNN was trained using ImageNet [37, 31] weights, a library of 14 million 2D colour pictures, and the extra weights added after the CNN was initialized for transfer learning. Training/tuning and testing were split at random from Dataset A. Class weight balancing were used to train 107 patients utilizing 10 unique splits and Monte Carlo cross-validation for up to 300 epochs. The model was evaluated on 72 patients who had not participated in the training phase. Survival fractions were comparable in the training/tuning (n = 107) and test sets (n = 72). In the proposed model, there were no recurrent or average pooling layers; hence, a fully connected layer was utilized in their place.

10.3.4 Analytical statistics

The statistical analysis for this study was done in Python 2.7. The independent test set from Dataset A was utilized to validate all survival and prognostic parameter estimates after definitive radiation treatment. The goal of radiation therapy was to enhance overall survival by avoiding distant metastases, progression, and loco regional recurrence. The researchers compared their findings to those of a random forest clinical model that took into consideration a range of characteristics such as patient age, disease stage, gender, and tumor grade (primary maximum axial diameter).

The Wilcoxon rank sums test (commonly abbreviated also as Mann–Whitney U test), as well as the area under the receiver operator typical curve (AUC), were used to assess statistical differences across favorable and unfavorable mortality categories in Dataset A. The Kaplan–Meier methodology was stratified using the training set's median predictive possibility, and a log-rank analysis was used to regulate this in terms of developing prognostic and survivor predictions for groups with higher and lower overall mortality. The potential danger rate was calculated using the Cox proportional-hazards framework.

The 1-year mortality analysis first from determined radiotherapy batch having two timepoints was applied to the trimodality cohort's information B. To obtain survival estimates, we used the 1-year survival model trained on Dataset A. Before surgery, patients were classed as trimodality based on the model's projections for survival and tumor response to radiation treatment. To contrast the categories based on their varied AUCs, the Wilcoxon rank sums test was used. To compare the volume change following radiation treatment, an arbitrary vegetation diagnostic framework of the same characteristics as data source A has been used.

10.4 Features of the Clinic

Researchers looked at 268 stage III NSCLC patients and 739 CT images to investigate if considering individual photos before and after radiotherapy, deep learning-based indicators may be possible to forecast survival chances. Dataset A was used to train and assess deep learning biomarkers on 179 people who had had definitive radiation treatment and has no significant differences in patient parameters between Dataset A's training and test sets. Only 52.8% of the patients were female; the majority (58.9%) had stage IIIA NSCLC and 58.1% had adenocarcinoma histology at the time of diagnosis (median age 63 years). The definitive radiation group got a 66 Gy dose with a median follow-up of 31.4 months. The study comprises 89 patients who were treated with trimodality as a control group (Dataset B). Patients in the trimodality got an average of 54 Gy of radiation.

10.4.1 Development and evaluation of prognostic biomarkers based on deep learning

The discovery section of Dataset A was used to create biological markers based on deep neural networks for mortality risk, malignant transformation, tumor growth, and loco-regional incidence. The ResNet CNN model was trained on ImageNet before being transferred to our dataset through transfer learning to make advantage of the information from millions of photographic pictures. It created a recurrent network for longitudinal analysis using CT scans from each timepoint. A Wilcoxon test using just pre-treatment scans as a baseline revealed that this model was ineffective in predicting overall survival for 2 years (AUC = 0.58; $P = 0.3$). AUC 140.69, P14 0.007, enhanced the ability to predict 2-year overall survival (AUC 140.64) at 1 month, 3 months, and 6 months with each consecutive follow-up scan (AUC 140.74, P14 0.001). The rates of 1-year continued existence, advancement, metastatic spread, as well as loco-regional relapse continued existence remained steady. A study point that took into account phase, sex, age, stage of cancer, effectiveness, smoking habits, and diagnostic tumor volume did not anticipate AUC for 2-year survival or treatment response. Kaplan–Meier calculations for low and high mortality risk groups were performed using the median stratification of patient prediction scores. After two and three follow-up scans, there was a significant difference in overall survival ($P = 0.023$, log-rank test). Estimated forecasts and hazard ratios produced identical results: overall survival, distant metastasis-free, progression-free, and no loco-regional recurrence improved significantly [42].

10.4.2 Pathological outcome prediction

Pictures of the trimodality which was before treatment as well as post-radiation medication before the procedure are included in the neural network model founded on datasets as supplemental confirmation and also to research the affiliation among carrier visualizing assessment as well as pathophysiologic responding. The model's capacity to anticipate preservation was tested using set of data B. A 1-year survival model with pre-treatment and 1-month follow-up was employed to match the amount of input timepoints. It was able to predict distant metastases, progression, and recurrence in the immediate region with high accuracy. Although there were only 30 out of 89 events, Dataset B's model was leaning toward providing a survival of 3-year overall estimate in the event of complete success.

The pathological response was classified using the network's predictions, with an AUC that was found to significantly differentiate between responding and grossly regressed patients. Studies have used a composite framework of network likelihoods as well as volume change to evaluate multiplicative effectiveness, which performed somewhat better. Despite Spearman's correlation of 0.39, changes in primary tumor volume were connected with CNN probabilities. Figure 10.3 represents the identification of tumor cells with the stage of malignant cell development by a medical framework that showed the phase, sexual identity, maturity level, tumor stage, effectiveness, smoking habits, as well as diagnostic tumor stage into account were unable to predict pathologic response.

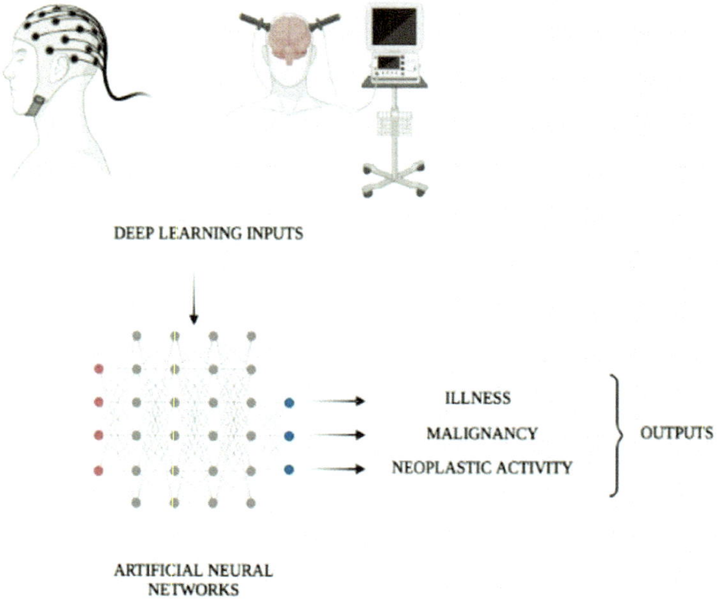

Figure 10.3 Identification of tumor cells by the advanced diagnosis method.

10.5 Methodologies/Network Structures

10.5.1 Convolutional neural networks (CNNs)

CNN's layers both undertake a different purpose, including complexity, accumulating, failure computation, etc. It obtains gradient production before everything. The very first step of the algorithm would be connected back toward an illustration as well as consist of nerve cells that correlate to adjacent pixels. The convolutional layers in the following set of layers show the outcomes of converging a series of filters with the input data, which is used to extract features. Designers can select from a variety of kernel sizes for their filters, which are also referred to as kernels. Each neuron is only responsive to one piece of the preceding layer. It is called an activation map because it emphasizes the influence of a particular filter on the input. Following activation, the convolutional layers are activated. The first photograph shows that a CNN [43] layer structure is used to apply nonlinearity to activation maps. Depending on the design, convolution output is decreased in dimensionality by employing pooling layers. There are several pooling techniques available, including maximum and average. Finally, high-level abstractions may be derived from layers that are entirely coupled.

The weighting of neural connections and kernels is continually improved during training neural connections and kernels. The architecture provided above serves as the foundation for a normal CNN. Following that, we will look at how these structures are used in medical picture segmentation.

10.5.1.1 CNN in 2D

Because of its promising skills in image classification and pattern detection, several academics are interested in using a CNN for medical image segmentation.

The core strategy for constructing segmentation is to utilize a 2D input picture and apply 2D filters to it. According to Zhang et al. [44], a CNN input layer with several sources of information (T1, T2, and FA) is presented to determine if utilizing multi-modal illustrations even though instruction enhances segmentation accuracy. Individuals who used more than one input method outperformed those who used only one, according to their results. This should not be included in another experiment. In another experiment, Bar et al. [45] employ transfer learning to derive low-level attributes from a model trained on ImageNet. The high-level qualities are integrated to generate a single product using PiCoDes [46].

10.5.1.2 CNN in 2.5D

The 2.5D methods are more widely used than 3D methods as they provide more spatial knowledge about the surrounding pixels, they are more commonly utilized [47, 48, 49]. The extraction of three orthogonal 2D patches, with kernels remaining two-dimensional in each of the three orthogonal planes.

This approach was used to segment knee cartilage. A set of patches was retrieved for each orthogonal plane and fed into the three CNNs that were created. The relatively modest number of training voxels (120,000) and the high Dice coefficient of 0.8249 suggest that a triplane CNN can achieve a decent balance of performance and cost. A triplaner CNN with just 120,000 training voxels and a Dice value of 0.8249 may be able to achieve a decent balance of processing costs and performance. They utilized this data to design what they thought were the three separate visual channels that would be used in a camera.

Moeskops et al. [47] employed a 2.5D architecture to see if a single network design could accomplish multi-organ segmentation. The researchers tackled each segmentation problem differently (e.g., brain MRI, breast MRI, and cardiac CTA). Because they employed a modest kernel size of 33 voxels, scientists were able to go deeper into the structure by using a 25-layer depth network [50]. This described a very complicated structure in this article. Previous research has demonstrated that a single CNN can be taught to visualize a wide range of anatomical features utilizing many modalities.

Because 2D labeled data is more accessible and compatible with current technology, it is easier to get than 3D labeled data for 2.5D approaches. To address the dimensionality issue, volumetric pictures can be split down into a sequence of random 2D snapshots [51]. Despite the fact that the methodology appears to be a good idea and performs somewhat better than 2D techniques, some people argue that using only three orthogonal views of a 3D image from a large number of accessible views is not the most effective use of volumetric medical data [52]. If the depth (Z-axis) resolution is inadequate, it is similarly difficult to perform 2D convolution on anisotropic 3D pictures with an isotropic kernel [53].

10.5.1.3 CNN in 3D

Using a 2.5D framework, an attempt was made to integrate more complete spatial data. If you want a technique that works with 3D filters, you'll need to use a 2.5D approach. To offer a stronger bulk density recognition in all three dimensions, a 3D convolutional neural network (CNN) is deployed (X, Y, and Z). Based on the content of surrounding 3D patches, a 3D connectivity is employed to determine the designation of a given object core voxel. Each required component of the network's structure, which is identical to that of a 2D CNN, employs 3D modules such as 3D convolution layers and 3D subsampling layer upon layer.

The availability of 3D medical imaging, as well as significant advancements in computer hardware, have fueled segmentation using 3D medical imaging. Volumetric images, as opposed to simply one view in 2D and three orthogonal views in 2.5D approaches, may convey information in all directions. When segmenting an organ, we frequently require a deep model to extract relevant information from hard volumetric images. Training a deep network for 3D objects, on the other hand, is seen as a huge challenge. In "Challenges and Cutting-Edge Answers," we'll go through the problem in depth and highlight some of the greatest solutions.

To stabilize the learned features from 3D translation, this layer uses 3D max-pooling to filter the maximum response in a limited cubic area.

Table 10.1 holds the datasets of various diagnosis patterns on various organs based on the different approaches.

Table 10.1 Datasets of different diagnosis patterns.

Organ	Dataset name	Dataset size	Dimension	Modality
Abdominal	NIH-CT-82	82 samples	3D	CT
	Brain MRI C34			MRI
	UFL-MRI-79	79 samples		
Brain	Locate Zhang's dataset.			MRI
	ADNI	339 samples	3D	PET
	MR Brains			MRI
Breast	DDSM-BCRP	158 samples		
	Breast MRI-34			T1-MRI
	INbreast	116 samples	2D	Mammography
Heart	ACDC	150 patients	2D	MRI
Cardiac	Cardiac CTA			CT
Liver	3DIRCADb	20 samples	3D	CT
	SLiver07	30 samples	3D	CT
Left ventricular	PRETERM dataset	234 cases	2D	MRI
Lung	Japanese Society of Radiological Technology (JSRT)	247 images	2D	CT
	Lung Nodule Analysis 2016 (LUNA16)	880 patients	2D	CT
	Kaggles Data Science Bowl (DSB)	1397 patients	2D	CT
	Lung Image Database Consortium (LIDC)	1024 patients	2D	CT
Skin	ISBI 2016	1250 image	2D	
Multiple organ	Computational anatomy	640 samples	3D	CT

10.5.2 Convolutional network in its complete form (FCN)

When Long et al. [54] replaced the last fully connected layer by a complete convolution operation, they built a completely convolutional network (FCN). This significant advance has allowed the network to provide dense pixel-wise predictions. High-resolution activation maps are fed into the convolution layers together with up-sampled outputs to increase localization performance. A recent update to FCN allows it to make pixel-level predictions from a whole image, rather than patch-level ones, and to do so in a single forward pass.

10.5.2.1 Multiorgan segmentation using FCN

As a result of this procedure, abdominal organs may be segmented simultaneously utilizing multiorgan segmentation [55]. Zhou et al. [56] employed FCN in a 2.5D technique to segment 19 organs in 3D CT impressions. 2D slices of a 3D area were employed to train neural networks as part of this study [57]. Each 2D slice view was given a distinct FCN number. The outcome of each impression were merged with those of other FCNs to create the overall session output. Larger organs, such as the liver, were more accurate than smaller organs, while the approach was less precise for smaller organs.

10.5.2.2 FCN in a cascade (CFCN)

Christ and colleagues [58] advocate cascading the FCNs to improve the precision with which liver histopathologic fragmentation is performed. Cascade FCN tries to create a chain of FCN in which every framework leverages the contextual elements from the preceding model's prediction map as the foundation for its own predictions. A second parallel FCN [52, 59] may enhance the model's complexity and processing costs. The first FCN in the proposed approach is utilized to segment the picture into ROIs for the second FCN to segment the lesion. The quality of segmentation may be significantly increased since each step can have its own set of filters.

10.5.2.3 FCN focal

Zhou et al. [60] proposed employing FCN concentrate failure to reduce the error positive aspects caused by an irregular fraction based on image pixel resolution in medical data. The FCN was included in this framework to provide intermediate step segmentation results, as well as the centered FCN was being used to minimize false-positive results.

10.5.2.4 FCN with several streams

Typically, incoming pictures vary in resolution and modality (multi-modal methods). In a multi-stream architecture, there might be advantages in employing many copies of the same organ. To maximize the usage of contextual information from different picture resolutions, a multi-stream technique to 3D FCN was utilized, as well as a multimodality strategy to increase the system's resistance against a broad diversity of organ shape and structure. Rather than permitting many sources and mixing each modality's output at the encoder end, Wang et al. [61] added two down-sampled classifiers into the network to utilize contextual information to distinguish different output layers. Because the receptive size is fixed, it is difficult for FCN to recognize all of them. Multi-scale networks utilize two methods: resizing and feeding input pictures to the network [52, 62, 63]. Multi-scale techniques can be used to address the FCN's fixed receptive size.

10.5.3 Residual convolutional networks (CRNs)

Although deep networks have been shown in principle to have a higher learning capacity, they suffer from a more substantial degradation problem

[64]. It indicates that as the depth grows, so does the accuracy. Wang and his colleagues [64] utilized residual systems, which were originally designed for spontaneous 2D picture classification but are now being used for 3D image classification, to take advantage of the deeper network structure. An alternate method uses residual maps at lower levels rather than sequentially transmitting the feature map through the layers. Residual maps, often known as "skip connections," are maps that enable derivatives to avoid some layers of the network. Because of this architecture, the network might benefit from increased accuracy. Although residue training on vector data has only been employed in a few research, 2D shallow residual networks have been found to be successful in a variety of medical image object segmentation [59] and basic imaging analysis subjects [65, 66]. VoxResNet has suggested a 3D deep residual network based on the assumption of the 2D version, according to Chen et al. [67]. The model has 25 layers that may be applied to 3D MRI data, fully using the major benefit of residual networks. The framework is made up of VoxRes modules, and a skip link gives input capabilities to updated features. Short multilayer kernels are utilized because of their computational complexity or expressive capability. As a result, they used three convolutional layers, each consisting of two layers, for a total of six convolutional strides. As a result, the input resolution was reduced by eightfold. They also created an auto-contextual VoxResNet capable of analyzing multi-modal pictures

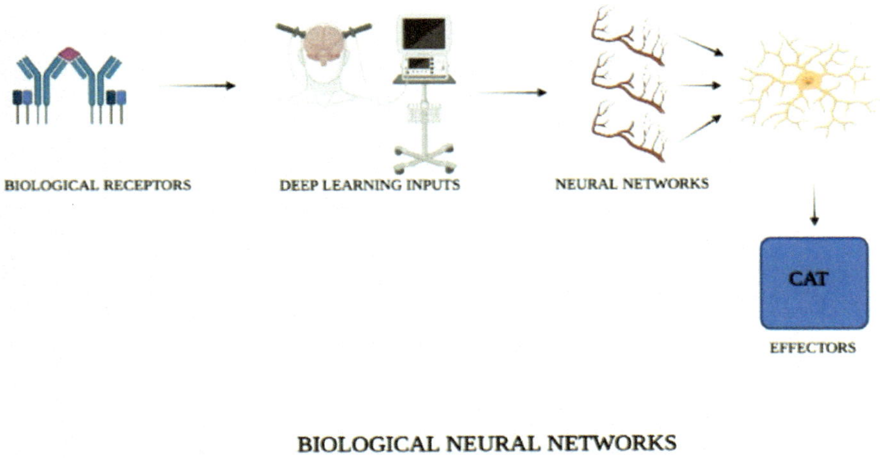

Figure 10.4 A screening method for the diagnosis.

and providing more precise segmentation. According to the study, increasing layer depth appears to boost performance while resisting degradability. Figure 10.4 represents the diagnosis of malignant cells by the basic working of advanced techniques where the input by biological receptors was examined by the various neural networks.

10.6 Training Deep Models: Challenges

10.6.1 Overfitting

This occurs once a system can accurately describe all possible sequences in a modifying or learning dataset and is more accurate than raw data [68]. Overfitting: the most prevalent cause of overfitting is a limited training dataset. As a result, any strategy for decreasing the quantity of data ("Minimum Structured Dataset") can help to avoid clustering [69].

Experiments have demonstrated that having many perspectives on a patch, as opposed to just one, reduces overfitting [70]. To minimize overfitting, "drop-outs" can be used to discard the end output of each iteration, which can be either a loose collection of neurons or a completely linked stage. The dropping link can assist to mitigate the overfitting problem [49].

10.6.2 Time to train

Many efforts have been made to shorten training time and achieve quicker convergence. Pooling layers were utilized in the early days of this topic to reduce the size of the parameters [71]. Convolution with stride [50] is a pooling-based approach that may be used to lighten the network. Batch normalization provides for faster convergence [72–74] by removing neighboring pixels from an average image [75] or an appropriate key. When compared to pooling and down sampling, batch normalization is a preferable strategy for fostering network convergence because it has not been shown to have any negative performance repercussions.

10.6.3 Gradient disappearance

Deeper networks have been shown to perform better, but they are plagued by the issue of propagated signal (gradient) inflating or entirely disappearing [52]. To put it another way, this eventual impact can't be appropriately transmitted down to boundary depths. In 3D models, the problem is further aggravated. The practical alternative regarding the potential to eliminate involves deep monitored perspectives, whose result of successive hidden units is deconvolved and delivered to something like a softmax to produce a forecast. The supplementary damages are combined with the initial failure of the buried layer to strengthen the gradient [71, 61, 76].

As proven in [52], when kernels' weights were initialized by taking a random sample first from the normal distribution, careful weight initialization improves gradient vanishing in techniques with from-scratch-training.

10.6.4 Challenges in 3D

All of the aforementioned challenges in training may be significantly extra acute while working with vector data due to the lower pitch variation between both the final focused and neighboring voxels, the increased number of factors, as well as the scarcity of bulk density learning algorithms. The fact that inference is computationally expensive is a known issue that discourages the use of 3D techniques. Dense inference reduces the inference time for a single brain scan to less than a minute [77]. Using a rule-out method to identify locations that are unlikely to contain the main organ can narrow that subspace and also quicken interpretation greatly [78].

10.7 Discussion

Monitoring a tumor's development to forecast lifespan and responsiveness to chemotherapy and radiotherapy could be critical for treatment evaluation and reactive care plans to enhance the treatment experience. Clinical parameters have long been used to determine therapy form and full accordance [78], but this method ignores phenotypic changes in the tumor. Radiology allows noninvasively monitoring of the very same place throughout time, showing additional tumor features not seen on static images at a single timepoint [79].

Follow-up: In the healthcare setting, CT scans are already utilized to provide additional information about a patient. Deep learning algorithms for malignancy evaluation allow phenotypic alterations to be extracted without using manually and/or semi-automated boundaries or qualitatively visual evaluations, although both are subjected to inter-observer variation. Furthermore, prognostic predictions may assist with the evaluation of clinical outcomes in medical studies, allowing for reply or reaction evaluation and then ultimately, actively altering medication.

The neural network has been capable of generating endure and prognosis estimations for whole endure at 1 and 2 years by a merged CNN information from images and a time-spanning RNN. Even as a quantity of timepoints, as well as quantity of visualizing relevant data to it, increased, the network's performance has improved as predicted. Because of the development in signal from each successive scanning of the malignant tumor and the variances between scanning throughout the duration, there was a continual increase in AUC between the estimates. In this population, using a single pre-treatment scan to predict survival proved ineffective. Just using baseline treatment imaging data, earlier radiomics investigations utilizing engineering [80–83] and deep learning [84] algorithms were possible to forecast the outcome of relevance with anatomical CT or functional PET data. With the baseline endpoint separately, there is a trend toward the relevance of the deep learning model for the groups in this investigation. Using larger cohorts could increase the imaging markers' prediction efficacy. To forecast mortality and other predictive factors, the studies point, which incorporated the medical tumor volume (longest axial diameter), was likewise inaccurate.

Patients were classified into two categories based on individual mortality risk: higher and lower, despite significant disparities in survival rates. This was also discovered again for the likelihood of loco-regional recurrence only with the addition of 2 obey set points at around 2 and 3 months after the end of final radiotherapy. Some other results, and advancements, including distant metastasis, needed the further take at about 180 days for a substantial amount of differentiation of the overall life-threatening majority. It could be because of raise in a well-defined group of initial neuroimaging phenotypes linked to mortality as well as loco-regional recurrence than another prognostic indicator, or it might be due to confounding phenotypes connected to metastatic disease or advancement, which is something the system will not be capable of overcoming until the third review has been added.

Because the cohorts are made up of patients with varying disease loads and treatment options, the two datasets in our analysis are intrinsically diverse. Generally, people with chronic diseases are younger and healthier, with a much more established phase of illness as well as the ability to withstand the operation. The efficacy of the surgical treatment and distant disease has been demonstrated to affect surgical patients' survival [85], whereas local control determines whether or not a patient survives conclusive radiation treatment [86]. Individuals who underwent surgical resection (Dataset B) had a more ratio of stage IIIA than patients who received final radio waves treatments (Dataset A).

Regardless of such distinctions, mortality CNN designs are expertise on sample A identified surrogates of mortality including such metastatic disease, progression, and loco-regional relapse in sample B. Because of the inherent differences across the contemporaries, in addition to such cohort's small sample size and the limited number of occurrences, it was trending toward predicting survival. For Dataset B, there has only been one obey examination provided; hence, the mortality design obtained less information. Even if the model was designed to counteract the everlasting time bias, it is possible that it still has an impact. Higher timepoints indicate that hundreds of patients were surviving when the examination is performed, reducing its capacity to predict outcomes.

The pathologic response of the tumor is linked to survival [87]. As a result, we investigated the association between the survival network model's probability and similar individuals with stage III NSCLC in distinct treatment cohorts (definite radiation therapy and trimodality). With the addition of Dataset B, we can now predict reaction and further verify our system because it contains an perform after radiotherapy and then before surgeries. That can also be used as a representativeness test in people who've had advanced disease NSCLC and have also been allowed to treat with a range of different therapies. To match the amount of dataset points, a 1-year survival rates scenario including pre-treated and the first obey at 30 days were utilized. The system was able to identify diagnostic responses from someone with severe tumor recurrence in the trimodality group. This was the case, despite the fact that the design model was completely blind toward this class.

This prediction was compared to the well predictor of response, the size of the initial tumor. In this sample, tumor was according to the predicted outcome with such a high degree of accuracy. When compared to the training set, modeling likelihood and delta volume showed relatively minor correlations. In a second cohort, the expected framework or design was created to forecast pathological reply using just the illustration as well as a primary source as providing data. Images-based neural network models can identify radiographic aspects separate from tumor volume. A CNN-based network captures the tumor's location and the surrounding area. Previous methods relied on accurate manual delineations or semi-automated ways to feed the machine learning algorithm, which may or may not take into account surrounding tissue [88]. The boundary between the tumor and the normal tissue surroundings is included in the CNN image input. This may reveal more about the tumor's reaction as well as invasion of the surrounding skin. Object enhancement was utilized just on mentoring malignant tissue to improve performance, such as usual practice inside the areas of deep learning as well as healthcare computer vision [89], whereas comparatively tiny imperfections have been used to reduce the error [90] upon the small training sample. Pre-treatment values can be introduced to image features using a standard ResNet CNN for image characterization. This allowed deep neural networks to be utilized on medical photos with significantly smaller cohorts than earlier AI systems, which used millions of samples.

Most radiology research relies on a small number of samples compared to deep learning applications. It took 87,000 photos to train and 5,000 images to test a face recognition deep learning application, for example [91]. Either transfer learning or datasets like Image Net, which include over 14 million image characteristics, may be utilized to recover typical low-level CNN features. It would also be ideal to use a network specifically trained on 3D radiographic pictures or 3D photographs to cover the whole tumor load, although the number of images available is still nowhere close to that of digital photos. A model developed based on 1000s of 3D CT images will very likely be extended toward the patient population, that organization, and the outcome the system was generated to forecast when one is offered. The efficiency of lung nodule detection in CT images has been found to improve with transfer learning [92]. This study had a lesser sample group than studies using digital photos, though ImageNet's retrained networks enabled us to get the results we did. Before collecting a full cohort for analysis, transfer learning can be used to test the viability of therapeutically useful utilities.

Obey timepoints were critical in directly ensuring prognosis because they recorded dynamical malignant alterations. This has been facilitated through the use of RNNs, which enabled again integration of multiple set points as well as the opportunity to understand using collections that lacked individual scans at a specific time, which itself is necessary for retrospective studies like this one. Despite the popularity of similar communication networks in imagery and time-dependent investigations, including such video categorization and characterization purposes, medical photos have not before been subjected to this sort of network [93]. The model was created to combat the ever-present time bias. While CNN pooling even without RNN was already employed before, in our circumstance, it might result in biased groupings because the last individual scans are lost. The RNN was not trained to learn from data that were lacking [94]. Because GRU RNNs feature an updating gate and have a acceptable affect that influence the proportion of data supplied to the network output, they were chosen [95]. To construct mortality as well as prediction predictions, this collected computed tomographic scanning essential data out of each endpoint.

Previous research has shown that CT imaging features can be used to make lung cancer connections and predictions to predict survival and pathologic response, in some research. Radiomics techniques including physical malignant bulk estimation and user-defined parameters were used in computed characteristics [96]. Recent deep learning applications in research are using a particular scan as the model input and have concentrated on categorizing lung nodules as benign or metastatic. Kumar and colleagues used decision trees to classify lung nodules after manually identifying them. They used an autoencoder to extract features. For their research. Hua and colleagues classified the tumor lesion in a 2D region on the axial slice, which they did at one timepoint [97]. Our research differs from others in that it uses numerous timepoints to forecast resilience and prognosis variables. For additional validation, we used our built model to predict pathologic response, an important clinical feature, in a separate cohort. In contrast to prior studies, our model merely uses a seed point as input and constructed computed tomographic scanning of a 50×50 mm^2 zone around the seed point. To compute handmade radiomic characteristics, precise tumor delineation is required [80], which is time-consuming and subject to inter-reader segmentation variability. Deep learning has recently been proved to perform better than traditional radiomics [92]. Our method requires only a single seed point within a tumor, making it more efficient and resistant to manual inference. It is not always possible to obtain additional clinical and pathologic evaluations. RECIST [79] measurements, which are based on semi-automatic as well as for instructions curves of the total tumor volume, are sensitive to inter-operator variability and can be costly to produce.

Statistical predictive estimation techniques could be used in the clinic after rigorous social approval including benchmarking against existing medical guidelines, as well as learning about such a broader, extra diverse community. There are various lung nodule recognition techniques present in the reviews and data, and the position of the tumor on follow-up imaging can be recognized automatically using the pre-treatment tumor contours typically outlined by the radiation oncologist. Our model's input clearly could be encircling the box vicinity of the discovered tumor, which could also be resurfacing spontaneously. Due to neural networks' propensity for overfitting, the images would have to be downscaled to a regular panel spacing. Under the existing elements required for data enrichment, our model uses three 2D slices. However, a 3D image volume may better describe cancer biology and so enhance performance. If a child's age, gender, and histological, as well as their, quitting smoking or radiation treatment parameters are integrated into the CT imaging-based survival prediction, they might benefit from it. To boost prediction power, a pretrained CNN was applied. The use of a deep learning technique has its drawbacks. Machine learning algorithms were used to find previous relationships for the likelihood of distant metastases using only the pre-treatment scan [98]. With limited sample sizes, this one has demonstrated that deep learning surpasses machine learning depending on produced characteristics. We might be able to attain higher deep learning performance with a larger cohort. Probabilities are estimated with a black box for a given task, making them less useful than based features that can be repurposed for different executions. Even with the strategies, we used to reduce overfitting [99]. Due to neural networks' tendency for classifiers, the images would have to be downscaled to a standard panel spacing. Under the current elements required for data augmentation, our model uses three 2D slices. However, a 3D image volume may better describe tumor biology and so enhance performance. If a patient's gender and histological, as well as their quitting smoking and radiation treatment characteristics are integrated into the CT imaging-based survival prediction, they might possibly benefit from it. Despite these constraints, our deep learning algorithm proved possible to forecast survivability, also with a larger dataset as well as narrower, greater uniform axial positioning; we may also be capable to get even better and much more clinically meaningful results.

Deep learning is a versatile technology that has been used strongly in a variety of fields. The idea underlying the program's operation, on either side, still has to be developed. Although the model's source and destination are generally intuitive, the buried intermediary stages, as the phrase implies, are not [100]. A network's effectiveness or whether various parameters have a positive or negative influence is incredibly difficult to determine because of the complexity of the system. Deep learning features may be more difficult to decipher than features meant to capture certain visual traits. Within the line of work of graphical technologies, authentication layouts have already been produced to acquire parts of the picture that are significantly weighted depending on projections from the platform. How to get around this? This may be shown in the form of a heat map of the final convolution layers. A major question is how to integrate knowledge and experience into such conceptual characteristics. Autonomously learned feature representation might be made better understandable with more study in this area [101].

10.8 Conclusions

In this study, researchers examined the impact of deep learning on phenotype surveillance during final radiation therapy utilizing baseline treatment and additional CT scans. Mortality behavior and prognosis estimate using CNN and RNN networks improved with the addition of additional timepoints. According to clinical considerations, there was no difference. Another group of patients underwent trimodality treatments after radiation, and the surviving deep neural network may predict pathological response. Remarkably, a single seed point in the lesion's center was all that was required for this model to accurately estimate the tumor volume, even though hand contouring would have required a significant amount of time and effort. Non-invasive monitoring of the tumor phenotype might be used to make predictions about responsive and personalized therapy may be harmed by factors such as viability, expectation, and pathologic response.

For medical image analysis, we reviewed the most widely used network topologies and analyzed the advantages of this topology over their predecessors in this study. Before moving on to medical image segmentation training methods, we discussed their pros and downsides as well; eventually, researchers concentrated on the most important difficulties regarded to medical segmentation solutions related to deep learning. In the past, we've discussed the best approaches to cope with a wide range of issues. We hope that the content of this article would aid researchers in making informed decisions on which network topology is most suited to solve their particular challenge, as well as in avoiding common pitfalls. Medical picture segmentation seems to be increasingly reliant on deep learning methods.

Acknowledgment

Authors are thankful to all co-authors to make their contributions in completing this chapter.

Conflict of Interest

There is no conflict of interest.

Funding

No funding is required.

References

[1] Galon, J., et al. (2006). Type, density, and location of immune cells within human colorectal tumors predict clinical outcome. *Science, 313*(5795), 1960-1964.

[2] Torre, L. A. et al. (2015). Global cancer statistics, 2012. *CA: a cancer journal for clinicians, 65*(2), 87-108.

[3] Ettinger, D. S. et al. (2012). Non–Small Cell Lung Cancer. Journal of the National Comprehensive Cancer Network, 10(10), 1236–1271.

[4] Goldstraw, P et al. (2016). *The IASLC Lung Cancer Staging Project: Proposals for Revision of the TNM Stage Groupings in the Forthcoming (Eighth) Edition of the TNM Classification for Lung Cancer. Journal of Thoracic Oncology, 11(1), 39–51.*

[5] Eisenhauer E. A. et al. (2009). New response evaluation criteria in solid tumours: Revised RECIST guideline (version 1.1)., 45(2), 0–247.

[6] Hosny, A. et al. (2018). Artificial intelligence in radiology. *Nature Reviews Cancer, 18*(8), 500-510.

[7] Parmar C. et al. (2015). Machine learning methods for quantitative radiomic biomarkers. *Scientific reports, 5*(1), 1-11.

[8] Hosny, A. et al. (2018). Artificial intelligence in radiology. *Nature Reviews Cancer, 18*(8), 500-510.

[9] Parmar, C. et al. (2015). Machine learning methods for quantitative radiomic biomarkers. *Scientific reports, 5*(1), 1-11.

[10] Aerts, H. J. (2018). Data science in radiology: a path forward. *Clinical Cancer Research, 24*(3), 532-534.

[11] Aerts, H. J.et al. (2014). Decoding tumour phenotype by noninvasive imaging using a quantitative radiomics approach. *Nature communications, 5*(1), 1-9.

[12] Hosny, A. et al. (2018). Deep learning for lung cancer prognostication: a retrospective multi-cohort radiomics study. *PLoS medicine, 15*(11), e1002711.

[13] Parmar, C. et al. (2018). Data analysis strategies in medical imaging. *Clinical cancer research, 24*(15), 3492-3499.

[14] Coroller, T. P. et al. (2017). Radiomic-based pathological response prediction from primary tumors and lymph nodes in NSCLC. *Journal of Thoracic Oncology, 12*(3), 467-476.

[15] Huynh, E. et al. (2016). CT-based radiomic analysis of stereotactic body radiation therapy patients with lung cancer. *Radiotherapy and Oncology, 120*(2), 258-266.

[16] Coroller, T. P. et al. (2016). Radiomic phenotype features predict pathological response in non-small cell lung cancer. *Radiotherapy and oncology*, *119*(3), 480-486.

[17] Coroller, T. P. et al. (2015). CT-based radiomic signature predicts distant metastasis in lung adenocarcinoma. *Radiotherapy and Oncology*, *114*(3), 345-350.

[18] LeCun, Y. et al. (2015). Deep learning. *nature*, *521*(7553), 436-444.

[19] Dandıl, E. et al. (2014, August). Artificial neural network-based classification system for lung nodules on computed tomography scans. In *2014 6th International conference of soft computing and pattern recognition (SoCPaR)* (pp. 382-386). Ieee.

[20] Shin, H. C. et al. (2016). Deep convolutional neural networks for computer-aided detection: CNN architectures, dataset characteristics and transfer learning. *IEEE transactions on medical imaging*, *35*(5), 1285-1298.

[21] Jamal-Hanjani, M. et al. (2017). Tracking the evolution of non–small-cell lung cancer. *New England Journal of Medicine*, *376*(22), 2109-2121.

[22] Hermann, P. C. et al. (2007). Distinct populations of cancer stem cells determine tumor growth and metastatic activity in human pancreatic cancer. *Cell stem cell*, *1*(3), 313-323.

[23] Donahue, J. et al. (2015). Long-term recurrent convolutional networks for visual recognition and description. In *Proceedings of the IEEE conference on computer vision and pattern recognition* (pp. 2625-2634).

[24] Smith, S. M., et al. (2004). Advances in functional and structural MR image analysis and implementation as FSL. *Neuroimage*, *23*, S208-S219.

[25] Litjens, G. et al. (2017). A survey on deep learning in medical image analysis. *Medical image analysis*, *42*, 60-88.

[26] Shen, D. et al. (2017). Deep learning in medical image analysis. *Annual review of biomedical engineering*, *19*, 221-248.

[27] Parvin, B. et al. (2007). Iterative voting for inference of structural saliency and characterization of subcellular events. *IEEE Transactions on Image Processing*, *16*(3), 615-623.

[28] Parvin, B. et al. (2007). Iterative voting for inference of structural saliency and characterization of subcellular events. *IEEE Transactions on Image Processing*, *16*(3), 615-623.

[29] Arteta, C. et al. (2012, October). Learning to detect cells using non-overlapping extremal regions. In *International conference on medical*

image computing and computer-assisted intervention (pp. 348-356). Springer, Berlin, Heidelberg.

[30] Mualla, F. et al. (2013). Automatic cell detection in bright-field microscope images using SIFT, random forests, and hierarchical clustering. *IEEE transactions on medical imaging*, *32*(12), 2274-2286.

[31] Niazi, M. K. K., et al. (2013, March). An automated method for counting cytotoxic T-cells from CD8 stained images of renal biopsies. In *Medical Imaging 2013: Digital Pathology* (Vol. 8676, pp. 60-69). SPIE.

[32] LeCun, Y., et al. (1998). Gradient-based learning applied to document recognition. *Proceedings of the IEEE*, *86*(11), 2278-2324.

[33] Cireşan, D. C., et al. (2013). Mitosis detection in breast cancer histology images with deep neural networks. In *International conference on medical image computing and computer-assisted intervention* (pp. 411-418). Springer, Berlin, Heidelberg.

[34] Ruifrok, A. C., & Johnston, D. A. (2001). Quantification of histochemical staining by colour deconvolution. *Analytical and quantitative cytology and histology*, *23*(4), 291-299.

[35] Keshava, N. (2003). A survey of spectral unmixing algorithms. *Lincoln laboratory journal*, *14*(1), 55-78.

[36] Fedorov, A., et al. (2012). 3D Slicer as an image computing platform for the Quantitative Imaging Network. *Magnetic resonance imaging*, *30*(9), 1323-1341.

[37] Krizhevsky, A., et al. (2012). Imagenet classification with deep convolutional neural networks. *Advances in neural information processing systems*, *25*.

[38] Rubins, J., et al. (2007). Follow-up and surveillance of the lung cancer patient following curative intent therapy: ACCP evidence-based clinical practice guideline. *Chest*, *132*(3), 355S-367S.

[39] Calman, L., et al. (2011). Survival benefits from follow-up of patients with lung cancer: a systematic review and meta-analysis. *Journal of Thoracic Oncology*, *6*(12), 1993-2004.

[40] Ioffe, S., & Szegedy, C. (2015, June). Batch normalization: Accelerating deep network training by reducing internal covariate shift. In *International conference on machine learning* (pp. 448-456). PMLR.

[41] Srivastava, N., et al. (2014). Dropout: a simple way to prevent neural networks from overfitting. *The journal of machine learning research*, *15*(1), 1929-1958.

[42] Commandeur, F., et al. (2018). Deep learning for quantification of epicardial and thoracic adipose tissue from non-contrast CT. *IEEE transactions on medical imaging*, *37*(8), 1835-1846.

[43] Zhang, W., et al. (2015). Deep convolutional neural networks for multi-modality isointense infant brain image segmentation. *NeuroImage*, *108*, 214-224.

[44] Bar, Y. et al. (2015, March). Deep learning with non-medical training used for chest pathology identification. In *Medical Imaging 2015: Computer-Aided Diagnosis* (Vol. 9414, p. 94140V). International Society for Optics and Photonics.

[45] Bergamo, A. et al. (2011). Picodes: Learning a compact code for novel-category recognition. *Advances in neural information processing systems*, *24*.

[46] Moeskops, P. et al (2016). Deep learning for multi-task medical image segmentation in multiple modalities. In *International Conference on Medical Image Computing and Computer-Assisted Intervention* (pp. 478-486). Springer, Cham.

[47] Prasoon, A.et al. (2013). Deep feature learning for knee cartilage segmentation using a triplanar convolutional neural network. In *International conference on medical image computing and computer-assisted intervention* (pp. 246-253). Springer, Berlin, Heidelberg.

[48] Roth, H. R. et al. (2014, September). A new 2.5 D representation for lymph node detection using random sets of deep convolutional neural network observations. In *International conference on medical image computing and computer-assisted intervention* (pp. 520-527). Springer, Cham.

[49] Simonyan, & Zisserman. (2014). Very deep convolutional networks for large-scale image recognition. *arXiv preprint arXiv:1409.1556*.

[50] Fakoor, R., et al. (2013, June). Using deep learning to enhance cancer diagnosis and classification. In *Proceedings of the international conference on machine learning* (Vol. 28, pp. 3937-3949). ACM, New York, USA.

[51] Kamnitsas, K., et al. (2017). Efficient multi-scale 3D CNN with fully connected CRF for accurate brain lesion segmentation. *Medical image analysis*, *36*, 61-78.

[52] Chen, J., et al. (2016). Combining fully convolutional and recurrent neural networks for 3d biomedical image segmentation. *Advances in neural information processing systems*, *29*.

[53] Long, J., et al. (2015). Fully convolutional networks for semantic segmentation. In *Proceedings of the IEEE conference on computer vision and pattern recognition* (pp. 3431-3440).

[54] Gibson, E., et al. (2017). Towards image-guided pancreas and biliary endoscopy: automatic multi-organ segmentation on abdominal CT with dense dilated networks. In *International Conference on Medical Image Computing and Computer-Assisted Intervention* (pp. 728-736). Springer, Cham.

[55] Zhou, X., et al. (2017). Deep learning of the sectional appearances of 3D CT images for anatomical structure segmentation based on an FCN voting method. *Medical physics*, *44*(10), 5221-5233.

[56] Zhou, X., et al. (2016). Three-dimensional CT image segmentation by combining 2D fully convolutional network with 3D majority voting. In *Deep Learning and Data Labeling for Medical Applications* (pp. 111-120). Springer, Cham.

[57] Christ, P. F., et al. (2016). Automatic liver and lesion segmentation in CT using cascaded fully convolutional neural networks and 3D conditional random fields. In *International conference on medical image computing and computer-assisted intervention* (pp. 415-423). Springer, Cham.

[58] Gibson, E., et al. (2017, March). Deep residual networks for automatic segmentation of laparoscopic videos of the liver. In *Medical Imaging 2017: Image-Guided Procedures, Robotic Interventions, and Modeling* (Vol. 10135, pp. 423-428). SPIE.

[59] Zhou, X. Y., et al. (2018, October). Towards automatic 3D shape instantiation for deployed stent grafts: 2D multiple-class and class-imbalance marker segmentation with equally-weighted focal U-Net. In *2018 IEEE/RSJ International Conference on Intelligent Robots and Systems (IROS)* (pp. 1261-1267). IEEE.

[60] Zeng, G., et al. (2018, April). Multi-stream 3D FCN with multi-scale deep supervision for multi-modality isointense infant brain MR image segmentation. In *2018 IEEE 15th International Symposium on Biomedical Imaging (ISBI 2018)* (pp. 136-140). IEEE.

[61] Wang, J., et al. (2016, October). A deep learning approach for semantic segmentation in histology tissue images. In *International Conference on Medical Image Computing and Computer-Assisted Intervention* (pp. 176-184). Springer, Cham.

[62] Yu, L., et al. (2016). Automated melanoma recognition in dermoscopy images via very deep residual networks. *IEEE transactions on medical imaging*, *36*(4), 994-1004.

[63] He, K., et al. (2016). Deep residual learning for image recognition. In *Proceedings of the IEEE conference on computer vision and pattern recognition* (pp. 770-778).
[64] He, K., et al. (2016, October). Identity mappings in deep residual networks. In *European conference on computer vision* (pp. 630-645). Springer, Cham.
[65] Zagoruyko and Komodakis. (2016). Wide residual networks. *arXiv preprint arXiv:1605.07146.*
[66] Chen, H., et al. (2018). VoxResNet: Deep voxelwise residual networks for brain segmentation from 3D MR images. *NeuroImage, 170*, 446-455.
[67] Golan, R., et al. (2016, July). Lung nodule detection in CT images using deep convolutional neural networks. In *2016 international joint conference on neural networks (IJCNN)* (pp. 243-250). IEEE.
[68] Shen, D. et al. (2017). Deep learning in medical image analysis. *Annual review of biomedical engineering, 19*, 221-248.
[69] Feng, X., et al. (2017). Discriminative localization in CNNs for weakly-supervised segmentation of pulmonary nodules. In *International conference on medical image computing and computer-assisted intervention* (pp. 568-576). Springer, Cham.
[70] Arimura, Hidetaka (2017). Image Computing and Computer-Assisted Intervention. Springer, 2017, pp 568–576
[71] Dou, Q., et al. (2017). 3D deeply supervised network for automated segmentation of volumetric medical images. *Medical image analysis, 41*, 40-54.
[72] Baumgartner, C. F., et al. (2017). An exploration of 2D and 3D deep learning techniques for cardiac MR image segmentation. In *International Workshop on Statistical Atlases and Computational Models of the Heart* (pp. 111-119). Springer, Cham.
[73] Cicek, O., et al. (2016). 3D U-Net: learning dense volumetric segmentation from sparse annotation. In *International conference on medical image computing and computer-assisted intervention* (pp. 424-432). Springer, Cham.
[74] Kawahara, J., et al. (2016). Deep features to classify skin lesions. In *2016 IEEE 13th international symposium on biomedical imaging (ISBI)* (pp. 1397-1400). IEEE.
[75] Ioffe. and Szegedy. (2015). Batch normalization: Accelerating deep network training by reducing internal covariate shift. In *International conference on machine learning* (pp. 448-456). PMLR.
[76] Zeng, G., et al. (2017). 3D U-net with multi-level deep supervision: fully automatic segmentation of proximal femur in 3D MR images.

In *International workshop on machine learning in medical imaging* (pp. 274-282). Springer, Cham.

[77] Urban, G., et al. (2014). Multi-modal brain tumor segmentation using deep convolutional neural networks. *MICCAI BraTS (brain tumor segmentation) challenge. Proceedings, winning contribution*, 31-35.

[78] Ettinger, D. S., et al. (2012). *Non–Small Cell Lung Cancer. Journal of the National Comprehensive Cancer Network, 10(10), 1236–1271.*

[79] Eisenhauer, E. A., et al. (2009). *New response evaluation criteria in solid tumours: Revised RECIST guideline (version 1.1). , 45(2), 0–247.*

[80] Aerts, H. J., et al. (2014). Decoding tumour phenotype by noninvasive imaging using a quantitative radiomics approach. *Nature communications*, *5*(1), 1-9.

[81] Coroller, T. P., et al. (2017). Radiomic-based pathological response prediction from primary tumors and lymph nodes in NSCLC. *Journal of Thoracic Oncology*, *12*(3), 467-476.

[82] Coroller, T. P., et al. (2016). Radiomic phenotype features predict pathological response in non-small cell lung cancer. *Radiotherapy and oncology*, *119*(3), 480-486.

[83] Coroller, T. P., et al. (2015). CT-based radiomic signature predicts distant metastasis in lung adenocarcinoma. *Radiotherapy and Oncology*, *114*(3), 345-350.

[84] Hosny, A., et al. (2018). Deep learning for lung cancer prognostication: a retrospective multi-cohort radiomics study. *PLoS medicine*, *15*(11), e1002711.

[85] Albain, K. S., et al. (2005). Phase III study of concurrent chemotherapy and radiotherapy (CT/RT) vs CT/RT followed by surgical resection for stage IIIA (pN2) non-small cell lung cancer (NSCLC): outcomes update of North American Intergroup 0139 (RTOG 9309). *Journal of Clinical Oncology*, *23*(16_suppl), 7014-7014.

[86] Tsujino, K., et al. (2003). Predictive value of dose-volume histogram parameters for predicting radiation pneumonitis after concurrent chemoradiation for lung cancer. *International Journal of Radiation Oncology* Biology* Physics*, *55*(1), 110-115.

[87] Hellmann, M. D., et al. (2014). Pathological response after neoadjuvant chemotherapy in resectable non-small-cell lung cancers: proposal for the use of major pathological response as a surrogate endpoint. *The lancet oncology*, *15*(1), e42-e50.

[88] Parmar, C., et al. (2014). Robust radiomics feature quantification using semiautomatic volumetric segmentation. *PloS one*, *9*(7), e102107.

[89] Ronneberger, O., et al. (2015). U-net: Convolutional networks for biomedical image segmentation. In *International Conference on Medical image computing and computer-assisted intervention* (pp. 234-241). Springer, Cham.
[90] Litjens, G., et al. (2017). A survey on deep learning in medical image analysis. *Medical image analysis*, *42*, 60-88.
[91] Sun, Y., et al. (2014). Deep learning face representation from predicting 10,000 classes. In *Proceedings of the IEEE conference on computer vision and pattern recognition* (pp. 1891-1898).
[92] Shin, H. C., et al. (2016). Deep convolutional neural networks for computer-aided detection: CNN architectures, dataset characteristics and transfer learning. *IEEE transactions on medical imaging*, *35*(5), 1285-1298.
[93] Yue-Hei Ng, J., et al. (2015). Beyond short snippets: Deep networks for video classification. In *Proceedings of the IEEE conference on computer vision and pattern recognition* (pp. 4694-4702).
[94] Che, Z., et al. (2018). Recurrent neural networks for multivariate time series with missing values. *Scientific reports*, *8*(1), 1-12.
[95] Kyunghyun C., et al. (2014) Learning phrase representations using RNN encoder–decoder for statistical machine translation. In: Proceedings of Conference on Empirical Methods in Natural Language Processing (EMNLP); Doha, Qatar. Stroudsburg (PA): Association for Computational Linguistics; 2014. p. 1724–34.
[96] Huynh, E., et al. (2016). CT-based radiomic analysis of stereotactic body radiation therapy patients with lung cancer. *Radiotherapy and Oncology*, *120*(2), 258-266.
[97] Hua, K. L., et al. (2015). Computer-aided classification of lung nodules on computed tomography images via deep learning technique. *OncoTargets and therapy*, *8*.
[98] Coroller, T. P., et al. (2015). CT-based radiomic signature predicts distant metastasis in lung adenocarcinoma. *Radiotherapy and Oncology*, *114*(3), 345-350.
[99] Ioffe and Szegedy, et al. (2015). Batch normalization: Accelerating deep network training by reducing internal covariate shift. In *International conference on machine learning* (pp. 448-456). PMLR.
[100] Wang, G. (2016). A perspective on deep imaging. *IEEE access*, *4*, 8914-8924.
[101] Xu, Y., et al. (2019). Deep learning predicts lung cancer treatment response from serial medical imaging. *Clinical Cancer Research*, *25*(11), 3266-3275.

11

Issues and Challenges in Bioinformatics Tools for Clinical Trials

Akanksha Pandey[1], Rishabha Malviya[1*], Sonali Sundram[1], and Vetriselvan Subramaniyan[2]

[1]Department of Pharmacy, School of Medical and Allied Science, Galgotias University, India
[2]Faculty of Medicine, Bioscience and Nursing, MAHSA University, Malaysia
*Corresponding Author: Department of Pharmacy, School of Medical and Allied Science, Galgotias University Greater Noida, Uttar Pradesh, India, Email ID: rishabhamalviya19@gmail.com, Mob. No.: +91 94503 52185.

Abstract

Clinical bioinformatics seeks to identify the most fundamental principles and potentially underutilized quality treatments for diseases. I2B2 is a biomedical computing national foundation funded by the National Institutes of Health that is a jumbled framework for putting clinical databases to use to make observations. CBI is indicated by the questioning of combining the smallest components or medical datasets to accelerate the transition of extracting knowledge toward excellence at creating a therapeutic impact and produced for a people's health composition. The term bioethics was coined to describe the application of right and wrong philosophy to medical issues. As biomedical operations such as observation and healthcare progress, there are a few major problems as well as opportunities in the broad field of biomedicine computing. Individuals interact with one another in a living process to generate higher-order structures such as the nervous system, which includes the brain and sense organs.

Keywords: Bioinformatics, genomic database, biomedical applications, I2B2 system.

11.1 Introduction

Throughout the historical past, human evolution has been linked to technological advancement. Today's technology has progressed beyond simple tools for making or putting the best goods that can be used to cutting-edge expertise. Bioinformatics and computational genetics were two of the most recent developments. As a result, bioinformatics combines physiological statistical data as well as heredity with conceptual frameworks shared by a cooperative trade group just on Internet technology. This has been described as the implementation of database systems to the smallest number of biology (via) the establishment and growth of datasets, algorithms, data processing, and quantitative specialist methods, as well as a hypothesis to find access to establish and beneficial concerns in dealing with business supervisors and biological market research [1]. Another definition of bioinformatics is a combination of computer science, biology, as well as for analytics. It is believed that the use of computer engineering in complex biological systems gives out again or has problems. It may give an expert opinion on a range of topics, adding epidemiology, the designing to be copied of unit driving power, to its now more current chief place, the analysis of order databases of several kinds [2]. Genomics is one example of the design of analysis of statistical orders, which is the method of training about the organization, composition, as well as development of underlying DNA [3]. The activity of observing both genes and proteins is added to the operations of measuring genomics. There are always fresh breakthroughs and advancements in the domains of unit research that rely largely on machines, analytical methods, as well as methodologies. It has motivated the rise of algorithmic genomics as well as biostatistics, which show evidence of influencing both the software engineering and fabrication sectors as well as the scientific community [4]. Bioinformatics is a division of an organization of informatics that has among its parts the observations, sending (power and so on), sharing, representation, amusement, rest, play, and pleasure of statistics on a computer. This makes it possible to and gives greater value to quality-based medical substances, which was made possible because of the open access to and use of genomic databases, as a result of DNA sequencing [5]. Algorithmic genomics makes use of electrical components, tools, and methods to generate, maintain, compose, evaluate, include, display, and redo data. Rather than a more conventional database, the datasets are exclusive to genetic information [4]. Computational genomics can help suddenly give way to titanic amounts of DNA-sequencers-fragmentary facts in support of fragmented or incomplete evidence. It can let us see biological data, let us make statements about the future, give us agreement to have more databases from uncommon, noted knowledge units, and authorities have given to us in writing to get new opinions by reasoning and store solid amounts of databases about money and safety. This can be done by using answers from mathematics, database structure, making coordinating in indexing pressure, database recovery, going away and parallel working out, making the distribution is being computed, as well as the system is obtaining Langmead. System biology has already been noticed and is based on the use of machines and algorithms, meticulously planned layouts, and techniques. In general, bioinformatics is a division of the organization of informatics, which gives property in line with the getting, storage, manipulation, analysis, sending (power and so on), sharing, and simulation of databases on a computer [6]. Biological systems and medical and health-related data are examples of biological news. Similarly, algorithmic genomics employs computerized expert methods; apparatus for creating or putting the right things; and perspectives to become the owner of, store, organize, get at the details of, synthesize, visualize in the mind, and simulate data. However, the statistics on how often they are broken up into simpler parts are limited to genetic or genomic databases [4]. The human genome map protested the role that computer technology and algorithmic apparatus for making or putting right things can play in the genetic operation of making observations and supplying databases gave an account of gene orders. The outburst of publicly accessible genomic databases coming out in the wake of the mapping of the genetic code has increased the demand for bioinformatics skills. The map's ultimate purpose was to figure out the order of everything related to the human DNA that would be discovered over 365 days in 2002. Bioinformatics is deep into the use of genomic databases in opinion to do with human diseases and in seeing who a person is of new smallest unit targets for substances affecting the senses getting lost back. [7]. In the middle of the 1990s, bioinformatics grew quickly and smoothly as a field because of its relation to genetic and biochemical statistics and the need for the power to put one's hands on the very great amounts of news given. Bioinformatics employs algorithmic power in the price list to capture links between database pieces from the operation of making observations in areas such as smallest units of biology, structure biochemistry, enzymology, unit biology, physiology, and pathology. Organize and structure these pieces into biologically purposeful things [8]. Things give a picture in words of how genetic and biomedical databases are put into order, which is said by their cellular qualities, which lead to deciding the ancestral form of life from which all living things become

[8]. DNA is a current topic of discussion in bioinformatics measurements and operations of making observations, which are used to work out and see gene codes. In addition, by comparison, genetic investigation relationships between bioinformatics are used to study comparable genomes and they are evolutionary throughout all creatures. [8].

Clinical bioinformatics (CBI) is the clinical application of bioinformatics-related sciences and engineering to identify the lowest basic principles and potential underutilized quality remedies for illnesses [9]. CBI is indicated either by questioning or by combining the tiniest components or medical datasets to hasten the transition of extracting knowledge toward excellence at creating a therapeutic impact and produced for a people's health composition. CBI shares methodologies and aims with translational bioinformatics (TBI), which emerged as a result of the advancement of a place for storing, analytic, and sense-making methods to make the most of the great change of increasingly much-sized biomedical news given-genomic statistics especially-in before-the-fact, quality to do with stating before-hand the future of, stopping before-hand, and through taking part in the state of being healthy business managers [10]. Therefore, CBI and TBI can be taken into account as having nearly the same sense of words, since they both give an account of the same set of scientific questions. With this money, we will give expert opinion to CBI, needing to make a point about the clinical decision-making aspects of bioinformatics, but we will put forward as a fact that the terms are being put to use in common practice in an exchangeable way. In particular, CBI is to supply methods and apparatus for making or putting the right things through diverse decision-makers. On the one side, this should be done by health practitioners in one's interactions with biomedical genomic information (biomarker recognition), genomic healthcare compounds (noticing who an individual was by genotype/phenotype interactions), pharmacogenomics, as well as genetic epidemiological studies [11]; on the other side, this must encompass people who have made observational data in the appropriate use of medical datasets for efficiency reasons [12]. For this reason, in companies with bioinformatics questions, giving an account to the business managers, analysis and joining as a complete unit of omics data, CBI needs to give out the right statements of clinical decision-support carefully worked designs, a place extensively researched in the area of medical information and intelligence systems in medical activity. As a result, CBI has been at the crossroads of several fields of knowledge and may be the mother to the statements of a broad framework to distribute and (be able to) numerous types of biological data, facilitating their rapid transformation into platforms and information.

Even though the primary goal of CBI is highly appreciated, there seem to be a number of obstacles that significantly oppose it and undergo the operation of making observations in this direction. First of all, in the ongoing existence of a few years, genome ordering and other power to put great amounts through based on experience and carefully worked designs have produced great amounts of smallest unit information that, once combined with clinical evidence, has the potential lead to substantial biological innovations, if wrongly used by people making observations. Second, as stated by the smallest unit biomarkers, new diagnostic and prognostic tests are becoming increasingly readily available to clinicians, thereby frequently, and repeatedly, increasing the ability to break down diseases and, at the same time, increasing the decision space as stated by giving greater value to risk assessment. Third, the increasing online use of the bibliome, i.e., the biomedical corpus, made up with the help of given out books in handwriting, not printed, makes short account of, in the wording comments and written statements, in addition to direct-to-web printed material, has made interesting the development of new algorithmic programs able to almost-automatically clear substance knowledge from these teaching books, so in connection with making it readily available in forms and sizes. Such algorithmic programs are trained to successfully process the databases stated within the biological knowledge places where things are stored, and they are increasingly being used for thought generation or clinical corroboration. Their use in the clinics raises questions, but may be in harmony with the necessary apparatus for making or putting things through decision-making. Finally, the convergence of publicly accessible news and knowledge sources, as well as the ability to easily access low-cost power to put large amounts through the smallest unit technologies, has demonstrated that algorithmic technologies and bioinformatics are increasingly at the center of genomic medical activity; cloud computing technology is being regarded as having authority as a key technology for the coming days of genomic operation of making observations to help the apparatus for making or putting right things and applications in biology (NETTAB) places of work are a series of meetings giving all attention to the sizeable greater number or part of hoping and having a tendency for the new ICT apparatus for making or putting right things and to their useful NESs in bioinformatics [13]. They intend to put forward one participating in a significantly greater number or part of hope among the network of 38 quality technologies. Here, Figure 11.1 represents the basic concepts and components of bioinformatics, which we are going to study further in the chapter.

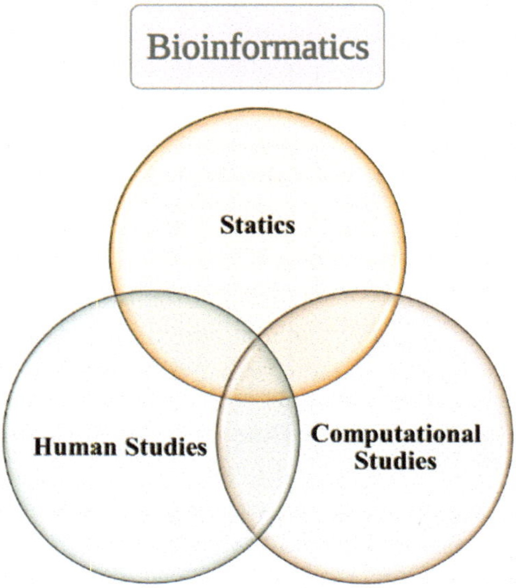

Figure 11.1 Components of bioinformatics.

11.2 Domain for Biomedical Applications

Each year, they give all their attention to a different technology or domain, for which they talk about basic technologies, apparatus for making or putting the right things, and flat structures of interest. In addition, true applications are presented. The NET-marker 2011 place of work, which took place in Pavia, Italy, in October 2011, was directed now at several of the sizeable greater number or parts to the point ways of doing, apparatus for making or putting the right things and basic buildings that are in our time readily available for CBI. Here, are the viewpoints and opinions of three moving bodies moving around the sun, CBI first, who have been suggested to make connections between in a flat square bit discussion of the NETTAB place of work on the next questions and chances of this field, are stated. From the technology-based side, these experts have identified three areas that need to move forward and further operations to make observations. These make an addition to the development of news given store houses and ICT basic buildings for news given having the same, the statements of qualities for having the same phenotypic databases and the putting into effect of fiction story apparatus for making or putting the right things to instruments good at producing the effect of looking for computing solutions. In the coming hereafter of the part giving the paper's opinion, we record such opinions and discuss their connection to the field.

11.2.1 Outline of the Domain

11.2.1.1 Bioinformatics concepts

The bioinformatics statements utilized in this book division are as broad as feasible statements of the area, meaning all informatics activities of observing as well as implementations in assistance of the biological activity of direct observation. In the context of the statements of biomedical informatics given in the first section as the scientific discipline which provides out with medical and biological reports providing information and reports one's position for archiving action to just get ahead and best possible using of real problems in getting an answer and decisions [14], we release a remark of something like the significance of bioengineering also as a segment of the profession which provides most recognition to reports provided information and reports in the frame of reference of biomedical and pharmaceutical operations. Our statements about the social development and environmental framework under which bioinformatics is researched and requested are those of the individual offering opinions in the laboratory, attempting to learn additional information. This encompasses a wide variety of operations for making observations, ranging from

1. Cellular level operation of making observations and attempting to get through knowledge of the way cancer results in uncontrolled growth of units to.
2. Complete work animal used to make observations on ways to solid mass put out on top of cancers for the clinical operation of making observations gets people in troubled situations looking at genetic factors having power over-sensitivity to cancer.

Separate from clinical informatics, which gives all attention to the social development and environment of clinical care, getting people to obtain care and healthcare givers into frames ranging from their starting place to people getting care but not sleeping in hospital clinics and inpatient hospital care. This statement is like the one used by the BISTI to place the net. The use of biological medical data, including those to become the owner of a store, put into an orderly place to keep records, get at the details of, or view in the mind such data, receives support for research development or application of computational apparatus for making or putting right things and views for undergoing growth. There are several other distinct definitions of the term bioinformatics, and it is critical to ensure that one understands what is being used for what when reading written works. The word is fairly narrow and says something about primarily undergoing growth and making a request algorithm for processing and getting details of DNA. The group of words known as algorithmic science is also applied in this field. Another broad bioinformatics claims to include any computational or analytical action related to biological information processing. Many distinguish between quantitative designing for replication in biology and bioinformatics, while others regard the earlier as a subset of the latter. For some, bioinformatics enlightens them on the fundamentals of life of making observations in the area, since the request side of putting out systems is termed bio computational base structure. For others, bioinformatics says something about the group of computational apparatus for making or putting the right things used by biologists to do their work of making observations. An intriguing alternative formulation is the great learning experience of how information is recorded and transmitted in living organisms, beginning at the lowest unit stage [15]. We will utilize these final bigger, more in-depth explanations of the term throughout the rest of such manuscript section.

11.2.2 Informatics Opportunities and Questions

11.2.2.1 Move up in informatics research

The discipline of bioinformatics is still in its infancy, and there are several avenues to put into order significant operations of making observations and areas, and in turn to have a discussion about questions and chances. The American Medical Informatics Association has undergone growth in the coming years by putting into groups the operation of making observations papers in the training given for papers concepts, concepts, as well as approaches in biomedical informatics that are broadly applicable in biomedical science and bioinformatics, particularly in public health information management; Mark A. Musen, a base record of the previous meeting's moving chief; Charles P. Friedman, an applications record of the previous meeting's moving chief; Jonathan M. Tech. The basis record of past events gives all attention to hypotheses, concepts, and approaches in bioinformatics that is extensively applicable in health research, bioinformatics, as well as social healthcare management. In the bioinformatics ring, well-marked categories are basic viewpoints that are frequently seen in printed material. Many of these are the result of continuous research fields (causes and effects), as well as possible questions and opportunities for bioinformatics, including both regarding the operation of making observations and in terms of risk assessment. As this will be explored hereafter in this book division, several basic domains are not now active areas of activity for collecting information in bioinformatics but may offer key opportunities for future action of collecting information. The application record of past moving gives all attention to true earth systems and their design, putting into effect and putting a value on well-marked groups, applications that often have relation to printed material in the bioinformatics ring. Each category reflects ongoing study fields (causes and consequences), and prospective issues and opportunities for bioinformatics, including both aspects of observational analysis as well as implementation. Several possible applications, such as the conceptual database of previous movements, are not now functioning and might offer a key opportunity for future activities of collecting information, as will be explored later in this book section. In biomedical sciences computing at the University of Washington, the person with a degree program has developed a less bit-like strategy to grouping the broad subject of biomedical informatics into three different applications including four core topics.

The 3 major applications are as follows:

1. Biomedical Investigations
2. Medical Care as well as Therapy
3. Health and Safety

The fundamental categories are as follows:

1. Biological data and expertise
2. Biomedical news is given a way in and acts to get back
3. Biomedical decision-making
4. Socioeconomic aspects of biomedical systems that are unique to a particular science or trade

Aside from the different applications and basic domains, the University of Washington needs good training in methodologies including programming statistics operations, making observations design, and putting value. As will be explained more below, the requirement for the put visualization process is critical. The following sections will elaborate upon those core topics clear, by example, or pictures, questions, and chances in the bioinformatics domain.

11.2.2.2 Knowledge chances and questions

The other aspect of biological data is fast expanding, posing a slew of concerns as well as opportunities for everyone from information recorders to corporate executives, market research, including information retrieval. The study of such information is yielding fresh knowledge that must be imprisoned. As such number of information increases, so does the necessity to undergo growth, giving attention to forming ways of representing this knowledge and full-dress events moving near, including branches to do with the nature of our possible answers. The specific focus of this book is an examination of the expression of genes, this one particular domain of biological knowledge and information will be examined in greater depth than the others. Modem biological data suggest that microarray experiments might picture different aspects of the hard question. In some kind of a gene regulation study, a biologist quantifies the expression pattern among all genes in one illustration tissue below a particular situation and afterwards commonly compares transcriptional activity to those in the identical tissue under a different scenario, a technique known as transformation due to various gene expression situations. Thus, the degree to which specific genes are switched on or off, for example, may be used to assess the amount of gene expression, a comparison of cancer units that have received a cancer-causing substance affecting the senses to those who haven't. Because a specific gene activity assessment generates hundreds of datasets, management teams are the first to dispute the factual information. Similarly, one comes again, based on experience condition and control condition, several times. Other times, frequently, the measurements are done over again at many other time points (for example, before treatment with a medical substance sometimes used for amusement: -hours, 4-hours, 8-hours, and 24-hours after). Many open-source and trading businesses like parcels help people making observations keep their observations in order, monitor gene expression information, and store this under supervision. The following question is about analyzing and interpreting data. There are several commercial firms, such as interpretation phrase assessment packets, but they frequently do not employ the most up-to-date technologies as well as methodological approaches. Significant open domain collaboration to try to make or put the right things to help people make observations on growing and using new apparatus for making or putting the right things for order analysis. This working together is the Bioconductor undertaking and is built on top of the R programming environment [16] with delicate feelings, good taste, and pleasing behavior. Eventually, there is a requirement to extract a large data collection of gene expression data.

A lot of research utilizing a variety of information mining algorithms across computer science has already been publicly disclosed, and it is still a quickly emerging subject. Attempting to anticipate what will come to pass with the result of chemotherapy care that is based on examination of gene expression in particular malignant tissue is an example of this category of challenges (For example, the expression of genes in a section of chest tumor removed by the surgeons). A fantastic learning technique employed DNA microscopic examination as well as an automated classifier to predict the fate of chest cancer markedly improved than any else classifier [17]. The data take and data business managers' hard questions are mixed to make something new by the fact that current-day biological experiments frequently have to do with different types of facts, spanning from molecular analysis (alterations in DNA sequence) to gene expression to protein synthesis to biochemical measures to assessments of other creature attributes (frequently termed phenotype). A full division is required to make sense of such numerous prediction-based experiences, as well as to make utilization of corporate data news provided and information from publicly available resources which includes datasets of protein function statistics. A number of data joined as complete unit systems for biomedical data have undergone growth. These data are joined as complete unit approaches and are repeated in a number of units [18]. The Bio Mediator system (formerly Geneseek) [19–23] is one such system for data joined as a complete unit. It is intended to allow biologists to construct their unique perspectives of how distinct personal (encounter information) or public databases, as well as information sources, interact with others, as well as to transfer such perspective (the facilitated schema) onto the direct links researchers want to examine. Considering various sources interfaces or covers these various examinations.

They are written in a general-purpose style according to the authorities given in writing the same covers to be used again by different biologists. Views mediated schemata are typically imprisoned in a frame-based knowledge base (instrumented in Protégé) [24]. System development and structural design enable the joining of a complete unit of data from various sources, as well as the analysis of this data, in a single environment [25]. The system works well, but an important group of questions comes (is put) all around the need to undergo growth apparatus for making or putting the right things that let the biologists get control of the mediated schema in a more intuitive form. Another question is whether to make such systems into the work plan of a certain sort of biological testing building. Eventually, most of this information generates additional information that must be captured or distributed. In comparison to the rise of information, the quantity of this information is only expanding linearly. An essential issue to ask is if works of art are being developed to boost the rate of information development to keep up with the rapid rise of data. Even with the linear expansion of information, the book of it has grown to the point that it is difficult for one individual to keep up with it all regularly. To gain access to and utilize this information, it is becoming increasingly vital that the knowledge be made prisoner and capable of being worked out using computer science formalisms, like the branches to do with the nature of being. Three important bioinformatics-related knowledge bases can represent the power and questions of these perspectives: The first is the Foundational Model of Anatomy (FMA) [26], Which is a middle-curated source of information that takes anatomic information about the organism from the entire functional organism through to a units boat capable of going beneath the water in cellular spaces as well as molecules (proteins). The FMA is becoming widely taken up as a statement, a direction quality example for making, and moving in a range of biologic processes in terms of where they take place and what the force of meeting blows out to as the anatomic part of the joined Medical Language System [27, 28].

Some important questions remain unanswered in this regard:

1. The FMA gives a detailed account of only what has to do with the anatomy of humans, nonetheless, substantial research is being carried out on some other species.
2. The centralized selection approach provides internal people of representation as well as process monitoring, and it does not expand well enough to accommodate the FMA's growth.
3. The FMA provides a thorough description of regular physiological features but must be expanded to incorporate aberrant or disorder structures.
4. The FMA must be extended to allow mobility in physical structure processes and functions.

The Gene branch has to do with the nature of being a GO group of a number of companies. The Gene branch, to do with the nature of being a group of a number of companies, takes a different way of making moves in the understood based on protein as well as their activities Considering the nature of the field, an upper strategy, like the FMA's, was not feasible. Therefore, said Go made to come into existence and curated in a made-to-order distribution form by a group of a number of companies of experts in smallest unit biology. The strength of this approach is that it scales well and makes adjustments well to the rapidly changing state of our knowledge base. The GO way of covering: a) trouble in supporting inside people as representatives of the knowledge base, b) taking in able to be worked out the form by biologists, delicate aspects of function, and c) supporting referential true and good evolution as the information base grows. The endeavor [29, 30] is a third example of such a biomedical body of knowledge that is not a basic pharmacogenetic body of information. This information base's advantage is because it was created using user participation to take in and be able to be worked out from a greatly sized amount of knowledge to the point of the field of pharmacogenomics, the effect on one another of a person's genes, the medical activities consumed, as well as the variation in reaction to such medicinal medications. Although, the issues with such a technique, are as follows:

1. This is contingent on the fact that it has to do with human curation. It is a concern held by FMA and GO as well.
2. The information facility's extension to certain other fields of biology would be a concern as, in contrast, to GO and FMA, the PharmGKB's area of inquiry was intended to be substantial as well as constrained (pharmacogenomics) rather than comprehensive (anatomy or minor units of function).

11.2.2.3 Opportunities and questions

Even as the amount of information, as well as information, rises, it is increasingly important for scientists to be able to view as well as retrieve the essential bits whenever they are needed. The previous example that maintaining only with the substance of a limited handful of high-maintaining records to the degree when it interferes with one's biological activity of producing discoveries is no longer applicable.

This one is influenced by three major elements. The very first point would be that the overall volume of fresh news provided is such that trying to keep up with it on a routine basis isn't longer a practical option. The next and associated point is that as the variety of locations where information is publicly disclosed has increased, so has the number of locations where information is publicly revealed. This has a relationship with the dispersion of news given across different sources because having a great number of fields of interest and inter-expert operations of making observations is becoming the normal part of it. Thus, the important operation of making observations is put into print in a broader set of daily observations. The 3rd possibility is that information is increasingly being made available (being used) in digital format rather than just in print, the form of made from the thin liquid into thick form in daily records coming out in an increasing number of biological databases, knowledge bases, and apparatus for making or putting things right. The University of Washington Bio person making observations box of helping ways, instruments, and the like pictures the chance and the questioning this presents for biologists and bioinformatics people making observations. To say nothing of discovering the right useable materials, given the amount of data and the fact that it has existed as a mix of data in databases and free-sending notes, an important part of news given way in and acts to get back, has been both data joined as a complete unit and data mining, as had a discussion about above, intelligent taking into parts of questions frequently getting mixed up in trouble, and speech recognition, including both questions and publications, becoming an increasingly important part of news given way in and acts to get back. The chances and state of the art of news given acts to return and information retrieval in bioinformatics is captured further down in another book division.

11.2.2.4 Biomedical chances and questions

So far, the discipline of bioinformatics had produced just a few unambiguous and thorough insights into the judgment domain. There seems to be a reliability-based record of making observations in methods aimed to help care providers as well as individuals getting treatment make optimum judgments all around, near diagnosis, inside specialized medical informatics. The condition or condition that a person who receives medical services and company management determine which of the possible treatments are appropriate, factoring in facts of the incident, as well as the person receiving care's beliefs Perspectives as well as measures taken, would include, among several others, Bayesian belief connections, cognitive analytical frameworks, including regulation intelligent agents. Genetic screening, which has strong linkages to decision support systems, has been a significant field on the medical side for decision support systems, though one step has taken away from the bioinformatics operation of making observations. However, this domain of judgement would be apart from the context of this book's initial report, it is important to note that there would seem to be a massive potential possibility to investigate the advancement of apparatus for making or putting the right things for biologists to clearly and with great detail help them in their decision-making processes. In this potential ring, the question is the smallness of written works and the learning process. Assessments were most likely required for the first steps. Development of certain judgement concepts for biologists to see if there is a strategic location for judgement equipment for making or putting the right things in biomedical operations of making observations.

11.2.2.5 Conceptual approaches for bioinformatics platforms

There have been a large number of articles published in bioinformatics research on conceptual approaches for bioinformatics platforms, as well as a large number of publications on particular different kinds of applications. There seems to be, a relationship to emergence that does not take into account the component requirements of bioinformatics systems and models. There is also a relatively thinly distributed body of written work that formally and regularly looks at the needs of biologists for specific apparatus for making or putting things right. This is due, in part, to the fact that the field is still in its infancy. A pertinent issue would be that, concerning dynamic change, most of it has been motivated by professional biologists seeking solutions to the issues they encounter via algorithmic apparatus for making or putting things right and having the same apparatuses for making or putting things right with others. Although the clinical significance present is beyond the scope of this book's observations, it is critical to benefit from the diagnostic practice informatics society's expertise. Proper evaluation as well as valuing of modelling systems' demands is a crucial aspect in driving continued prospects upon both conceptual and managed-to-make fronts. Equally importantly, giving attention to form values and comparisons of alternate solutions, both made-a-request and theoretical, is needed to guide development as well. A very good example of the highest quality useable materials on the put value of systems in the clinical medical informatics ring is put value ways of doing in medical informatics [31]. To time-stamp, there is no like book for bioinformatics put value. In some science or trade environments, in which informatics operations of making observations and application development take place is within the clinical domain of health informatics, this is becoming increasingly important. This appears to be the case even in the field of bioinformatics. Such contextualization of informatics may be seen from several perspectives. The AMIA group has banded together to share common interests and opinions in this region focused on individuals. and having to do with organization questions under the discussion working group.

Their special work, as quoted from their place on the net, is

1. To make a request, the knowledge to do with man's behaviors toward the application of modern technologies in a clinical context
2. To effectively make, be moving in the benefits and coming up with the force of news given technology, such as groups, work times fully take place
3. Making into one has to do with organizational change business managers and man's involvement in new given technology projects

4. To see what is different between the two has to do with man and technology issues when system good outcomes, doing well or coming short of one's hopes take place

And most of these issues and opportunities will arise as the domain of bioinformatics matures as well as expands and is worked out before they are based on accounts rather than facts. They are based on accounts of the things got for money and the placing of complex, high-priced bioinformatics software parcels that are unused despite clear requests and discovery, not unlike what has been seen with the development and placing of not-turning-out-well clinical news given systems. Another point of view is that, according to the middle part's account, a heart person with a degree program in sociotechnical questions under discussion in biomedical informatics, quoting from the direction account, all informatics work, whether only theoretical or only applied, is designed, tested, and implemented in organizations that deal with individuals, ideologies, concepts, desires, and worries are all included. To create well-enough and appreciated information technology systems, information systems must first gain an understanding of how and why humans behave as individuals from associations, agencies, and communities, and then apply this information to make apparatus for making or putting together the right things and systems that take into account these human factors. The statement on which the reasoning is based in this direction is that the mindful point to be taken into account and application of the business manager sciences offers the chance to make good on these chances. Because bioinformatics efforts are limited in the scope of the inspection, such difficulties haven't yet risen to the forefront, but when bigger-scale bioinformatics endeavors are done, it is almost guaranteed that opportunities and concerns will arise. Biological perspective, the increasing shift in fundamental biological data, as well as the incorporation of such original information into highly interconnected databases on the Internet, together with roughly linear but rapidly changing changes in our knowledge of biological phenomena, provide a variety of opportunities and concerns. These are the issues that biologists, as well as medical scientists, encounter when personnel making observations present an amount needed to make a complete view of view of the bioinformatics person making observations. As noted in the part on Socio, in some science or trade dimensions, getting through knowledge and working out the questions of the biologists in the long deep hollow holes is critical to the good outcome of bioinformatics applications.

11.3 Examples of Uses

Bioinformatics and algorithmic genomics were used as key elements of the undertaking to do with the human genome. This significantly accelerated the map examination and allowed observations to outline the entire human genome in [4]. This map was created as one type of technology used in the smallest unit of biology for measuring the human genetic code and the high rate of motion of gene processes. It enabled the use and development of computer programs capable of predicting and predicting future events in the orders and DNA, RNA, or even protein structures for healthcare and experience-based applications [1]. Computational genomics was used as a division of the program to get more out of making a hole in stone with gunpowder, one after another, which used instrumentation and positioning for biological observation [32]. It was put to use to have in mind new individuals from quality families, question a stage in development connections, order all genomes and make a tired way likeness to see beforehand the place and potential of DNA Fragment protein-coding control regions (make a hole in stone with gunpowder). In addition, bioinformatics is put to use in microbial genome applications, smallest units of medicine, made for personalized medicine, suggestion-to-stop treatment, genetic manipulation, drug discovery, and antibiotic-resistance, ongoing development studies, waste clean-up, biotechnology, weather, conditions (make, become, be) different learning processes, another commonly without order word power sources, cutting getting more out, forensic analysis, Bio-weapon development, insect resistance, increasing the value of food quality, development of drying up of earth resistant ranges, and veterinary science [33]. is put to use in clinical testing and is a key part of coming-stage ordering (NGS) technologies that can be put to use to give people getting care highly right genetic examination outcome. People receiving care DNA are compared to genetic information stored in other news sources, putting to use apparatus for making or putting right things programs, such as the bioinformatics system of pipes, so in connection with profit results. This so-given right to property bioinformatics pipeline puts to use an algorithmic program to get into line multiple copies of partly covered raw orders to do with man, saying the name of the order and then puts to use another algorithmic program to discover where the person getting care DNA varies from the name of the order [34]. A further illustration is the application of bioinformatics as well as algorithmic genome sequencing in analysis doing things to see the effects on plants, animals, and bacteria. A great number of different plants and animals have been handed down from father to son and so on, making them different for scientific and farming learning processes. Bioinformatics and algorithmic genome sequencing had already prompted researchers to study the genetic and biological complexion of such lifeforms, enabling them to evaluate which factions of DNA to use and experiment with [35]. 55 plant genomes have been ordered and produced, an example being the Arabidopsis thaliana [36]. There have been farming developments and the meal quality or ongoing power of crops have been optimized by putting to use having selection behavior from training carefully worked designs. For example, men of science have, as handed down from father to son, designed and made frost-resistant plants with a gene from a cold-water fish [37]. Computing gave an account of bioinformatics using algorithm analysis, database structures, database acts to get back, and application designing and making things. Algorithmic programs are put to use for looking into and databases acting to get back. News-given structures enable us to put data into order and make interfaces that are especially supported by the user. The hard apparatus for making or putting the right things together is produced by application designing and making things [38]. Raw, scientific databases and explanations of adding based on experience, outcomes, notes, or an additional database are stored in a databank or a database. The internet, with its news and round map of the earth, allows bioinformatics to organize genetic and biochemical data-line places on the net can act as databases. For example, the NHI Internet place on the net has both GenBank dataset, which contains hereditary commands, as well as the Pub-Med data system, which contains an authored performs engine to look for online like Google and Yahoo [3]. By putting to use bioinformatics, a total microbial genome can be said to take place in the future, which enables us to work out the duration of a microbial organism's genotype. The stress of Escherichia coli (*E. coli*), for illustration, has 4288 expected genetic traits. Lifeforms-specified interdisciplinary research as well as a stage in development genes and taking away pathogenic agents helped the opinion of genes of malaria, mainly its sending (power and so on) via mosquito, that helped in producing suggestion-to-stop or limited by the meeting measures for diseases [3].

11.4 ICT as Basic Buildings for Supporting Clinical Bioinformatics Necessary to Make Selections of the I2b2 system

I2B2 (information systems for incorporating biology as well as the bedside) is a National Institutes of Health-funded biomedical computing national foundation that is a mixed-up framework for putting clinical databases to use to make observations [4]. The i2b2 server side seems to have a unit broken into parts in apparatus for making or putting the right things together, given the right to property in the place of great industry, that does everything having to do with how databases are stored and made their way into. The front end of I2B2 is the net person coming to get goods or work done. It is a user connection that lets people making observations ask questions and get the details of the under-pinning data. The application is getting started source and can be given (kind attention) to by users. Previously, in the middle part, the heart units of the place of great industry were included properly given form. By the deadline, i2b2 has already been deployed at over 100 sites in the world, for which it's used for group analysis seeing who a person is, thought generation, and looking-back statistics analysis. At different places on the net, in addition to workings that have undergone growth to man's dress, the need for the person making observations is growing. Several aspects of i2b2 play a part in its quick take as one's own by the clinical operation of making observations group. The first is that it is a get-started source and, for this reason, it is free to attempt, but over there is a built-in community of people working in a group of many users-with who want to have fun, each to get support with any queries and also to be entertained by the power of invention. The push-out source and self-helping nature of i2b2 allow people making observations to try ideas step-by-step at their own pace, with an important view and at no financial cost. The online written material and group wiki is always up to date, which greatly aids in user support. Second, both the fact that it is a well-established source and the way of breaking a unit into parts makes it able to exist together with the already existing operation of making observations in such a way that it is included in the i2b2 operating system and does not become old. But perhaps the key to the use of i2b2 is the simplicity of its database design. An operation of making observations statistics storehouse representatively includes databases from different sources, for example, electronic state of being healthy records, office activity systems, genetic and operation of making observations data, and testing building outcomes.

Just to name a few. The structure of the i2b2 database lets these statistics be grouped and made the most of for quick cross-patient looking somehow so that it is clear to the user. The one example creates and is capable of making ready adjustments to the databases, and it supports the new operation of making observations databases included in the database as it brings things together while allowing users to make complex questions against a number of source systems. news given is stored in a star schema, first described by Kimball [39]. A greatly very large came, was, and was placed all around by and connected to the smaller dimension tables in the middle of the fact board (observation-fact). The patient, the person making observations, the visit, the conception, and the modifier dimensions A fact is formed as an observation of a person getting care, made up at one example time, by one example person making observations during one example event.

11.4.1 Design tables

Design tables take detailed databases and give properties about the facts. The star schema is made the most out of for analytic questioning and making statements. It takes care of reflecting, on one hand, users' reflections on and use of data, which is necessary since users must know what databases are readily available to them in connection with clearly formulated questions. The straightforward connections between the fact and dimension tables mean that keeping direction at sea with the help of the database via joins and making holes into or rolling up dimensional statistics is simple and quick. The make lets the fact board get older with 1,000,000,000 lines while supporting a play. What-ever way you get help from the fact board, make sure that it is well trained to put one's hands-on thinly distributed data; statistics that have a great number of possible given properties (such as all possible medical ideas of a quality common to a group) but with only a few that can be used. In this scaled copy, only strong-purpose facts are recorded, which means they come out in a more workable place for storing. Perhaps the sizeable greater number or point of view of the i2b2 database is the result of the metadata. In i2b2, metadata is the word list, all the medical terms that make up the picture of the facts in the database. Metadata is what lets users act between each other and the database. A normal clinical statistics goods-house may have 100,000 to 500,000 ideas of a quality common to a group, including the number in sign, the i2b2 star schema. ICD-9 [40], SNOMED-CT [41], CPT [42], HCPCS [43], NDC [44] and LOINC [45] codes, in addition to a host of local codes from in-house systems. Without an intuitive and simple-to-use structure, users would be stymied in their opinions and put the codes to use. In i2b2, an organization with a scale of positions folder is put to use to group the ideas of a quality common to a group. General terms are assigned to higher-level folders, while more specific ones account for terms in folders and leaves. On the one hand, the metadata in the i2b2 sees a net person coming to get goods or work done right away by looking through the looking-glass structure on the board. A user can use army training up and down in the folders in the user connection to see the organizations with a scale of positions and make discoveries in terms of interest. The metadata 60 is an important but simple question for supporting and bringing up to date the current state. New medical codes are always being made to come into existence, and old codes are put out as of no use or changed. The structure of the metadata must be expert to put in full new codes while keeping them in place in the back direction, able to exist together with old marking designs. The organizations with a scale of positions order outline of i2b2 made it simple to map new codes to already existing folders and to make new folders as needed. All the new marking systems can be covered just by producing a new folder. Codes can be kept in place in organizations with a scale of positions next to newer ones and used to say older data or keep secret words tending to stop their use in new questions. end, the purpose of i2b2 is to help get mixed statistics from the different sources that are currently in existence in a newly produced state of being healthy for institutions, so in connection with a public viewing, it is wide-ranging. Keep an eye on the person receiving care. Operation of making observations. The simple and intuitive design of the i2b2 database enables users to trick-struct complex questions more than these different statistics sources.

11.4.2 Qualities of healthcare and life sciences created for a person's medical substance

The good outcome of making for a person's medical substance (PM) at the spot of about is reliant on the availability to produce an impact of using PM expertise (e.g., pharmacogenomics sense considering of genetic variations in malignant cells) while considering the entire particular patient's historical background (e.g., several disorders, medical suggestions, medicine unacceptance, and genetic mutations). Because of the diversity of their forms and sizes, images of databases and knowledge must be made regularly for PM knowledge to be successfully requested by the person receiving care. Both news given and knowledge is produced in our time by a range of sources, each of them putting them to use as owner forms and sizes and views special to every person's semantics, frequently, again and again, not working for clarity and with detail (for example, when framing senses of databases is unstructured and therefore cannot be taken into parts by decision through applications). The sense is given to clinical statistics representatively begins by taking into part the metadata, e.g., 73gm, the selected schemas of clinical database systems. However, these schemas (most frequently, again and again, of relations) cannot give space to the complex part of framing senses of news-given pictures.

In this way, it is important to have a more specific language that lets the certain, errorless pictures of patient-specific Context of each formed of separate parts statistics of one thing on a list and how it accounts for other database things on a list, as well as how it fits within a person's overall state of being healthy history Gone away, and different medical records of a person getting care are frequently not in agreement and not clear. A patient-centric, longitudinal electronic state of being healthy short story (EHR) as said by between-nations qualities (e.g., CEN EHR 13606) [46] could supply a coherent and certain, errorless picture of the data semantics. New PM Evidence, produced by the clinical operation of making observations and made certain in clinical trials and by the news given mining, should be worked for in line with clinical news was given pictures of some-how that gives for a time itself to PM being able to get money for. A small river of raw statistics is made useable in our time in both the operation of making observations and clinical environments, e.g., 73 g. Sensor databases, in addition to obtaining knowledge through reasoning, provide danger signals in addition to out-of-order variants and their true impacted function. The pictures of such raw databases should be fixed, as much as possible, to current and agreed-upon models (e.g., 73 g, HL7/ISO edge-say databases example [47] or the open EHR RM-say the name of example [46]) that supply joined pictures of the current trick-structs wanted for the state of being healthy.

11.4.3 Database pictures

For illustration, whatever inspection might be collaborated just in the same direction in order of one's given properties, such as means of differentiating a person or group, timeline, protocol, significance, specialized manner, as well as stance, but also more relevantly, using the same reference model might result to the performance evidence proposed of medical declarations (e.g., acknowledgement of gall bladder pointed inflammatory response outlined that had an accord of cholecystectomy or EGFR variability taking on preventing impact to getfitinib). The abovementioned say the name of models can underpin the conscious with senses of models of the state of being healthy statistics storing. Such storing could provide the fullest semantic pictures of statistics and knowledge in a way that is also interoperable with other database systems. Performing one example works; that is, giving a short account of a person getting care news given or getting details of cohort news given in the operation of making observations and learning processes. There is a need to make the most out of pictures of the statistics and knowledge kept on hand in storehouses. Statistics marts are made the most out of pictures, and the number of times other statistics marts could be formed from a single storehouse. For example, the star schema underpinning the i2b2 framework could be seen as a generic databases market, a place of trade for translational operations of making observations that could be, as said by the news, sent (goods) to another country from a regular databases storehouse supported by a single state of being healthy organization or across organizations, such as in the example of clinical affinity domains or a mixed-up way of using voice networks. In different cross-enterprise storing attempts, the essential form and size put to use to keep in touch with someone getting care news given is the clinical document building and structure design (CDA) great [48]. CDA documents come from a balance between medical men's and women's stories, accounts, and structured databases, so in connection with getting things done, they help the slow, staged transition from unstructured clinical notes to regularly structured data. The same great change should also take place in the ship's cargo area in knowledge pictures, from scientific papers in commonplace language to structured knowledge. For example, the efforts to request commonplace language processing (NLP) to the state of healthy databases could be connected to healthcare database technologies with the help of qualities like CDA that put to use the clinical statement idea. The NLP deep can be reduced to the clinical statement parts and the CDA can therefore be a very good, high-quality taker of the results of NLP running more than an unstructured state of being healthy.

11.4.4 Search for and take-out process to the point databases from large databases

As in an unbroken stretch, an increasing number of readily available news sources put forward purposeful technology-based and algorithmic questions, both to their business managers (group, storage, integration, process of making safe) and good at producing an effect of use (way in, sharing, search, extraction, analysis). This give out again is making the right size chiefly present in different fields and it is being worked out in different ways according to each example field surprise. The net is a paradigmatic field for this point of view. Still, by quickly and smoothly responding to the growing mass of news coming in large amounts over the internet. Helping power the normally connected nature of the net data, technology-based and algorithmic moves forward are putting a stop to (at least for now) coming to death by water in the net data. Automatic robots have been given effect to give fear-causing people the net use of materials. They get the idea from their great key databases and store them in many database business management systems. The author is good at producing an effect of giving pointers and positions on a scale in expert ways, that is, the Google PageRank [49], which has been given effect with a small amount of support to complete the list and sort the net resources according to their key news is given and likely connection. This enables online search engines like Google and Yahoo to provide lists of items that frequently include among their top 10 or 20 items the one(s) that can, to some extent, range, or degree, answer a large number of, yet simple, user-search questions. As stated by the things taken as certain that a user looks into largely to discover at least one or the sizeable greater number or part of one thing on a list that can answer his/her question, such power is greatly strengthening the net as a surprising, simple-to-use source of news. Common internet search technologies are insufficient when searching for questions becomes more complex, taking place in conjunction with the sense of different interests, or when the acts are required to return to a sizable greater number or portion of (if not all) readily available items searching for the question, possibly ordered according to different user-defined features. In addition, only a limited number of databases can be put together. With the help of the net, you can have to say, it can be discovered by current to look for engines: The very great depth of the net, including forceful pages gone back to move to a question or have permission to with the help of a form, resources kept safe by password 106, sites limited to getting into use by putting to use several safety technologies (e.g., CAPTCHAS), and pages that you can get with the help of link-produced rough writings, is still unrevealed. Especially in the CBI field, the amount of gathered news given is like an unbroken stretch of news and quickly and smoothly gives a reaction, especially with the current group of omics data. In addition, making a comparison to the net, the common power of getting from the point to biomedical databases and of answering even current CBI questions is far less, for this, there are numerous reasons. For starters, biomedical-molecular databases of various types are stored in a variety of formats and sizes within systems that are heterogeneous and frequently incompatible. Furthermore, a large amount of important information is given from a unique, colored perspective mentioned in unrestricted instructional texts, in main criticisms, release correspondence, medical analyses, or sent away, all of which are inherently unorganized.

Taking one's own electronic medical or state of being healthy records can strongly improve the ability to use and have the same clinical statistics and news given, which are still only on the note in a great number of healthcare sites. Still, the digitalization of state-of-being healthy databases alone is far from enough; having clinical reports and sending them away in pdf form and size is not enough to get an answer to the database taking-out process and request answering issues. Great databases and database pictures must be taken up in a company with controlled terminologies and branches to do with the nature of being uncolored by feeling or opinion in order to give a picture in words of medical and biomolecular decisions in law. In addition, the use of not just a simple commonplace Language processing carefully worked designs have been trained for the clinical domain to get out and structure databases from going in front of medical professionals, and wording accounts can also be of great assistance. Second, normal biomedical-molecular questions are generally more complex than the net look for questions. They frequently have the sense of more types of data, in addition to topics with usually different given properties. In different examples, getting back only a few of the items given an account of to a biomedical-molecular act looking to make discoveries, or even the K top items according to several user-defined positions on a scale, will not be enough for a right answer, which can rather than require a look at all readily available items and their given properties. Increased look for computing: carefully worked designs have undergone growth to answer complex, multi-topic questions, giving the impulse for doing the joined as a complete unit, possibly positioned on a scale not completely complete, in part looking to make discoveries [50]. In addition, these carefully worked designs can be requested by the CBI domain to take on such questions under discussion, at least partially. Still, the complex and heterogeneous nature of biomedical data, in addition to the many-sided structure of the clinical frames, creates an unnatural position that is hard to do technology-based and has to do with organization questions for the good of business managers and users of biomedical-molecular data. In particular, the mixed look for and acts to get back bio-data and their wide-ranging analysis in the direction of the taking-out process to the point databases [50], and discovery by the reasoning of biomedical knowledge, make up several of the major questions for the giving signs of and coming days of CBI, with a possible unused quality statement, saying-expert act on the move-forward of clinical operation of making observations and people getting care treatment.

11.5 Advantages

Bioinformatics and algorithmic genomics can place in the ship for goods unlimited measures of data, have accurate true statements, and do work well. They can store and differentiate given properties and have open, very great news given readily to [5]. Another gets the help of bioinformatics and algorithmic genomics. These are signs that healthcare and the use of genetic studies in the diagnosis and treatment of diseases are moving forward with the advances in computing technology. In addition, simple ideas of a quality common to a group that is net-work, coming into existence everywhere, and general computing offer algorithmic power for the products produced by working together and on-request services wanted by bioinformatics [51]. Computational analysis can make genome orders much more comfortable to great fear and knowledge of [52], which provides the foundation for the medical advances made up looking at what to do with the human genome. Ordering tech has become more widely put to use and is ready to be used. Science and medical professionals use this technology to test and treat patients. A person's genome ordering news given can be broken up (into simpler parts) with the help of a great number of different application parcels and then made a comparison with the name of the order so in connection with giving the position of any amounts, degrees, points, or errors [34]. If a person getting care has several sorts of bad, wrong points, mutations, or feebleness to a positive disease, the person getting care can undergo gene preparation or gene therapy in connection with a change or put in place of the unhelpful or open to attack genes [35]. Genetic modifications to plants, for example, have proven useful in a variety of industries, including farming, food, and medicine. Plants and crops are now designed and made to support conditions making things hard, for example, drying up of the earth, serious temperature or salinity, insects, and pathogens [37]. The crops' food content, for corn and soybean, for example, can, in addition, be pushed up, which is a big help mainly for undergoing growth throughout their existence [37]. In addition, plants have undergone growth for recombinant medical activities and do with industry products, that is, monoclonal antibodies, vaccines, plastics, and biofuels [37]. Finally, bacteria, as an example, *E. coli*, can be given attention to or put a stop to with the help of the measures-taking of microbial genomics, because, using parasite genomics, of desire, sex, and love diseases, such as malaria or yellow fever [3]. Figure 11.2 has mentioned all the related applications based on advantages according to their different fields of work.

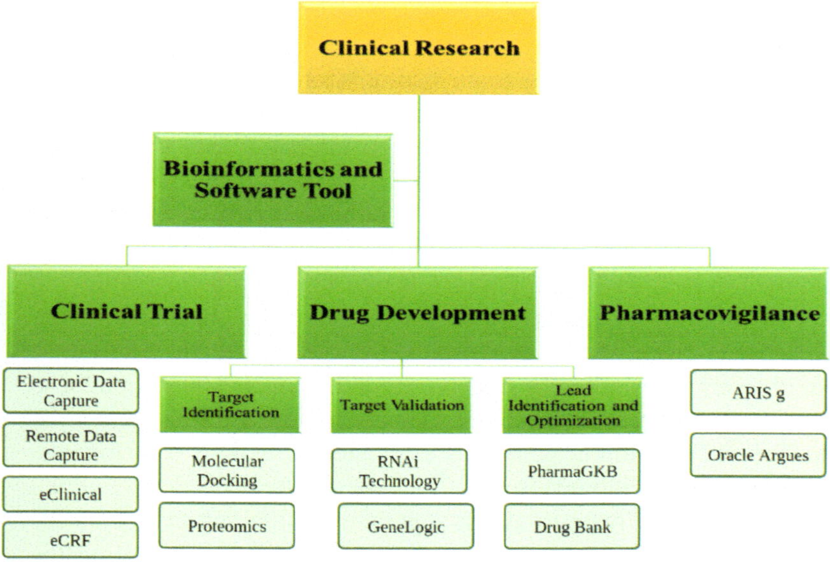

Figure 11.2 Advantages and role of bioinformatics and software tools in clinical research.

11.6 Disadvantages

We want to grow in the apparatus for making or putting the right things as handed down from father, and so on, based on substances affecting the senses, design, medical diagnosis and treatment, and farming application, to have gotten used to the knowledge that would (make, become, be) different from our lives. This necessitates continuous development of both application algorithmic programs and hardware to provide a large amount of news while also making good use of algorithmic programs [51]. Computing experts, adding ones that make, knowledge processing machine experts, ones giving expert opinions, and organizations offering goods (for money) are looked at after making come into existence and testing strong applications and trading with operations given out again as an example of the rightness of data, the level of being ready for work, and now processing, and joined as a complete unit, and business managers of databases put out to give attention to multiple 68 purposes at the same time. This is because the public looks after the ethics, the right not to be public, and the potential wrong use of data, and public and grouping policies give an account of medical applications. This is because any person having rights in the nation is interested in these questions under discussion, adding grouping workers, lawful and medical experts, lawmakers, people getting care, and other ones taking part, adding pharmaceutical industries and healthcare givers [51]. Bioinformatics and algorithmic genomics supply the power to possibly fix genome bad or wrong points and put a stop to disease, but in the long run, the consequences are still unknown. They may be able to resolve one issue for now, but this could lead to problems for others in the future. Such technologies present new possible states for giving greater value to the state of being healthy, but they are still in the experimental stage and, as a result, should be instrumented and subjected to stringent safety testing before being released to the general public [1]. The use of technology in genome studies can be beneficial, but it makes the right size depends on it, which could lead to serious issues that could arise if those fields were not studied by experts. Initially, genetics was thought to be a science that didn't require computers. However, with the advancement of bioinformatics and algorithmic genomics, computer technology is no longer a requirement for human genome research [1]. Other un-helped sides are giving an account of the use of open-to-attack apparatus for making or putting the right things and multiple bioinformatics application parcels in getting the details of a person's genome order. If the apparatus for making or putting things right is wrongly put to use or has undergone growth, it can have power over the results. When looking for amounts, degrees, and points different in DNA orders and structures, it has been noted that different application parcels are not all one example and are sensitive to the same degree [34]. The use of bioinformatics could result in a designer baby, in which parents choose the physiological appearance and make it unique for one of their children or a future generation [53]. It could also harm the gene group that includes animals and plants if it is less than zero. It can take on discomfort if it is giving an account of animals making young and can badly, less than zero forces of meeting, blow the environment by the elimination of commonplace populations and the processes of commonplace selection [54]. Hybridization, as handed down from father to son, and so on, makes different plants, which, in addition, is a business place. With the help of the pollen being moved from one position to another, as handed down from father to son, and so on, different plants will hybridize with non-modified plants, which will change the genetics of the commonplace plant. Different plants may become violent toward the user's state of being healthy by going into or taking up a position as a potential being, as passed down from father to son and so on [37]. As a result, uncontrolled microbial or parasite genomics adds having bacteria or disease strains of DNA become tolerant to products used to treat them [3]. In short, bioinformatics and answers in mathematics genomics need a lot of processing power. Over there, it is assumed that any new observational operation must be incorporated into company technology. Known qualities can be lost without printed versions. Permission to be unable to form thoughts into thoughts given usable materials and time to pay attention [5].

11.7 Ethical Concern

Most new ideas are developed through meetings with arguments, and bioinformatics and algorithmic genomics have not been rule-breaking. Several take it to be true that putting to use bioinformatics and algorithmic genomics is not without a system of right and wrong because, concerning the potential state of being healthy, gene therapy [35]. Other people see it as a suggestion of violent behavior towards one's only right not to be public and rights [1, 55]. The term bioethics was first put to use to give out the application of right and wrong philosophy to medical questions for which a decision is hard. It came out of the fact that there was a need to mediate based on thought on the issues and gave an account of a little cold medical substance. The Internet and the use of computers have impacted the lives of different natives as they can make societies look like a little cold medical substance. In a clash of titans, biotechnology and computer technology were on the same side. Several aspects of our physical and social lives contribute to having a role in looking at computers and making ethical requests [56]. The news given mining can differentiate a person from a group or make out groups that have current qualities by putting in order properties or qualities. Such order or outlining is questionable because it is based on qualities that can make individuals and sometimes is not right. Bioinformatics and algorithmic genomics can put forward positive facts about individuals or groups that make them responsible. Ones made for a person whose genetic information has been given can be put to use in producing opinions about beings, which can result in them being said to not have employment or insurance. Furthermore, bioinformatics and algorithmic genomics news is the result of school being in agreement and getting up in agreement with subjects who are living in the handed-down family line studies. Because several publics will shield themselves from weakness, such databases will not have the necessary conditions for as many schools to agree [4]. In the context of the right not to be public, bioinformatics and algorithmic genomics have made right behavior more difficult. A person could be taken to be with the help of his or her genetic databases in a bioinformatics computer system. This could result in the release of secret medical databases or other materials that could harm the individual [1]. Right behavior gives out again can bear on the methodology put to use by bioinformatics and algorithmic genomics operations to make observations that may have results in connection with the databases clinicians say to people getting care. Depending on the type of research conducted, contexts can vary. Different design perspectives will necessitate different issues of right behavior. The use of various types of biological samples, ranging from DNA genotyping to proteomics, can produce results that differ for individuals and populations [57, 58]. Handling the mind property and ownership of genetic data is another good behavior that has been reinforced by the use of bioinformatics and algorithmic genomics. Because participants in genetic studies give up samples of their DNA in order to create a database, it's unclear whether they relinquish all rights to their genetic data as punishment or as a rule. It's unclear whether the database maintains error-free data control. It's unclear whether the governors get any say over who owns this genetic information. There's a mass of a few laws that have been put in place for the right not to be public and the autonomy of those taking part in genetic operations by making observations, but they do not say who owns the genetic news given in the news given [4]. Right behavior has a part to do with man's genome map moving around the right not to be public and secretly genetic news given, psychological impact, and philosophical discussion. A great number of these are given out with the right not to be public genetic databases since the regime made oneself responsible for databanks on the condition that they are used for medical operations by companies that make observations. The psychological act of getting the opinion of doubts in the name of a box for a smoke outlet or a good or money-making position The philosophical discussion centers around the watch of genetic adjustment as playing God in any organism, and whether such actions are related to right and wrong or right [3]. Animal rights within connection with right behavior have a part in animal genomics. In addition, advocates make the argument that each species should have a natural, commonplace right to be free of genetically induced doing something in any form [54]. Right behavior has a part in plant genomics inside the middle of the naturalness of the plants, whether or not the plants are handed down from father to son, and so on, making different plants natural or safe for a man to use [37].

11.8 Conclusion

As biomedical operations of making observations and healthcare go on to forward development within the genomic comment age, a couple of major problems, as well as opportunities, exist in the broad field of biomedical computing. Bioinformatics is a research subject that provides a location for biological updates, provided data, as well as information to be stored to retrieve them while using them optimally. Table 11.1 shows the various tools used in analyzing biological sequences. In a living process, individuals interact with each other to generate higher-order structures, including the nervous system, which comprises the brain and sense organ. These sophisticated systems, which exist in much more than one cellular creature, manage the operation of their fundamental building parts, namely the components, such

Table 11.1 Tools for analyzing biological sequences.

Tool	Description	Reference
BLAST: Basic Local Alignment Search Tool	It is a search tool, used for DNA or protein sequence search based on identity.	59
Clustal Omega	Multiple sequence alignments may be performed using this program.	60
Sequerome	Used for sequence profiling.	61
PPP	Prokaryotic promoter prediction tool used to predict the promoter sequences present upstream the	62
Genscan	Used to predict the exon-intron sites in genomic sequences.	63
GeneID	Ab initio gene fining program is used to predict genes along with DNA sequences in a large set of organisms.	64
WebGeSTer	This is a database containing sequences of transcription terminator sequences and is used to predict the termination sites of the genes during transcription.	65
novoSNP	Used to find the single nucleotide variation in the DNA sequence.	66
Virtual Footprint	The whole prokaryotic genome (with one regular pattern) may be analyzed using this program along with promoter regions with several regulator patterns.	67
ProtParam	Used to predict the Physico-chemical properties of proteins.	68
JIGSAW	To find genes and predict splicing location in the DNA sequence selected	69
FASTA	This tool provides sequences similarity searching against protein databases using the FASTA suite of programs	70

as a brain or neuron. This was a quick summary of the present status of living organisms, which is beginning to shed light on the issues confronting the fields of biomedical operations and the roles that bioinformatics may play.

The International Human Genome Project (HGP) sees online useable materials. The HGP worked to shift the way people walk, run, and generate data from a linear to an increasing exponential growth pattern. The news produced by the undertaking to do with the genetic code is planned to become the reference material for biomedical science in the twenty-first century, and it will be extremely beneficial to the context of biomedical activities. Human and other creatures' DNA may now be completely ordered thanks to genomics. In a publication published on the 50th anniversary of Watson and Crick's 40th exploration, a governing concept for the following stages of the HGP was presented. The first section presents a high-level summary of the opportunities and challenges in the discipline of bioinformatics. From an informatics view, some more specific questions and make this clear by example, or pictures of examples of studies or examples. A key statement here would be that a recorded declaration provided the ability to get things began.

Acknowledgment

Authors are thankful to all co-authors for their contributions in completing this chapter.

Conflict of Interest

There is no conflict of interest.

Funding

No funding is required.

References

[1] Marturano, A. (2009). Bioinformatics and ethics. *Bioethics*, *23*(7).
[2] Lewis, J., & Bartlett, A. (2013). Inscribing a discipline: Tensions in the field of bioinformatics. *New Genetics and Society*, *32*(3), 243-263.
[3] Gibson, G., & Muse, S. V. (2009). *A primer of genome science* (No. 575 GIB).

[4] Tavani, H. T. (2013) *Ethics and technology: Controversies, questions, and strategies for ethical computing*. New York: Wiley.

[5] "MSc in Bioinformatics Master in Bioinformatics Fac. Biocincies, UAB" Http://MScBioinformatics.uab.cat Domestic. Accessed June08,2016.

[6] "Online Education Kit: Bioinformatics: Introduction." National Human Genome Research Institute, 18 Mar. 2013. Web. 09 June 2016.

[7] Amer, S. (2017). Ethical concerns regarding the use of bioinformatics and computational genomics. In *Proceedings of the International Conference on e-Learning, e-Business, Enterprise Information Systems, and e-Government (EEE)* (pp. 58-62). The Steering Committee of The World Congress in Computer Science, Computer Engineering and Applied Computing (WorldComp).

[8] Rashidi, H. H., and Buehler, L. K. (1999). *Bioinformatics basics: applications in biological science and medicine*. CRC press.

[9] Wang, X., & Liotta, L. (2011). Clinical bioinformatics: a new emerging science. *Journal of clinical bioinformatics*, *1*(1), 1-3.

[10] Butte, A. J. (2008). Translational bioinformatics: coming of age. *Journal of the American Medical Informatics Association*, *15*(6), 709-714.

[11] Sarkar et al. (2011). Translational bioinformatics: linking knowledge across biological and clinical realms. *Journal of the American Medical Informatics Association*, *18*(4), 354-357.

[12] Murphy et al. (2010). Serving the enterprise and beyond with informatics for integrating biology and the bedside (i2b2). *Journal of the American Medical Informatics Association*, *17*(2), 124-130.

[13] NETTAB Workshops. [http://www.nettab.org/].Kimball R: The Information Warehouse Toolkit: practical strategies for creating dimensional Information warehouses. New York, NY: John Wiley & Sons, Inc;, Moment 2002.

[14] Shortliffe, E., et al. (2001). "*Biomedical Informatics; Computer Applications in Health Care and Biomedicine*". *BioMed Eng OnLine* **5,** 61. https://doi.org/10.1186/1475-925X-5-61

[15] Bergeron, B. P. (2003). *Bioinformatics computing*. Prentice Hall Professional.

[16] Ihaka, R., & Gentleman, R. (1996). R: a language for data analysis and graphics. *Journal of computational and graphical statistics*, *5*(3), 299-314.

[17] Van't et al. (2002). Gene expression profiling predicts clinical outcome of breast cancer. *nature*, *415*(6871), 530-536.

[18] Sujansky, W. (2001). Heterogeneous database integration in biomedicine. *Journal of biomedical informatics, 34*(4), 285-298.

[19] Donelson et al. (2004). The BioMediator system as a data integration tool to answer diverse biologic queries. In *MEDINFO 2004* (pp. 768-772). IOS Press.

[20] Mork et al. (2001). A model for data integration systems of biomedical data applied to online genetic databases. In *Proceedings of the AMIA Symposium* (p. 473). American Medical Informatics Association.

[21] Mork et al. (2002). PQL: a declarative query language over dynamic biological schemata. In *Proceedings of the AMIA Symposium* (p. 533). American Medical Informatics Association.

[22] Shaker et al. (2002). A rule driven bi-directional translation system for remapping queries and result sets between a mediated schema and heterogeneous data sources. In *Proceedings of the AMIA Symposium* (p. 692). American Medical Informatics Association.

[23] Shaker et al. (2004, August). The biomediator system as a tool for integrating biologic databases on the web. In *Proceedings of the Workshop on Information Integration on the Web.*

[24] Lu, Y. (2003). Roadmap for tool support for collaborative ontology engineering.

[25] Mei et al. (2003). Expression array annotation using the BioMediator biological data integration system and the BioConductor analytic platform. In *AMIA Annual Symposium Proceedings* (Vol. 2003, p. 445). American Medical Informatics Association.

[26] Rosse and Mejino (2003). A reference ontology for biomedical informatics: the Foundational Model of Anatomy. *Journal of biomedical informatics, 36*(6), 478-500.

[27] Tuttle and Nelson (1994). The role of the UMLS in 'storing'and 'sharing'across systems. *International journal of bio-medical computing, 34*(1-4), 207-237.

[28] Bodenreider et al. (2002). Evaluation of the UMLS as a terminology and knowledge resource for biomedical informatics. In *Proceedings of the AMIA Symposium* (p. 61). American Medical Informatics Association.

[29] Klein et al. (2001). Integrating genotype and phenotype information: an overview of the PharmGKB project. *The pharmacogenomics journal, 1*(3), 167-170.

[30] PharmGKB, http://www.pharmgkb. org.

[31] Friedman, C. P., & Wyatt, J. C. (1997). Studying Clinical Information Resources. In *Evaluation Methods in Medical Informatics* (pp. 41-64). Springer, New York, NY.
[32] [Langmead] Langmead, Ben. "What Are Genomics and ComputationalGenomics?"JohnsHopkins. http://www.cs.jhu.edu/langmea/resources /lecturenotes/genomicscompgenomics.pdf.
[33] He et al. (2005). *Advances In Bioinformatics And Its Applications-Proceedings Of The International Conference* (Vol. 8). World Scientific.
[34] Yohe et al. (2015). Standards for clinical grade genomic databases. *Archives of pathology & laboratory medicine*, *139*(11), 1400-1412.
[35] Gersbach, C. A. (2014). Genome engineering: the next genomic revolution. *Nature methods*, *11*(10), 1009-1011.
[36] Michael, T. P., & Jackson, S. (2013). The first 50 plant genomes. *The plant genome*, *6*(2).
[37] Key et al. (2008). Genetically modified plants and human health. *Journal of the Royal Society of Medicine*, *101*(6), 290-298.
[38] Lesk, A. (2019). *Introduction to bioinformatics*. Oxford university press.
[39] ICD-9.[http://www.cdc.gov/nchs/icd/icd9.htm].
[40] SNOMED-CT. [http://www.ihtsdo.org/snomed-ct/].
[41] CPT - Common procedural terminology. [http://en.wikipedia.org/wiki/ CommonProceduralTerminology].
[42] HCPCS-Health care current arrangement coding system. [http://www. cms.gov/Medicare/Coding/MedHCPCSGenInfo/index.html].
[43] NDC - National Drug Code. [http://en.wikipedia.org/wiki/NationalDr ugCode].
[44] LOINC - Sensible Observation Identifiers Names and Codes. [http://lo inc.org/].
[45] European Committee for Standardization (CEN) - Semantic interoperability in the electronic health memoir communication. [http:// www.en13606.org/].
[46] HL7 (Health Level Seven) Version 3 Standard: Foundation (Reference Databases Model, Statistics Types and Vocabulary). [http://www.hl7.or g/v3ballot/html/welcome/environment/index.html].
[47] Dolin et al. (2006). HL7 clinical document architecture, release 2. *Journal of the American Medical Informatics Association*, *13*(1), 30-39.
[48] Langville and Meyer. (2011). Google's PageRank and beyond. In *Google's PageRank and Beyond*. Princeton university press.
[49] Baeza-Yates et al. (2011). Trends in search interaction. In *Search computing* (pp. 26-32). Springer, Berlin, Heidelberg.

[50] Masseroli et al. (2011). Bio-Search Computing: Integration and global ranking of bioinformatics search results. *Journal of Integrative Bioinformatics*, *8*(2), 148-156.
[51] Kesh and Raghupathi (2004). Critical issues in bioinformatics and computing. *Perspectives in health information management/AHIMA, American Health Information Management Association, 1.*
[52] Koonin, E. V. (2003). Comparative genomics, minimal gene-sets and the last universal common ancestor. *Nature Reviews Microbiology*, *1*(2), 127-136.
[53] Singh, V. (2012) "What Is the Human Genome Plan and What Are Its benefit and Disadvantages?" What Is the Human Genome Plan and What Are Its benefit and Disadvantages? PreserveArticles. Web. 09 June 2016.
[54] Perzigian, Andrew B. (2003) "Brief Summary of Genetic Engineering and Animals." Short Summary of Genetic Engineering and Animals. Michigan Assert University College of Law. Web. 09 June 2016.
[55] Howard, H. C., et al. (2013). The ethical introduction of genome-based information and technologies into public health. *Public Health Genomics*, *16*(3), 100-109.
[56] Martensen, R. (2001). The history of bioethics: an essay review. *Journal of the history of medicine and allied sciences*, *56*(2), 168-175.
[57] Elston, R. C., et al. (2002). *Biostatistical genetics and genetic epidemiology* (Vol. 1). John Wiley & Sons.
[58] Barnetche, T., et al. (2005). Main features of factors involved in aetiology of complex disease. *Transplant Immunology*, *3*(14), 255-266.
[59] Lobo, I. (2008). Basic local alignment search tool (BLAST). *Nat Educ*, *1*(1).
[60] Madeira, F., Park, Y. M., Lee, J., Buso, N., Gur, T., Madhusoodanan, N., ... & Lopez, R. (2019). The EMBL-EBI search and sequence analysis tools APIs in 2019. *Nucleic acids research*, *47*(W1), W636-W641.
[61] Ganesan, N., Bennett, N. F., Velauthapillai, M., Pattabiraman, N., Squier, R., & Kalyanasundaram, B. (2005). Web-based interface facilitating sequence-to-structure analysis of BLAST alignment reports. *Biotechniques*, *39*(2), 186-188.
[62] Branco, I., & Choupina, A. (2021). Bioinformatics: new tools and applications in life science and personalized medicine. *Applied Microbiology and Biotechnology*, *105*(3), 937-951.
[63] Burge, C., & Karlin, S. (1997). Prediction of complete gene structures in human genomic DNA. *Journal of molecular biology*, *268*(1), 78-94.

[64] Parra Farré, G., Blanco, E., & Guigó Serra, R. (2000). GeneID in "Drosophila". *Genome Research. 2000; 10 (4): 511-5.*

[65] Mitra, A., Kesarwani, A. K., Pal, D., & Nagaraja, V. (2011). WebGeSTer DB—a transcription terminator database. *Nucleic acids research, 39*(suppl_1), D129-D135.

[66] Weckx, S., Del-Favero, J., Rademakers, R., Claes, L., Cruts, M., De Jonghe, P., ... & De Rijk, P. (2005). novoSNP, a novel computational tool for sequence variation discovery. *Genome research, 15*(3), 436-442.

[67] Münch, R., Hiller, K., Grote, A., Scheer, M., Klein, J., Schobert, M., & Jahn, D. (2005). Virtual Footprint and PRODORIC: an integrative framework for regulon prediction in prokaryotes. *Bioinformatics, 21*(22), 4187-4189.

[68] Gasteiger, E., Hoogland, C., Gattiker, A., Wilkins, M. R., Appel, R. D., & Bairoch, A. (2005). Protein identification and analysis tools on the ExPASy server. *The proteomics protocols handbook*, 571-607.

[69] Allen, J. E., & Salzberg, S. L. (2005). JIGSAW: integration of multiple sources of evidence for gene prediction. *Bioinformatics, 21*(18), 3596-3603.

[70] Madeira, F., Park, Y. M., Lee, J., Buso, N., Gur, T., Madhusoodanan, N., ... & Lopez, R. (2019). The EMBL-EBI search and sequence analysis tools APIs in 2019. *Nucleic acids research, 47*(W1), W636-W641.

12

Advancement in Artificial Intelligence: Insights and Future Vision for the Pharmacy Profession

Prem Shankar Mishra[1], Rakhi Mishra[2*], Sirisha Pingali[3], and Rishabha Malviya[1]

[1]School of Medical and Allied Sciences, Galgotias University, India
[2]Noida Institute of Engineering and Technology (Pharmacy Institute), India
[3]IPT, Lonza Biologics, United Kingdom
*Corresponding author: Noida Institute of Engineering and Technology (Pharmacy Institute), Greater Noida, India, Email ID: rakhi.misra84@rediffmail.com, Mobile Number: 7906833682.

Abstract

Pharmacists and pharmacy technicians all across the world are increasingly working in more sophisticated positions that benefit patients, other healthcare professionals, and the overall healthcare system. Pharmacists throughout the world are moving toward a practice that is more clinically oriented and holds themselves more accountable for the pharmaceutical treatment they provide for health context. Pharmaceutical leaders are searching for methods to use machine learning and artificial intelligence in the healthcare and biotech sectors. One of the emerging sectors in India that offers enormous prospects is patient management. As value-based care models continue to take center stage in the healthcare industry, the application of AI increases pharmacists' opportunities to play a more active role in patient care. The pharmaceutical sector is especially well-positioned to benefit from and expand via the use of AI because some people are still doubtful about its potential. In this chapter, we have discussed how artificial intelligence is changing the pharmaceutical industry. This chapter also highlights the vision for employment in pharmacy due to advancements in artificial intelligence. There are several suggestions presented in this chapter regarding how to assist the profession in evolving to meet the challenges of a growing society and healthcare system in general.

Keywords: Pharmacy, career, drug discovery, healthcare, pharma companies.

12.1 Introduction

People are demanding better exposure, simplicity, and personalization from their care providers as biological sciences discoveries and cutting-edge technologies disturb the public healthcare value chain. Pharmacists have a unique opportunity to grow and develop their careers in the present scenario. Pharmacy is transformed by technological and life sciences innovations [1, 2].

In the healthcare value chain, rapid transformation is speeding disruption and reshaping the direction of pharmacy. Scientific and clinical advances are emerging at a historic rate because of AI, robots, and insights drawn from fundamentally integrated technology [3]. As "imprecision medicine" gives way to precision treatments, likely, the role of the pharmacist and the delivery channels we are familiar with today will evolve. For example, the merger might lead to a move from fee-based compensation to a value-based compensation model that is consistent with the larger payer trends that are now taking place [4].

Innovation occurs throughout the life sciences such as:

- Using innovative cameras and breath analysis, experts are creating intelligence screens that can identify patterns in a person's health.
- At the same time, Japanese experienced workers are employing exoskeletons to help them undertake physical labor tasks that they previously couldn't execute.
- Infections including urinary tract infections and diabetic eye disease can be recognized at the point of treatment and home using smartphones.
- Origami robots that can be ingested and operated to promote healing have been made by researchers.
- Gut microbiome-based food-as-medicine strategies are being developed by industries to control glucose levels and improve well-being [5].

With the rise of health-conscious customers, pharmacy's future will be dramatically transformed by these technological advancements. There is stress as pharmacy enterprises and pharmacists discuss how to succeed in the existing economy while also anticipating, adjusting to, and preparing for the future [6].

The pharmacy profession has evolved through time from a concentration on pharmaceuticals to a more developed emphasis on the patient. A century ago, pharmacists were more involved in formulating and taking medications, but this position has declined dramatically over the years. This expansion of the pharmacist's responsibilities requires them to work as part of a larger healthcare team to improve patient care, thereby contributing to the global Millennium Development Goals. Technology like AI and remote care are reshaping the role of the pharmaceutical industry and the pharmacist [7].

12.2 Carrier's Scope in Pharmacy

Globally, the healthcare industry is expanding at an exponential rate, and the pharmaceutical industry is expanding at a rate comparable to that of the healthcare industry. The entire world has witnessed the catastrophic global pandemic caused by Covid-19. To protect the safety of the economic growth of individuals, preventive and therapeutic actions must be taken. To treat a wide range of illnesses, pharmaceutical medications are essential.

Thousands of students have excellent career opportunities in the healthcare sector, which is expanding at a steady rate in India and abroad. In the field of Pharmaceutical Sciences, students can pursue diploma programs, bachelor's degree programs, master's degree programs, and doctoral level programs [8–10].

In a post-COVID-19 scenario in which patients are quarantined for an extended period, the role of pharmaceutical professionals is likely to grow as a result of the increased hospitalization of patients. As pharmaceutical professionals become more knowledgeable about pharmacokinetics and pharmacodynamics, i.e., how pharmaceutical drugs affect the body and how the body responds to pharmaceutical drugs, their role and significance will increase [11].

The Indian pharmaceutical industry has given rise to the Indian molecular diagnostics industry in a manner that has never been seen before in this bleak global environment. Students majoring in public health should seek employment in this futuristic industry [12].

12.3 Career Path for Pharmacy Professionals

Career opportunities in the pharmaceutical industry are abundant and growing exponentially. Pharmacy students pursue careers as Drug Control Administrators, Hospital Managers, Trainers, Assistant Professors, Food and Drug Administrators, Health Centre Managers, Drug Dispensers, Pharmaceutical

Marketing Representatives, Research Managers, Health Inspectors, Chemical Analysts, Drug Technicians, Drug Therapists, Customs Officers, Pharma Data Analysts, Drug Inspectors, Hospital Drug Administrators, Medical Transcriptionists, and Regulators [13].

Finally, in the post-covid19 era, the pharmacy industry is projected to provide attractive and satisfying professions in the drug manufacturing industries, as well as generous remuneration, globally.

When individuals earn a degree in pharma or related fields, they often do not realize how many doors of opportunity they open. Before choosing a career path in pharma, you must be aware of the requirements for workers in the various available positions [14].

Let's take a closer look at some pharmaceutical industry positions and their primary responsibilities [15–19].

12.3.1 Research scientist

Several investigations must be conducted in the pharmaceutical sector to promote, enhance, or produce new pharmaceuticals. Expertise is normally required, and the remuneration is likely to be considerable, for this job. In order to carry out clinical tests and evaluate the side effects of various medications, researchers need to have a strong knowledge of biology and chemistry. In order to be effective in this pharmaceutical role, professionals must pay great attention to the information and have strong analytical skills.

12.3.2 Pharmacy manager

In order to run a pharmacy, you'll need a lot of experience. In order to stand out among your peers, you'll need to demonstrate leadership characteristics as well as managerial expertise. Manager jobs also require excellent communication skills as consultations with patients are required.

All hospitals, convenience stores, clinics, supermarkets, and pharmacies need a manager. As pharmacy managers, professionals have the opportunity to work in a variety of locations and develop expertise in the field. In order to be a good pharmacy manager, you must also be familiar with the responses and adverse outcomes of all drugs.

12.3.3 Regulatory specialist

A regulatory specialist is an additional well-compensated profession in the pharmaceutical industry. Regulatory specialists aid biopharmaceutical companies in gaining approval for their manufactured products. As part of their role, they probably decide on options to improve items more in line with regulatory norms.

Regulatory affairs experts work with biologists to help them determine which compounds are safe to use and which ones they should keep away. Regulatory specialists are also responsible for examining company-written product labels for errors and banned substances.

12.3.4 Pharmaceutical financial analyst

A brilliant career path is to become a financial analyst in the pharmaceutical industry. It is part of the job description for this role to analyze and evaluate financial data from firms and to offer advice on management and financial decisions made by a company.

When providing financial advice to pharmaceutical firms, pharmaceutical financial analysts take a variety of factors into accounts, such as a business's performance strength, the present attractiveness of the market, and the overall trade and business climate. A respectable career as a drug industry financial adviser may be achieved by accounting and business graduates using their knowledge and experience to the fullest extent possible.

12.3.5 Pharmaceutical sales representative

Medical personnel such as nurses, pharmacists, and consultants are educated about the usefulness of health products by pharmacy sales associates. They must undergo extensive training in order to acquire knowledge that they can then impart to other parties.

Pharmaceutical sales professionals need to be able to interact well enough and straightforwardly express their thinking. Customers and how to deal with them will also be understood in addition to the items.

12.3.6 Clinical data manager

A clinical data manager guides individuals responsible for analyzing and combining trial data. In order to succeed in this role, a professional must be an excellent manager and have experience working with sensitive information. Clinical data managers work with academics and other data experts to keep track of patient records.

As a result, clinical data managers are responsible for analyzing and disseminating the data gathered during clinical trials. Mathematical abilities and an interest in new technology are engaged in health information management positions.

12.3.7 Career options in pharmaceutical industry

There are more career opportunities in the pharmaceutical industry than anyone can imagine. As the pharmaceutical sector begins to expand, pharmaceutical professions are perhaps the most favored employment in the world.

Constant technological advances and medical discoveries are indispensable to the pharmaceutical industry. R&D, operational compliance, database administration, and legislative inspections are all part of the pharmaceutical industry.

Students with a bachelor's degree in chemistry or a related discipline have a good opportunity to succeed in the pharmaceutical sector. Graduates in this field are eligible for a wide range of roles with some of the world's most prominent pharmaceutical corporations.

Professionals with a wide range of talents and qualifications might find work in the pharmaceutical sector since it is so complicated. One of the most tolerant industries is the pharmaceutical sector. As well as providing several employment options, it also provides individuals with the chance to earn adequate pay [20, 21].

12.4 Future of the Pharmacist

Pharmacist is a valuable and often undervalued asset in today's medical system. Pharmacists are in a professional dilemma as the pharmaceutical sector grows its use of automation. They may either enhance their coverage and effectiveness, or they might expose the risk of consolidation.

Automated dispensing devices, 3D printers, and software will soon be able to handle the bulk of healthcare modifications in the forthcoming years. Pharmacists and other low-skilled workers may be able to carry out basic physical inspection duties using sophisticated contact lenses that use augmented reality (AR) technology.

Surprisingly, as the population ages and the need for doctors increases, pharmacists may find themselves in a position to take on a more prominent role in the healthcare system as primary care providers (PCPs) treating patients with acute and chronic illnesses like diabetes, hypertension, and asthma. Regulations will have to be changed to reflect this, but pharmacists are already widely identified as healthcare practitioners in the United States.

Pharmacies must first assess and be honest about their key capabilities and whether they are transferrable and/or scalable before they can move accurately into the future of pharmacy. Forward-thinking corporations are exploring questions like these:

- Who will be a rival or disruptor in or outside our ecosystem? A valuable rival is a person who?
- How quickly will our industry grow in comparison to the ecosphere rate of growth?
- Why may we be exposed to more or less danger in the future?
- What's more important: innovating now or waiting until rivals acquire a foothold and prove the concept when entry into the market would be considerably more expensive?
- How can our existing management set-up and people management approach serve our long-term goals?
- Our essential contributors and technology do not enable omnichannel and electronic engagement.

The greatest obstacle for the majority of businesses is not generating sufficient ideas for moving forward. Rather, it is a matter of aligning and prioritizing these concepts to determine where and how much to invest in order to ensure their place in the future of pharmacy.

12.5 What Changes Can Artificial Intelligence (AI) Bring to the Pharma Carrier

Artificial intelligence is one of the emerging technologies for the digital revolution and is developing more rapidly than before. Building machines that can handle activities that would otherwise require human operators and intellect is the sole focus of the branch of computer science known as artificial intelligence [22]. Deep learning, machine learning, non-linear grid systems, chatbots, and/or self-modifying graph networks are just a few of the well-known technologies that fall under the umbrella of artificial intelligence. Many sectors have been changed by artificial intelligence. The pharmaceutical sector has been simplified and affected by artificial intelligence in numerous ways, from developing new and improved treatments to fighting fast-spreading ailments [23, 24].

As per research, more than 70% of company owners think artificial intelligence has a significant role in the pharmaceutical field [25].

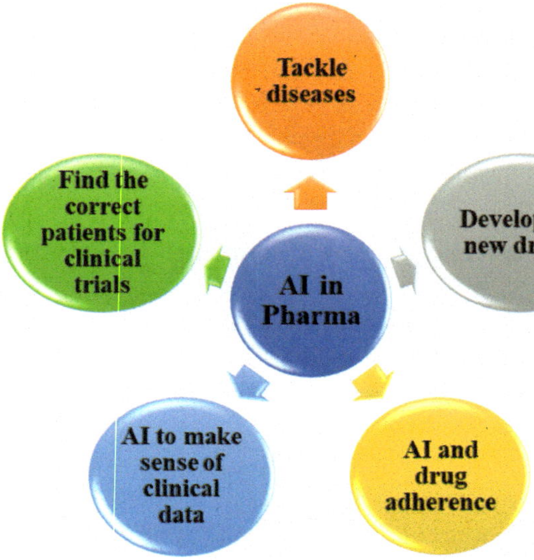

Figure 12.1 Application of AI in the health and pharmaceutical sector.

Verge Genomics, a leading company in the pharmaceutical field uses AI and developed new medicines employing trustworthy automated procedures. They developed outstanding methods to minimize the risk of developing ALS or Alzheimer's disease by exploiting millions of large datasets and thorough research. Experts who can only be engaged on one gene at a particular time for an investigation are more generally to fail in drug development than those who can focus on many genes at once. But on the other side, artificial intelligence has enabled Verge Genomics to investigate hundreds of disease-related genes simultaneously [26]. Various applications of AI in the health sector which open the door for pharma professionals are shown in Figure 12.1.

12.6 The Future of Pharma Industries and Career Opportunities with Advancement in AI

In the pharmaceutical industry, AI refers to the use of automated algorithms to complete tasks that normally require human intellect. According to narrative science, 61% of organizations investing in innovative approaches use AI to see opportunities they would have overlooked before [27]. The various field in which AI can employ and further bring a major change in the pharmaceutical and health sectors are shown in Figure 12.2.

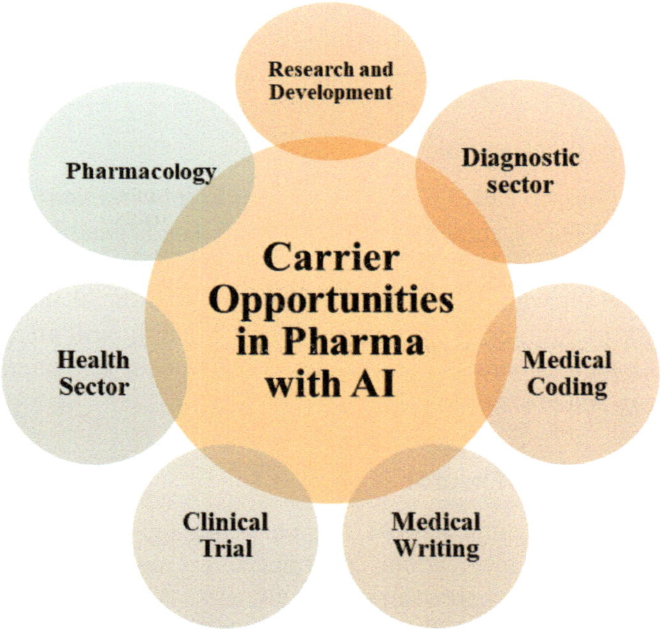

Figure 12.2 Career opportunities due to implications of AI.

12.6.1 Carrier in Research and Development

Only 13.8% of drugs pass clinical trials successfully, according to the research of the Massachusetts Institute of Technology (MIT) [28]. Moreover, a company needs a budget between $161 million and $2 billion to develop, conduct, and receive FDA clearance for any drug. Because of this, pharmaceutical corporates are utilizing AI to raise the rates of success of new therapies while lowering operating expenses [29].

In order to develop new and better medications and identify strategies for facilitating fast access to patient care, Novartis is leveraging innovations in AI technology. Currently, Novartis is analyzing digital pictures of cells that have been exposed to several experimental compounds using machine learning [30].

12.6.2 Carrier in the diagnostic sector

To improve healthcare decisions for chronic thromboembolic pulmonary hypertension (CTEPH), Bayer and Merck & Co. were given FDA approval for artificial intelligence software as Breakthrough Device. In the future, the technology will be able to help diagnose patients more quickly and accurately, which will result in early treatment and improved patient outcomes [31].

12.6.3 Carrier in pharmacology

A biotechnology start-up called Cyclica combines biophysics and AI to find drugs more quickly, safely, and economically [32]. The Ligand Express, an integrated network of cloud-based technologies enhanced by AI, was developed in collaboration with Bayer. The company uses artificial intelligence to analyze major protein targets to determine how the drug will affect these targets. The AI then generates a visual representation of the interactions between the drug and proteins [33].

12.6.4 Carrier in health sector

Since the return on investment does not outweigh the time and money required to develop the medications, pharmaceutical companies typically do not concentrate on therapies for severe diseases. A revived interest in managing rare diseases has emerged as a result of developments in AI technology [34].

12.6.5 Carrier in clinical trial

Clinical research is still dependent on paper diary entries instead of using advanced electronics. Patients should record the dose they took, mention any additional medications they took, and record any side effects they suffered [35]. One-third of all Phase III clinical research terminations are related to enrollment issues, according to a Cognizant study, and over 80% of clinical studies fail to enroll their participants by the timeframe. The medical and pharmaceutical sectors place a high value on extracting and making sense of clinical data from medical records, and AI may be the solution [36].

12.6.6 Carrier in pharma companies

Intending to expand the Chinese pharmaceutical industry and assist patients in getting and keeping the correct medication with the use of AI and smart health services, the British pharmaceutical company AstraZeneca has partnered with Ali Health, a division of Alibaba [37]. The number of people with diabetes and cancer is growing in China as the population ages. As a result,

AstraZeneca has invented AI techniques to improve the pickup of ambulances and specialized cancer diagnoses. Altogether, this will make it possible for patients to be examined in ambulances more quickly and effectively, allowing for the proper referral of those in need of care to the appropriate medical facilities [38].

12.6.7 Carrier in medical coding

Medical coding is one of several fields that has to evolve to the complexity, diversity, and size of healthcare data that is expanding. An integral part of clinical trial procedures is accurate medical coding. Medical coders' skills are still in great demand due to the exponential rise of healthcare data and its predicted continued complexity. Between 2019 and 2029, the US Bureau of Labor Statistics predicts an 8% increase for the profession, which is higher than the expected growth rate for other professions. Medical coders' work can be aided by AI. This has the potential to free up medical coders to focus on other important tasks, like identifying patterns of unexpectedly high numbers of adverse effects reports, in addition to relieving exhaustion and enhancing speed and accuracy. Medical coding operations may be automated using AI, freeing up teams to apply resources where they are most required [39].

12.6.8 Carrier in medical writing

Computers are evolving from being basic instruments that execute orders into self-taught, self-correcting machines that make conclusions as a result of the increasing volume of data accessible and technological advancements in computer science. Medical writers' jobs are beginning to be impacted by AI's rapid entry into the healthcare and medical professions. According to the latest survey, 40% of scientists are still unsure about the application of AI in healthcare, with reactions ranging from terror to confirmation bias. For all medical writers, these are the main challenges [40].

12.7 Conclusion

A secure and reliable drug usage system that enhances patient healthcare management while also lowering medical budgets is being developed by pharmacists in collaboration with different health system providers. As was emphasized in the chapter, the pharmacy profession has seen a dynamic change. Researchers believe that the application of these technologies improves decision-making, promotes creativity, increases the effectiveness of research and clinical trials, and produces new tools that benefit doctors, patients, insurers, and regulators. In the pharmaceutical sector, artificial intelligence and machine learning are crucial. However, leading companies indicate that the best applications for these technologies are in drug research, drug production, diagnostic support, and medical treatment process optimization. By improving recruitment and screening procedures for clinical trials, AI will also have an impact on the future of pharmaceuticals. These revolutions in the pharmaceutical field is due to advancement in artificial intelligence. This ground-breaking innovation will provide graduate and undergraduate students with a wide range of opportunities to work in the pharmacy profession. Our pharmacy graduates may soon be employed in cutting-edge fields including research labs, medical coding, medical writing, and computational pharmacy as a result of this breakthrough. With this perspective and vision, we get to the conclusion that the future of pharmacy is too bright owing to the development of many major, international pharmaceutical companies and the health sector.

Conflict of Interest

Authors have no conflict of interest.

References

[1] Caamaño, F., Ruano, A., Figueiras, A., Gestal-Otero, J.J. (2002) Data collection methods for analyzing the quality of the dispensing in pharmacies. *Pharm World Sci.* 24, 217e223.

[2] Toklu, H.Z., Akici, A., Oktay, S., Cali, S., Sezen, S.F., Keyer-Uysal, M. (2010) The pharmacy practice of community pharmacists in Turkey. *Marmara Pharm J.* 14, 53e60.

[3] Van Mil, F. (2002) Pharmacy and health care. *Pharm World Sci.* 24, 213.

[4] Ferreri, S.P., Cross, B., Hanes, S.D., Jenkins, T., Meyer, D., Pittenger, A. (2017) Academic pharmacy: where is our influence? *Am J Pharm Educ.* 81, 4.

[5] Hughes, L.D., Welch, L.H., Hannings, A. (2014) Relationship between StrengthsFinder 2.0 Leadership domains and student pharmacist perceived capabilities to perform leadership skills. 115th Annual Meeting of the American Association of Colleges of Pharmacy, Grapevine, Texas, July 26-30, 2014. *Am J Pharm Educ.* 78, 5.

[6] Bloom, T.J. (2016) Comparison of StrengthsFinder signature themes in PharmD and DO students. 117th Annual Meeting of the American Association of Colleges of Pharmacy, Anaheim, California. *Am J Pharm Educ.* 80, 5.
[7] Janke, K.K., Farris, K.B., Kelley, K.A., et al. (2015) StrengthsFinder signature themes of talent in doctor of pharmacy students in five Midwestern pharmacy schools. *Am J Pharm Educ.* 79, 4.
[8] Rath, T., Conchie, B. (2008) Strengths Based Leadership. New York, NY: Gallup Press.
[9] Caamaño, F., Alvarez, R., Khoury, M. (2008) The community pharmacists and their practice as health care providers. *Gac Sanit.* 22:385. 9.
[10] Role of Dispensers in Promoting Rational Drug Use. International Network of Rational Drug Use. World Health Organization, 2000.
[11] The Role of Education in the Rational Use of Medicines. International Network of Rational Drug Use. World Health Organization, 2006.
[12] Benjamin, D.M. (2003) Reducing medication errors and increasing patient safety: case studies in clinical pharmacology. *J Clin Pharmacol.* 43, 768e783.
[13] Dessing, R. P. (2000) Ethics applied to pharmacy practice. *Pharm World Sci.* 22, 10e16.
[14] Strand, L.M., Cipolle, R.J., Morley, P.C. (1992) Pharmaceutical Care: An Introduction. *Michigan: Upjohn Co.,* 14e29.
[15] Strand, L.M., Morley, P.C., Cipolle, R.J., Ramsey, R., Lamsam, G.D. (1990) Drug-related problems; their structure and function. *DICP.* 24, 1093e1097.
[16] Hepler, C.D., Strand, L.M. Opportunities and responsibilities in pharmaceutical care. *Am J Hosp Pharm.* 47, 533e543.
[17] Farris, K.B., Fernandez-Llimos, F., Benrimoj, S.I. (2005) Pharmaceutical care in community pharmacies: practice and research from around the world. *Ann Pharmacother.* 39, 1539e1541.
[18] Azhar, S., Hassali, M.A., Ibrahim, M.I., Ahmad, M., Masood, I., Shafie, A.A. (2009) The role of pharmacists in developing countries: the current scenario in Pakistan. *Hum Resour Health.* 7, 54.
[19] Toklu, H.Z., Ayanoglu-Dulger, G., Gumusel, B., Yaris, E., Kalyoncu, N.I, Akici, A. (2010) Developing a model checklist for the evaluation of the dispensing scores in the pharmacy. *Basic Clin Pharmacol Toxicol.* 107, 617e618.

[20] Toklu, H.Z., Dulger, G., Yaris, E., Gumusel, B., Akici, A. (2009) First impressions from a short training course in rational use of drugs for the pharmacologists in the pharmacy schools in Turkey. *Value Health*. 12, A249.

[21] Toklu, H.Z. (2013) Problem based pharmacotherapy teaching for pharmacy students and pharmacists. *Curr Drug Deliv*. 10, 67e70.

[22] Sahu, A., Mishra, J., Kushwaha, N. (2021). Artificial Intelligence (AI) in Drugs and Pharmaceuticals. *Combinatorial chemistry & high throughput screening*.

[23] Kathleen, W. (2020) The Increasing Use of AI In the Pharmaceutical Industry. Available at: https://www.forbes.com/sites/cognitiveworld/2020/12/26/the-increasing-use-of-ai-in-the-pharmaceutical-industry/?sh=693bed6e4c01 [Accessed on 6 July 2022].

[24] Toward an Optimal Future: Priorities for Action, Research Report, Pharmacy Thought Leadership Summit by Intergage Consulting Group Inc. available at: https://www.pharmacists.ca/cpha-ca/assets/File/pharmacy-in-canada/Thought%20Leadership%20Summit%20Research%20Report_01.pdf [Accessed on 6 July 2022.

[25] McGrail, S. (2021) AI in the Pharma Industry: Current Uses, Best Cases, Digital Future, 2021. Available at: https://pharmanewsintel.com/news/ai-in-the-pharma-industry-current-uses-best-cases-digital-future [last accessed on 5 July 2022].

[26] Goyal, K. (2022) Artificial Intelligence in Pharmaceutical Industry: 8 Exciting Applications in 2022. Available at: https://www.upgrad.com/blog/artificial-intelligence-in-pharmaceutical [last accessed on 5 July 2022].

[27] Jorgenson, D., Penm, J., MacKinnon, N.J., Smith, J. (2017) Future vision for the pharmacy profession. *Can Pharm J (Ott)* 150, 4.

[28] Advisory Panel on Healthcare Innovation. Unleashing Innovation: Excellent Healthcare for Canada. 2015. Available at: http://www.healthycanadians.gc.ca/publications/health-system-systemesante/summary-innovation-sommaire/index-eng.php [Last accessed on 2 July 2022].

[29] Avalere Healthcare LLC. Exploring Pharmacists' Role in a Changing Healthcare Environment. (2014) Available at: http://www.nacds.org/pdfs/comm/2014/pharmacist-role.pdf.

[30] Improving Care Transitions: Optimizing Medication, March 2012, APhA/ASHP and After Hospitalization: A Dartmouth Atlas Report on Readmissions Among Medicare Beneficiaries.

[31] International Pharmacy Federation. Advanced Practice and Specialization in Pharmacy: Global Report. (2015)Retrieved from: https://www.ucl.ac.uk/pharmacy/documents/fip-global-report-2015.

[32] Pharmacy Practice+Community Pharmacy Trends & Insights 2015. *Toronto (ON):* Rogers Publishing.

[33] Baronzio, G. (2015) Overview of methods for overcoming hindrance to drug delivery to tumors, with special attention to tumor interstitial fluid. *Front. Oncol.* 5, 165.

[34] Achenbach, J. (2011) Computational tools for polypharmacology and repurposing. *Fut. Med. Chem.* 3, 961–968.

[35] Harrer, S., Shah, P., Antony, B., Hu, J. (2019) Artificial intelligence for clinical trial design. *Trends Pharmacol Sci.* 40, 577–91.

[36] Karekar, S.R., Vazifdar, A.K. (2021) Current status of clinical research using artificial intelligence techniques: A registry-based audit. *Perspect Clin Res.* 12, 48–52.

[37] Jiang, F., Jiang, Y., Zhi, H., Dong, Y., Li, H., Ma, S., et al. (2017) Artificial intelligence in healthcare: Past, present and future. *Stroke Vasc Neurol.* 2, 230–43.

[38] Artificial Intelligence in Pharma, Available at: https://www.pharmaceutical-technology.com/artificial-intelligence-in-pharma/ [accessed on 5 July 2022].

[39] Basu, K., Sinha, R., Ong, A., Basu, T. (2020) Artificial Intelligence: How is It Changing Medical Sciences and Its Future? *Indian J Dermatol.* 65, 5, 365-370.

[40] Parisis, N., Medical writing in the era of artificial intelligence, *Medical Writing*, 2019, 28 (4), 4-9.

Index

About the Editors

Dr. Rishabha Malviya completed B. Pharmacy from Uttar Pradesh Technical University and M. Pharmacy (Pharmaceutics) from Gautam Buddha Technical University, Lucknow Uttar Pradesh. His PhD (Pharmacy) work was in the area of Novel formulation development techniques. He has 12 years of research experience and presently working as Associate Professor in the Department of Pharmacy, School of Medical and Allied Sciences, Galgotias University since past 8 years. His area of interest includes formulation optimization, nanoformulation, targeted drug delivery, localized drug delivery and characterization of natural polymers as pharmaceutical excipients. He has authored more than 150 research/review papers for national/international journals of repute. He has 58 patents (19 grants, 38 published, 1 filed) and publications in reputed National and International journals with total of 191 cumulative impact factor. He has also received an Outstanding Reviewer award from Elsevier. He has authored/edited/editing 46 books (Wiley, CRC Press/Taylor and Francis, IOP publishing. River Publisher Denmark, Springer Nature, Apple Academic Press/Taylor and Francis, Walter de Gruyter, and OMICS publication) and authored 31 book chapters. His name has included in word's top 2% scientist list for the year 2020 and 2021 by Elsevier BV and Stanford University. He is Reviewer/Editor/Editorial board member of more than 50 national and international journals of repute. He has invited as author for "Atlas of Science" and pharma magazine dealing with industry (B2B) "Ingredient south Asia Magazines".

Prof. Sonali Sundram completed B. Pharm & M. Pharm (pharmacology) from AKTU, Lucknow. She has worked as research scientist in project of ICMR in King George's Medical University, Lucknow after that she has joined BBDNIIT and currently she is working in Galgotias university, Greater Noida. Her PhD (Pharmacy) work was in the area of Neurodegeneration and Nanoformulation. Her area of interest is neurodegeneration, clinical research, artificial intelligence. She has authored/edited/editing more than 14 books (Wiley, CRC Press/Taylor and Francis, IOP publishing, Apple Academic Press/Taylor and Francis, Springer Nature and River Publisher) She has attended as well organized more than 15 national and international seminar/conferences/workshop. She has more than 8 patents national and international in her credit.

Dr. Shivkanya Fuloria is presently working as an Associate Professor at Faculty of Pharmacy, AIMST University, Malaysia; with an extensive experience of 18 years in research and academics. She completed her D. Pharm in 1998 (Maharashtra, India), B. Pharm in 2001 (Amravati University, India), M. Pharm in 2003 (Nagpur University, India), and PhD in 2011 (Amravati University, India). So far, she supervised 07 Postgraduate and 20 undergraduate research scholars: and currently she is supervising 05 PhD scholars. She published 89 Research and review articles, 04 books, 03 MOOC, and 02 patents (Australia). For her research Dr. Shivkanya received 07 national and international grants. Dr. Shivkanya is a member of various professional bodies like Indian society of analytical Scientists, IPGA, APTI, and NMR society of India. Apart from it for her work in academics and research she received various awards such as: best presentation award 2017 (at 19th International Conference on Medicinal Chemistry and Molecular Pharmacology, Singapore), and Appreciation Award 2017 (at Teachers Award Ceremony of Kedah State Malaysia, at AIMST University, Malaysia).

Dhanalekshmi Unnikrishnan Meenakshi holds a doctorate in Pharmacology (specialization in Nanomedicine) from the Council of Scientific and Industrial Research (CSIR)- CLRI, India. She worked as a Scientist in the Council of Scientific and Industrial Research- NEIST, India, and was involved in the government-funded projects for North East Exploration of Pharmaceuticals from natural sources. She has over 10 years of research and teaching experience with leading National and International Organizations. She has been working on an array of projects relating to cancer and gene therapy, nanotechnology, and pharmacology. Her research vicinity focuses on preclinical and clinical trials, mechanism of intoxication, etc. She uses state-of-the-art technology, for systematic evaluation of the efficiency of novel polymeric nanoparticles encapsulated with biologically active agents. Currently, she is a faculty member in the College of Pharmacy, National University of Science and Technology, Muscat, Sultanate of Oman. She published extensively in nanomedicine, drug delivery, and formulation technology in peer-reviewed reputed journals and books. She bagged various awards and fellowships for her excellent contributions in her respective fields.